An

Extraordinary

Year

A Journal of a Student Abroad

1956-1957

For Amy!
a fellow art
traveler and adventurer!
Best wishes -
Judy Hoodell Hauman
Dye!

An Extraordinary Year

A Journal of a Student Abroad

1956-1957

Judy Woodall

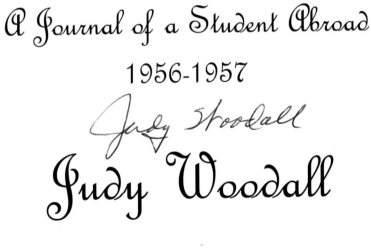

TATE PUBLISHING
AND ENTERPRISES, LLC

Published by Tate Publishing & Enterprises, LLC
127 E. Trade Center Terrace | Mustang, Oklahoma 73064 USA
1.888.361.9473 | www.tatepublishing.com

Tate Publishing is committed to excellence in the publishing industry. The company reflects the philosophy established by the founders, based on Psalm 68:11,
"The Lord gave the word and great was the company of those who published it."

Book design copyright © 2015 by Tate Publishing, LLC. All rights reserved.

Book design by Irish Cabrini Creative

Published in the United States of America

ISBN: 978-1-68187-475-3
1. Biography & Autobiography / Personal Memoirs
2. Travel / Europe / General
15.05.05

Dedication

To the memory of my parents,
Alma and Howard Woodall,
who encouraged me to participate
in the Newcomb JYA program.
They bravely sent me off and supported me
throughout my year-long, life-changing adventure.

Acknowledgements

Thank you to the late John Hubbard, Dean of Newcomb College at the time of this journal, for being such a supportive mentor to me and to the other young women in this JYA program, which he founded. Years later he told me that he thought of us as his "Renaissance women", and in a sense, our year abroad was a kind of re-birth.

Thank you to Canadian author Muriel Gold Poole, whose writing workshop encouraged me to proceed with not only this project, but to continue my interest in creative writing.

Thank you to my loving and patient husband, for helping me learn how to use Word and PDF files, and who guided me through other mysterious computer challenges.

Thank you to my daughters Constance and Carrie Hauman for their encouragement, with special thanks to Carrie, who introduced me to my editor.

Thank you to Jeanne McCafferty, my editor, without whose guidance and enthusiasm I could never have completed this project. She shepherded this project through its various stages, beginning with the scanning of old typewritten pages, through the editing process, all the way to production. In so doing, she taught me a whole new vocabulary!

Thank you to my longtime friend (and graduate school roommate) Constance Lewis, Newcomb classmate and English major, for her careful proof reading.

Thank you to Beth Willinger and Susan Tucker, editors of "Newcomb College, 1886-2006, Higher Education for Women in New Orleans", who offered me encouragement and provided me with the history of the JYA program at Newcomb.

Foreword

On September 6th, 1956, twenty young women from Newcomb College set sail on the S.S. Liberté for the big adventure of our Junior Year Abroad. Eight of us were headed for Paris; three of us to further our musical studies and ambitions; the others would be concentrating on French Literature and Art.

I had arrived at Newcomb in the autumn of 1954, fresh from graduating high school in my hometown of Paducah, Kentucky. My parents preferred that I attend a women's college, and I wanted to go to a big city, where there would be many cultural opportunities, along with the advantages of a co-ed university. Newcomb College of Tulane University in New Orleans, Louisiana filled all our requirements.

The year before my arrival, Newcomb Dean John Hubbard, (later president of USC) and Dr. Peter Hansen, chair of Newcomb's music department, had suggested the creation of a Junior Year Abroad program. In 1954 the program began in England, then expanded within two years to France, Spain, and Germany. By my sophomore year I knew I wanted to be part of the JYA program in France. My parents agreed it would be a great opportunity for learning and traveling, so I applied and was accepted.

The year-long program began with a six-week intensive language and cultural immersion. After a brief stop in Paris, we went on to Dijon, where a local director was hired to guide and advise students. In Dijon we would live "solo" with non-English speaking host families of varying economic situations, ensuring that we would learn to speak and cope with the French language in everyday life.

Classes at the Sorbonne began on November 1st, and we returned to Paris a few days beforehand. There some of us chose to be housed with a French family and a Newcomb roommate, while the others chose Cité Internationale Universitaire housing. The program provided a resident director, Madame Andrée Alverhne, who helped with social and academic life as required.

Spending a year in Europe meant we would be able to take advantage of breaks in the academic calendar to travel around the continent. We had a magical Christmas in Switzerland, an adventure in Spain, then a trip to Italy including a memorable Easter in Rome, and a whirlwind tour of Northern Europe and the British Isles before heading home.

This is the daily journal I kept in letter form and mailed home, where my darling mother typed them. I still have those original letters and typed pages, and this edited version is drawn directly from them.

The year provided me with many fascinating encounters with acquaintances and friends, many of whom I never saw again. But I was able to visit my Paris family after I had a family of my own, and I have remained in touch with Jean-Louis Baut, whom you will meet in this journal, and have had the privilege of meeting his family and visiting with them on several occasions. Sadly, John Donaher and I lost touch with each other after returning to our "state-side" lives. All the other people I met during that year remain vivid to me.

Most special, of course, are the memories of those young women with whom I shared this experience. Louise Slaughter (Geiss), my Paris roommate, remained my very close friend up until her recent death. She had a long career as a piano soloist, chamber music performer, and piano teacher. Over the years we continued to enjoy performing together.

My friend Eugenie Ricau (Rocherolle) is an internationally known composer of every musical genre. We are still in touch, and she continues to amaze me with her talent.

Ann Coco, an intrepid traveler, has been a teacher of French in foreign lands as well as a lawyer, a master gardener and an activist – and the only real Cajun I've ever known. We, too, have remained in touch through all these years.

Martha Johnston (Bancroft) is an artist, a retired teacher of art, and a dedicated choral singer. She, like her Paris roommate Eugenie, lives in the East, and we have recently re-connected.

Sandy Sutherland (Messersmith), who sadly died much too young, was an artist and designer, and also sang and played the guitar. She was a true friend to us and gave of herself to her community.

After college we went in various directions, living in different parts of the country, and like most young women of our generation, we all became wives and mothers. We've shared heartaches, disappointments, and successes, and we are forever bound through our mutual experience of our extraordinary year.

From

the

S. S. Liberté

to

Paris

Friday night, September 7, 1956

Dear Mother and Daddy,

It was a mighty strange feeling to pull out from the Pier on this mammoth ship. It all seemed so unreal, even though I certainly felt on my way to somewhere! I took two pictures of the Statue of Liberty as we passed her. I had forgotten she was green.

The afternoon was quite confusing in all the rush of trying to find out the status of everything. We were shown to our cabins in 3rd (cabin) class, which were disappointingly tiny, with extremely narrow hallways. There are 4 of us in our tiny room, which has a small sink in it, but the bath and the toilet are in separate rooms, for everyone's use.

We were also assigned to our tables in the dining room, which is quite nice and large. We are to sit at the same table with the same people and have the same steward for every meal. Our first dinner was delicious, and we met other passengers, including a dozen French boys, some of whom are aviators! I also met a girl who recognized me as having the lead in the operetta at Interlochen in 1953! (She was in the orchestra.) What a coincidence!

I finally bought a deck chair – ($3.50). It was cold on the deck as soon as we got moving, and the wind is oh so chilly.

The cabin stewards are very attentive. Tonight when I got ready for my bath M. le steward ran my water and did everything for me except put me in the tub!

Today we were confined to our lowly class habitat but tomorrow we get passes to go most any place we want. Our lowly class does have movies, "race horses" and Bingo, and dancing. Today I did not participate in any of that.

Before supper tonight we visited the lounge and sat with a lot of the Smith College girls. While we were there two French boys came and sat with us. They were very kind with us and spoke slowly so we could comprehend. One of them knew his English very well, the other was like we are about French with his English. There are about 10 French aviators in our class. Some of them are precious. Martha Johnston has already become great friends with one! They will provide excitement perhaps.

After dinner tonight (ending at 9:30) Louise and I went up on the deck – all wrapped in coats and scarves and sat in the deck chairs and talked until eleven. It is wonderful on deck at night. It's so cold and the salty smell is so strong. I love it. I didn't care about flirting tonight – it's too much work!

There is not as much to do as the folder said in the tourist class. Perhaps now that we have met some more girls and boys there will be better times around the corner. Being freer to go in different parts of the ship will be a help.

Saturday, September 8, 1956

Last night was the most horrible night I've ever spent! It was (still is) so hot down here that we nearly died. With four in a tiny room there was no spare oxygen, but plenty of body heat. There is almost no way to get air even though there are air vents like those on airplanes only larger. In our room they couldn't be aimed to hit those on the lower berths. I never went completely to sleep. To top it off, the ladder for the upper berths was on the opposite side of the room and during the night it fell over and hit my knee. It nearly scared me to death. I screamed bloody murder. It bruised my knee pretty badly, but I'm sure I'll manage. Louise had a rough night of it too (as did everybody I think). So this afternoon we went to see the Purser and he let us change cabins. Louise and I each moved to single cabins, just across from each other down the hall from our first cabins. They are much cooler because there are two portholes nearby which cool things greatly, also the air vents work and they cool things too. Also, you're not in anybody's way. I'm really glad we did it – smartest thing I've done in a long time!

This morning was very short because I didn't get up until eleven fifteen. After a long lunch we went up on the deck and read for a while. At four o'clock the whole ship had an emergency drill – life jackets and all.

After the drill Louise and I went to the Purser, who had sent for us about entertaining. It was arranged by Dean Hubbard that Louise would play piano and I would sing for the Gala parties. He (the purser) gave us a pass to go to 1st class and practice in the private music room which we immediately did. We can use it at any time. We're going to perform for the cabin and tourist classes at the Gala party the night before we land. Maybe 1st class too, but I doubt it.

We stayed in the music room until time to freshen up for dinner. Dinner was good and very large and very fattening. After dinner Susan Shelley used a pair of scissors to unlock the door and about 8 of us filed up to 1st class. We went to the music room and Louise began to play, then we played and sang some of the things we know. A little crowd gathered around outside the window and listened to us and applauded. I think there aren't many people of 1st class since this is off season. I didn't see but a few, and those I saw looked as if they had nothing to do. They really seemed glad to see us. That's why I think we might get to perform for their Party too. The Purser told us that a professional opera singer was on board – she sings in Europe – but I haven't seen her.

We left 1ˢᵗ class about ten and came back to tourist to the Gala get-together dance which wasn't very gala. So some of us came down to Louise's and my rooms and talked.

Sunday,

Another day has gone slowly, but quickly, but slowly because of the lack of something to do – quickly because now that it is over it seems short. It was a day of failure once again where men are concerned, Louise and I seem to be the only two who lack the nerve to brazenly corner one! We did meet a very nice and attractive architect from Florida who is going to study for a year in Europe. We decided that tomorrow we'd skip this "partner" business and see how we do alone!

I slept so wonderfully well in my new room that I didn't wake up till noon! After luncheon (which is always huge) I didn't do much of anything, although Louise and I met with the orchestra about our performing. We decided to perform without their accompaniment because they don't have or know any of our music, and we know it all by heart. Speaking of our music, tonight we were up in first class reading their magazines and the man who listened to us play and sing the other day came to us and asked when they could hear us again. We told him tomorrow night, so we're giving a private concert for him and his wife and another couple. He thought we were professional musicians. He said he couldn't understand why the young men weren't flocking at our feet because we were so beautiful and charming. We like him!

The swimming pool has been made open to us from three to five and of course I don't have my bathing suit! It really doesn't matter that much. We also have passes to cabin class.

I think I've gained ten pounds already! I've got to stop eating so much. Both lunch and dinner are so long! First there is soup, fish, salad, meat and vegetables, cheese, dessert, then fruit. Red wine is served with each meal. It's very good – not very strong. There is always French bread too of course. Today we asked for milk, and our dining steward nearly died. He said it was only for babies. But he gave it to us anyway.

These people really speak fast French. I'm having a hard time understanding it all but I hear more every day!

Monday, September 10, 1956

I started off the day at 11:15 a.m. with a continental breakfast in bed – which consists of juice, coffee, toast with butter and jam. It was a relief after all these heavy meals! Louise and I decided we'd try breakfast and skip the big lunch, but by 8:00 (dinner time) we were so famished we decided not to do that anymore. It was fun though – very luxurious.

Spent the afternoon in the music room practicing and reading on the deck. At 4:00 our group had a meeting about our trunks. We pay $1.50 to the French line and they handle all the customs for us for our trunks. Then they store our trunks in Paris while we're in Dijon. We pay about six cents a day – all in all about $2.00 for storage fees. It's nice to know we don't have to worry about it.

At 4:30 this p.m. our group was taken up to the bridge of the ship to the pilot house and to meet the Captain. It really was a thrill to look at the water from way up there. They showed us how the radar equipment worked, how they plot the ship's course, the weather maps, the depth reading machines, etc. The Captain was very nice and quite Captain-ish looking.

The man and woman I sang for tonight in first class were so nice. They loved us – thought we were wonderful, said I was better than Julie Andrews when I sang "I Could Have Danced All Night." They are musicians themselves, amateurs that really love music. They live in New York now, but spent most of their life in Buenos Aires. They have a daughter who was a model in Australia and who is meeting them in Europe. She is quite attractive and drips diamonds. He is really clever and looks like poor dead Louis Calhern. We were so disappointed because they didn't ask us for dinner or lunch, but they did say they were coming down to either cabin or tourist to hear us perform, so maybe they'll invite us yet. Anyway it was fun singing for them.

The boat is really rocking tonight, more than ever.

Tonight I had a drink with an architect from Florida whom I met last night. He has a Masters from Columbia. Very intellectual and interesting. I enjoyed him very much.

Tuesday, September 11, 1956

We were really sleepy heads this morning. 12:30 when we finally arose. After the delicious luncheon we spent a few minutes on the deck – then bought a beautiful picture of the ship leaving the New York Harbor with all the little tugboats ($1.00). Then we went to first class to practice – then

6

stayed up there to hear the little orchestra's concert. While we were sitting there teatime (4:30) arrived, so we had tea in first class. So elite and exclusive we were! It was fun. They had much better sandwiches and cakes than we do in tourist.

Dinnertime rolled around soon so we dressed and went. Since this was the Big Gala Evening we had an extra special dinner – the best we've had so far. First we had cantaloupe with wine in the center in a cutout hole, then consommé which was delicious, then filet de sole with a hollandaise sauce with shrimps and mushrooms, then asparagus tips cooked, drenched in butter, then delicious chicken in a casserole with peas, carrots, and potatoes, then a green salad, then ice cream with cherries and fresh peaches on top with little thin French cakes, then fruit, then coffee! It was all delicious. Surely I gained pounds from that one meal.

After dinner I put on my green satin dress to sing in at the party. The party was quite gay. There were balloons, noisemakers, paper sailor hats, dancing, drinking and entertainment, of which Louise and I were a part. We performed only for the tourist class after all – I don't know why. We were first. I sang and Louise played "On The Street Where You Live," "I Could Have Danced All Night," "You Made Me Love You," and "What's The Use of Wonderin'." Everyone liked us. They yelled "more" and "bravo." Several people have asked me all about where I'm going to study and told me I have a lovely voice and all that. It was really fun. I hated to stop singing. Also on the program was a young woman who is professional – has a job waiting for her in Paris. She did some things from *Carmen*. She has a good voice but is very affected. Then a black boy of about 20 who has a beautiful tenor voice sang some, a spiritual, a French song, "For You Alone" and an aria. They loved him. I think he's on a scholarship to study voice in Paris.

After the party I went out on deck for some fresh air. The ocean is really amazing. At night it is really terrifying and beautiful. The whitecaps and foam make such odd shapes and figures. It's fascinating.

I met a darling steward from first class today. Think I'll visit him tomorrow.

Wednesday, September 12, 1956

Another leisurely day. I didn't get to visit the cute steward after all because I didn't get up until about 12:20. Luncheon wasn't as good as usual, so I didn't eat a lot (for a change). After lunch we just sat on the deck in our deck chairs and read, dozed and all the things one does on a deck chair (well, not all the things). We even had our tea on deck today. It tastes much better out there

from General Foy Street. The station was very busy – full of people reuniting or saying goodbye. After we left the train and got our baggage altogether (all of our group), we were standing waiting for instructions from Dr. Smithers when I heard a man say, "Judy Woodall." I couldn't imagine who would know me in Paris. I turned and saw Dr. Smithers pointing me (and Louise) out to this man. Then the man and the woman with him came over to us and introduced themselves. They were M. and Mme. Rémond, the family we are to live with! They had come to meet us – the only ones besides Mme. Alvernhe and the American Express people.

Well, Louise and I were flabbergasted that the Rémonds had come. They are so wonderful, charming, and warm. Louise and I couldn't speak much French, so we all spoke English. We told them that we hoped to be able to speak French to them fairly well after our time in Dijon. The Rémonds had come back from their country place to meet us. The two little girls (age 3-6) were still there, and they are going back tomorrow at noon. They asked us to come to their house tomorrow morning before they leave, so we are. It doesn't look far from the hotel on the map. Mme. Rémond looks much younger than I had expected. I would guess her age at 34 or 35. He is about 6 feet, has gray hair and I think blue eyes. He is very jovial and distinguished looking. He is about 45 years old I would guess. They were both so wonderful to come down and meet us. It really made us feel good. I'm looking forward to seeing them tomorrow.

We were also met at the station by Mme. Alvernhe, our sponsor and French advisor here in Paris. She is also very charming and attractive – speaks beautiful English, of course. Also meeting us were the American Express people, who took care of our bags, loaded us and our bags into four cars and brought us to our hotel, The Francia on Lafayette Street.

The Francia is a small, tourist-catering hotel, not expensive. The bellboys can speak English. There is a spiral marble staircase, one of those old, old elevators that are mostly glass with a little iron, and look like a little box. If you leave your shoes outside the door at night they will be polished in the morning. (A custom in all Parisian hotels.) The rooms are very nice, each with a bath, but no washcloths or soap. Louise and I are in a room together.

After we got here we walked up the street and got a sandwich (ham on that long French bread with butter) and beer, which costs 140 francs, about 45 cents. This hotel isn't located in a very exciting place, so we came in from our snack at about 10:15 and started getting ready for bed. Now since I've written this epistle it's nearly 1:00 a.m. We're getting up early in the morning and washing our hair, walking to the Rémonds, and then walking all over until 2:30 when we have a meeting at Dr. Smithers' place of residence – a pension (like an apartment hotel, not luxurious), on the left side of the Seine. We're going to take a tour of the city during this 3-day stay too, to get a good view of everything and an idea of locations.

September 14, 1956

This has been a wonderful day. We have just done everything, and so far, Paris has been just as marvelous as I had expected it to be.

After breakfast, we started out on our day of walking. Our first destination was the Rémonds' home. We walked and walked for about an hour, and finally with our trusty map, found it.

The house is an old 4 or 5 story building on a street with other old 4 or 5 story buildings. It is right off the Place de St. Augustin, where the beautiful St. Augustin church is. You walk through the big doors with huge brass doorknobs into a sort of courtyard where the garages are – it used to be the place where the carriages were kept. The concierge lives in a small apartment next to the stairs, which are to the right as you enter. The Rémonds live on the second floor (what we would call the third floor in the US). The staircase is winding and carpeted.

The Rémonds met us at the door with their beautifully charming manners. We had the nicest visit with them – nearly 2 hours. They are the loveliest people! They're so interesting and interested in us. Our conversation was a mixture of French and English. They are very helpful – they speak their French moderately slowly so that we can understand. M. Rémond was busy making arrangements for their forthcoming trip to Scotland. He has to go on business, which is cultural relations and developments, and they'll be gone about 10 days. He has been to the US nine times, and she once.

They served us the most delicious wine I've ever tasted, some sort of port. They were surprised with both Louise and me. They expected us to be very tall because most of the Americans they know and have met are tall. They don't think we look American – they think we look more European. They were surprised (and pleasantly I think) that we didn't smoke and that we had walked all the way to their house. We showed them our families' pictures and they thought all of you were so attractive. Mme. Rémond thinks all the Woodalls have beautiful, interesting eyes. They invited us to their country place anytime we want to go with them.

They showed us their apartment and our room. Their apartment has a large living room, entrance hall, dining room, kitchen, maid's room, three bedrooms, each with a bath (one is ours) and a long hall leading to our bedroom. The entire apartment is furnished with fine, authentic 18th century furniture with very worn fabric. The living room has some beautiful pieces. None of it is lavish or fancy however. In the dining room they have a 1790 piano forte, a beautiful little tinkling thing. Also in the dining room they have a huge painting of their country place depicting each member of the family in 18th century times, which a friend painted for them.

Our room is nice, but like the rest of the house, nothing lavish. There are two beds, made up like couches, a huge old mirror over a beautiful marble fireplace, a large round table, shelves, an old dresser with a marble top. Our bathroom is very big with an old tub sitting on feet (like the one in our hotel), a lavatory, an old dresser, two chairs. The toilet is next to the bathroom in a little closet sort of. Mme. Rémond told us that the toilet was seldom in the bathroom. We were very pleased with our abode. Oh yes, they have central gas heating, which only a few families in Paris have. It hasn't been turned on yet though. We left the Rémonds and our future home very elated and excited.

We then started on our second long walk. Destination: a meeting of our group at Dr. Smithers' residence across the Seine on the Left Bank on Rue de Babylone. We walked to the Place de Madeleine and saw the beautiful church, then down Rue Royale to the Place de la Concorde where you see the monument where the guillotine used to be, and also The Louvre, the Eiffel Tower, the Place du Carroussel, and the Arc de Triomphe, all in the distance. Also you can step into part of the Tuileries Garden, which we did. It really was a thrill to be standing there at last. It just did not seem possible though. Then we crossed one of the bridges over the Seine and were in the Left Bank. We walked down Boulevard St. Germain to Rue Bellechasse, down Bellechasse to Rue de Babylone. It was quite a walk – a little over an hour, which convinced us that we won't be able to walk to school at the Sorbonne.

At the meeting Dr. Smithers and Mme. Alvernhe discussed some of our problems. Dr. Smithers said that by the time we are back from Dijon, he will have contacted our money man so we can get a good exchange rate. Then we will give our traveler's checks to Dr. Smithers, and he will take them to the man, get our money, bring it back to us. Also he and Mme. Alvernhe are going to investigate piano and voice teachers while we're gone, their prices, and a place for Louise, Eugenie, and me to practice. Mme. Alvernhe knows a voice teacher who sounds like just the thing I need – not expensive either.

When I get back from Dijon I'll find out. We also discussed courses at the Sorbonne.

After the meeting Louise and I walked back as far as the Place de la Concorde. On the way we bought some bread, ham, butter, and a bottle of wine for our supper, then took a taxi back to the hotel, came up, ate our food, rested, and went to the opera with Sandy Sutherland and Ann Coco.

We saw *Faust*. It was fabulous! I've never seen such a production. The staging was terrific, so was the singing, the costuming, and there was a long ballet in it that was breath-taking. They had three marvelous prima ballerinas. We bought the cheapest tickets they had, which were up in the 5th balcony. We stood almost the whole time, because you couldn't see in the seats. But it was worth it. Louise and I are going back to see our first Wagnerian opera tomorrow night – *Lohengrin*.

September 15th

Back to my story: after the opera, the four of us walked back to the hotel. We stopped on the way back at a sidewalk café to have café au lait (coffee with milk which is like the coffee at the French market in New Orleans). When we got in we wrote in our journals (obviously) and finally went to bed.

We got up this morning at noon, and it was hard to do then. We decided that today we would splurge and we started out by having breakfast in bed. Then we dressed and got ready to go on the tour of historical Paris. I must say the tour wasn't quite what I thought it would be. The guide spoke English and German and he had such an accent it was difficult to tell when he stopped speaking English and started speaking German.

But the tour was of course interesting and we saw so much. We saw the monument to Joan of Arc, Place du Carrousel, French Academie, St. Germain du Luxembourg, Île de la Cité, Place des Vosges, Latin Quarter (crowded with beret-headed students), Roman Villa 1500 years old, Church of the Sorbonne, Luxembourg Gardens (beautiful), Louvre, Tuileries Garden, Palace of Luxembourg now the Senate, Pantheon, the Sorbonne (which is just like everyone has said and like I expected – right on the street, dirty, old – but so interesting), Notre Dame (a miracle in itself), Hotel de Ville, Place de la Bastille, Monument of the Republic, the famous Sacré-Cœur Church from where you can view all of Paris, and finally, the Montmartre district where all the artists live and where all the night clubs (including the Moulin Rouge which is built like a red mill) are situated. The tour lasted nearly three hours. It adjourned at the L'Opéra, from where we walked home.

We stopped and ate dinner on the way. Louise and I got back to the hotel, freshened up and walked back to L'Opéra to see *Lohengrin*. We bought good seats and rather expensive ones – 880 francs which is about $2.50, but you have to tip the ushers before you can sit down, and the better your seats the more you have to tip, so it ended up costing about $3.00. But it was worth it, especially since it was the first Wagnerian opera I've seen. It really was good. The soprano was terrific. *Lohengrin* was the typical looking tenor – the banty-rooster type and he sang flat several times, but other than that he was pretty good. After the opera we walked back to the hotel, stopped on the way for some café au lait.

We plan to sleep till 10:00 tomorrow. The American Express people are picking us up and taking us to the train, which leaves at about 1:20. I think it takes about 4 or 5 hours to get to Dijon. All this walking we've been doing, has really been fun (we needed the exercise) because we've seen so much. The streets are all fascinating with the many foreign cars that nearly run over you. (At night they drive with their dim lights on and then instead of honking their horns, which is against the law, they switch their bright lights off and on.) The whole city except the churches, are buildings not more than 8 or 10 stories high, which are all old, gray, and ornate. The people of course are terribly fascinating. I'd love to just spend a day sitting in a sidewalk café watching all the people go by.

I'll write tomorrow from Dijon. What a gad-about!

Dijon

Sunday, September 16, 1957

Dear Mother and Daddy,

Your little traveler is now in Dijon. We arrived at about 3:30 this afternoon after leaving Paris at 1:10 on the fabulous all first class train, The South Wind. It is one of the best trains in Europe.

There was a stop of only a few minutes in Dijon for us to get off, so three of us were still on the train holding bags when it started again. It picked up speed so quickly that we practically had to fly off, bags and all. Everyone was yelling and jumping up and down for fear we wouldn't make it, but we did.

We were met by Mme. Lucien Herard, who is a darling woman. She's 50-ish and the best dressed woman I've seen yet in France. There was a bus for us and we rode in it to our respective residences. All of us are alone with one family. I'm staying in a small apartment with a widow and her 28 year old daughter. The woman, Mme. Delmas, is very sweet. She's about 50, a little over, very short and plump and speaks no English. Of course that was the purpose of putting us alone with people who can't speak English, so we'll have to speak French. So far we've managed all right with me running to my dictionary all the time.

The apartment is only two rooms with a small kitchen and tiny bath with a tub which is full of clothes. My room is plenty large with a nice bed, a table, a beautiful hand-carved chest from China (Mme. Delmas lived in China a while) and an equally beautiful hand-carved armoire with a long mirror also from China. However there isn't much of a place to hang clothes, so I didn't unpack much. Mme. and her daughter's room is the same size of mine. It is decorated very gaily and brightly with lots of flowers and knick-knacks.

There is a tiny balcony in their room and a window-box in my room, both with lots of flowers. We are on the 4th or 5th floor (I've forgotten) and have a beautiful view of Dijon, which is the prettiest little town I've ever seen. All the roofs of the houses are of red tile and all the houses are sort of a beige color. Leaving the station we passed through the center of town and saw the decorations of huge bunches of grapes for the wine celebration, which unfortunately ends today. The streets were packed with people. All the shops are so pretty and there are lots of beautiful churches.

I love the view from my window. The moon is coming up now and everything is really beautiful.

I panic every time I realize that I'm going to be here 5 weeks with this poor

everywhere we've been in Dijon it has been colder inside than out. I suppose the day is drawing near when all the heat is turned on.

After class this morning I walked back to my abode (a good long walk) for lunch. Lisette was there and we talked for about an hour. She really is a sweet, attractive person. I asked her where I could rent a bicycle, and she told me that I could use her bicycle. Wasn't that nice of her? I asked her to let me pay her something for it, but she wouldn't hear of it. Then she told me it needed a very small repair job on the wheel and that she would go to the garage tomorrow with me to get it fixed before she goes to work. I'll probably have to pay about a dollar to get it fixed which is much cheaper than renting one. I can hardly wait to ride it. Ann Coco and Martha Johnston rented bicycles today and came to school on them this afternoon. They were so funny riding them. The traffic is very confusing and the first time on a bike isn't easy. Also the streets are cobblestone which makes it difficult to sit very well.

After lunch and my conversation with Lisette, I walked back to the tourist office and met Eugenie, Sandy, and Louise. We all needed to buy notebooks, ink, stationery, envelopes. We went in a darling little book and stationery shop. A sweet gray haired middle aged man ran it. We had the best time talking to him. We left there and went in one of the large department stores and Sandy and I bought of all things, a washcloth.

We left the department store and headed for a bank so Eugenie could cash a travelers cheque. On the way we ran into the man of the family where Eugenie is staying, and he gave us all a ride to the bank in his little car. All the cars are very small. Everyone says to us, "En Amerique les voitures sont très grandes and très longes, n'est-ce pas?" (In America the cars are very big and long aren't they?)

After Eugenie got her money we walked to a café and had some coffee. While we were sitting there, Coco and Martha rode by on their bicycles yelling "Au secours, au secours!" (Help, help!) They were so funny we nearly died laughing. We all went on over to school then for the lecture nobody understood. It was over about 6:15 and I walked back home with Coco and Martha, who live only a few streets away from where I live.

Pretty soon after I came back we had supper. We had soup, eggs and bacon – more ham than bacon if you know what I mean – bacon cut like Canadian bacon. Then we had noodles cooked with tomatoes, cookies, then fruit. Mme. Delmas knows how to make the best of what she has.

Mme. Delmas and Lisette are so good and patient with me. At dinner our conversations were broken with my references to my dictionary during which they were very understanding. After our delicious dinner, I said "Oh, je suis si pleine," thinking I had said "I'm so full." Both Mme. and Lisette looked horrified, then started to laugh, realizing I had translated literally, but what I had said in French was a very coarse way of saying "I'm so pregnant." Will I ever learn?

Lisette works very hard. She works all day in an office and before and after work she makes little figures (like dolls) of animals and skaters and dancers. She makes them out of wire and a straw-like material and sells them at a store here in Dijon for four hundred francs a piece – which is about one dollar and thirty cents. She is very proud of them.

I doubt if we'll be going out much at night in Dijon. Since we are separated we would have to go alone at least part of the way. We may go to the ballet tomorrow night with M. Brahm, the man of the family with whom Eugenie is living. That would be O.K. We can't go out with any boys unless they are first approved by Mme. Herard, which is an excellent thing.

Everyone rides bicycles in Dijon. Today we saw a fat, fat nun riding one with her habit flying in all directions. Later we saw a priest riding with his skirts tucked up around him. Very amusing.

Oh, I told Mme. Herard I had no place to take a bath and she told me this P.M. that the woman where Eugenie lives said we could take a shower (hot) in her bathroom anytime for 75 francs (22¢) which is cheaper, more private, and everything else than going to the public baths. So my situation is better already.

Tuesday, September 18, 1956 2:20 PM

This is a gorgeous day! The sun is bright and the sky a beautiful blue. A perfect day for taking pictures!

This morning I rode to school on a bicycle! It was one lent to me by the woman next door until Lisette's bicycle is fixed – which it will be in a few minutes. The ride was very exciting because the bike is old, the brakes are bad, and the traffic is heavy. Lisette's is in good condition – fairly new, good brakes, etc. Now that I'm bike riding I wish I had brought a shoulder bag instead of the one I have. I put it on my shoulder anyway but it doesn't stay very well. Anyway – I made it to school safe and sound. I love to ride – very good exercise – also saves money on the trolley.

Our lecture with Mme. Herard began at 10:00 and lasted until 12:00. Before she started speaking in French, she spoke to us in English about our housing – what to expect and not to expect. One thing led to another, and pretty soon she was telling us about life during the war. I pray God we never have another war! She had to live like an animal, scraping garbage out of the tins the Germans and Americans threw away – going without soap for months – starving. She and her husband lost all their furniture, their silver – everything! I couldn't help but cry as she told us. She said the French in the small towns especially had the feeling of "what's the use to rebuild – to try to improve our towns and homes it will be bombed and destroyed again." I don't see how after so much horror, hardship, pain, privation, and suffering these people have existed, have continued to live, to be happy, contented and friendly to Americans – because we bombed the French in our effort to get rid of the Germans. It is a mystery and a wonderful miracle. We can't know, we can't understand even part of the meaning of war in America because we have been fortunate not to have to learn about it the hard way. Pray God we shall never have to.

September 19, 1956

I'll start where I left off. After Mme. Herard's lecture – which was on the province of Bourgogne (Dijon is in Bourgogne which we translate Burgundy) and which I understood quite well – I pedaled home on my bicycle for lunch. Lisette always comes home for lunch (everything closes from 12:00 to 2:00 for lunch) and after we ate, we all talked while Lisette was busily making her straw animals to sell. I'm really lucky to be with two such fine people as Lisette and Mme. Delmas.

Yesterday at 3:00 we met Mme. Herard at the tourist office and she took us around to visit some of the beautiful buildings of the 13th, 14th, 15th, and 16th centuries. It is amazing they are in such good condition. Tomorrow Mme. Herard is going to lecture to us about the buildings we saw, the architecture, etc. The little trip was over at 5:10, so four of us stopped at a little place for some tea and pastry. Everyone always looks us over when we go in a place like that. We look so typically American with all our feet in the same kind of shoes, all with huge pocketbooks, and looking very wide-eyed!

After one of Mme. Delmas' delicious dinners, I dressed to go to the ballet. The man with whom Eugenie lives, M. Brahm, his wife and daughter took Louise, Sandy, Eugenie and me with them to the ballet – we paid for our seats of course. This ballet company was a group of Hungarians who do folk dances. The costumes were so colorful, as were the dances and songs – everything was happy, gay, carefree. It is hard to believe that this is the first time, since

Hungary became Communistic under Russia, that these young (17 or 18 yrs. old) people have been allowed to leave Hungary. Last night was an extra performance which they were not supposed to give – they were supposed to have returned to Hungary yesterday, but because they were so well received here in Dijon, they decided to stay.

Since we don't have to be at school until 10:00 A. M., I have been sleeping till about 8:30. It's wonderful! This morning our class wasn't a class – it was a tour of the palace of the Dukes of Burgundy, given to us by M. Le Professeur France. He of course talked to us in French and I could understand most of what he said. The palace is very big and ornate. It's hard to realize that such richness and grandeur existed in the midst of such pitiful poverty. We even climbed 315 stairs to the top of the old tower, from where you can see the whole of Dijon – even past where Dijon stops. We saw lots of places we want to visit on our bicycles.

After lunch today I talked a few minutes to Lisette. I am improving rapidly in my French. It's amazing that in three days I can see so much difference.

This afternoon Mme. Herard is taking Louise, Susan and me to the showing at the very exclusive shop in Dijon of the new collections of Dior and other designers. Of course we're all thrilled. Tomorrow the other five are going, but without Mme. Herard. I'm glad we're going with her because she can explain so many things to us. I'm stopping now to get dressed to go. After the "collections" we have a lecture with M. Herard, Mme. Herard's husband who is also a teacher.

10 PM – September 19, 1956

Well I'm all clean – I've washed my hair, my clothes, and me – with hot water from the kettle of course. It's amazing how much water one uses without realizing it until he can no longer have it anytime he wants it!

I didn't get Lisette's bike – decided to wait until the morning before school. But I did go to the "collections." It was much fun and so elegant – the first elegant thing I've seen or done since I've been here.

We met Mme. Herard in front of the Oudebert, where the showing was held. The store is very exclusive and expensive for the people of Dijon. They carry all the Dior products, etc. The higher you go in the store, the higher the prices. They did have some beautiful things! The showing of the collections was held in the rooms in the very upstairs of the store, which were filled to capacity with all women, most well-dressed. Mme. Herard said that the store never let people have tickets to come unless they thought they might buy something.

The "collections" were of Dior and Pierre Balmain (never heard of him). There were three models and they walked out one at a time, stayed a good while, walked away. There was no one to describe the dresses or anything, and Mme. Herard said that they never give the prices of expensive clothes like they presented today. Two of the models were very good and very Parisian, but one, a blonde, must have been a substitute. She walked clumsily, didn't have a good figure, looked embarrassed, and had no poise.

The clothes were beautiful but not as "different" as I had expected. There were dress and coat outfits, suits with the new loose fitted jackets, dresses with lots of detail in the front (which I dislike very much – makes the stomach look big), there were *My Fair Lady* necklines, full skirts, but not as full as they have been. The materials used were mostly tweed, taffeta (or peau de soie), and soft wool. There were two coats of Persian lamb trimmed with mink. Very different, but not very pretty in my eyes.

There were three things I really liked. A gray suit with a full skirt and loose fitted jacket – take off the jacket and the skirt turns out to be a dress. A gray cocktail, party dress with a gorgeous neckline – a sheath with an over skirt that makes it almost an entirely different dress. A green taffeta cocktail dress with a beautiful neckline and semi-full skirt. There were probably all terribly expensive. It really was nice – I probably won't have another chance to see an original Dior showing.

Afterward Mme. Herard, Susan, Louise, and I went for some tea and pastry. I learned from Mme. H (who speaks beautiful English – did I tell you?) that Mme. Delmas and Lisette have had a sad life. They were well off – the husband died (I don't know how) and then came the war and they lost all that they had. The older daughter was married to a soldier who had to go to Indo-China. When he came back he had changed so radically they couldn't get along – so they divorced each other. Later the girl was engaged to a doctor here in Dijon, but his parents wouldn't let him marry her because she was a divorcée. This grieved the girl so much – and also she was quite ill anyway – that she died. The doctor tried to get her to marry him on her deathbed, but of course she didn't. After her death Lisette and Mme. Delmas nearly died of grief. They cried all the time and would not live in the present – always in the past. Finally Mme. Herard persuaded Mme. Delmas almost a year ago to take in boarders to help make money. At first Mme. Delmas did not want to – her pride was too great. Finally she agreed, and has been much happier since. For Lisette – she doesn't like Dijon and wants to leave. Mme. Herard said that perhaps she will be able to leave now that her mother has a way of making a living. Isn't it all sad? Yet Mme. and Lisette smile, go about their work cheerfully, go out of their way to be helpful and kind – it is wonderful!

At 5:15 we had to go to school – a lecture with M. Herard. He is the cutest man! He has a real deep voice which is unusual for a Frenchman. He is most charming. He lectured on French contemporary poetry – a very interesting lecture – simply delivered so we could comprehend and we did. I wish we could have him every day instead of M. Mery the Monkey and M. France the Owl!

Thursday, September 20, 1956

I've been in France exactly one week and it seems like I've been here at least a month. I wonder why?

This morning I finally got Lisette's bicycle. It rides well and the brakes are good but it, like all the bikes here, has the most uncomfortable seat and handle-bars. The seat is high and the handle-bars are low, which explains it.

We had class at 10:15 this morning at the municipal Library, where the head man who is famous in France as an expert on manuscripts, took us up in the special rooms of the library – rooms only entered by persons with special permission and accompanied by this man. (I've forgotten his name.) It really was interesting. He showed us all the valuable and old books, old maps, globes. Manuscripts with beautiful printing and gorgeous illustrations, called illuminations – of beautiful, rich colors. It's hard to believe they are so old, they're so well-preserved. We saw many books written about and dedicated to many of the French about whom we studied this year – Napoleon (of course), Gilbert, Duchess de Berry, Duke de Berry, etc. The only drawback to our library excursion was the man – the expert – he talked so rapidly we could hardly follow him, and he stammered terribly. It looks as if all the professors we have (except Mme. Herard) have some physical defect.

Our lecture at 5:00 was with M. Mery – the little monkey looking man. I guess I'd best explain my statement about the defects of our professors. M. Mery talks so that saliva gathers on his bottom lip in a little white spot and nearly drives us mad. Isn't that awful! M. France, who looks very much like an owl, blinks his eyes all the time. Then the man in the library stammered. I hate to be crude – but he not only stammered, he had B.O. Poor men. But they are so nice and anxious to help us. I should be ashamed of myself for noticing such things – but they're so obvious! Anyway, today M. Mery spoke more slowly than he did the other day and we all understood him much better. Tonight at dinner Lisette and Mme. Delmas told me my French was greatly improving!

After the lecture I pedaled home, had dinner (very good as usual) and got ready for bed. I love this going to bed early, it's quite a change. You can't go out at night even if you wanted to because there's no one to go with. In Paris it's different because it's such a big city, girls can go out safely in twos and threes at night in Paris. You can go in twos and threes here too, but we're separated and we'd have to go part of the way alone even if we met somewhere. It's a good thing because we need the night for study and we need to be in a good rested healthy condition when we go to Paris.

The weather has been so peculiar lately. It's cold in the morning, warm in the afternoon chilly at night. There's been lots of wonderful sunshine – no rain and I hope not any for a long time. (Rain that is.)

Friday, September 21, 1956

Right now my legs are aching so badly from riding my bicycle that I can hardly move. I've ridden all day long. First to school where dear Mme. Herard talked to us in French about Beaune, the town we're going to visit tomorrow.

After lunch I pedaled to Louise's house. She wanted me to meet the woman she lives with, Mme. Herz. They are in a new apartment building with all the conveniences. It would be a wonderful place if it weren't for the woman. Now she knows that Louise is going to leave next week. Today they were still eating when I arrived. Mme. Herz had asked another lady and her two children to lunch also. They found out from Mme. Herz that Louise was moving and during the meal – at least while I was there, they hardly spoke to Louise. She can't wait to move and I don't blame her at all.

When they finished lunch Louise and I rode to the shop where she was going to get a bicycle to rent. It isn't far from where I live. This whole section is very picturesque because it's so old. We passed some darling little cottages with lots of flowers and vegetables growing in the yards. After we got her bicycle we went to the Swiss Consulate to see if we could have any travelers checks exchanged at the Swiss rate. We can't, but we learned about a huge, splendid wine festival to be held next week in a colorful town in Switzerland near here (about 4 hours on a train). All 8 of us may go there next weekend for that festival and to exchange money!

We left the Consulate and rode to this beautiful park not too far from school. Then we saw a beautiful street lined with tall trees and street lamps, so we rode down it. It must be where the few rich people of Dijon live parce-que (because) there were some fine looking houses with big lawns and wrought iron fences that looked as if they belonged to richer people than we have seen here yet. At the end of this long avenue we came to the most gorgeous park! It was nothing but lots and lots of trees, so thick and green and the sun was shining through like you always see in pictures of forests and such. There were lots of buckeye trees and so many buckeyes on the ground. Reminded me of the necklaces I used to make out of the buckeyes in our neighbor's yard. Buckeyes and red corn. We walked around in the park a little then rode back to school to meet the boy for the library instruction. This same boy is going with us to Beaune tomorrow to explain everything there and on the way. Mme. Herard cannot go because she wants to cook things for us to have Sunday at her house. The library instruction was short and simple, but we stayed and talked with Pierre (about 18 or 19) till 6:30. He gave us some helpful hints about our French. (He told us all this in French.) He's really very nice and charming – the only boy I've seen that I would like to go out with. Funny how male companionship makes things so much more interesting! After that, I pedaled home and here I am waiting for supper, after which I intend to take a bath – not really a bath in a tub – but a bath, and go to bed. We have to leave at 8:45 in the morning, which means I'll have to get up earlier than I have been.

Mme. Delmas is so sweet. Today she bought some beautiful carnations to put in my room. She always has lots of flowers in the apartment – even in the kitchen. It makes things very cheery.

Riding a bicycle makes me so hungry! I'm starving. I don't think I've gained any weight. I look the same to myself, and my clothes fit the same. I'm surprised, because it seems like all I've done is eat, but I guess all the exercise keeps me from gaining. Hurrah!

Saturday, September 22, 1956

Our trip to Beaune was very successful and also tiring. We left this morning at 9:00 on a public bus. We rode to a little town called Nuits St. George and visited this old, old château in the middle of a beautiful vineyard called Clos de Vougeot. It used to be – ages ago – a monastery for the Cistercian monks. It was begun in the 11th century, then another part was built in the 13th century and still another in the 15th! It's wonderful to see three different styles of architecture in three different centuries in the same place! In the oldest part there were four of the huge wine pressers the monks used to use to make wine. There were barrels so large that the monks had to climb down into them, naked to do whatever they had to do to help the grapes ferment. The guide told us that sometimes the men died in the barrels from the carbon dioxide of the fermentation, but that they used that wine anyway after they pulled the body out! Ugh!

We left Clos de Vougeot and took another bus to Beaune. When we got there we were starving, so the first thing we did was to find a café where we ordered wine to drink with the sandwiches we had brought. We chose a café right by the marketplace, which was in full operation since this was Saturday.

After lunch we went to the Hotel Dieu – a hospital built at the beginning of the 15th century. It is noted for its beautiful tile roof of many colors. The tile roof is on the front of the building, inside a court so that they can't be seen from the street. Tours are given so you can see it. We went in a marvelous room which is just like the rooms used now for the patients. It has the old wooden bed with red curtains that draw, the old side tables, and the tin dishes used. At one end is a beautiful chapel with an altar and stained-glass windows. We also went to the kitchen and a wonderful museum of the hospital. In one of the museum's rooms was a huge painting of angels, etc. with people at the bottom of the painting going to Hell. The expressions on their faces were fabulously horrible! It really is an extraordinary work. The nuns who are nurses at this hospital still wear the same type habit which was worn in the 15th century – huge white hats that look like wings. It really is a wonderful sight.

From there we went to the caves where thousands and thousands of bottles of wine are stored. It was so cold and damp in there I nearly died, and the fumes were enough to intoxicate anybody! The caves have been used since the 13th century and I think they have not swept the cobwebs out since then!

After the caves we went to the bus stop to catch the bus and missed it of course. We waited another 45 minutes for the next one – we sang all the way back to Dijon to the amusement of some of the passengers and the chagrin of others! But we had fun.

The bus stopped in Dijon near the tourist office. Sandy and I were dying to go to the bathroom so we went to the tourist office and asked if they had a "toilette." They sent us around to the back of the building. It was down lots of steps and in a dark corner, but the door was locked! We were so bad off and so tickled that we had to go right then. There was a drain outside the door so we just used it. Ann and Martha were waiting at the top of the stairs for us. When they heard us (the place echoed terribly) and realized what we were doing they burst out laughing. They started telling us to get up – some boys were approaching, but we couldn't get up then! Two boys walked right in front of the steps and looked right down at us. We couldn't do anything but just stay where we were. By then we were so tickled we were dying – and embarrassed. I guess now that we've gone to the bathroom in (almost) public we're really French! They do it all the time – well practically in public. The public places on the street are strictly public! Poor us.

Sunday, September 23, 1956

This morning Eugenie, Susan, Louise, and I all went to High Mass at St. Bénigne Cathedral. We went mainly to hear the music. It was the first time I've ever been to a Catholic service (beside a wedding) and I found it very moving and beautiful. And the music was exquisite. The church is very large with tall, tall ceilings and stone walls, so when the organ sounded it was as if there were 100 organs instead of one. It was beautiful! There were two organs – one in front and one in back, and when they played together it was divine. I haven't been so moved religiously, in ages.

The service was conducive to prayer. I really felt like a better person spiritually after having come to the Mass. (Don't worry, I'd never be a Catholic.) After Mass we four walked down to the Protestant church – the one Protestant church in Dijon – to meet Sandy, Ann, and Martha. Then all of us went to a café for café au lait then I came home for lunch, changed from my suit to my blue silk dress and walked to Louise's abode. We then walked on up to Eugenie's house, which contains a piano. Martha met us there and we practiced some songs arranged for four-part harmony. We really sounded good and it was such fun.

We sang for about an hour and a half, then walked to Mme. Herard's for tea – with everything good to eat. Mme. Herard had all of us, Pierre Quintallet (our guide to Beaune), another boy, two French girls, an older couple, and she and husband – whom I dearly love. We had wine red and white and cassis, all sorts of pastry – I had entirely too much to eat. We looked at art projects, read poetry, sang, talked and had a wonderful time. I hated to leave. M. and Mme. Herard's home is very nice – not lavish, but very, very nice. It's so hard to picture their living as they did during the war.

Monday, September 24, 1956

This has been a confusing day emotionally because I've been very gay and happy and very sad and tearful. My day started with an unsuccessful attempt to pump up my bicycle tires with this strange little pump that goes with it. I rode to school with them flat and luckily Pierre was in front of school talking with some of the girls when I got there, and he pumped them for me.

Lots and lots of students were at school today taking their examinations for their degrees. Most of the exams are oral and public. I think I'll listen in tomorrow morning since we have no class. This morning we had a lecture with Mme. Herard. I can understand her almost perfectly. Her lectures always end up being on many subjects because we have so many questions for her. After school I came home, ate lunch, washed my hair, some clothes, sat out on the petite balcony to let my hair dry and read over my notes.

I was expecting Bernard Paulien, one of the two boys at Mme. Herard's last night, at 4:00. Last night Bernard, his mother, father, and two sisters drove me home from Mme. Herard's and on the way Bernard asked me if he could call on me at 4:00 today and we would speak French. He told me this also in English, which he speaks very well. He studied last year at Oxford. Anyway, I was going to get dressed at 3:30 so I'd be ready when he came. As I said – I was sitting on the balcony in my robe, with damp hair, when I saw him coming across the street all dressed in his blue suit at 3:20! I nearly died. I ran to Mme. Delmas and asked her what to do. She said she'd let him in and tell him I'd been detained and therefore still at my "toilette." (Doesn't that sound awful?) Well, I dressed in a jiffy (believe it or not) and walked in to greet him. He asked me if I were ready to go. I had no idea of what he was talking about, but I said yes, went to get my purse, and we left. After a block and a half of walking I finally asked him where we were going and he said to the Place Darcy for something to drink at the sidewalk café. We walked, talked and finally had tea. He asked me to come to lunch Thursday at his home, and also to go dancing some night. Of course I'm tickled pink even though his name is Bernard and he isn't at all attractive to look at. He's very tall, very nice, and very intelligent. He is wonderful to talk French with because he can tell me the equivalent French word for English words I know. He walked me back to school for my 5:00 class (for which I was 10 minutes late) and then took his leave till Thursday. On the way to school I learned that he is going to school in Paris in October to study business administration at a school very close to M. and Mme. Rémond's house. He said he and his friends (yay!) would come to see Louise and me there.

Tuesday September 25, 1956

This has been an educational day in more ways than one! We had no class this morning, so I stayed in my pajamas until lunch time. I spent the morning writing an essay in French on our trip to Beaune, Saturday. It took me two hours to write it although it isn't that long. It was the first long piece of writing in French that I've done since my final exam in May, and there were lots of little things I had to look up.

After lunch I went to the post-office and then rode to the Tourist office; from there Mme. Herard took us to the old, old monastery of Chartreuse, which is now a mental institution. The purpose of our going was to see the marvelous masterpiece of sculpture, *The Well of Moses* (in French, *Puits de Moise*). It was done in the 13th century and it is magnificent. The expressions are very realistic, so much so that it does not seem possible that is was made in the 13th century. Mme. Herard explained everything about it to us. She makes everything so interesting. We also went to the beautiful gardens which used to be part of the monastery but are now public gardens.

After our little trip we came back to the museum where M. Quary gave us a lecture on the old Monastery of Chartreuse and *The Well of Moses* and illustrated it with slides. It would have been wonderful except we were so tired and he showed so many pictures and he mumbled his French. But the main drawback was that we were pooped!

After the lecture, which lasted until nearly seven, we decided to meet at nine at the café at the Place Darcy for some coffee – five of us, Louise, Ann, Sandy, Eugenie, and me.

After supper and our usual after-supper conversation, I met Ann at the Place de la Republic and we walked to the Place Darcy where the other three were waiting for us. There were a lot of French boys sitting around and they all made comments. Finally we decided to move inside where we wouldn't be conspicuous. We moved. The boys, three of them (one real good looking) followed us, and sat down at the table next to us. They tried to talk to us in French and English but we never said a word to them. We tried our best to keep straight faces but it was almost impossible. They did everything to try to make us talk to them, but in vain. After 45 minutes they finally moved and sat with two French girls. Since other boys had come in and were also eyeing us, we left. We were scared to walk home, so Sandy, Ann, and I took a taxi – Louise and Eugenie had their bikes and they live very close to each other. One reason we were sort of scared was because Mme. Herard told us that many of the students who were crowding the streets are Communists. I think I told you that the students were thick because this is exam week. Anyhow, we know not to ever go out at night to a café. A movie is all right, but not a café. Mme. Herard didn't know we were going, or she probably would have disapproved. We really didn't dream it would be like it was. Live and learn – always!

Wednesday, September 26, 1956

This has been our first day of bad weather for it has rained and drizzled all day – very cold and damp. Brrrr!

I slept until 8:30, got up, dressed slowly, ate my breakfast, read some French, went to St. Bénigne Cathedral where M. France, the Owl, took us through the church and into the old church, which is sort of underground. The old part was begun in the year 1000! Part of it that we saw was completed in the 9th century. It really is unbelievable. There are several pieces of sculpture on the pillars that are the only ones of their kind in the world, and the first in Europe! I enjoyed that visit very much, it would have been wonderful had it not been so cold and damp. But you can't have everything.

After the tour of the old church, I came home and had lunch, after which I went to Mme. Monjaux's, where Ann Coco lives, to take a real bath – my first in Dijon! It was really luxurious – should have been because it cost me thirty cents to take it.

After my bath Ann and I sat and talked awhile, then she and I rode over to my abode. She loved Mme. Delmas, as everyone does, and thought my room was so cheerful, which it is. We stayed here until four o'clock when we had a lesson with Mme. Herard. She had received word from Dr. Smithers and Dr. Woods that we are to start reading a book a week, in French of course, and writing an essay on each book. Bye, bye spare time! We were already supposed to write an essay this week – which I've already done. I'm glad they're sending us instructions. It's hard to make ourselves study when there is so much to see and do.

After our lesson with Mme. Herard, 5 of us went to see the pastor of the Protestant church here. Last Sunday Coco, Sandy, and Martha attended this Protestant church and noticed there was no music except for the hymns. No one played the organ or sang. They had the bright idea that we could sing for them and Louise could play the organ. We told Mme. Herard, she wrote a note to the minister, he told us to come today. They (he and his wife) were very nice, but finally we got the hint that they didn't really want us to sing in the service. Of course they appreciated our gesture – but no thanks anyway. We felt sort of silly afterwards. Live and learn.

All in all this hasn't been an exciting day. Oh, Mme. Herard received our "laws" today from Dr. Smithers, the "what we can and can't do" laws. They're no different from the way we've been doing!

Thursday, September 27, 1956

This has been a very enjoyable day. We had a session with Mme. Herard this morning from eleven to twelve. She gave us dictation – I didn't do so hot.

At noon I pedaled home very quickly, changed clothes, put on my shrimp-colored outfit for it was such a pretty day, and by some miracle was ready at twelve thirty when Bernard Paulien came for me to take me to lunch at his home. His father had come with him in the car, which was very elegant to me since I've pedaled and walked now for 2 weeks everywhere I've gone (nearly).

We went to his house which is up on one of the hills of Dijon. It's a very nice house, not pretty on the outside, but the inside is beautifully furnished with reproductions of French Provençal furniture. Our déjeuner was very good. Before dinner we had an aperitif of that deliciously smooth port wine, after dinner some coffee and a liqueur that nearly tore my throat up, it was so strong. After dinner also we played records on the phonograph most of them were American songs. There was even some New Orleans jazz! We walked back to my little place and were here by four thirty so I could change and be at class at five.

I really did enjoy the afternoon. His family is delightful. They think I speak French well, especially for having studied only two years. I was very flattered and pleased to hear this.

M. Paulien asked me if Daddy were in commerce. I found it very hard to explain "automobile dealer" in French. Finally Bernard, who speaks English very well, came to my rescue. You have a concession of Ford cars, Daddy! Bernard studied last year in Oxford. He speaks French, English, Spanish, and reads German and can speak it a little. Amazing isn't it?

Friday, September 28, 1956

I've been putting off telling you this because I thought it was only temporary. But for the last week I've been itching with the itchiest little mosquito-looking bites. My legs are covered and they're also on my arms, my back, my stomach! I thought perhaps they would go away – but no! And every morning when I get up I have new ones. I showed them to Mme. Delmas and she said she couldn't imagine where I was getting them – certainly not in her house! Well, finally today I was just nearly dying they itch so badly, so at school I showed them to Mme. Herard. She was much alarmed and wrote a letter to Mme. Delmas hinting for her to check my bed, etc. She'll get the letter tomorrow. I dread it because I don't want Mme. Delmas to think I'm insulting her cleanliness – but something has to be done before I itch to death!

Saturday, September 29, 1956

What a day!! At 11:00 we all met at the tourist office to go on our day's journey. First mishap: Martha decided not to go. Second: Susan and Ellie couldn't find bicycles to rent. (They waited too late to see about them.) So five of us – Louise, Sandy, Coco, Eugenie, and moi started out with our bicycles and our little lunches. Before we got out of Dijon Louise's bike went haywire. We got it fixed at a not-so-nearby shop, and started off again.

The weather was beautiful – so was the scenery. There were lots of wildflowers, pretty little farms. We rode for about 45 minutes or more – an hour I guess, and then stopped at this little quaint village called Couchey. We stopped in a tiny café, bought some wine, ate our lunches. While we were there a man came to the little village square, played on a little drum and yelled out advertisements, for the forthcoming fiesta. The church bells chimed and two little boys watched us during our whole lunch.

We mounted our bikes and started out to Fixin, a little village famous for a park and an unusual statue of Napoleon, besides having an interesting history and being quite colorful. The wine had been pretty strong and we were all laughing, singing, and riding very fast – up a slight hill. At the top I started coughing a little. We got back on our bikes – my cough got worse. I lagged behind, I tried to rest and make it stop but the cough turned into that dreadful wheeze. I stopped and sat down on the side of the road, but by that time it was so bad I could barely breathe.

The girls had gone on and not turned back because they thought I'd stopped to go to the bathroom. By some miracle I managed to ride to Fixin, which was only about 1½ miles away, and the girls were waiting for me in front of the café. I nearly passed out when I got off my bike – I couldn't breathe! They took me inside and gave me some water. I saw myself in the mirror and I looked like I was about to blow up. My face was red as fire with little white spots all over it. Of course I had no medicine with me.

By then it was quite obvious that I was having an asthma attack – it was the real thing this time. Sandy and Eugenie stayed there with me while Louise and Coco made it to the nearest drugstore, which was nearly 1½ miles away.

Louise came back with some wonderful pills for asthma and hay fever that helped me within 15 minutes! Coco rode on further to tell the man who owns the vineyard we were supposed to visit that we couldn't make it. Then she came on a bus to Fixin so I could then take that bus and come back. They were all so good to me. They really were good friends. I hated to leave them to struggle with my bike, but they insisted, and since I was in such bad shape I agreed.

The bus was so crowded and more people got on along the way. We were packed like sardines. We got back and I walked home.

I was met by Mme. Delmas who looked as if she'd been crying. She was getting ready to go out. She showed me the letter Mme. Herard wrote to her about my bites. Mme. Herard had said she would write a very tactful letter. Well – Mme. Delmas showed me the letter and it was anything but tactful. I was mortified. It said "Please check Judy's bed. I think there might be vermin in it!" It was so insulting! Mme. Delmas told me I could find another room perhaps. I was speechless! She left and I cried and cried which did the asthma no good! Finally I washed my face, dressed, and went to the park across the street. Then I walked up to where I thought I might find the girls if they had returned, and sure enough they were there at the Café Glacier drinking tea.

I joined them, told them my sadness. We all decided Mme. Herard is not the perfection we thought she was. She has written letters to Ellie's family and Louise's ex-family (she moved yesterday) which were very tactless.

The girls found a man at Fixin who brought my bike back absolutely free to Dijon. He was on a motor scooter, so he had to leave it at the Ford-Mercury place (I haven't seen it) because it's against the law to carry bikes and ride scooters at the same time. So, Monday morning I'll have to go get it before school.

Anyway, after the café I came home. Mme. Herard had been here in the meantime. Mme. Delmas and Lisette told her how insulted they were, etc. Apparently she realized it too from what they said. I told them I didn't want to leave them. I liked them very much, and I knew they were very clean. We got everything straightened out and have forgotten the whole matter.

But – I still have my bites. It may be some sort of allergy, but I don't think so. The bed was changed today and I know it's clean – it's really a mystery. Anyway, after dinner Mme. Delmas fixed me some hot tea – only it's not tea – it's made from some sort of green herbs and is yellow when it's ready to drink. If my bites don't go away and if I keep on getting new ones, I'm going to a doctor or somebody. As for the asthma, I'm sure it was brought on by too much wine and by getting hot and tired immediately after eating and drinking! Anyway – I know what not to do now.

Well – that's the reason I said "what a day." I hope I never spend another one like it. The really bad part is that we rode all the way back and I didn't even see Fixin's claim to fame; and because of me the girls didn't get to see much of it. And none of us got to the vineyard where we wanted to go most of all!

But – I guess there have to be days like this to make you appreciate the really good days. Don't worry about my asthma. I'm sure it won't happen again, because I'm sure I know what caused it today.

Sunday, September 30, 1956

Compared to yesterday this was a dull, but very pleasant day. I went to St. Bénigne Cathedral (same as last Sunday) with Louise, Ellie, and Eugenie. The music there is absolutely magnificent! Of course, I don't understand anything else that's going on (except the collection), but the music is so beautiful and I like to go and just pray when and for as long as I can.

After church we met the others at the café and sat there till about 12:20 then Louise came home with me for lunch. Her family went to the country today, so last night (after the storm) I asked Mme. Delmas if Louise could come for lunch. She and Lisette seemed so pleased that I asked and said they'd love to have her. I think it proved to them that I really do like them and I don't think they are dirty or surely wouldn't invite my friends to come see!

After lunch Louise and I went to her new home to do some studying and play the piano. She lives now with a very rich young widow with three little girls. They have a fine apartment. But I repeat I am glad I'm living where I am, although there is a disadvantage as far as meeting new French people through Mme. Delmas and Lisette. But I'm getting along and I have no complaints.

After we studied, it was so gorgeous outside we walked through the park and down the main street of the town, looked in all the shop windows. Sunday is walking day in Dijon – everybody was walking and sitting at the café.

I have a few new bites today. I'm really stunned as to where they're coming from. The mosquitoes are bad now as everyone says, but I haven't seen one even near me. I'm sleeping with my windows closed so they don't get in that way! Really a mystery.

By the way – how's election news these days? I wrote for whatever it takes

for more information or to place an order, contact:

TATE PUBLISHING
AND **ENTERPRISES**, LLC

www.tatepublishing.com/bookstore
888.361.9473

An Extraordinary Year
A Journal of a Student Abroad 1956-1957

Judy
Woodall

Judy Woodall

An Extraordinary Year

to vote by absentee ballot. Are Ike's chances more or less? Over here they pronounce "Ike" as "Icke" as in picnic. Really sounds funny.

Monday October 1, 1956

I haven't had a drop of milk since I've been here. I do have milk (Carnation) in my café au lait every morning. Café au lait is practically half coffee and half milk. At the other meals we have red wine (and white too on special occasions) but I've been drinking mostly water with my meals lately. For breakfast I always have café au lait with 3 or 4 slices of toast with butter and jelly or preserves. For lunch we always have some sort of salad (not necessarily green), meat and one or two vegetables, cheese, dessert, and fruit. And of course French bread with every meal. At supper we always have soup plus the courses we have at lunch. At the end of the week when the money is low we don't have meat but maybe once a day. Then we eat lots of ham for ham is dirt cheap. So I am well fed – too well fed, I'm afraid. Mme. Delmas is really a good cook. But right now I'd love to have some country ham, turnip greens, green onions, cornbread and a big glass of milk! Just dreaming I guess.

I got up at seven-thirty, ate breakfast, dressed, went to the post office and started out to find the Ford-Mercury place where the girls told me my bike was left on Saturday. I walked, and walked in the direction they told me to take, but never saw the place. I asked one little man in a fishing tackle shop about it and I had the hardest time making him understand "Ford." They pronounce it with a French accent so that it sounds like "Forte" when said very quickly. He told me it was back near Place de la Republic which is where I live. By that time I had to hurry to school to be there on time. When I got to school I asked the girls where the Ford place was and learned I didn't walk far enough. So Louise said she would go with me after lunch to get it.

After our course with Mme. Herard this A.M. I came home to lunch, which was really good. For vegetables we had boiled potatoes cut up in little pieces with lots of butter and mixed with cooked carrots. I remember being told that French carrots are delicious, and they really are!

After lunch I walked to Louise's and met her new family, part of it, the mother, grandmother, and one of the little girls, the one not old enough to go to school. Today was the first day of school for the French children. Then Louise and I went to get my bike. I wanted to tell the man that my Daddy was also a Ford dealer, but the owner wasn't there. The chain was off its track so I took the bicycle a few doors down the street and had that fixed.

Then we went to the library to check out some of books to study for this week and write a report on. Unfortunately the book assigned to me is one that cannot be taken out of the library which means I'll have to do all my reading there. After reading in the library for about an hour and a half (my book is on "Songs of Bourgogne"), we went to our last (hurrah!) class with M. Mery – the monkey. I understood pretty much of the lecture today. Afterwards I rode home on my bicycle. I had on my black suede flat shoes and one of them fell off and was nearly crushed right in the middle of the street. It really was very funny. I had to pull over to the side, put down my bike, and run to pick up my shoe. Several people on bikes nearly had accidents trying to watch my maneuvers.

About my money. I haven't touched any of the $400 worth of travelers checks. Out of the $150 I had in cash I have $42.05 left in francs, which means I've spent $107.95 so far on the boat, in Paris, and here, which is pretty good considering what all I had to pay for in tips on the boat, my meals in Paris, three weeks of my rent here, a little side trip, a paper bound notebook, a satchel for my bike, Kleenex, toothpaste, asthma pills, and a few other necessities. I dribbled out a few 15 cents on tea and pastry which I'm cutting out for money and weight purposes. I have 14,495 francs, which will cover my rent for the last two weeks with 495 francs left over which is $1.45. I'm afraid I'll have to get into my $400 because we want to take a trip between the end of our courses here and time for us to be in Paris, which is a week. I think I've told you about that. Our five weeks of study are finished here on Friday, October 21, but the Paris families and dormitories aren't expecting us until the 26th, so we all want to either go to the South of France or perhaps Switzerland. We can't decide. But I'll need more than $1.45 to do either! About our money – we've all gotten so stingy and Silas Marner-like – we quibble over 50 francs and less which is 15¢ and less. Strange how money affects people when they have to watch most every penny.

Tuesday October 2nd

This has been a very profitable day! It didn't start out that way but it ended up as such. I got up early so I could be at the library at nine and study for an hour before class. I pedaled there only to find the library is closed on Tuesday mornings. I went on to school, just around the corner from the library and read on the special report I'm to give this week – Friday in fact – on the statue of Napoleon I was to have seen in Fixin, but didn't because of my asthma! After class I came home, ate lunch, then at three Bernard came for me to go play tennis. I rode my bike and he rode beside me to the Parc des Sports.

After our tennis, which lasted nearly 1½ hours, we pedaled back to the café at the Place Darcy for some tea and met up with one of Bernard's friends, Jean Bourland (a boy). He sat with us a long time and talked. He also speaks English and Spanish. He is quite attractive and I must admit I greatly prefer him to Bernard – he's so much more charming.

Eugenie, Sandy, and Martha came by (all the girls were returning from the "Collections") and sat for a minute. They left and Jean, Bernard, and I sat until it started raining, then we couldn't leave. Bernard said he was going to get up a dancing party for us soon. I'm so glad. Jean is also going to be at the school in Paris near the Rémonds and he's going to live on the same street, General Foy! Very nice. Jean saw a friend of his, Felix Guillot, sitting nearby, so he brought him over and introduced us. He is very attractive also. He had a car, so he, Jean and Bernard all took me home in it since it was raining. I will have to admit that after being without a date of some sort for so long, it was very nice being the only girl with three boys! You know I said Bernard was only about 18½? Well, he's 21. I found out today. So are his two friends I guess, because they're all in the same year in school. Jean asked me if I liked to dance. Of course I said very much. He then told me about a dance the upperclassmen give the lower class men at this school in Paris. I don't know whether he told me because he might invite me or what. It's a nice thought anyway.

Tonight I found out more about Mme. Delmas' husband and how they lost their wealth. He was head of the customs offices in Indo-China, where they lived for 20 years. Lisette was born there. They returned to France in 1939 because of the war. There was war in Indo-China too with Japan. Her husband remained in Indo-China alone, with all their furniture, money, etc. The war grew worse, the Japanese invaded Indo-China and took all of the Delmas' furniture, money, property, etc. Her husband died later, alone there of some sickness – I didn't understand the French word. Isn't that awful?

I also learned from Mme. Herard that M. Herard was taken prisoner twice by the Germans during the war, and escaped both times. Can you imagine!

Today I woke up with more little bites than ever, only today they really look like some sort of hives, which Mme. Delmas has been saying I've had all along. She said there was a lot of it in our group last year because of the change in diet. So tomorrow Mme. Herard is going with me to the doctor to see what is wrong with me. I hope it's something easily and quickly cured. Depend on me to have all the ailments!

Wednesday October 3, 1956

This morning we went to the museum with Mme. Herard. It is really a fine museum with so many wonderful things. I only wish I knew more French and Bourgogne history.

We spent our time looking at statues and paintings dating from the 12th and 13th centuries to the present. There are thousands of other things to see, but you just can't see much in one little morning. We also saw the very elaborate tomb of the Dukes of Bourgogne. One of the coat of arms of the Dukes is very much like the Woodalls'! I'm sure there's no connection.

It rained all this morning and I paddled around in my raincoat and boots. It has stopped now, everything is much colder now.

I've been to the doctor. He examined my bites and said they were not bed bugs, not from something I've been eating, but aoûtat (sounds like out) bites, which is a little bug something like a chigger, only it isn't. It gets under the skin the same way, and comes from trees, grass, etc. I still don't see how I could be getting them because I'm not around trees, grass, etc. much. The only thing I can figure is that maybe they come from the flowers in the window box, but I don't keep my window open very much. I told, rather Mme. Herard told him all this, and I told him some (he speaks English, a little). The little visit cost me about $4.50 and $1.50 more for some salve to put on the bites and stop the itching and some pills which are given only to people who have bites to make them sleep better – not to wake up scratching, as I have been doing. So maybe now things will be better. I'm glad it's not something I'm eating because it would be hard to get something different!

Thursday, October 4, 1956

This has been an ugly, messy, rainy cold day. It really feels cold to me, but Mme. Herard said just wait until it's really winter! I think I've told you that no one turns their heat on until November 1st no matter what! Right now I'm in my pajamas, tommy coat, house coat, and a blanket wrapped around me.

I didn't do much today but study at the library for the report we have to write on our book and on the report I have to give orally, tomorrow in class.

At five we had another lecture with M. Herard who is just fabulous. I can understand everything he says. It's such a nice feeling.

After the lecture Sandy, Louise, Eugenie and I met Jean and Bernard at the café. Jean asked me if I'd like to go to that ball at his school in Paris and I said "yes." He said he'd send me tickets. I have a feeling the plural of ticket means that he was inviting not only me, but all of us, which is very nice of course but it will still be fun. It will be at the end of October or the first of November.

We were all excited today because we learned that Kid Ory, the King of Jazz, is coming here in Dijon Monday night to give a concert. We've made our reservations. He was on our ship coming over, in Paris when we were and now we'll finally hear him here.

We're going to try to see him before the concert and tell him we go to school in New Orleans. Won't that be fun!

Friday October 6, 1956

This has been a wonderful day. In a few minutes we're all going dancing with Bernard and his friends.

We went to Mme. Herard's to ask her permission and she said we could go. So I'm waiting (what a switch) for them to come and pick me up in my little coral or shrimp outfit which is going to be dirty by the time I get to Paris.

It rained this morning something terrible and we were afraid we couldn't go on our little excursion, but it cleared up – so we did. Eugenie couldn't go because she hadn't finished reading her book. We – Sandy, Louise, and I – met Bernard and Jean at 2:30. We drove through the magnificent countryside they call "little Switzerland" – beautiful and mountainous. We drove through lots of tiny villages and also went to see the grand Château of Lamartine, the famous French poet. It is private property but we snooped around anyway. Jean (especially) and Bernard are so nice and entertaining.

We came back to Dijon by way of Fixin, and I was able to see the famous statue of Napoleon I missed the day I had asthma. I really just can't explain how gorgeous everything was. Oh, before the weather cleared up we drove through a hail storm – quite exciting.

Oh, I knew I had something to tell you. Mme. Delmas is sick. The doctor is with her now. I really don't think there is anything wrong with her but fatigue. Anyhow, she won't be able to cook, so for a few days I have to eat lunch and dinner at Mme. Monjaux's, where Ann Coco lives. For the days I do not eat here, I will be paying Mme. Delmas only 350 francs, and Mme. Monjaux 650 francs, so I'll still be paying the 1000 francs a day.

Well, I've got so much to catch up on tonight. First, Friday night was so much fun! There were nine boys and seven girls. We went in three cars to this little village just outside Dijon to one of the boy's little country cottage. There was a record-player, a "pick-up" as they call them and the boys brought lots of records. We all danced to mostly American music.

I danced most of the night with Jean-Louis Baut, who was the nicest one there I thought. He isn't handsome, but very cute and has so much charm and wit – dances well too. He is going to Paris to study this year too. I rode home in the car with him and others and he said he'd like to take me to the theater when we're in Paris.

At the party we had our equivalent to potato chips and Cokes – bread, cheese, and wine. It really was so much fun! We had all been dying to dance for so long! We danced to mostly fast music. Once they played the Charleston and Coco and I started Charlestoning. When the music stopped they all clapped and begged us to do it again, so we did. They (the boys) didn't know how at all. I guess they never had even seen it before. We didn't get home until around one-thirty A.M. It really was a good old party-ish party!

At five-thirty A.M. Saturday morning I got up in the freezing cold of morn, put on my slacks, three sweaters (long sleeves) my blazer, long socks, and my wool scarf and gloves, boarded my bike and rode to Louise's to have petit déjeuner with her. Then we rode to the station to Châteauneuf. Sandy, Coco, Louise, and I had our bikes put on top of the bus for riding back. (Susan and Ellie don't have bikes.) So we decided to ride the twenty-six miles back (46 kms). The bus left at seven and we got to Châteauneuf about eight fifteen.

I'm sure you're wondering what Châteauneuf is. It is a beautiful old château, the first one I've seen so far in Europe. It really is marvelous. It sits on the tip top of a high hill, which we had to climb up, and it looks like Cinderella's castle from a distance. There are only a few pieces of furniture left in it now, but it's so easy to visualize how things were. The walls of the little chapel are terribly faded, but you can still see the red, white, and blue panels which were the colors of the Duke of Bourgogne.

But the most wonderful thing about the château was the moat – a real moat. There is no water in it now, but the drawbridges are still there – you walk over them to get in the château. I could just see the knights in their armor galloping over them with the enemy close behind and then the drawbridge pulled up leaving only the water confronting the pursuers. Very exciting. Another interesting thing were the little seats in the windows used only for knitting. The windows were made in sort of coves and the seats were so that one could see out the window and in the house from the same position. The guide who took us through was wonderful. He took us in the tower and we could see for miles and miles. The countryside is marvelous there – mountains, lakes and trees and vineyards and shepherds.

We left the château at about nine-thirty and expected to see interesting things in the little village. There was nothing of note – many of the houses were in ruins. Of course everything was quaint. Down the hill was the little village Vandenesse-en-Auxois, so we decided to go there and see what we could see. Sandy and Coco rode on and Louise and I rode slowly so Ellie and Susan wouldn't get so far behind us. On the way down the mountain the four of us just had to go to the bathroom, so, as has become our habit, we began looking for little secluded spots. We came upon the perfect place – a little bit of a stone wall, about as high as my waist. It even had a little door! We all visited this charming place. I was last and Louise took my picture! Oh well, she claims only my head was showing.

We went on and met a shepherd driving his little herd of sheep. We threw down our bikes, grabbed our cameras and took a picture of the wonderful sight. Later, Louise and I passed a little cottage with a small apple orchard. The apples looked so good that we stopped and asked the little old dried up lady with two teeth in her mouth, who was standing in front of the door, if we could have an apple. She told us to take all we wanted. She begged us to take more, but we had no room to carry them, so we couldn't. It was so much fun though. Things like that are the experiences that really make you feel good.

Finally we got to Vandenesse-en-Auxois. Sandy and Coco had been there a long time because we had taken the longest road, we discovered. About 15 minutes later Ellie and Susan came too. We all went to this little café and ate our lunches and drank tea. We didn't have anything else to do but sit there until time to start back. We laughed so hard while we were sitting there eating and talking that we nearly got sick. Susan, who always has "control" trouble, laughed so hard she wet her pants which is nothing unusual with her.

Finally we decided to leave at 11:45. Coco and Sandy went on since they had seen the little church while waiting for us to come. The rest of us went in the church and looked around. There wasn't anyone in there, so we played the little organ, climbed up the stairs to the priest's pulpit, and went in the confession booth. It sounds like we were being sacrilegious, but we weren't. I've always wanted to see the inside of a confession booth! We started to leave when the two boys who ring the bells at noon came in. The ropes are right there in the church. They started ringing them and they were magnificent. The best thing – they let us ring them, too. After you pull the rope down it goes back up so fast that it pulls you right off the floor. It was really a thrill to ring those glorious bells.

About 12:10 Louise and I mounted the bikes and started out. Susan and Ellie waited for the 2:30 bus. I have news for Mme. Herard. It is not all downhill from there to Dijon. We had to walk our bikes up so many hills! But I don't regret it. The scenery was just gorgeous – we were up so high and could see so far. Everything was so still and un-20th century – until a car would pass us. The mountain weather was grey and misty looking and so, so, cold. But it gave everything a faraway fairy tale look.

After we were almost to the half way mark we started hitting all the downhill part. The hills were nearly mountains! The sun came out so we put on our raincoats – not because of the sun, but to break the wind. It's amazing how warm I can keep with my raincoat on top of everything. We practically flew down those hills and it was great. The air was so cold but it felt so clean and good. I was so happy I could have yelled and yelled. Nature was so splendid and God was so evident!

Our downhill road was lined with beautiful trees and a little blue canal was running alongside the road. We stopped to have hot chocolate after we passed the half-way mark by about 2 miles. It was the best hot chocolate! We pedaled on in the cold until finally at four forty-five we pulled up at the café Glacier in Dijon. We rode and walked in all that trip about 30 miles! Imagine riding a bike past Mayfield. If I had done it at home, people would have thought I was crazy!

We went from the café to Louise's and I met the three little girls of the family. Fabienne, Florence, and Fredericka. They are so darling and sweet. I'm really envious of Louise for living with them. When I left they all hugged me goodbye. I went to Coco's to eat supper. She and Sandy had been about 20 minutes ahead of us all the way. After supper I rode home and wrote part of my book report – finally could not hold my eyes open and went to bed.

Oh, just as I was getting in bed, Sandy, Bruno and Jean-Louis came by for me to go somewhere but I couldn't then. Today, Sandy told me they went with a gang (as is the custom here) to two different houses for dancing and wine – one was Jean-Louis'. She said it was a mansion and that all the group were the very elite of Dijon. I wish I could have gone.

Today wasn't so wonderful. I had to get up early and finish my report. At noon I met Sandy at the café and she took my report with her to Mme. Herard. As we left the café, we saw the crowd she was with last night, including Jean-Louis. I went to lunch at Coco's, came back and went to bed. Soon I got up at one, dressed and left. I couldn't stand it here alone. Lisette had gone and Mme. Delmas was in the bed. She has the strangest disease or something. She doesn't look sick, but she has both her thumbs bandaged up. I wish she would recuperate for her sake, and because I hate riding to Coco's for supper, especially the ride back here after supper.

I know I am going to need another pair of wool slacks, especially if we go to Switzerland and Germany for Christmas as we're thinking about doing instead of Italy. Also for the weekends at the Rémonds' country home. It's soooo cold.

Tuesday, October 9, 1956

You've asked about the Protestant church. The one here is not like any of our denominations. It's a mixture of all our Protestant churches. I haven't been to any services there – only that one afternoon that we all went to see about singing for them. They have an organist but she was away for a few weeks. I prefer going to St. Bénigne and hearing beautiful music to going to the Protestant church and hearing worse than we have at home! I am going to try to go to one service at least at the Protestant church.

It looks like I'm going to have to move from Mme. Delmas' anyway. She's still sick with liver trouble and an abscessed thumb. She can't stay up very long because she's dizzy and has terrible head-aches. Mme. Herard called them this afternoon (unknown to me) and asked how Mme. Delmas was. They told her she wasn't much better and that they doubted if she would be up the rest of this week. Mme. Herard seemed to think it would be best for me to move. I sort of agree with her, because I don't like riding my bike back alone from supper at Coco's, and there's no one here for me to talk to and improve my French. So tomorrow I will talk to Mme. Herard about it. Who knows, tomorrow night I may write from somewhere else!

Last night was the Kid Ory jazz concert. The place was full of young students like ourselves. Because we were from New Orleans we got to go back and meet them before the concert started. Coco (because she had bought our tickets for us and met the man who sort of managed it) got to present Kid Ory with a bottle of wine on the stage! We all enjoyed everything – all that New Orleans music really hit home. Our friends Jean, Jean-Louis, Bernard and some others sat behind us. Afterwards they took us to the café for chocolate and then Jean took us all home in his car. They really look out for us because Mme. Herard told them that when we're with them we're their responsibility.

Today I bought a little beret (black) for 325 f. nearly $1.00! It's real cute and it keeps my head so warm! Nearly everybody wears them – especially the older men.

This afternoon I went to the gymnasium of a girls' school near where I live to practice. They have a piano there. Mme. Herard had received permission for me to go. It was so big and there was so much echo it sounded like a choir of 100! After practicing I went to the library and started on my book for this week. At five Sandy, Eugenie, Martha, Louise and I met Jean-Louis, Jean, Bruno, Yves, and some other boys at the café. Jean-Louis had invited us all to his house last night to play the piano and sing. So we all went. He lives in a beautiful old home – very richly decorated inside – they are obviously wealthy. We had delicious port wine and little cookies.

We played the guitar and sang for a while, then all moved into the room with the piano. Eugenie played some of her compositions, and some boogie woogie. Louise played some classical music, then Louise played for me while I sang. They really enjoyed Louise and me, so we did almost our whole repertoire. They begged Sandy and me to Charleston for them. They really are fascinated by that. So we did until we nearly dropped from exhaustion.

Jean-Louis had a darling French girl there named Monique. They stayed together the whole time. She is the cutest French girl I've seen here in Dijon. We finally decided they were engaged. I was crushed! I thought he was interested in me – he asked me to go to the theater with him in Paris! I asked Jean if they were engaged and he said not exactly. They've gone together for two or three years – dated – and they're considered as engaged to be engaged!

Anyway – we left at seven and Jean-Louis took Monique, Louise, Sandy and me home in that order. He told Monique he'd see her tonight when she got out. Oh, boys never open the car doors or see you to your door – it's very bad manners! When he stopped to let me out he started talking – I was in the back seat still. He asked me why I wasn't very friendly today – I hadn't noticed that I hadn't been. Anyway – I told him I thought he was the one who was unfriendly – one thing led to another and I told him I knew why he was unfriendly today. He begged me to tell him, but of course I wouldn't. He said he thought someone had told me something and that I shouldn't believe everything I hear. We carried on that way for about 20 minutes – half flirting. I enjoyed it. His parting words were that he had to work in the library, too, tomorrow so he'd see me there. I'm glad.

Saturday, October 13, 1956

Well, I guess you're wondering what on earth has happened to me! I've been busy! Let me see if I can catch up now. First – I've moved. I moved in yesterday with M. and Mme. Grepey, the family with whom Martha Johnston lives. They had an extra bed in Martha's room, and agreed to let me come. They are so nice, especially him. He loves to tease. They are well to do. We have a private entrance to our room, which is just a plain room, but quite comfortable. We have a sort of dressing room – not really – with a lavatory. For baths etc. we use the big bathroom. They have hot running water and a telephone and heat. They have two sons away at school. M. Grepey is so cute – about 55 or 56, grey hair and twinkling eyes. Mme. is about 45 or 46, very vivacious and kind of prissy. She is very gracious. We have good food, which she cooks herself. They speak very proper French and are so willing to help us. They told me they thought I spoke French very well! Better than Martha, who has studied much longer than I! I was quite complimented. Lately lots of people have been telling me that my French is improving. I gave an oral report the other day and Mme. Herard was quite impressed. I can tell that my French has improved too. It's a good feeling.

Back to the subject. I hated to leave Mme. Delmas and Lisette, but it was the best for everyone. They wanted me to be more comfortable too. I intend to go back and visit them.

Speaking of weight – I weighed the other day. I weigh 45.5 kilos (with my clothes on), which converted into pounds is 100. I don't seem to have lost weight, but I guess the marathon walking I've been doing has taken it off, or maybe I scratched it off scratching my bites!

I received the first Time magazine so far today. So glad to see it! Still haven't received anything about voting in November.

Now, for my recent activities! Wednesday night I was getting ready for bed when Sandy came bounding in telling me to get dressed quick because Jean-Louis wanted me to go with him, Bruno and Sandy, Yves and Eugenie, to their friend's house to listen to records. She had gotten Mme. Herard's permission, so I dressed and went. The friend's name was Max. He lives in a huge house which has a room apparently used only for listening to records and talking and sipping wine, which we did. Jean-Louis and I talked and talked, and I learned that he is not engaged. The girl at his house is an old family friend – nearly like his sister. Anyway, he is so cute, sweet, and polite and witty that we had a grand time talking. I've really learned lots of French from him. They wanted us to go out Thursday night, but we couldn't for reasons of overdoing a good thing and study reasons.

Friday morning we went with Mme. Herard to a gorgeous château near

Dijon which is now a boarding school for girls. The château is splendid with marble, paintings, gilt, tapestries, draperies, etc. The grounds are exquisite with all sorts of delightful (as Susan Shelley would say) little gardens. The château still has its look of grandeur that belonged to the eighteenth century. It's hard to believe things were once so riche and plentiful! We also saw the rooms where the girls live and some of their classes. When you enter a classroom in France all the pupils immediately stand. It's a good custom.

Last night I went with Jean-Louis, Sandy, Bruno, Felix, Yves, and Eugenie (with Mme. Herard's permission) to a boy's house – Philippe somebody (they never tell you people's last names) for a party. It was a huge old house. There were lots of young people there – we danced and talked and had lots of fun. I learned from Jean-Louis that a girl never dances with her head close to the boy's head unless she wants to flirt with him. He was appalled that Americans dance that way with everybody. We learn something new about what not to do every day!

Jean-Louis took Sandy, Eugenie, and me home afterwards in that order. We sat and talked for a long, long time before I went in. He is quite smitten with me and I'm glad because he's so nice. I love to talk to him because I can speak so much easier with him. My French surprises me sometimes when I'm with him. He told me last night that he liked me so much because I am (so he said) discreet, genteel, intelligent, pretty, little, because I'm not noisy like some of the other American girls here, because I don't flirt with all the boys. What do you think of that!

I'm so glad he's going to be in Paris. I've come to know him quite well this week because I've had to spend so much time in the Library – we all have – and so has he – at least he's always here and always sits with me. He helps me with my reading and writing. Tonight I'm going out to dinner with him in a real live French restaurant. It will be the first nice one I've been to since my arrival in France!

Of course I had to get Dr. Smithers' O.K. to go. He's here now – as of last night – and we have to ask him instead of Mme. Herard. Tomorrow afternoon we're all going to an old château for the ceremony of the hunt. There will be hunters, horses, dogs, hunting horns and the men who play them. There is even a Mass to bless the dogs! I will tell you about it after I see it. I'm in the library now waiting for six o'clock. (I've finished my report.) At six the library closes and we all meet at the café. We meet there usually after twelve and after six. Everybody is there. We see all our French friends and all sit at several tables arranged lengthwise, and talk and laugh and drink tea (not wine). It's so much fun. That's where we've met practically everybody because the friends we know bring new friends and then they become our friends.

Monday morning – October 15

Saturday night I went out to dinner with Jean-Louis. We went to the most exclusive place in town called The Chapeau Rouge – red hat. I had my first snails and they are delicious! I'm dying for more. While we were sitting there Dr. Smithers came in and had dinner, too. I'm so glad he saw me at such a wonderful place.

Jean-Louis is terrific. I learn so much French from him, as well as art, literature, etc. He's so intelligent.

After dinner we went into the bar to drink our coffee. Jean-Louis is studying law and of course he knows lots of the lawyers in Dijon. There was a big dinner for the lawyers that night at the Chapeau Rouge and he had been invited – but he preferred taking me. Anyway, all of his lawyer friends were in the bar with their wives. Jean-Louis introduced me and they were all very gracious. It was the first big group of really fine people that I've been with.

Oh, we started the evening off quite nicely! Sat. afternoon in the library Jean-Louis and I were talking about French poetry. I told him I liked Paul Verlaine's poetry and that I had several Debussy songs to Verlaine poems. I also said I would like to learn more about French contemporary poetry. So when I got in the car he reached in the back seat and took a package out and handed it to me. He had bought me two books – one is about Verlaine – his life, style and his poems – the other is Rimbaud and other contemporary poets! He is so sweet.

Sunday morning I went to St. Bénigne with some of the other girls to hear the boys' choir sing. Jean-Louis met me there and sat with us. He's Catholic like the rest of France, and he had the most gorgeous prayer-book with him. The music in the church was so beautiful I just couldn't help but cry. The organ is magnificent and the organist plays wonderful contemporary music, which seems to take on a deeper meaning and is more beautiful in the church. After church we all took the bus to Nuits-St.-George, from there we walked to Quincy to the château for the jumping competition and the Mass for the hunting hounds. It was the most exciting thing I've done yet. It was like stepping back into the 19th century – the château, the huge green and brown trees, the misty fog of the afternoon, the statues in the garden, the buckeyes on the ground and the best of all, across a little lake stood two groups of piqueurs, the men who play the cors de chasse – hunting horns. One group was dressed in navy blue coats and black jodhpurs, the other in red coats and black jodhpurs. They were reflected in the lake. With their brass horns, their uniforms, and the hunting calls – oh, it was so exciting! It really was so colorful, and as I said, so non-20th century-ish.

We rode home with friends of M. Grepey. M. Grepey took some of the other girls home, and M. Herard the rest, so none of us had to ride the bus. When we got home we had an aperitif with the Grepeys and two of their friends. Then, Martha and I ate dinner after which the Grepeys took us and Eugenie (who lives on the same street) to the Cloche Hotel, where we had a meeting with Dr. Smithers. He told me they have found one voice teacher for sure for me in Paris, and that by the time we get back there will be others for me to look up.

After the meeting we all went to the museum with the Herards to listen to the music of Rameau, the great 18th century composer. After some of his music we went into the room of the Tombs of the Dukes of Bourgogne, which looks like a small cathedral, and listened to gorgeous church music – this was all on records. The church music was fabulous – organs, boys' choirs, Gregorian chants. I could have stayed there all night.

I don't think I have mentioned anything at all about French table manners. They're quite different from ours. You never put your hands in your lap – always keep them lightly resting on the table. You put your knife not on the side of your plate when you're not using it, but only the tip end of it rests against the plate. When you eat fish you have a special knife to use. You push the fish on the knife with your fork and eat from the knife. When you cut something up you don't change hands to eat with your fork, you keep it in the left hand with the round end up and eat like that. You never wait for everybody to be served the first time before you start eating, but if you want a second helping you must wait until the others are ready. This is true only in very formal places. When you eat bread you break off only what you can put in your mouth – you then eat that – you never pick up a large piece, take a bite, and put it back! Complicated n'est ce pas?

I received my application for absentee ballot today. It had gone to M. Rémond in Paris and he forwarded it to me. I have to have it notarized, so I'm going to take it to Jean-Louis' father, who is a notary here.

Oh, about our trip after our studies here. We've decided to stay here in Dijon and visit every day the places in Bourgogne that are so famous and wonderful, because Bourgogne is such an important and rich (in history, folklore, art, literature) section of France, that we feel, as does Mme. Herard, that we should see all of it we can while we're here.

Which reminds me, we've about decided to go to Switzerland, Germany, Austria for Christmas instead of Italy because they have snow, etc. but mainly because they have a much more colorful, warm Christmas season – also we heard Christmas was usually a rainy season in Italy.

P.S. We leave here on the 26th at 10:30 A.M. Registration starts November 1st – classes the 3rd at the Sorbonne. Did I tell you Jean-Louis goes to the Sorbonne too? His family has an apartment in Paris where he lives alone during the week – his parents come on weekends. He has invited me to come for dinner one time when his parents are there. Isn't that nice? He's also going to help me with my French and I'm going to help him in English since our classes will be in each other's native language.

Wednesday, October 17, 1956

Why does everything happen to me? I guess by now you think I'm a nomad – because I've moved again! Yes, moved. It's all very complicated and so unpleasant that I don't want to go into detail because I don't want to remember the unpleasantness.

Anyway, it just didn't work at the Grepeys for so many reasons. I had a feeling they didn't like me very much, but the boiling point came last night. I went with Louise and Mme. Darbois, whom I adore, to the movies. I had asked Mme. Grepey's permission to go – she had very sweetly said yes, so I went. It seems that while I was gone Mme. Herard called. She was upset for some strange reason because I wasn't there. Then Mme. Grepey told Mme. Herard that she didn't want to keep me next week – she'd keep Martha, but she just couldn't get along with me. I was absolutely astounded this morning when Mme. Herard told me.

Mme. Herard has been making life miserable for me lately. I really don't understand what's wrong – why she all of a sudden dislikes me. Everyone has noticed her behavior, we're all disgusted with her. I'm so glad Dr. Smithers is here and knows how mean she can be. Anyway, Jacqueline, Mme. Darbois, got so angry when she heard from Louise the way Mme. Herard talked to me this morning, that she called Mme. Herard and me and insisted that I come live with her. I was so glad because I wanted to leave the hypocritical Grepeys as fast as I could. So, Jean-Louis helped me move this afternoon with his car. He is so utterly wonderful. So here I am and I'm so happy to be here. I adore the three little children and they love me.

Mme. Darbois is only 32, she's a widow and her mother, who is very sweet, lives here too. They are very rich – her husband owned this huge factory here in Dijon. She is so much fun and so eager to be sweet and obliging. I'm in the room with Louise and the smallest girl – Fredericka, who is 4 and sleeps through anything. The other girls are Florence, 5, and Fabienne, 9. Their father was killed in an automobile accident. There is a young girl who is their maid, cook, nurse, etc. and she stays here all the time. The food is delicious. Please don't worry about me, because everything will be OK now.

I hope you're not thinking there must be some reason for the Grepeys and Mme. Herard not liking me. I'm sure there is something, but I swear before God I have not the faintest idea. I have been nice and kind and obliging as I know how. That's the honest truth. I have not ever been rude. It is a mystery. But soon I'll be going to Paris and starting my real life here in Europe. I can hardly wait! But I love this family – especially the three girls. They are so lovable.

I'm also getting a sore throat – perhaps the result of much chagrin lately.

Jean-Louis went to Paris today to take an examination for this year in law school. He'll be back Saturday – he's driving back with his mother and we're going out Sat. night. Mme. Darbois knows his family and is glad I know him. She and Louise already had planned to go out with some friends of hers Saturday night – a young man for Louise, so it's alright for me to go out. Jean-Louis is so nice – I can't get over it!

Again, don't worry about me – I'm really growing up fast here in the last few weeks!

Sunday, October 21, 1956

I'm now fighting a terrible cold. It's in its last stages now, and I hope it's soon gives up. Mme., the grandmother, just gave me some tea with alcohol to drink. It was awful, but I can tell it helped. She is so sweet. The cold has gone to my chest, so I've got Vick's salve rubbed all over my chest now.

I haven't written since Thursday I think. So – Friday morning before class we went to the marketplace to see and hear a famous merchant of plates, cups, saucers, etc. His name is Fernand, and he's famous here because he rattles off his fast sales talk and if no one buys the plate or saucer he is holding, he throws it down and breaks it! The whole marketplace is very colorful. Everything is under tents – sort of like a fair, only this takes place twice a week. It seems that Fernand is really very rich and can well afford breaking his wares.

Friday afternoon – after our last class here Friday morning – I spent an hour in the library, then came home because I felt so awful, and went to bed. Saturday morning I felt a little better, and after lunch I worked on my theme till about 3:00, when I took Fredericka with me to get Dr. Smithers at the University to bring to our house for tea. Fredericka was so cute – they never get to go outside to play and she had the best time playing in the leaves and finding different colored ones. The leaves are all gold and red now – the first autumn I've seen in two years. I didn't realize how much I've missed it! Dr. Smithers came for tea, and we all had a nice social chat with our tea and wonderful pastry!

At 8:00 I went out with Jean-Louis Baut. We went to have dinner at this little place near Dijon. It's in a tiny village, is only one small room with a potbellied stove and checkered tablecloths. Across the narrow little road is the kitchen where the food is prepared. An old man and woman own the place. The man does all the table waiting, the woman does all the cooking. Everybody in Dijon goes there to eat "country cooking." Bernard Paulien's family was there last night and also some lawyer friends of Jean-Louis. We had delicious, simple food – scallops of veal with mushrooms, fried potatoes, salad and tarts – which is really open face pie. The little village is so pretty, and it looked so fairy like last night because the moon was bright and pretty.

Jean-Louis is so wonderful. I really like him a lot, and I'm glad he's going to be in Paris too. He went to Paris Wednesday of this week and came back Saturday. He had to take some sort of exam. So Saturday night he had on a tie he bought in Paris – it was real pretty – sort of a maroon color with a tiny light pink stripe diagonally across the top – and on the little stripe in white letters was "I Like Ike" – all for my benefit of course. Which reminds me – everyone here is so concerned, and peeved with the US because Ike and Dulles have not taken a definite stand on the Suez Canal issue. It's certainly difficult to try to explain!

This morning Dr. Smithers, Eugenie, Coco, Louise, and I caught the train at 9:30 to go to Flavigny, an old town of the 13th century, high on a hill, surrounded by a great wall. We had to walk a long way from the train station to the town – all uphill. The town is marvelous – it's so unbelievably old! In the walls were places for the warriors to put their bows and arrows when they were fighting the enemy. All the little houses were so medieval. We first went to see an old château which is now a boys school for the priesthood. A darling young priest took us through it. He was a pupil of M. Herard's. We went to see the old church which was beautiful, especially interesting were the "misericords" which are places where the priests have to stand with little hidden seats, so they can sit and still look like they're standing. The carvings on the seats are quite amusing.

After the church we went back to the school, because our friend the young priest had offered to drive us to Alesia. That's the little town where the great Vercingetorix, the Gaul, surrendered to Julius Caesar. We went up the hill to the battlefield where the surrender took place. There is a huge statue of Vercingetorix – really tremendous – on the very top of the hill. It's quite impressive, very sad to think that Julius Caesar marched the great Vercingetorix through the streets of Rome as a common captive and then had him executed! We also saw the excavations of Roman ruins at Alesia. There are parts of an old road, houses, public baths, and even an old villa. Of course now what is left standing are only walls about three feet high, deep basement like places, a few pillars, etc. But it's wonderful to see these things and realize that they have been there since the time of Julius Caesar.

From Alesia we walked to the nearest train station, where we took the train for Dijon at 5:30. We were all absolutely pooped! My legs are still aching from all the climbing. I met Jean-Louis near the station here at 7:00. He took me home and asked me to play tennis in the morning. I'm dying to, but if I'm not better I simply can't.

The countryside is so gorgeous now with all the artistry of Nature – the colors are magnificent, the air wonderful – it would've been worth our walking today only to see the autumn in full bloom. The marvelous thing is that a week ago everything was still green! God is so awesome when he makes himself so evident in Nature!

Tuesday, October 23, 1956

Well – I'm slow about writing again. I think my cold is finally going away. I still have a terrible cough, but I feel a hundred percent better. Yesterday I had that asthmatic wheeze that's so terrible. Jean-Louis was going to try to find a doctor who would give me a prescription for some chlor-trimeton today, but he didn't. He's going to try to find one again tomorrow because it's the only thing that relieves that wheezing. Anyway I guess I'll be okay by the time we leave for Paris Friday. I can't understand why I have had all the bad luck – I wonder for what I'm being punished with three moves, terrible bug bites, asthma, cold, etc. Oh well – that's life.

Yesterday morning Jean-Louis took me to visit the Cathedral of St. Michel and the Cathedral of Sacré Cœur here in Dijon. I had not yet seen them. The first one – St. Michel, is famous for the beautiful sculptures above the doors – the portal. The interior is not extraordinary – just huge. Sacré Cœur is a new church – about 10 years old. It is very modern and I think marvelous. The stained glass windows are so unusual, and the murals at the altar is breathtaking. It's so huge! There are two huge gorgeous organs.

In the afternoon the six of us (we are minus Susan and Sandy now) and Dr. Smithers went to the town of Châtillon on the bus. We went to see mainly the Vase de Vix, a relatively newfound excavation treasure – it was discovered in 1953. It is the only vase of its kind in the world. It's made of pure bronze – which is green, like green marble. It's almost 6 feet tall, and was made in the sixth century before Christ! It was found in the tomb of a princess near Châtillon, but it came from Greece (Gallic) at least it is Grecian – it could have come from a Greek colony. It really is marvelous. The town of Châtillon is not very interesting – unfortunately because it was completely destroyed during the war and everything is brand-new. Oh – we also saw the old church of the 13th century. It was quite interesting as all the churches are. The Vase de Vix was worth the four hours on the bus. People from all over the world come to Châtillon to see it now.

Today Dr. Smithers rented a car (we all paid, of course) and took us to Autun, a city built by Augustus Caesar, at the bottom of the hill on which was located the city of Bibracte which Augustus destroyed before building Autun. Unfortunately this was a terribly foggy day, and we couldn't see things as well as we wanted to. On the way we stopped in the little village of Sully to visit a magnificent château, which has a real moat with water in it! We couldn't go inside because someone lives there now, but we walked all around it. It has three different façades, each of a different style – really beautiful. At Autun we had lunch at the cutest little atmospheric restaurant and the best food. Afterward we saw the school where Napoleon and his brothers came to learn French – they were Corsican you know.

Then we went to see the famous Cathedral of St. Lazare. It has one of the most famous portals in all sculpture – the "tympanum" is called *The Last Judgment,* and is of the 12th century. It really is marvelous. The Cathedral is the most beautiful I've ever seen. It was started in the Romanesque period! 12th and 13th centuries – and finished in the Gothic – 14th and 15th centuries. The exterior is gorgeous with one of the most beautiful spires I'll ever hope to see. The interior is beyond my ability to describe. The stained glass windows, the arches, the altar, everything is breathtaking. No wonder the Europeans are such devout Catholics – with such beautiful places to worship which are so full of the beauty of religion! I wonder what a European thinks when he sees pictures of churches like some of our Protestant churches?

At Autun we also visited the museum which contains some interesting pieces of sculpture dating from as far back as the Gallo-Roman period, before the sixth century! One piece was from the third century. It's so incredible to see these things and truly realize their antiquity. I know I've said that over and over but it's true. We also visited the ruins of a Roman theater. It's still in good enough condition to be used for summer theater – which it is. To think that at one time, in the same spot where I was Frenchmen and Romans sat in their tunics and thong sandals watching some tragedy or comedy by the great Greek writers. It's really a strange feeling. We also saw the old Roman gate that is still standing – looking so typically like European travel-lure. We spent all afternoon in Autun – mostly at the Cathedral, it is so beautiful. We didn't leave until about 5:00. We stopped in Beaune on the way home so Dr. Smithers could get a look at the Hotel Dieu which we had seen on our previous trip.

The others stayed in the car, and I went with him and told him all I remembered from being there before. We returned to Dijon at 7:00.

The drive was so enjoyable both ways. Even with the thick fog the autumn colors were gorgeous. I think they even outdo our beautiful Kentucky autumns. It's absolutely fabulous. I wish you could hear Eugenie, Coco, and Louise go on about autumn – they've never seen a real one before.

Oh, the New Orleans paper is going to publish an article of Newcomb's Junior year abroad with pictures of us and the TV station is going to show movies of us! Probably next month. Maybe you could write to your friend Lillian and ask her to be on the lookout for them and send you the article, pictures, etc. I'd like to have them.

I hate to leave Dijon Friday – there's so much I still want to do and see. I hate to leave the Darbois family too.

Return

to

Paris

Friday, October 26, 1956

Dear Mother and Daddy,

I'm in Paris now! It was almost like "coming home" to come back here. We left Dijon this morning at 11:00 and were here by 1:30 this p. m. We were driven to our respective homes and abodes by American Express limousines – one last such luxurious ride until we come home to the U. S. A.!

The Rémonds were awaiting us. They seem so anxious that we like everything here. We talked for a while, then Louise and I walked to the French Line office to get our trunks out of storage. We could have telephoned, but we preferred walking. Then we walked to the American Express where I picked up my mail. It seems so strange to see so many Americans there! I felt like I'm back in modern civilization after being in Dijon. We went from the American Express to the department store, Au Printemps, where we bought some coat hangers. We had lots of closet space but no hangers. Now we have both. We came back and started unpacking – trunks and all. It was such a good feeling to finish. Dinner was nice – but not nearly so tasty as in Dijon. The Rémonds are trying to find a maid – I hope they find one who cooks well. We have been confirmed in what we already suspected – Mme. Rémond is expecting! I'm sure that wasn't planned for when they decided to take us in. We suspected it, then this afternoon Isabelle, the oldest (6) girl said that her mother was again going to buy her a sister or brother if she worked really well in school this year.

M. Rémond is so attractive and such a talker! They both are so proud of our progress in French. We were really smart by not speaking French the first time we met them. Finally it got too late to chat anymore, so they went to bed and we finished getting settled. We have so much space for all our things it's so nice. Our bathroom is wonderful, we even have a little clothes rack for hanging clothes after we wash them. Our room looks like a student's room – very conducive to study! Right now the house is cold. We do have a fire in a little stove, but the central heating isn't turned on for another week.

We saw the little girls yesterday – they are darling. Isabelle looks like her father and talks all the time. Anne, who is only three, looks just like her mother and is really beautiful. She was so shy at first but now she's just as friendly as Isabelle. Everything is just perfect except for Mme. Rémond's being pregnant. Oh – the food wasn't nearly as good as in Dijon, but I think a maid is coming to work sometime this week, so maybe it will improve. This morning she (Mme.) served us our breakfast on a little tea cart in our room. I wonder if it will be habitual!

Saturday, October 27

Let's see – what did I do in Dijon that I haven't written about. Wednesday night Jean-Louis took Louise and me to the ballet. Thursday night Louise and I took Jacqueline out to dinner at the Chapeau Rouge. So our last day was really a splurge as far as food and money goes. I also bought a pair of leather gloves lined with warm wool the last day.

Friday Jacqueline took us to the train. She was so sweet to me, I hated to leave her. She comes to Paris right often and so we'll see her here, and also she wants us to come to Dijon for a weekend in the spring, and she's going to give us a big party. At the train station whom should I see but Jean-Louis, who decided to go to Paris, too, and pay his tuition for school. We sat together for the ride. Mother, I appreciate your advice on French men, but really, there's nothing to worry about with Jean-Louis! Honest!

I had two Time magazines waiting for me here, and was so pleased to find the one of October 29th for two reasons: I love Maria Callas and I'm so happy to see such good pictures of Bourgogne. I do hope you saw them. Everything looks exactly like the pictures.

Today we were going to buy some little fur-lined boots but we didn't have enough money and the banks are all closed on Saturdays. Isabelle took us on a little tour of shoe stores so we could see our boots à la window. We bought her some roasted chestnuts – which, by the way, are the same things that we called "buckeyes." It was so cold she wanted to go home, so we brought her back, then we walked some more.

We bought the little book *A Week in Paris*, a Herald Tribune, a bottle of Benedictine (for my cold as well as pleasure). We played with the children till supper time. Supper was more proof that Mme. Rémond is not a wonderful cook! After supper we played and sang old French songs. Their piano is one of the 18th century – 1740! It has only three octaves and sounds like a bad harpsichord.

After supper, M. Rémond came in from a day of hunting which had been successful because he had a beautiful pheasant and a huge hare. He looked so country gentlemanish in his tweed knickers and jacket.

Sunday, October 28, 1956

I can hardly wait till November 1 and the heat! The beds are so cold at night it's just awful! We use Louise's heating pad and a hot water bottle to warm them.

This morning our breakfast was rolled into us on a little tea cart. Breakfast isn't very tasty because the coffee is Nescafé, the water is never hot enough and right now there is a milk strike in Paris, and we have to use concentrated milk. But it wouldn't be bad if the water were just hotter. Mme. doesn't seem to know how to make things get really hot. After breakfast we went to Mass at St. Augustine, right around the corner to hear what we thought was the Mass with choir and organ, but turned out to be only organ. It was gorgeous, but I don't care to go back there. After that Mass we went to the Church of the Madeleine for the short organ recital at 12:30. The organist played works of Buxtehude, Franck, Saint-Saëns, and Widor. It was really beautiful.

For dinner we had the hare that M. killed yesterday. It really was good. Afterwards we had a little fête for Louise's and my arrival in Paris with some France-Amerique champagne. It was so delicious. Also some wonderful pastry which is called "religieuse" which is the French word for a nun, a sister. The little cream puffs have a top which is the head of the nun and a bottom which is the full skirt.

After lunch and a long conversation (M. loves to talk!) Louise and I started out walking with the idea of going to a concert at 5:45 at Salle Pleyel on rue Faubourg St. Honoré. Only we didn't realize there was a Faubourg in the name, and we walked down the whole of rue St. Honoré, a different rue, before it dawned on us that we had walked down the wrong street! By then it was too late to go to the concerts, so we walked some more – by the Louvre, the Tuileries Garden, down the Champs-Élysées to the Arc de Triomphe and then home. We had walked for nearly 3½ hours! The Champs-Élysées was so crowded with Sunday strollers, in fact, the whole city was being walked upon. It was so much fun seeing all the people so typically Parisian.

It was dusk by the time we got to the Champs-Élysées, and all the lights were suddenly flicked on. It was really magnificent. The Eiffel Tower and the Arc de Triomphe looming up in the sky, the lovers walking arm in arm and hand in hand, the berets, everything. C'est magnifique!

Supper tonight wasn't so hot. The salad was good and I do love salad. Maybe I won't gain a lot of weight anyway.

Tuesday, Oct. 30, 1956

First I want to talk about money. We have to pay nearly 25 dollars to the Rémonds (as does everyone else) for this time in October plus the $125. for November, which I'm going to do tomorrow. I will then have $160. I think maybe you should send me money pretty soon, but please, tell me how you're going to send it and to what bank. You haven't told me yet for sure. M. Rémond told us he would prefer having his money in dollars because he has to go to the United States often, once every couple of years or so, and the French government won't allow Frenchmen to take over $300 with them to America. We went to the American Express to try to get our travelers checks changed into dollars, but they won't give you but $50 at a time. So we're going to pay M. Rémond $50 a month in dollars and $75 in francs. Mr. Smithers has contacted the man who gives us the world market rate, and tomorrow I'm getting $200 worth of francs on which I'll make a little money. Unfortunately for us, the franc is getting more solid, therefore going down. The world market was 389 yesterday. So much about money.

Yesterday morning we had little individual meetings with Dr. Smithers to straighten out our schedule. The meeting lasted until noon. We rode the Metro for the first time yesterday morning to go to the meeting and to come home from it. The Metro is wonderful, so easy to take and you can go anywhere in the whole city. Of course you see nothing while you ride, but it's such fun! I had thought it would be difficult, but it's easy!

After lunch we met Susan in front of the Theatre de Paris to buy tickets for the Ballet de Paris en Revue for last night. It was the famous Ballet Revue of Roland Petit and the Zizi Jeanmaire, who was in *Hans Christian Andersen*, *The Girl in the Pink Tights*, and in several articles Life Magazine has published about Parisienne Ballet. I'm sure you've seen her picture thousands of times. The ballet was modern, and in some places almost Broadway-ish. There was a girl who sang in between some of the ballets. Roland Petit and Jeanmaire were wonderful. Their version of *Carmen* was excellent. We really enjoyed it. The theater was so elegant and beautiful. We didn't have elegant seats, but just being in an elegant place was wonderful. It was raining when the ballet was over. We tried to take the Metro, but I think from that spot to our house is the only place in Paris where there is no Metro line, so we took a taxi because the bus to our house had stopped running by then.

This morning we all met at Dr. Smithers' for the purpose of going to the Sorbonne and registering, but when we arrived at his office he told us that complications had come up, and we couldn't register until tomorrow. So we discussed schedules. I made a change in my schedule from the Literature Course to the theater course given by Mme. Alvernhe. It will be so interesting because we will go to the plays we study and of course it will be wonderful ear training for our French. So here is my schedule as it now stands:

Voice lessons – (I'm going teacher hunting Thursday. Mme. Alvernhe gave me the name of a woman who sounds wonderful)

History of Art – (My only course at the Sorbonne)

History of Music – (Privately with a man and four others of us.)

French Theater with Mme. Alvernhe

French Composition with Mme. Alvernhe

I'm very pleased because I like everything I'm taking so much. I hope I'll be able to sing normally again soon – my cold is still hanging on slightly. I do wish it would completely leave.

After our meeting we went to the equivalent of our Dime Store – Au Bon Marché – nearby to have our pictures made on those horrid little machines of our profile with our right ear showing! In France there are two methods for identifying foreign persons, criminals, etc., by fingerprints and by the ear. Since our pictures will go to the police, the school, etc. we had to have our right ears showing!

After that Louise and I walked over to the Invalides, which was only about three blocks away. The Invalides is a huge beautiful hospital built by Louis XIV for wounded veterans, etc. It was restored by Napoleon and it is there that Napoleon's tomb is found. It is magnificent. The outside alone is gorgeous but the inside far surpasses the exterior. Besides Napoleon's tomb there are the tombs of Joseph Bonaparte, Napoleon's brother, who was on Spain's throne, Napoleon's son, Marshall Foch, and two generals whom Napoleon had loved most. I'm sure the great Napoleon is happy lying amid such splendor and grandeur. It really is fabulous. Napoleon and his legend thrill me anyway.

We left Les Invalides and went à la Metro to our abode. We ate lunch which was delicious – steak and potatoes. Mme. Rémond was in such good spirits because a maid is now with us. Mme. was all fixed up with lipstick even. She really is a beautiful woman, and when she smiles she is exquisite. I'm so glad she's feeling better. She had too much work to do.

After dinner we had liqueur and M. Rémond showed us pictures he had taken of Canada and I showed off little old Paducah. Then M., Mme., the children, and Louise and I all went into the living room, where M. built us a fire in front of the fireplace! It's wonderful. After not having any heat since we arrived, you can imagine!

My Parisian life is rolling on. Oh, no one sent me any sort of ballot to vote for Eisenhower. If he doesn't win I just don't think I'd want to come back to America to stay!

Wednesday Oct. 31, 1956

We registered this morning at The Sorbonne. It was the simplest registration I've ever been through! The Sorbonne is so exciting. Its appearance is deceiving. Like many buildings in France, the main part cannot be seen from the street. It is inside a courtyard – very old, very cultural and very scholastic. The students were swarming everywhere – French and foreign. There were students at the entrance handing out hand bills for the Communist party on the Suez affair which, by the way has come to an appalling head! Our courses at the Sorbonne are for foreign students only – there will be no French students in our classes – which will make things easier for us.

After a delicious lunch (I don't know what happened to Mme. Rémond's cooking, but I'm sure glad it happened!) Louise and I went shopping for boots. We bought some darling ones – both the same kind – for nearly $15.00. They fit right on your foot, and luckily I had no trouble finding my size. I wear a 34 in French shoes! Obviously the sizes run differently. The boots are black leather lined with warm, warm, fuzzy wool. They come about 2 inches above my ankle bone, and have a band of fur about 2 inches wide around the top. They really are good looking and so marvelously warm. We also bought little slide viewers for our pictures.

Tonight at dinner we had a new personage Claudine, M. Rémond's godchild who is our age. She is so nice. Tomorrow afternoon all of us (including Claudine) are going to the Rémonds' country home for the weekend. It's a long weekend because tomorrow is All Saints Day and Friday is All Souls Day. They are always holidays in France. I'm sure it will be fun – very relaxing.

November 2, 1956

Here I am in the country – huddled beside the fireplace trying to keep warm.

Yesterday was started off with Claudine having breakfast in our room with us. I simply can't talk much at breakfast right after waking up – much less in French! Neither can Louise, so I'm afraid we weren't very entertaining hostesses.

After breakfast the three of us went to the Mass of All Saints Day at Notre Dame. It was magnificent. Claudine is Catholic and naturally wanted to participate in the Mass, but Louise and I paid 50 f. to go up to the balconies above the altar and transept so we could see everything. The priests were all in their richly ornamented robes and were really a gorgeous sight. Behind the altar was the Notre Dame Seminary Choir of about 250 boys ranging from the age of 8 to 20 (my guess). They were marvelous, sang beautiful Agnus Deis and choral works from Palestrina's time. Also behind the altar were about 40 or 50 archbishops in ornamented robes. Some of them were so old they couldn't stand up. Also near them, on a special chair, with a special place to kneel, was the Cardinal, the first one I've ever seen. You know there aren't but about 20 or so in the Catholic Church. He had on the Cardinal robes of "Cardinal" red with the long train! Really beautiful.

We saw the whole ceremony, the choir, the little "un-churchly" incidents, the especially sweet and beautiful parts of the ceremony that could only be seen from our perch in the balcony. It was the most magnificent religious ceremony I've ever seen. At the end of the ceremony the boys' choir sang the Hallelujah Chorus (which was moving, but not perfectly executed), the priests, the altar boys (dressed in solid white) the archbishops, the young priests all recessed in pairs, after making a turn around the altar, then, following them all came the Cardinal in his flame red robes – truly magnificent to see. I really think the Catholic Mass is the most sense-satisfying ceremony of all – that is, for the eyes, the ears, the heart – it has more to offer of true beauty, even when you don't understand all of the ceremony and the reasons for certain parts of it.

After Mass we walked home as far as the Place de la Concorde, then took the Metro the rest of the way. It was so cold! I've never been this cold before! After lunch we all piled in the car to come to the country. Mme. Rémond came later on the train because there wasn't room in the car – a Renault. We left Paris a little after 3:00 pm and arrived here two hours later.

The little village is called Champscenest. Its population is about 200, and its mayor is none other than M. Rémond. The house we're in is large and furnished very carefully to suit the "particular taste" of M. and Mme. Rémond. He also owns two other old houses on this land, but they are still in a very demolished state, as was this house until six years ago, when M. Rémond. started fixing it up. It has three bedrooms, a large kitchen, and two large living rooms. One of the living rooms is not yet quite furnished, but it is my favorite. The living room we use has the dining table, etc. at one end. There is also a bathroom – a very modern one for the country. But there is no central heating only little stove-like things, in the fireplaces. The bedroom Louise and I are sharing is the smallest and has no heat at all. Of course we have loads and loads of covers on our beds, but getting up nerve enough to dress and undress is the hardest thing I've ever done!

Mme. Rémond came about an hour and a half after we arrived with magazines which we immediately read, also the newspaper. All the news is very upsetting lately with England and France rushing into Egypt. I'm also anxious about the election and because I haven't received any sort of directions about voting absentee. I don't understand why I haven't been sent anything. It's quite disturbing to think I have a right to vote and may not get to now.

November 3, 1956

We drove to Provins this afternoon to see the big market – it's one of the oldest of all the old towns in France, and I had no idea there was so much to see there. Unfortunately, we were only there for two hours, so naturally we left much unseen. But the things we saw really were amazing for their ancient-ness.

Practically the whole town dates from the 12th and 13th centuries. There are magnificent remains of the great walls and towers which fortified the city in the middle ages. They are the best ruins I've seen yet – only the very tops of the walls are missing. After the fortifications we visited the Tour de César – a great tower which was used as a prison, among other things. It's amazing how nearly perfectly intact it is. From the top you can see for miles and miles – really a gorgeous view.

After the Tour de César we visited an old, old church where Joan of Arc took communion with King Charles VII on their way to Reims. It isn't a particularly beautiful church, but is interesting because of its age. We visited two other churches which can be described in the same manner. The town of Provins was all decorated for some sort of forthcoming festival – there was music playing in the streets over loudspeakers. The market was an open one, under little tents. There was everything to sell in the way of food and old clothing. Ugly old people were everywhere. That wasn't a very complimentary thing to say, but they were all ugly and old. And it's no wonder. If I had to live the hard life they've lived I'd be ugly and old too. Many of them have lived, as have the poor people in this tiny village, without comfort, without enough money, enough food, etc. They've farmed with the most primitive of tools, they've always known only one way of life – the hard one – and neither they nor their children will ever know anything better. It's all very sad I think.

For dessert tonight M. Rémond bought some pastry in Provins that is only made on the 2nd of November in the section of Provins – only on the day of All Souls. They were so good – I hate to think I'll never have another one!

The weather has been cold and rainy, but the worst part was that the toilet plugged up and we had to walk through the mud to use the horrible outside toilet, which was right next to a bunch of cows!??

Sunday, November 4, 1956

Well, we're back in Paris, and I was never so glad to get back to any place. My ballot for voting was waiting. I have to do it before a civil officer tomorrow – which means it can't possibly reach the US in time to be counted. But I'll do it anyway, it makes me mad that they waited so late to send it to me.

We have our first class tomorrow at 11:00 at the Sorbonne – art history. I'm sort of scared of it.

Monday, November 5, 1956

Well, I've had my first class at the Sorbonne – so exciting! The Sorbonne is swarming with foreigners. We chummed with an English girl this morning hunting for our class. It was held in a huge amphitheater which had at least 500 of us in it for that one class! Everyone was a foreigner to France and yet all of us spoke and understood French. It was a really a strange sensation.

Our professor, M. Gaillard, is wonderful. Naturally he understands the problems of foreign students, he speaks clearly, precisely, not too quickly. I understood every word he said today. We really didn't have a class, he just talked to us about what the course would include, books for us to use as references, and books which would be helpful for us to buy. I really was impressed with him. He told us we could ask him questions about our personal needs after each class or we could write the question and he would write the answer back. We usually would have class on Tuesday morning, but tomorrow is some kind of special day at the Sorbonne and there are no classes.

At 3:00 I went to the American Embassy to have my absentee ballot notarized. I mailed it right after I had it notarized but I'm sure it won't get to the US by tomorrow. I'm so anxious about the election. I've read everything I could get my hands on about it.

At 5:00 we had a meeting with Dr. Smithers followed by our first class in composition with Mme. Alvernhe. In the little meeting we found that the piano at the pension where Dr. Smithers lives is to be ours for practicing. Of course Louise, Eugenie, and I have to pay for the renting of the piano and the room which will run to about $9.00 a month for each of us, which is cheaper than we could've done it any other way. Tomorrow we're all practicing.

We have a schedule all made out for this week. I'm going to call Mme.

Milleret tomorrow and ask if I may see her the first of next week. I figure I'll be in good enough shape by then, after practicing all week. I can't wait to get started. Mme. Milleret is a very good friend of Mme. Alvernhe, who is a pretty well-known literary woman. She says that Mme. Milleret is a marvelous teacher that she has prepared many students for careers, that all the musician friends of Mme. Alvernhe know Mme. Milleret and praise her work, that she doesn't have a famous name, that she has never been a famous singer, that she charges $3.00 for 45 minutes, which I think is grand and reasonable. I'm going to try to take two lessons a week I think.

We're really going to have to work this year. It's certainly not going to be a picnic!

My schedule as it stands so far with everything but voice lessons is:

History of Art – Monday 11:00, Tuesday 8:45, Friday 8:45

French Composition – Monday 2 – 4

History of Music – Wednesday 8:45

French Theater – Thursday 2:30 – 4:30

So you see my schedule leaves me plenty of time to study and see ballets, operas, concerts, etc. I'm going to try to get my voice lessons on Tuesdays and Thursdays. Then I'll have from Friday noon to Sunday night for short weekend trips.

Our room – the whole house – is delightful now that the heat is on. The weather has been much milder too. Must be the calm before the storm.

The world situation is really alarming. However no one over here seems too alarmed. The situation in Hungary is so appalling. To think Hungary was brave enough to revolt – a little country like that – revolting, hoping for help from the "free," "democratic" Western world, and not getting that help because the free, democratic world is so afraid of Russia. It's horrible. I pray God will keep us safe and bring back peace soon. I'm so uneasy living this close (which isn't really close) to danger. Think what these people who have lived in real danger have been through!

Tuesday, November 6, 1956

I'm dying to know about the election! I can't wait till tomorrow so I can find out.

I've had a very enjoyable day today. I practiced this morning, then after lunch I called Jean-Louis. I had received a letter from him asking me to call him. We made a date and met in front of the Madeleine. I was there first, and was walking around whistling. When Jean-Louis arrived I was so glad to see him, but he was appalled that I was whistling. He said that is what the putains (prostitutes) do, and I should never whistle when alone and in public! Live and learn!

I was really glad to see Jean-Louis. It's so much easier for me to speak French with him, much easier than with anyone else. He had his sports car, which he'll have all the week. His mother has gone to Belgium to visit her sister and left him her car. He had tried to call me last night because his mother wanted me to come to their apartment so she could meet me. I wish I had been home when he called.

We got in the car, drove bravely through this horrible traffic to the Eiffel Tower. I had never seen it up close. It's quite unusual, but not at all pretty. We rode in the lift to the top – from where you have a gorgeous view of Paris. Luckily the sun was out, the sky was blue, and it wasn't very cold. It was, in short, delightful! Afterwards we drove to their apartment. He wanted me to see it. The maid was there, so I figured it was all right to go in. It's a lovely apartment – four pretty large rooms, a kitchen and a bath. The inside is all new. The maid is there all the time just to cook and clean up for Jean-Louis. Tough life!

On the drive back to my house we talked about the world situation. I became so frightened I nearly cried. It almost seems inevitable that there will be another war. Oh God, I hope not. I'm such a coward I guess. Jean-Louis doesn't think there will be a war because of the Suez but because of Hungary – if there is a war. I don't know what to think.

After Jean-Louis brought me home I changed clothes and got ready for our dinner guests. One of them couldn't come so there was only Marie-Louise somebody – I never get last names! She's 20, very cold, very sophisticated. Louise and I worked like dogs trying to get something out of her. Finally she did talk to us a little. She's studying to be an interpreter – speaks English and Spanish. She is very big, much older looking than 20 – as are most of the girls that age here – and they are all more advanced than we as far as education goes. I hate being inferior in that respect, but I can't blame myself – I guess I can't blame anyone, although I think it's really partly our educational system that is at fault. Then I think – which would I prefer – a few beautifully educated people (like in France) or many mildly educated people – obviously USA. I've decided we Americans have more innate common sense and know-how, but certainly lack that desire and respect for learning which permeates every person here who has an intellectual curiosity.

So many of my opinions have changed since I left home. There's so much about the U.S. that rubs Europeans the wrong way – I never understood why before, but now I think I do. It's because so much of the publicized America is the America of garbage disposals, washing machines, luxury items. Unfortunately much of America, especially in the lower middle classes is becoming just that. In France people do without those luxury items in order to be able to have beautiful works of art, attend concerts, spend their money visiting the museums. Which is the most worthwhile set of values?

Back from my tangent – I did enjoy Marie-Louise finally. I think she's Mme. Rémond's cousin. She also has something to do with France-Amerique (of which M. Rémond is president – I asked him). Tonight they discussed having a dinner dance for us and the Hollins girls. It sounds wonderful. Louise and I are going to have to help get the girls together and let the Rémonds know about it.

Thursday, November 8, 1956

Hurrah! Ike won! You can't imagine how relieved I was when I heard of Ike's victory on the radio early yesterday morning, and then bought the special edition of the Herald Tribune with everything about the election in it.

Yesterday morning Louise and I met Jean-Louis at the Sorbonne at 10:00 and went to buy tickets for the ballet last night. We went to a place where students get reductions, but we found out after we got there that they give reductions only for theater. So we got out the Semaine de Paris and tried to decide where we wanted to go instead. Louise and I have been dying to see the play *Cyrano de Bergerac*. It's such a classic. Jean-Louis knows it practically by heart but he said he'd go. So, he called the theater, they had tickets, but said he must come to pick them up and he did. (He's afraid to drive his car in Paris now because the government passed a law this Tuesday that no cars could be driven outside of their own departments because of the shortage of gas resulting from the Suez affair – his car is of course from Dijon and has a Cote d'Or number.)

For dessert last night Mme. Rémond had told us she was going to have a surprise – an American surprise – for our dessert. It was grapefruit. It tasted so wonderful.

At 8:10 Jean-Louis came to take us to the theater. We had a hard time finding it. I think all men everywhere must be alike. Louise and I knew how to get there by the map, but J. L. was determined to do it his way. He got lost, refused to ask anybody the way, wouldn't listen to us. Consequently we were 10 minutes late! But not too late to miss a lot of the play which was marvelous. Naturally I couldn't understand all of it, but I understood enough to know what was going on. It's such a romantic and sentimental play. I was feeling sort of blue anyway, so it really got to me. The sets, the costumes, the actors were superb. Afterward Jean-Louis took us to a delightful café on the Champs-Élysées for a drink. We had hot chocolate and J. L. had a beer. He really was nice to take both of us last night. That is the custom here – the boys don't mind at all if there is a third-party. We really did have a good time.

I'm getting ready to call Mme. Milleret about voice lessons. Then I'm going to practice. I wish I didn't have to go so far.

Thursday night

I'm really disturbed about everything. The world is in such a mess – and I'm right here in the middle of it all of it. Last night there were demonstrations in some of the streets of Paris against the Russians and the Communists action in Hungary. Some of the demonstrations were violent. They tore up the Communist newspaper press, thirty people were seriously injured in all the ruckus (a word). Tonight there is a Communist rally against the anti-Communist rally last night. They really have no importance except it's the only way to show Hungary that the French are in sympathy with them. Not only is France doing it, but all over Europe there are such demonstrations. What good will they do? Everyone here seems to believe the next war will come from Hungary. So do I. The Rémonds don't think there will be another world war for four, maybe five years, but they – like everyone else – are certain of the inevitable war. It is a repetition of history. In 1939 Poland cried for help and no one came. In 1940 France cried for help – no one came. In 1941 England and Greece cried out – and no one came. As a result of waiting, of hoping to avoid war an even more terrible war developed. Perhaps if the victims in Poland had been helped at first, the horrible war that developed could have been avoided. Now, in 1956, Poland wanted help – no one answered. Hungary pleaded on her knees and was refused. England and France would have loved aid in Egypt but had none. So total war has been avoided, but for how long? And what can be done? And who will be the first to do it? I'm scared. I want to be at home if I'm going to die. I certainly never planned on the world being in such a state when I left home! If I just had someone to talk to who could reassure me – I'm afraid no human could do that. There's so much inside me right now I can't seem to find a place for it all.

I called Mme. Milleret today and she was so nice on the phone. I have an appointment to meet her and I suppose sing for her tomorrow afternoon at 2:30. I'm not as ready as I would like to be but I have no choice. I just hope I like her and she likes me and my voice. Tonight Louise has gone to meet her piano teacher. I'm writing, and reading and listening to the radio. After supper I played with Nanou (Anne) and Isabelle a long time. They love for me to dance for them and with them. They begged me to do acrobatics all the time. Isabelle has been really sweet lately – I hope she stays that way. That's all for now.

Saturday, November 10, 1956

I'm a little relieved today about the world affairs. Things seem a little more calm. I really have been living in fear.

Yesterday morning I practiced for an hour before lunch, after which I took the Metro to see Mme. Milleret about my voice lessons. I didn't know it until we rode past it, but the Metro stop I wanted was out of order and I had to ride to the next one, which was about six blocks from where I wanted to go. I was a little lost at first, but finally I got my bearings and proceeded to walk to 138 Rue de Rennes.

Mme. Milleret lives in an apartment house (as does everyone in Paris!) similar to this one on the outside. She lives on the second floor. I was greeted by her husband who obviously stays there all day long because he was the one who answered the phone when I had called her. He showed me into the room where Mme. was giving a lesson to a Chinese girl (French too – I mean she lives in France – is from Indo-China I suppose). The room is large with too much furniture in it. There are autographed pictures of students and friends who have made careers of their singing. There was a ballet shoe (toe) hanging from a picture frame, a poster of a symphonic concert. The piano is a grand piano – a Pleyel – the best French-make piano maker.

After about ten minutes she finished and Mme. asked me several questions about myself and my singing. Then I sang. Mme. liked my voice – told me it was "very pretty ravishing, charming, beautiful timbre." She said of course there were things that needed perfecting but no great fault. She said my high notes had too much vibrato sometimes – which was – still is true. I explained that I was out of practice and she said that probably was part of the reason for the vibrato. She complimented the way I used my diaphragm, told me that I obviously had studied with good teachers.

Anyhow she gave me a lesson right then. I sang several things – a couple of French songs. She said she couldn't understand a word I sang in French, but she could understand my spoken French. She made me sing some exercises. I had been told that if I studied voice in Paris I would learn an entirely different method. I believe it now!

Although Mme. Milleret is aiming for the same results, her methods are different. She wanted me to hold my mouth in a different position for several of the vowels – the pronunciation of ah, e and u all entirely different in French. It means I'm going to have to work very hard not only on tones but French diction. Mme. Milleret herself is large, about 50 or a little over, has bleached blonde hair, is a dramatic soprano. She stops you all the time to make correction, which is of course very good. I am going to have two lessons a week with her at $3.00 – each is a 45 minute lesson. I think that's very reasonable. My lessons are on Monday afternoons at 5:00 and Thursday mornings at 11:00. I'm not convinced yet that she's the teacher for me, but I'll know in a couple of weeks. She seemed so enthusiastic about me.

I met Louise at the American Embassy to register. It took so long – we came straight home and I dressed to go out with Jean-Louis. Mme. Rémond had me come to her room and model my dress (the bright pink jersey) and coat (black) for her.

Jean-Louis came at 6:30. We drove to the Champs-Élysées, parked the car and walked up the Champs. That time of evening is everybody's favorite time for promenading. We ended our little walk at the restaurant where we ate. After dinner we drove toward Sacré-Cœur. We wanted to go to the top of the hill and see all of Paris at night, but we got lost and never got there. We were driving to the Montmartre section where all the nightclubs and little hot spots are. You really can see some strange sights there! I was dying to go to the Moulin Rouge, but didn't dare suggest it. We had a good time just driving around looking though.

When I came in Mme. Rémond had forgotten to leave the key for me under the second step (the secret place) and I had to ring to get in. I hated to wake her up at 1:00 A. M. She came to the door all apologies for having forgotten.

After lunch Louise and I went to see Sainte-Chapelle, but it was just closing, so we didn't get to see it. Then it began to rain, so we came on back home. Paris is really beautiful in the rain. It doesn't rain hard, just enough to let you know it's really raining. The flower markets were in full swing with all their gorgeous glorious smells and colors. The fishermen who were always there but never seem to catch anything were fishing. It was all quite dreamlike.

Sunday night, November 11, 1956

Happy Armistice Day. This really has been an enjoyable day. There were only four of us today because M. Rémond has gone to Champscenest to hunt and took Isabelle with him. After lunch Louise and I hurried to catch the Metro to the opera. We went to the matinee performance of *Carmen* at the Opéra-Comique. It was very good. The woman who played Carmen was excellent. She looks so much like Risë Stevens. The singing wasn't as good as in the *Carmen* I saw at the Met. The tenor was horrible. He sang so sharp so many times! But as a whole it was very good. I love the music so much.

Jean-Louis met us in front of the Opéra-Comique after the performance and the three of us walked up and down the boulevards a little. Sunday is walking – rather strolling day. All of Paris walks on Sundays. We went to the Café de la Paix and had ice cream. I've been craving ice cream for several days now and this was the best I've ever tasted. We sat and talked a long time – until 7:30, then we took the Metro to go home. So we had a very enjoyable afternoon. Jean-Louis is so nice to Louise and me.

At dinner we had a long intimate talk with Mme. We found out why the family is so unfriendly to each other. I've told you that the whole family lives in this one big building, but they all feel hard toward each other because of the problem of the fortune to be inherited. It seems M. Rémond is the oldest and therefore gets a larger part or something. It's all very complicated anyway, Mme. doesn't like the set up at all – the unfriendly atmosphere that is. She also told us about their courtship, marriage, about her schooling, her life during the war etc. It was the first really intimate talk we've had. She really is a wonderful woman

Tuesday, November 13, 1956

I have a new complaint. My wisdom teeth are giving me trouble now! The upper left one is coming all the way through, I guess, and it hurts like the devil! My jaws are so sore and my neck feels like it is trying to swell. Of course that's just what I need! The Rémonds told me that there are American dentists in Paris, if it gets any worse I guess I can look them up.

Yesterday morning I had my first real lecture in art history. It is so interesting, but it's so hard to take notes in French! I guess I'll eventually learn. Before class I practiced for about an hour. After lunch I studied until time to go to my voice lesson. I was a little early but Mme. Milleret wanted to start a little early since I was there, so we did. I was so encouraged after my lesson. We seemed to understand each other so much better. I surprised her because I had already learned a song sheet she gave me on Friday. She complimented me again. Her husband came in and told me that I had a voice for concerts, that I remind him of a famous German singer of Schubert songs. I left feeling like a million after being so encouraged. In fact I left in such a daze that I forgot to pay Mme. Milleret!

Jean-Louis met me in front of Mme. Milleret's after my lesson. It was raining and neither of us had an umbrella, but we walked anyway. Paris rain never pours – it just falls lightly. We walked to a café and had hot chocolate. It was so good. We were both in a good mood and everything was so funny – the rain, the people, everything. We really had a good time. He told me that my French had improved so much, he was really amazed. He said that he has no trouble understanding me now.

After dinner Louise and I performed for Mme. Rémond. She (Mme.) had me sing in French, German, Italian and English. She said she could understand my French perfectly – also my English. She kept me singing for about half an hour. It was the first time I've ever really sung for her because I had my cold for so long. Thank goodness it's gone away.

Yesterday it started getting really cold again. It's been sort of mild and the sun has been shining a lot, but now winter's coming I guess. M. Rémond told me that it is always like this during the vacation for All Saints and All Souls Day since the time is sad, so is the weather, it rains, etc. That's exactly how it was the whole time we were in Champscenest during the All Saints All Souls Day holidays. Then after the holidays, when the sadness is ended, there is a time when the weather's mild and pretty. It's strange that the weather should comply with the morale of the people.

Today we had another art history course at 8:45. That means we have to get up at 7:00. We have to do that three times a week. It's still dark at 7:00! I was going to go practice after lunch, but my jaws were hurting so that I didn't. I studied here instead. We had our theater course at 4:00 and before I went to class I went to get my camel's hair coat from being repaired. It had a little hole in it where it got caught in the chain of my bike in Dijon. It looks fine now.

After our theater course I met Jean-Louis. I had the toothache, headache, and didn't feel like being very amiable. So, of all the terrible times to pick, Jean-Louis announced that we were going to meet his mother at the Place de la Madeleine and then go to have a drink together. Well, since I've never met his mother I naturally wanted to make a good impression, the first time, but there I was with a dull mind, my very un-elegant big purse, camel hair coat and plaid scarf around my neck. I was so mad at him for not warning me. Of course I couldn't blame him because he hadn't known in time to tell me. His mother has just returned from Belgium. Anyway, I said I simply would not go. He said O. K. if I wanted to be that way. I explained that I simply couldn't be very charming and couldn't think enough French because I was too tired. So then he said for me to come with him to the Madeleine, he would go tell his mother that I couldn't come, and then he'd walk me home. We started walking toward the place where he was to meet her. I stopped as he started to go near the place where she was supposed to be, when all at once Jean-Louis said "She's already seen us and is coming this way." I was trapped.

In a second she was there, and I was pleasantly surprised to see a very attractive woman of about your age, Mother. She's medium height, blonde, blue-eyed. She had on a gorgeous black suit, beautiful mink stole, mauve colored velour hat, and a huge diamond ring. I was completely at ease with her. She complimented my French, which encouraged me. We went to an exclusive bar and had champagne and caviar! We talked for over an hour and poor Jean-Louis didn't have a chance to say a word! I really do like Mme. Baut. We left at 7:30 and all walked to Place St. Augustin where they took the Metro and I came home. I was so glad I went on and met her even looking as slouchy as I did. I really was awful to Jean-Louis refusing to go etc.

After supper I heard the Rémonds singing together so I went in to listen to them. We had a long conversation. They are so wonderful. We're very lucky to live with them.

I received the money orders. That's the simplest method of all. I've been doing really well with my money. I still have about $75 in francs and I have $50 in travelers checks. Then $200 in money orders. I really didn't expect you to send it so quickly.

Wednesday night November 14, 1956

I have a horror of catching cold! I've got the same sort of sore throat that I had when I had the last cold. Maybe it's just a reaction from my teeth.

This morning we had our first class in music history with Monsieur Handemann. We went to his apartment at 9:00. He is so charming – about 53 or 54, gray curly hair, a little gray moustache, about Daddy's height, rather slim, and a beautiful speaking voice. We listened to several records which he said gave an over-all idea of the width of the range of variety in French music. It was so nice to sit quietly in a lovely room and hear some beautiful music. He has become quite famous in music history during the past few years, and agreed to take us only on the condition that we be very serious, hard-working students, which means work with a capital W! We have to (among other things) attend at least 2 concerts a month and write a short critique on all that we hear at those concerts.

After lunch I studied until four, when I met Jean-Louis. I had errands to run – pick up my shoes. Speaking of shoes, the only ones I wear to school and for walking are my two black leather pairs of little heels (wedgies included). People nearly laugh in your face if you venture out in saddle oxfords. Jean-Louis is always teasing me about my camel hair coat because it's so typically American. Today we saw five obviously American girls from the North with camel hair coats exactly like mine. It was really funny.

Friday morning November 16, 1956

Just call me sore mouth now. I suppose I'm just scared over nothing, but I have visions of getting pyorrhea (or however you spell it) and everything else. I'm so worried about my teeth. I wish you'd call Dr. Donoho and ask how my wisdom teeth look on the X-rays he has. I think he has some. I am telling myself the pain will go away soon. My glands are a little swollen and I have a sore throat a little.

Yesterday morning we had no classes, so I slept until 8:30, then wrote the little theme due for composition class. After lunch we went to Composition class. On the way I stopped and bought some penicillin throat tablets which Jean-Louis told me were good. So far they've worked no miracle.

Yesterday afternoon we worked on grammar and I was so glad. I know our French will really improve rapidly with Madame Alvernhe. After class at 4:45 I rushed to catch the bus home. I had an appointment with Jean-Louis at 6:00 in front of Mme. Milleret's. The only thing was I didn't go to Mme. Milleret's for my voice lesson because my throat was too sore for singing. I called her and told her and she was so sweet. Then I tried to call Jean-Louis but couldn't get anyone. So I had to rush home from class, quickly change my clothes, and rush all the way back on the Left Bank side to be in front of Mme. Milleret's at six. I was 10 minutes late and so pooped after the race I could hardly stand up. Dear old Jean-Louis was there waiting for me. The purpose for our meeting was to have dinner with his mother, but he hadn't told me if we were going to eat out or at their apartment. When we met he said we would eat at their apartment, then go to the musical shows. So, we went back across town to get tickets, then back across town to their apartment. His cousin Edith was also there. She's 18, very nice and rather pretty. We had a wonderful supper of – I don't know what to call what we had first, but it is in a pastry shell and is a cream cheese filling. It's always served hot, and is so delicious. Then we had some delicious green peas, ham, sausage, and dessert was fresh peaches. I don't know where they came from but they were delicious. After dinner Edith left and we took a taxi to the theater – my first really long ride in a taxi through Paris. The show was wonderful. Its star is Charles Trenet, the famous singer since back in 1930. He's the one who wrote and sings "La Mer." He was marvelous. He didn't come on until eleven and then he sang until twelve-ten. Everyone yelled bravo and clapped until I thought the walls would cave in! I was afraid he wouldn't sing "La Mer," but after about four encores the crowd was begging him to sing it, so he did. It was so marvelous. There's something about French songs that is irresistible. They are so smooth and subtle and easy to listen to. Charles Trenet has a trademark – an old hat he has had since he first started out. He wears it for every performance. He put it on for nearly every song last night or else put it on the piano next to him.

I really think French popular music is more genteel than our popular music of today – 1956. There were other attractions on the bill last night. The main two stars besides Charles Trenet were a comic, who was excellent, and a girl who sang beautiful old French folk songs. There were also dancers, quartets, a juggler, like a T.V. variety show. It was really an enjoyable evening.

About my classes. Art History meets 3 times a week for one hour a session. There is no outside "assigned" work, but we have books and they expect you to follow the lectures in the books. Then too, we all are to take excursions to see examples of the art they speak of – here in Paris of course. I think I told you about music history. In Composition we study grammar and write – this week we wrote a résumé of a story by Guy de Maupassant. We are to do a lot of writing and reading on our own too. We have grammar exercises to do also. In theater we study of course "plays." Right now we're studying Molière's *Bourgeois Gentilhomme*. We've had to write about what we read besides discussing in class. I'm sure I'll have more to say about my classes as the year advances.

Saturday night. November 17, 1956

Well, Louise and I are really having a hard time! Last night we went to the opera to see *La Bohème*, it was to be Louise's first time to see it. She said she was sort of sick at her stomach before we went, but we went on anyway. As soon as we got there she started having diarrhea and vomiting too. All during the first act she ran back and forth to the bathroom. I thoroughly enjoyed the first act. It was the first good tenor I've heard in France! But poor Louise!

She was so pale and weak and exhausted that she couldn't stay any longer. I hated for her to have to go home alone. She might faint, so we both took a taxi home. Madame Rémond fixed her some tea and she went straight to bed. I sewed some buttons on my coat, wrote letters, and went to bed.

Today I was more uncomfortable than I have ever been with my mouth. Last night I woke up three times in a cold sweat. I noticed my glands were more swollen this morning and that I had blisters on the end of my tongue. It was so difficult to talk and eat – but I went on to Versailles anyway. When we came home I examined my mouth again – because I had been so uncomfortable all day. This evening the top of my mouth behind my upper teeth had nice white blisters and also my gums were inflamed – and there were white blisters in several places. Louise looked and said it looked like trench-mouth. I burst into tears. I just can't take having to fight something new every week. Louise insisted that she call the American Hospital. She did – they told her they could send a doctor or I could come there Monday. They said to call them back and tell them my decision. I decided to have a doctor come.

Louise had to dress to go to see France-Amerique headquarters with M. Rémond. I was supposed to have gone too, but of course I didn't. I called the hospital and talked with a Dr. Keenan. He said he wouldn't come unless it was really urgent. I described everything to him. He said he didn't think it sounded like trench-mouth, but obviously was some infection. He said he didn't think it would get worse by tomorrow and that I could come to the American Hospital at 10:30 in the morning and he would see me.

Right now I'm in the bed. I really can't chew anything, so Mme. Rémond brought me some wonderful hot soup and café-au-lait – and here I am. I really hate to be pessimistic, but I always fear the worst for my teeth. I guess it's because I wore those braces for so long that my teeth are of such concern to me. If I ever get rid of this whatever it is I pray to Goodness I won't have anything else wrong with me – at least for a while.

I had been told that an entirely new life, climate, food, habits, would do strange things to one's health, and I believe it now!

Aside from sickness we had a wonderful day. We left for Versailles at 9:15, caught the train at Gare St. Lazare which is just about 3 ½ blocks from us. There are trains leaving every half-hour for Versailles. We got there about ten. We took a long walk through the vast and absolutely magnificent gardens. The colored leaves were still hanging on the trees – the only place (I think) where they still remain. Of course the flowers were not in bloom, but the gardens were still beautiful. I am going back in the spring though to see them in full bloom. The plan of the garden is perfect, symmetrically and geometrically. There are elaborate marble fountains in large pools everywhere. Statues are everywhere. But the splendor lies in the trees, the planning and the perfection of everything. We walked to the Trianons, but they are open only from 2 to 5. Also the little hamlet where Marie Antoinette played milkmaid. So we decided we would come back to see them in the spring too. We then went to eat lunch in a restaurant nearby before we went to the château itself. It is so huge, so vast, so ornate, that words don't do it justice. The ceilings are all carved in gold and satiny white. They are exquisite, lavish, so rich that I had never even imagined it would be like it is. The marble everywhere is overwhelmingly beautiful – black, white, green, pink, and red marble are used throughout the palace. We didn't get to see all the rooms because several of them are closed for reparations, but we saw enough to be blindly dazzled.

The famous Hall of Mirrors is just as I thought it would be, but even more lavish. Marie Antoinette's bedroom, the King's apartment, everything is unbelievable – and to think, all that splendor was constructed for one little measly human being to live in! The chapel itself (where Louis XVI and Marie Antoinette were married at ages 16 and 15) was worth the trip there. What furniture that is still left in the Palace is exquisite.

In Marie Antoinette's bedroom is a desk made of mosaic pieces of mother-of-pearl! It was my favorite of all the furniture too. The tapestries and paintings are for the most part all very beautiful and interesting. There were lots of American tourists taking tours through the Palace, and we sort of latched on to the tail end of several of the tours and learned a lot more than we ordinarily would. We had a little guide book that told us everything about all we saw, but by hanging on to the tours we got a lot of little details that weren't in the book. I really would like to go back and see the whole castle again. I feel sure I will in the spring. There really is no way to justly describe Versailles. You simply have to see it for yourself.

M. Rémond wants to have a party for us Newcombites and seven Hollins girls – equal number of French boys. The party is planned for Friday night Dec. 14, and will be a dinner-dance. He wants those of us who know French boys to bring them. I guess I should bring Jean-Louis but I'd like to meet somebody new!

I'll let you know the doctor's verdict tomorrow.

Sunday night November 18, 1956

Well, I went to the doctor this morning. I was an hour late because I went to Avenue Victor Hugo first instead of Boulevard Victor Hugo. Dr. Keenan is so divine – I knew he would be – unfortunately he's married. We became good friends. He drove me to the Metro stop after my call. My case is just as Louise thought – trench mouth. Of course there's not much that can be done for it. At first Dr. Keenan suggested I stay in the hospital for about two days and let them fill me full of penicillin, etc. Then I told him I have other classes besides singing – which I can't do in this condition. So he said he'd just give me a big dose of penicillin that would last nearly all week. If I had gone into the hospital it would have been covered by the health insurance policy, under hospitalization, but I just didn't feel I could afford to miss all those classes right here at first.

Dr. Keenan gave me horrible hydrogen peroxide to wash my mouth out with, which nearly kills me because everything in my mouth is so raw. He also told me to wash my teeth well – even making my gums bleed. He said he couldn't say how long it would last, because you just never know. Fortunately, it was caught in its early stages. So, there it is. I really am uncomfortable with it. I can't eat anything but liquids and soft stuff. But worst of all I can't sing – again. It seems as if it weren't meant for me to sing anymore!

Of course I know things could be worse. Oh, the doctor cost me about $7.00 including shot, visit, etc., which is much cheaper than at home for that price isn't it? I hope by the time you get this that I'll be well again. Oh, my wisdom teeth don't hurt so badly now.

I spent from ten to one doctoring. After lunch we all met at the dormitory where Sandy, Ellie, and Coco live to discuss our plans for Christmas. We're meeting tomorrow with a travel agent whom Mr. Smithers knows, who handled all the girls' trips last year.

November 19, 1956, Monday

I've spent the whole day in bed and I'm going to again tomorrow. It really has helped. I've been using lots of peroxide and I hope in a few days my tongue at least will be back to normal. I have to be well enough by Thursday – Thanksgiving. Louise went to see a friend of her uncle, who is a very important major in the army here – he is in charge of two hotels whose clients are all American army personnel. Anyway he has invited both of us to a big Thanksgiving dinner-dance Thursday night – formal dress! There probably won't be any young people there, but we don't care!

This major (Annan is his last name) is about 50, unmarried, one of those men who knows everybody and everybody knows him. He also told us that he can get us francs for our dollars at least at the rate of 390. They do it through the army, so it's all legal. We're going to let him get our next money for us. Also, there's a PX at the hotel where his office is where we can get Kleenex, toothpaste, and all the necessities at an American rate, which is so much cheaper than the French one. He said for us to tell him anytime we need something and he'll get it for us. Also, Louise and I want to go to Frankfurt, Germany for a week-end because Louise has a friend whose family lives there now. He has invited us to come and stay at their house and see Frankfurt. I would like to go because that part of Germany won't be on our itinerary for Christmas. Major Annan said that he might be able to let us fly over in an army plane for practically nothing! Wouldn't that be great!

Now I'm going to write an "I want" paragraph. Our trip Christmas is going to be on a half-pension deal which means that we'll stay in very nice inexpensive hotels and we'll have two meals a day included in the price. It will probably cost about $80.00 for the 18 days in three countries – Germany, Austria, Switzerland, which I think is remarkably inexpensive. Of course that won't include the third meal, the extras, the souvenirs, etc. I figure $125 for the whole trip would do marvelously. Now, I've got $30.00 in francs, about $34.00 in American money, $60.00 in traveler's cheques, and $200.00 in money orders. For the month of December we're not going to pay M. Rémond for the whole month because we won't be here. We figure we'll owe him about $80.00 for December and $100.00 for January. Our vacation is from December 20th to the night of January 6th. So, I know I can finish this money and still have some of the $30.00 in francs. If I take $180 out of the $200 for paying for Dec. and January's rent, I'll have about $80 of $90 So, why don't you send me another $100 money order soon. I'll give all three money orders to Major Annan who will get nearly 400 f. to the dollar. I can then make about $45 off the $300 in money orders! That I'm sure will do comfortably probably to February. Oh, I forgot. For myself I'm dying to buy a gold signet ring for my little finger. The most elegant people wear them and they have such beautiful ones. I don't want to pay over $30 for one, but I guess – Oh – I can buy it with the profit from the money deal with Major Annan!

Now, what do you think of all this? Thursday I'll know the definite itinerary of our little trip and I'll write you about it. I got the chlor-trimeton today – it took only four days for it to come. Hope I never have to use it. I don't have anything else to tell since my day was spent totally in the bed unfortunately, because it was beautiful outside today. I'll be glad when I can eat normally again. I'm afraid I've lost weight again. I'm taking pills now, so maybe I'll be saved.

Do send the money orders soon so I can give them to Major Annan. Oh, I got my first pictures back today and they are really good.

Friday, November 23

Worry no more, my trench mouth is gone – thank the Lord. I stayed in bed Monday and Tuesday, took really good care of myself, and I'm sure that helped it go away. I had to be well by Thanksgiving Day, and I was.

We had a lovely Thanksgiving Day. The weather was pretty, but horribly cold. We went for noon dinner to Reid Hall – as I told you we were. All the Reid Hall girls were there, lots of girls from Smith, many of whom we met on the ship, many American adults, but not many – rather any – boys. Everything was decorated with Pumpkins filled with fruit, leaves, and flowers. Very Thanksgiving-ish. We had a wonderful meal of turkey, dressing, sweet potatoes, broiled onions, cranberry sauce, and pumpkin pie. There was a little orchestra of a piano, violin, and bass fiddle that played during dinner. Several times they played such good old American songs that everyone simultaneously burst into singing. After dinner several of us stayed and played the piano, sang, and chatted. It was really delightful. We left there about four thirty and Sandy, Susan, and Ellie came home with Louise and me to see our room and drink Benedictine – the bottle Louise and I bought when we first got here. They stayed while we changed to go to our second Thanksgiving dinner.

First we all had to go to Mrs. Smithers' (who has sprained her ankle) to meet the man who's arranging our Christmas trip and get the final word on it. Then Louise and I took a taxi to meet Major Annan at the Continental Hotel. I can't remember if I told you about Major – oh yes, I remember now I did. Well, he's tall, gray-haired, red-faced, typical old bachelor in the Army – and so nice. When we first arrived at the hotel we were escorted into the cocktail room where everyone was having cocktails. Major A. came up to us immediately and began introducing us to everybody – who was either an Ambassador, Colonel, General, Minister, or something with their wives.

Everybody was speaking both French and English, since the crowd was made up of both. After cocktails we went into the dining room, which is beautiful – like a room in Versailles almost. We sat at a table for 12. Three men had their wives, three didn't, and then Maj. Annan and Louise and I. All the men were old men who have been in Paris for years. One was married to a Frenchwoman.

They have certainly led interesting lives – don't seem to care if they get back to the states or not. One of them is an honorary something or other in the French government. Everyone there was dressed in silk, satin and mink. The food was delicious – turkey, dressing, cranberry sauce, green peas, sweet potatoes, salad, mince-meat pie with ice-cream. To drink we had red wine, champagne, Benedictine, and coffee.

After dinner there were several speeches made by such people as the Minister Plenipotentiary of the U.S. Embassy to France, His Excellency the U.S. Ambassador to N.A.T.O., the President of the Senate Delegation to N.A.T.O, Monsieur de Minister de France Gerard Jacquet, and other notables. Everybody there was somebody important. It was so late by the time the speeches and everything was over that we didn't stay for dancing.

Major Annan took us and one of our table companions home. He took the gentleman home first, then, because we had told him that we had no heat half the time in our house, he insisted on taking us to his apartment and giving us an electric heater he had but didn't use. He was so insistent that we went with him. He has a tape recorder, so he recorded our voices talking about how we like France. Then he pulled out his accordion and played for us, we sang, recorded our singing and playing, and sang Christmas carols. Poor Major Annan. I felt so sorry for him playing his little accordion, loving so having us there listening to him. It was so late and we were so tired, but we just couldn't ruin his evening by not listening to him. Just think, he's got nobody in the way of a family. His only hobby is playing that little (it's really sort of big) accordion and playing with his tape-recorder. It's so sad. He is so nice!

Besides giving us the heater, he's going to give us milk – real drinkable milk that they get at the PX. He told us to come by whenever we wanted it. The heater doesn't do such a great job, but it's better than nothing. Right now I'm in my room practically sitting on the heater with my boots, my long undies, two sweaters, a skirt, and my house coat on – and I'm freezing. With the fuel shortage from the Suez they just can't turn the heat on all day. As soon as the ships start coming from the U.S. things won't be so bad. About my clothes, I have plenty of the right things. I do think I'll have to buy some heavy wool underwear sometime soon. It's so cold outside that even with wool lined leather gloves my fingers get so cold they really truly hurt.

About our Christmas trip. It sounds just marvelous, but will cost more than I wrote. The man planned everything so we'll be going to the places that are prettiest in winter. We're staying everywhere half-pension, which means breakfast plus one other meal are included in the price, except in the place where we're spending Christmas we'll be on whole pension – all meals included. We're not going to Austria after all because it's too far out of the way from the places we're going.

Our itinerary takes us to Zurich, Tschiertschen (sounds like Churchen), Innsbruck, Munich, Heidelberg, Frankfurt, and back to Paris. Doesn't it sound wonderful! The whole trip includes almost all the meals, the train fare, sightseeing, hotel, etc. It comes to 40,500 francs, which is about $120. What do you think?

I think we're going to have to pay M. Rémond for part of the time that we're gone, there's something in the contract that says we get a reduction of 600 francs a day for 10 days during our Christmas vacation. He may give us more but I doubt. it. So I guess you'd better send me more than $100 in the next money order – or if you've already sent it – send more. I'm sure $150 or $200 would do it, leaving me some left over. This means I'll pay rent, trip, everything with this. Send me what you think is best.

The 14th of December M. Rémond is giving (not really a gift because we pay $3.00 each) a grand soirée for our group and some of the Hollins girls. There will be 16 of us in all. Then the girl who had dinner with us, Marie-Louise, has invited 16 French boys from the best families to come. It really will be nice. I've been calling the Hollins girls this week and it's been such fun talking to them.

You know I really thought I was being original coming to France for my Junior year, but it's not at all original – there are hundreds of girls here doing the same thing – probably much better.

Sunday night, Nov. 25, 1956

It's so cold here and we have so little heat that Louise and I are sitting in the bathroom with a little electric heater on, running hot water. The steam from the water helps to heat the room. It's the only warm place in the whole house. I'll be so glad when the American ships come bringing fuel. If M. Rémond were here he would build us a fire in the little stove-like thing in our room, but he isn't here and we don't know where any wood is. As a matter of fact the whole family has gone to the country – they went for the week end, will be back in the morning. They took one of the maids, Nicole, with them, but Nicole's sister – the other maid, Josieanne, stayed here and cooked for us. It's been kind of nice being alone for a while.

Friday I met Louise, Susan, Ellie, Sandy, and Coco to go to a cocktail party to which Madame Alvernhe invited us. She is the Vice-President of the organization called the Friends of Guy de Maupassant – a famous organization. They were celebrating a recent accomplishment of one of the members, who has published for the first time some papers written by Guy de Maupassant. The party was in their club rooms and was so nice. We had wonderful things to eat and drink and all the people were so nice and cocktail-ish and fun to talk to! The man in whose honor the party was made a little talk. It was really so nice.

Afterwards both Louise and Ellie wanted to go to a party we heard the Sorbonne was giving for its foreign students. We finally found the address for the party – inside a big old building in a not so big room on a weird little uninhabited looking street. Everyone was packed in and we didn't like the looks of the people there – some of them looked like the outcasts of the Sorbonne – so we sneaked out as soon as we could. It was still early, we didn't want to go home, and besides, it was Sandy's birthday and we had to celebrate. So we called Jean-Louis and asked him if we could come over. He said he'd be delighted. I had told him it was Sandy's birthday, so when we got there he had Scotch, cognac, Cassis, grapefruit juice, tomato juice, pretzels and some other little goodies all sitting on the coffee table for us. We drank a little of almost everything, sang "Happy Birthday" to Sandy, warmed ourselves by the wonderful heater at Jean-Louis'. Nobody including Jean-Louis had eaten, so we boiled potatoes for all five of us, and ate them with butter and salt. We really did have a good time. Jean-Louis is just about the nicest person in the world to everybody – not just to me. So Sandy had a little party after all. I was the only one going my way on the Metro when we got ready to leave, so J.L. went with me. Perfect gentleman.

Saturday after lunch Louise, Susan and I went to Sceaux, which is a suburb of Paris. We went on the Metro – part of which is just like a train and is not underground. We went to see the château and park of Sceaux. It was the strangest afternoon – cold, the sun was just a little orange ball that gave no light. It had snowed Saturday morning and there were little patches of white still on the ground. Everything at Sceaux was so quiet. I guess it was the contrast from Paris that made it so different and strange. The château and the park were lovely, but that's all. The inside of the château is a museum now, but not a very interesting one. We were the only people in it except for the guides, who scared us so that we got out as quick as we could. The guides really didn't do anything, but it was just the idea of us being there alone with them that we didn't like. One old man kept trying to get me to come look at different little things with him. He was probably just being helpful, but I didn't want it! We left the château and went in the cutest little old restaurant and had tea and pastry.

By that time it was past time to come home, so we hurried to the station and took the next Metro home. Susan had a date with a boy from Houston who is here, and Louise and I had dates with Jean-Louis and his friend to go to the dance given by France-Canada, which is a club like France-Amerique. It was held at France-Amerique in the downstairs ballroom. I almost felt like I was back at school at a party. Everybody was our age, of a nice caliber, everyone was in sort of cocktail dress, there was a wonderful little band which played great jazz. I even jitterbugged almost like at home! The French really go whole-hog on jitter-bugging. They do all the acrobatics you see in pictures of Elvis Presley orgies etc. We really did have a good time, though. It was too late to take a Metro after the dance (they stop running at one) so we took a taxi home.

We slept too late this morning to go to church. About twelve the phone rang and it was for me. I was surprised when I found David Kaufman on the other end of the line. I wrote David a note this week but sent it to the address he gave me before we left this summer. Then I got your letter with the other address in it – not the one he had given me, so I just figured he wouldn't get my note but he had, and I was so glad to hear from him. We talked for a long time, then decided to meet at a concert this afternoon at five forty-five. I told him Jean-Louis would be with me and he said he'd like to meet him, so we arranged to meet. After lunch I met Jean-Louis and went to the Louvre – my first trip to the museum itself. It's so huge it takes days to see it all. We saw only about half of the first section this afternoon. There are six of them. In the first section (which we saw) was the famous statue of Venus de Milo the original one. I really can't see that Venus is so beautiful. Her face is plain, but her body really is magnificent. She's so old! It's unbelievable. It was so exciting to see the original Venus. I also saw the famous original *Winged Victory*. We went through the section of Roman and Greek sculpture and part of the Egyptian section. I can hardly wait to go back and see more.

We walked from the Louvre to the concert, which wasn't too far. It was so cold! We passed a big store which had Christmas windows all fixed up, like St. Louis. Crowds were standing around with children on men's shoulders trying to see the fascinating windows. Wonder on a child's face is the same heart-warming sight everywhere. The streets around this store were decorated with

Christmas lights and Christmas trees. It was all very pretty. It's hard to realize Christmas is so near.

We met David in front of the concert. He looks so good. He's gained weight since summer and it really becomes him. Of course his French puts mine to shame. He and Jean-Louis got along beautifully. Jean-Louis told me later that David really did speak well – but that there were some words that I said better! I think he saw my ego had fallen and he was trying to build it up for me. David is doing fascinating things – studying voice with a famous baritone, mime with Marcel Marceau's teacher, has a course taught by a Marxist. Depend on David. We're going to try to get together again this week. It seemed so strange to see someone from Paducah in Paris and talk as calmly and un-excited as we did.

The concert was very good. The orchestra played Shubert's Unfinished Symphony better than I've ever heard it, Brahms' 1st Symphony worse than I've ever heard it. The most famous French cellist played Schumann's concerto for cello. It was fabulous. The piece itself isn't so wonderful, but the cellist, Pierre Fournier, was wonderful. His tones were so pure and his technique marvelous, I really did enjoy it. I'm glad David talked me into going – I was going to a Beethoven festival. Jean-Louis came home with me on the Metro, we had supper, and here we are in the bathroom.

P.S. I think I told you we weren't going to Austria for Christmas. Well, I just made the brilliant discovery that Innsbruck is in Austria, so we're going to Austria too.

Monday night, November 25, 1956

Art class this morning was more interesting than it ever has been, and I understand more – and I took better notes. I really feel better about it now.

My voice lesson was a success. Mme. Milleret goes into almost fits because I vibrate too much sometimes but then I know that's the best way for me to learn to correct it. She tells me the vibrato is horrible, then she'll say, "But you have a ravishing voice!" So, she tears it down, builds it up, tears it down, etc. I really do like her. Wednesday night she is giving a recital with a pianist, a cellist, a violinist, and the composer. I suppose I'll go – I'm so curious to hear her. I just can't imagine her singing in public – she's so stooped and non-singer-ish looking. Maybe she's transformed in recitals.

After my lesson I met Jean-Louis and we walked and walked. It wasn't very cold today for some odd reason. It rained last night and that's the reason. It never is as cold after it rains. We bought some hot-roasted peanuts and ate them while walking along the street. I also bought some pastry to eat after supper. I've had a huge appetite lately. Jean-Louis was really cute tonight.

All the lights went out in our part of the house this afternoon and when I came back at 7:30 the Rémonds had not come back, so they still weren't fixed. We sat in the kitchen with Nicole and Josieanne for a long time. Finally the R's came back about 8:15. They seem to think it was our fault that the lights went out. Mme.'s pregnancy is making her cross again. Anyway they fixed the fuses, so we're in the light again.

Wednesday, November 28

At theater class yesterday afternoon I found out more about Mme. Milleret. Monday at my voice lesson Mme. Milleret asked me to come to her recital. She kept saying "we" have worked so hard and "we" have done this and that. Well, Mme. Alvernhe told me yesterday that the man I thought was M. Milleret who was always there is not M. Milleret at all. M. Milleret found him a new young novelist who naturally is younger than Mme. Milleret and he lives with her now. He is a well-known artist. So Mme. Milleret rents two rooms in her apartment. I don't know who lives in one of them, but this sweet man who raved over my voice lives in the other one. I really think everything is quite innocent between him and Mme. Milleret because they are old family friends – of course I may be wrong. Anyway this man, M. Belliard, is a composer and it is his works that Mme. Milleret is singing tonight at the concert. Of course I'm definitely going now.

We didn't have to go to music history this morning because M. Handemann is sick, so we're going next week for two hours instead of one. I really was so disappointed not to go this morning because it's my favorite class. I'm getting ready to go practice now till time for lunch. The sun's out today so I guess it's cold, cold, cold again. But I prefer the cold sunshine to the rain and dampness. I'll finish this tonight.

Thursday morning November 29, 1956

Well I went to the concert last night. It was really enjoyable although very long. I had a hard time keeping awake. M. Belliard's music was very good – not great, but certainly admirable. Not only did Mme. Milleret sing songs he has written, but one of the best-known female Parisian pianists played a concertina he has written. She was marvelous – more so than the piece itself.

As to Mme. Milleret's voice – I was quite surprised to hear such a lovely voice from a woman her age. Some of her tones are exquisite. The only thing I dislike is the way she makes such faces and gestures! I really nearly laughed aloud several times because she looked so ridiculous. So I listened with my eyes shut and really liked what I heard. When I came back last night I told Mme. Rémond just what I've told you. She told me that in France, concert singing is always exaggerated and artificial – the gestures, facial expressions, etc. She said that is why the first thing she said to me after I sang for her the other night was that I sang so naturally and with such ease.

This morning I had a voice lesson and of course I told Mme. Milleret and M. Belliard how much I enjoyed the concert. They were so pleased that I had gone. Mme. Milleret told me that Sunday afternoon, December 9th, she is having a little recital for her pupils and she wants me to sing. She said it would be international because there will be French students, a Chinese girl, a Yugoslav and me! I'm glad she's having it though. It's much nicer to have something to work toward like a recital.

After my voice lesson Jean-Louis met me in front of Mme. Milleret's and we went to have chocolate and croissants – a type of breakfast roll. I really didn't want to see him, but he insisted that I meet him there. After a while we got into a terrible argument. He insisted that I meet him tomorrow and I insisted that I could not. Finally he said, "Why don't you tell the truth and say you just don't want to?" So I said "Okay – I just don't want to." That did it – he was furious and so was I. Finally, I got so tired of hearing him fuss that I just told him goodbye and left. We were in the Metro then. He's going to Dijon for the weekend – so I won't see him at least till Tuesday – maybe not for a long time after today. I just get kind of tired of him. That's terrible to say because he's about the nicest person I know.

I guess you've been reading about the shortage of sugar, gas, fuel, cooking oil, etc. which we now have here. We haven't suffered from anything but the heat because the Rémonds foresaw the shortage and bought up a lot of sugar, oil. M. Rémond has some friend who somehow gets him gasoline.

For Christmas Louise asked her mother to send her some Gillette thin razor blades to give to M. Rémond. He asked us if we ever could send him some next year he would appreciate it. I'm going to pay Louise for what half of them cost. Also – Louise bought some hose to give Mme. Rémond for Christmas – I'm going to pay for half of them also.

After our composition class today I went to Mme. Rémond's beauty operator (the shop is so near here) and had my hair tinted again. It was getting horrible looking – about an inch on each side of my part was so dark it looked awful. I couldn't stand it. The woman did a good job – I'm so glad I went on and had it done!

Saturday, December 1

On September 7th, December seemed so far away that I can barely believe it is come. Time really flies – using a not-so-profound statement.

Yesterday and today have been really busy. After class yesterday morning at the excruciating hour of 8:45, Louise and I went to the Bon Marché department store and had our pictures made in the Photomaton. I'm sending them to you to show you my long hair and French airs. They're not wonderful pictures, but they're not bad considering how they were taken (and of whom). Before coming home for lunch we stopped to buy more Christmas cards and some cookies.

Yesterday afternoon Louise and I went to a jewelry store recommended by the Rémonds and bought ourselves gold rings like we've been wanting. For once we chose differently! Louise's is a very plain and round one, and mine is a little more decorative and square. With initials the cost will come close to $30. It's so good looking, real gold, and so Continental. They had to cut it down for me – especially since I'm having it made for my little finger – so I won't get it until late next week. I can hardly wait for it!

After our ring buying we decided to go to the Prefecture of Police to get our identity cards – which we were supposed to have gotten about two weeks ago. After standing in line for half an hour we finally got to the main window just as it closed. I was so mad I could've chewed nails! So since we were across the street from La Sainte-Chapelle and since it was a sunny day, we went to see it. It has to be seen on a sunny day because it stands surrounded by buildings and the only light is from the sun coming through the stained glass windows. Sainte-Chapelle was built by St. Louis to house the original crown of thorns, which is now in Notre Dame. It is a treasure of Gothic architecture. It really is so gorgeous – I can't remember seeing anything more beautiful. The stained-glass windows are breathtaking. The shelter for the crown of thorns is magnificent. The huge rose window is unique. I hadn't expected it to be so wonderful. The tympanum over the main door is marvelous. I just don't know enough adjectives to describe it. I always feel so little and unimportant in such magnificent monuments.

After seeing Sainte-Chapelle (The Holy Chapel), we went to the Smithers' and practiced. I practiced in the office, which doesn't have a piano, and Louise naturally practiced on the piano. After about an hour and a half we walked to Sèvres-Babylone to have some ice cream at the wonderful little corner shop there. French ice cream is so delicious. It's not so heavy as ours. I just love it. Of course it's more expensive than ice cream is at home too. After ice cream we went home to supper.

Last night after supper we really had a delightful time it all started simultaneously with Nanou wanting to "faire la danse" – which for her is to hold hands and run around in a circle. She was doing it with Louise and me. Then we started singing "Here we go round the Mulberry Bush." Isabelle joined us. We changed to "London Bridge." M. and Mme. sat down to watch the show. Then Nicole and Josieanne joined in. Then they taught us French folk dances and songs. All six of us – Nicole, Josieanne, Nanou, Isabelle, Louise and I danced and sang for almost an hour. The Rémonds really got a kick out of it. Then somehow I was imitating Mme. Milleret the other night and I thought the Rémonds would fall out of their chairs laughing. We are lucky because we have two elements – the aristocratic, educated, very refined Rémonds and the simple peasant element of Nicole and Josieanne. From them we can learn something of their kind of people even without going to the country to meet them. We all really enjoyed the after supper fun.

This morning I got up at 7:00 so I could be at the Prefecture of Police by 8:30. I was determined to get that over with. I was there from about 8:45 to 10:00! The bad thing was – I was to meet Susan Shelley at 10:00 to go to a wax museum. I was half an hour late meeting her. We went to a museum in Montmartre called the Histoire de la Montmartre, in which the history of Montmartre is shown in fabulous scenes with wax characters. I just love wax museums! There was a scene of Berlioz, Lizst, Chopin, Harriet Smithson and George Sand. Another scene of Toulouse-Lautrec and many of the people from La Moulin Rouge whom he painted. It was all unbelievably real. Susan and I were the only two going through and the guide was so interesting – we just learned so much from him. I'm so glad we went.

After the Museum we walked a few blocks to see the last of the original windmills which were once all over the hill of Montmartre. Montmartre is so fascinating. It is here that all the famous painters made their hangout. Everything is still so old and quaint – you really forget you're in a busy bustling Paris. We walked down the hill right into a big street market – they are so fascinating. The vendors are practically like barkers in a circus. I loved Paris so especially much today.

Later we went to a café and drank hot chocolate till time for the concert we had tickets for at 5:45. Susan didn't go. We heard the pianist Malcuzunski play Chopin's Concerto No. 2 and Tchaikovsky's 1st Concerto. The orchestra also played the *Rosamunde* Overture of Schubert and Ravel's *Alborada del gracioso*. It was a great concert. The pianist was one of the best I've ever heard. Such control and strength! I really enjoyed it. I enjoyed my whole day!

Sunday, December 2

After dinner today, Louise and I went to the Comédie-Française to see *La Bourgeois Gentilhomme*. We're supposed to see it for theater class. We've missed it twice now. We didn't buy tickets before hand because we were told we could get good seats just before we went in. Well – there were no more tickets left for the play by the time we got to the window. I was so mad. It seems that lots of schoolchildren had come, and helped fill the seats.

So – we decided to go to the opera tonight. We saw *Tosca*, which I had never seen. It was wonderful. I love Puccini's music. For the first time since I've been here I liked all the leads' voices. The tenor was the best I've heard in ages. Everything was perfect – we even had good seats – except a poor idiot girl sat behind me and kicked me during the whole opera. Once she kicked me so hard that I said "oh" out loud. I didn't have the heart to fuss at her, poor thing, but she sure did kick hard!

Tuesday, December 4

I was so busy yesterday I didn't have time to write. Yesterday morning I practiced until I went to art class. Then after lunch I met Eugenie and we went to the Palais Chaillot to the Museum of French Monuments to go on a little tour for art history class. It was so interesting. The girl who explained everything to us couldn't have been over 22 and she was so interesting. After the tour Eugenie and I walked around on our own. Everything in the Museum is a reproduction. There are so many things there that I have seen in Dijon and the surrounding area – only I saw the real thing. I'm so proud to have seen them, especially since we're studying them.

I like Madame Milleret better every time I go. I had a good lesson. She told me that she'd like for me to give a concert myself later in the year. She said she'd put out a notice in the paper and everything. I really do want to do it – naturally. And it will be something to work for. M. Belliard is so sweet. He kissed my hand when I left yesterday. There is among the many autographed pictures to M. Belliard and Madame Milleret one to M. Belliard from the famous violinist Nathan Milstein. I was really impressed.

After my lesson I took the Metro to come home. It was at the peak of the rush-hour when the Metros are horrors. It took me nearly an hour to get home – it usually takes 20 or 25 minutes! It was horrible – I've never been in such a mess. I was squished between about six huge men. I couldn't breathe or see. When I got to my stop I couldn't budge. I was saying very politely, "Pardon me, excuse me, I'd like to get off." No one moved. So I raised my head and voice and yelled as loud as I could, "Descendant," which is "I'm getting off." I flailed my arms and made everyone mad, but I finally got off. I was so whipped when I finally made it, that I had to sit down and rest a while before I went on!

This morning I had a class at 8:45. I hate those early classes because it's always dark when we get up and just barely light when we leave. But once we're outside it's delightful. Paris is beautiful all gray and sleepy eyed in the early morning.

After lunch Marie-Louise Bernard came and we decided on the menu for the soirée next week. Everything is going to be so nice.

I met Jean-Louis after theater class. I hadn't seen him since Thursday when we had our big fuss and he left for Dijon. We were both a little peeved with each other still, but we finally got over it. I just have absolutely no feeling for him anymore of any kind. We walked all the way from Sèvres-Babylone by way of St.-Germain-des-Près, to here – General Foy. It was so delightful walking because it wasn't too cold. It was clear and brisk and invigorating. I love Paris at seven in the evening. The Seine was so beautiful with all the lights on it – the Eiffel towering over everything. I loved Paris so much as we crossed the Seine – I wanted to run and shout and sing and laugh and dance. I don't see how I'll be able to leave this summer knowing that even if I come back some day, things will never be the same.

Sunday, December 9

I haven't written since Wednesday – I've been so busy!

Thursday after class Louise and I went to see Major Annan. He did the typical American "I close my eyes to foreign things." He has been in Paris for over five years and still hasn't absorbed any of Paris. He is so nice though. He took us in the PX and we bought soap, Kleenex, candy, and other things at almost below American prices. This week he's getting us some sugar and salt for us to give Mme. Rémond, and the next week he is invited to have dinner here with us. M. and Mme. asked us to invite him since they knew we had no way of repaying his kindness by other means. "Major" Annan is really a colonel we discovered. He asked us to go to an Italian restaurant with him that night, but we couldn't – darn it.

Friday morning I went to get the money from the Hollins girls for the party Friday night, then I went to Mrs. Smithers' to get the money I had exchanged. This time we got a rate of 395 to the dollar, and on the $300 I had exchanged into francs I made $38 – more than enough to pay for my ring.

Friday afternoon Louise and I went to buy tickets for the opera for Saturday night and tickets for the Comédie-Française for Wednesday night. At 4:00 we met Jean-Louis and the three of us went to the Grevin Wax Museum – the most famous one in the world. Every famous personage is there, but I just thought it was kind of boring. The first little wax museum I saw with Susan was so much better and ten times more interesting. I was really very disappointed in the famous Grevin.

Friday night the trio of Louise, Jean-Louis, and I again met and went to hear the pianist who is very famous in Europe but not so famous in the US – Julius Katchen. He is young and plays brilliantly. His technique is marvelous. He lacks some of the emotion that comes with age and experience, but as a whole he is the most exciting pianist I've ever heard. He played the Bach Italian Concerto and left me hanging in the air – it was so wonderful.

Saturday morning we slept relatively late, then I went to practice. After lunch we went back to Mrs. Smithers' to have a meeting with Mr. Hochwald and get our train tickets. I'm so excited about our trip.

Saturday night Louise and I went to the opera to see Mozart's *The Magic Flute*. I loved the music, the costumes, the scenery. It really was a spectacle, but the voices weren't equal to the general production. The baritone was excellent, but he was the only one of whom I can say that. We were sitting by a boy from Australia who is traveling all over the world this year. He was so nice. He asked us to have coffee afterwards, but we had other plans. We met Jean-Louis and Jean-Pierre (a young man Louise met), and the four of us went (on foot) to a little private nightclub of which Jean-Pierre is a member. I loved it. It was very small, with a wonderful hi-fi and hundreds of wonderful records – mostly American. There was a bar and cute little tables and chairs. We danced, drank, talked, and stayed till 3:15 a.m.! We came home in a taxi – I simply couldn't punish my feet by walking again. Louise and I found Jean-Pierre rather exciting, but the ever-knowing Jean-Louis said he wasn't very "bien-éléve" which is probably true, but the change from Jean-Louis was delightful. Jean-Louis is nearly driving me crazy. I simply can't stand him much longer. He likes me so much more than I like him and he acts like a child about it. I've got to be nice to him until Friday night so he'll come to the soirée, but after that I don't care if I ever go out with him again!

Sunday morning we slept till 11:30, got up and piddled round until noon. M. Rémond went to Champscenest Sunday morning early. I love when he's gone because we get to talk with Madame more. She really is wonderful; loves for us to go out and have a good time. After dinner Sunday, Louise played and I sang for her. I sang everything from opera to "You Made Me Love You." She asked me why I didn't sing on Broadway or in a nightclub, instead of studying seriously. She loved to hear me sing popular songs.

After giving her the concert, Louise and I left to go to the recital at Mme. Milleret's. It was the strangest thing I've ever been to. Not all of her pupils sang – most of the ones who did sing have not studied real long. But – I've never heard such horrible singing in my life! Most of them had absolutely no natural talent and those that did simply weren't trained well. I decided then and there that I would change voice teachers after my Christmas trip. I think I'll find someone well known. If it's more expensive I'll just take one lesson a week or one every 10 days or something, instead of two a week. Marie-Louise, the Rémonds' friend, takes voice from a famous Austrian teacher at something like five dollars a lesson. I could maybe take once a week from her. I think I'll inquire about the people Dr. Hansen gave me and their prices, etc. I have definitely decided I don't want to stay with Mme. Milleret.

This morning we let ourselves sleep late again since we don't have class until 11:00 on Mondays. Class was awful today because we had a substitute and I couldn't hear her talk she spoke so softly.

It's colder today than it has been in over a week now. Buying an electric blanket would be a blow to the Rémonds' electric bill I'm afraid. I'm going to buy some more long underwear and some slacks before I go to Switzerland, but that's all I'm going to need.

I'm glad you're getting a TV for your bedroom. I'm not going to know what TV is when I get home. I guess that's all for this time. I'm feeling fine and dandy now – still skinny, but I feel good.

Tuesday, December 11, 1956

I'm so excited because I finally got my gold ring today. It's so beautiful – I just love it. I feel so very cosmopolitan and continental now! I've been just dying for it and now I finally have it. Louise is equally pleased with hers. Mine looks so good with my watch. It came to 10, 480 francs, which is about $30.50. They did a wonderful job of engraving it. I had all three initials put on it like this sort of – **JHW**. Only of course it looks 100 times better. I really am pleased with it. I feel so elegant now – until I look down at my hose – each with a run in them. I wear the "runny" hose to school and on rainy days!

Yesterday afternoon I had a lesson with Mme. Milleret. I'm so confused now. Everything she says make sense, and I can hear that I sound better when I do the things she tells me to do, but I'm just afraid it would be better if I changed. I'm so confused. I wish Rodgers and Hammerstein would come to Paris looking for talent – I'd surely pay them a visit. Such a problem!

This morning we struggled to get out of bed at 7:00. It's the biggest battle I have to fight every day. We were on the same bus as our professor for Art History – he was opposite us. He wasn't in class yesterday and the woman who took his place was horrible so we were pleased to see him today. If we had been at school we could have said "Hello there sir, we miss you in class yesterday," or "I'm sorry you were ill yesterday" or something. But here you don't dare say anything. Of course I'm sure he didn't recognize us out of all that huge mob in his class!

After class I went to buy the verb dictionary Mme. Alvernhe has been after us to buy. It's a wonderful little book for only 73¢. I'm really pleased to have it

After lunch Marie-Louise Bernard came over and we made final plans for the party. We found there would be room for some more boys. So M. Rémond told me I could ask my American friends. So I called David Kaufman and invited him. He said he'd love to come. I also told him to invite his two roommates. He's going to call me tomorrow and tell me if they can. I hope they can.

We had theater today from 4:00 to 6:00. She gave us back some of our themes and I had one with the highest mark Mme. Alvernhe gives. Of course I was pleased. After class Louise and I took some shoes to get them re-soled. Then we stopped at the patisserie very near Mme. Smithers' and bought some flan – a little individual custard. It's the best thing I've ever tasted and I can only find them at that one pastry shop. We then walked to Sèvres-Babylone where wearisome Jean-Louis was waiting for me. He went with us to get our rings – which was practically at our house. Then he walked us home. I just hated and despised him tonight. I told him I just couldn't see him again until the party Friday night – but I'm going to make it a point not to see him much then. I didn't want to invite him, but we needed all available men. I told him when I invited him that he wouldn't be with me. I'm beginning to think he's thickheaded. If I had some sort of stick I think I would have hit him tonight. Isn't that awful?

Thursday morning

I'm waiting for Marie-Louise Bernard to come so we can plan the seating arrangement for tomorrow night. She's already half an hour late.

Yesterday morning after our music history class (which I adore) Louise and I went to see Major Annan. He is really a character. He was showing us some funny papers in which he is a character. The cartoonist Stoky somebody, I can't remember his name, is a good friend of Major Annan's and is always using his name for some silly character. Major Annan is so proud of it. Every time I've seen him he has shown me that funny paper! We bought some things at the PX to take to the birthday party, which I haven't told you about, Saturday night – cheese spread, Ritz crackers, and Planters cocktail peanuts. We thought they'd enjoy a little American food. Sweet Major Annan has bought us some sugar – a 10 pound box, and salt – two boxes of Morton's, for us to give to the Rémonds. Sugar isn't so hard to find now, but salt is impossible to find. We decided to just give it to them as part of their Christmas present. We also bought M. four little boxes of extra thin razor blades that he's been dying for, because we're afraid the ones Louise's mother is sending won't get here until after Christmas. He was so cute. He went down on his knees and kissed our hands to thank us. They really were pleased to have the things.

Yesterday afternoon I spent working on a theme for composition class today. Last night Louise and I finally went to see *La Bourgeois Gentilhomme* at the Comédie-Française. It was so really wonderful. The costumes, the music, the little ballets, everything was delightful – the actors were superb. I'm anxious to see another play soon at the fabulous Comédie-Française.

7 p.m.

Well, Marie-Louise came – an hour late. She had forgotten. We're having so much trouble with this party because people keep calling and saying they can't come. I never had this much trouble with a party before.

This afternoon I had composition. I was so pleased on the homework we got back – themes – I had the highest grade of anybody – even Sandy! who usually gets the best grade. It really encouraged me.

After class I had a voice lesson. Mme. Milleret gets so excited when I have a good lesson. I just don't know what to do – whether to change or not. I guess I'll let that be my big problem to contemplate on my vacation.

I came home from my voice lesson a different way tonight – I got off the Metro at Gare St. Lazare instead of the Madeleine. St. Lazare is so much nearer and much more interesting for walking. There are so many people in that quarter – all in a hurry, trying to get home from work. There are lots of grocery stores, bakeries, butcher shops, and everybody is buying things. I just love being in the midst of all the humdrum – there are so many interesting things to see. I enjoyed walking too because the weather has been so nice lately – not cold at all – at least not like it was. Paris is at her best anyway around 5:00 to about 7:00. Her majestic hours.

I'm going to try to get some sleep tonight since we have such a big weekend ahead of us. Tomorrow night is the party for us. Saturday night the eight of us are going to a huge birthday party given by a boy (for himself) whom we met at the cocktail party for the Amis de Guy de Maupassant. He is having about 40 Americans and 50 French people. He lives in a suburb of Paris. It's going to be sort of a potluck supper and dance – that's why we bought some of the things at the PX. I really think it will be fun.

I'm getting kind of lonesome for Christmas at home about now.

PS. Louise's mother sent her the article on the Newcomb Junior year abroad. There are some pictures of me in the article (with other girls). I hope Lillian sends them to you or something because I'd love to have them and for you to see them too.

Saturday afternoon December 15, 1956

We had the most fabulous party last night! I've not had so much fun in ages. After all my worry and stewing about not having enough boys, yesterday morning I found out about some young interns at the American hospital who had heard about us and wanted to meet us, so I called up at the hospital and invited them. Four of them came and saved the day. The party was a huge success – all the Hollins girls were cute and of course all the Newcomb girls are too, nobody was left sitting instead of dancing. The boys were all delightful. They were all good dancers. I danced with nearly every one. I'll have to start from the beginning.

There were 42 people there, including the Rémonds. We sat at individual tables – 3 tables of 8 and 3 of 6. Everybody spoke French. Our meal was delicious. It started off with mushroom soup that was divine. Then we had this delicious cold fish, called Colin, with lemon and French mayonnaise – which has no equal. Then we had wonderful roast beef and a hot dish of mixed vegetables. Then the cheeses. Then dessert – a sort of English rum pudding with custard sauce that was the best I've ever put in my mouth! We had white wine, red wine and champagne – and of course French bread. It was so delicious! I'm getting to be a real wine drinker.

At my table was one of the young doctors I had invited, who turned out to be French. He had studied in the U.S. for five years. I found him so charming. He's much older than I, but so, so nice. I danced with him a lot, but he had to leave early (around 1:00) for work today. I certainly wish he'd call me for a date. I think I told you I asked David Kaufman to come. Well, he forgot that last night he was supposed to go to a play – he had already bought his ticket and everything. So – he didn't come to the dinner, but his roommate for the past two years at Dartmouth, Mike Margulies, came. David then came for the dancing part.

Mike is tall, handsome – so intelligent. He's a fabulous dancer and we had so much fun dancing together. We usually ended every dance weak from laughing. I really am smitten by him. I don't know why Jewish men have such a fascination for me, but they certainly do. I think David was smitten with Louise. Tomorrow night we're all four going to the theater together. Mike speaks beautiful French, and sounds just like David.

Jean-Louis was there last night too. I put him at the same table with the Rémonds and they found him delightful. M. Rémond got just a little "grise" (tight) last night and was really funny.

Everything came to a halt about 2:30 a.m. But then seven of us (Eugenie went home with some boy, she is always the one to pick up any and every man) went with two of the American doctors to the apartment of one of them and scrambled eggs, fried bacon, ate Campbell's vegetable soup, peanuts, peanut butter, homemade fudge and cookies (his folks had sent him). He got all the other things at the PX. We ate and talked and laughed until 5:00 a.m. Then they brought us home. By the time we got in the bed it was almost 6:30 a.m. We slept until 12:30 got up, ate lunch. Then M. and Mme. Rémond and I listened to Louise play the newly tuned piano. M. Rémond was asking me to sing for him because he has never heard me. But I just couldn't today. I promised I'd sing for him Monday night. Then Tuesday night we're going to sing Christmas Carols for them and Major Annan.

In just a minute Louise and I are going to a reception for American and

French students given by a very elite group of French people. M. and Mme. Rémond have an invitation but can't go, so they gave it to us. After the reception we'll go straight to the other party – the birthday party. This is fun – all the partying, but sort of tiring!

Sunday, December 16, 1956

Last night turned out to be not so successful. We got on the bus to go to the afternoon reception and just before we got off the bus I happened to read the invitation again. Both of us had looked only at the address on the top of the invitation, which was the address of the club itself. We were to go to a private home, which was of course an entirely different address. After we discovered our stupid, juvenile mistake it was too late to try to go to the right place, because we had to meet the other girls soon to go to the other party.

I had had qualms about last night's party all week because everything was so indefinite. Sandy was the only one who had actually talked to the boy when he invited us. Well, Louise and I were the first to show up at the Metro stop St. Cloud, where we all were to meet. There were supposed to be some people to pick us up there and drive us to the party. Susan finally came, then Sandy, Coco, and Ellie. Two boys and a girl came up to us and asked if we were the Americans waiting to go to the party, and they drove us to the party in two cars. We were the first to arrive.

It was in the most interesting house! The parents of the boy, Christian (who is I think more of a girl than a boy) own a travel agency and have gone on just about every cruise and to every country there is. Their house is furnished with all the things they have brought back from every country. It really is fascinating. We had all sorts of party food, wine, liqueur, etc. Finally a few more people came – but nothing like the huge numbers they had told us were coming.

The boys were all rather strange. A couple of men were there with their wives – one with his fiancée. There was an older man there who is an artist and painted two of the paintings in the living room. He was shorter than I am and had the bug for jitterbugging with me! He was kind of cute – like a teddy bear. Another boy there who seemed to take a liking to me – tall, blond, not at all bad looking. Guess what he does! He's a woman's hairdresser! I nearly laughed out loud when he told me. We ate the food, danced some, and in general were rather bored. At 11:00 Coco, Louise and I insisted that we had to leave, since we were tired from Friday night. We finally persuaded one of the boys to drive us back to the Metro stop. Susan decided to go too. We took the Metro and were home by 12:30. I'm so mad because we never made it to the reception. I'm sure we would have had a much more enjoyable evening. Live and learn I guess.

We slept this morning until 10:30. The Rémonds have gone hunting together at a friend's château in the Valley of the Loire. Josieanne spent the night with her sister who lives in Paris. She called this morning and talked to Nicole. Nicole hung up the receiver and ran to the kitchen crying. Louise and I thought something terrible had happened. We ran to see what was wrong. It seems Josieanne had promised Nicole that she would come back this afternoon so Nicole could go out, but on the phone she said she wasn't coming until tonight. Poor Nicole cried as if her heart would break. We told her to go on and go out, that we would take care of the children since we would be here anyway. So now she's happy.

We're listening to music from *Oklahoma* on my radio. It's music like that that makes me homesick. And it also makes me sad because I'm not singing it on the stage! I want to do that more than anything else in the world! But how! I've decided that after I finish school I want to go to New York and try to get some sort of a part in something. I've got several ideas on how to go about doing it. I think about it all the time now – it's become an obsession!

Monday morning December 17, 1956

We had the best time last night! It started off with the wonderful surprise that Mike has a car! I was so shocked. I think he's really wealthy. He's been here since August, is over here on his own – not with a group like David is. He's already been just everywhere. I think he's so handsome and so much fun. Anyway, Louise and David went to one theater and we went to the Comédie-Française Salle Richelieu. The two plays were wonderful especially, *Les Fourberies de Scapin*. The man who plays Scapin, Robert Hirsch, is superb, absolutely. I never laughed so hard in my life! I understood much more of it than I had expected to.

After the play we drove back to get David and Louise at Salle Luxembourg. Then we went to the Caveau des Oubliettes.

Caveaux are sort of like night clubs – they are usually down in a basement-like room, some caveaux have dancing. There are usually singers, etc. This one used to be a prison in the 12th century, and it was used in the Revolution. The caveau is in the part where all the torture chambers used to be. Nothing is changed – they have simply added tables and chairs. There are performers who sing folk-songs, tell jokes (risqué ones) and sing songs that are a little risqué too. One woman recited poetry. Mike got up and announced that he had with him two young American girls who had performed on Broadway and he thought they should perform for the little group (only about 20 people there – it's very small). Everyone clapped, so Louise and I paraded to the little stage, they put the spot light on me, and I sang "You Made Me Love You." They seemed to like it very much. One of the male singers there asked if we were professionals! It was fun. Mike is so fascinating. He not only speaks beautiful French, but also Spanish, Italian, and he can get along in German! I'm so jealous of people who can do things like that. He plays the piano and sings. He's singing in a choir once a week at the Alliance Française. I've been dying to do some choir singing, so I'm going to meet him Wednesday morning and go to the rehearsal with him. He's just so nice. I hope we can cultivate our friendship this year!

Yesterday at dinner Louise and I talked with Nicole and Josieanne about the Rémonds. Josieanne told us that she is getting married at the end of January, she was going to wait until June, but she can't stand it here any longer because of Isabelle.

I haven't mentioned it before, but Isabelle is one of the meanest children I've ever met. I feel sorry her in a way. She's only 6½, she's two years ahead of herself in school and is first in her class because the Rémonds force her and push her so much in her school work. They throw fits when she makes mistakes in her work. Therefore, she is confused I think, half of the time. She has been stealing some of our things – soap, etc. Yesterday one of my two bottles of Revlon makeup was gone. I told Josieanne and Nicole about it. They said their things were missing, too. They said Isabelle insulted them and kicked them and then when they tell Mme. Rémond she doesn't believe them. So – Nicole is leaving too when Josieanne does. Poor Mme. Rémond. She'll have so much trouble finding someone else.

After we murdered witch Isabelle with our words – I must add something here, Isabelle can be the perfect lady, charming, and sweet when she wants to be! – we began discussing M. and Mme. Rémond. We found out that Mme. Rémond is M. Rémond's third wife! When they told us Louise and I just screamed. I've never been so shocked in my life! They didn't know any details, but they have some friends who know all about it and they're going to find out more for us. We had the longest talk – and all came to the conclusion that while the Rémonds are certainly lovely people, they are curious and, unusual. But the crowning blow came when we left the dinner table. Louise and I went in the bathroom and Louise said, "I know Nicole has on my black leather belt, because she pulled her sweater up to adjust her skirt and I saw it!" So we looked in her closet (Louise's) and sure enough Louise's belt was gone. Nicole heard us whispering and fumbling in the closet, so when we went back in the bathroom we heard her fumbling in the closet. Louise's closet is next to Nicole's. The hallway is real narrow – Nanon was trying to get through, so Nicole opened the closet door as if to help Nanon get by, but we saw her put her hand in the closet. We came in our room, stayed a few minutes, then looked in the closet, and sure enough there was the belt! Well, we got hysterical. We laughed and laughed until tears were running down our cheeks. Here was Nicole "borrowing" things and we had just told her about all our things being missing. So now I don't know whether it's Isabelle or Nicole to accuse. I know Isabelle broke our bathroom drinking glasses (furnished by the Rémonds) and I know she has taken a few packages of my travel soap, but I doubt if I'll ever see my makeup again.

Today is the most gorgeous day I've ever seen. It's just like early spring. I suppose that means that January and February will be horrible.

Wednesday Dec. 19, 1956

It was really a thrill talking to you this afternoon. Do you realize that our voices went clear across an ocean? The telephone is really a marvelous invention! There was so much I wanted to tell you – so much I would have liked to have said, but of course I was completely taken aback when I heard your voices. All of a sudden it seemed like years since I had seen you and next August seemed years away! I could hear you all perfectly, but you didn't seem to hear me well. I thought it was well worth the money even if we didn't say much.

Last night Major Annan came for dinner. Also a couple who are the Rémonds' friends. They are similar to the Rémonds in that the man is much older than the woman. We spoke a mixture of English and French all night because the Major doesn't speak French and the other two don't speak English. We had a wonderful meal. Mme. had all her nicest things out and they are really gorgeous. The dining room looked so pretty. All the Christmas decorations are up and we put the tree up yesterday. The tree is on a table and is beautiful. Instead of lights there are little candles on it. Monsieur lit them all last night and it was so beautiful. Mme. has some gorgeous decorations. Which reminds me. I bought some unusual little decorations to bring home and use on our tree next year.

We had such a good time last night. Major Annan was so funny. He really is pathetic in some ways and he says such outlandish things. He brought us a box of Whitman's Sampler from the PX last night. After supper (dinner) Louise and I played and sang for everybody. After we had run through our repertoire we all sang Christmas Carols. It was really wonderful. Louise had a date with one of the doctors we met at the party the other night. He came about 11:00 and had a drink with us. Then the two of them left. I was fascinated with the other male guest – I've forgotten his name. He is so charming. After the other guests had gone M. and Mme. Rémond and I sat up and talked until 12:30. I found out that the guest with whom I was so fascinated was a hero during the war – a resistance hero. He was hunted and spied upon and nearly captured by the Germans. The war has broken his spirit and now he has no interest in living as he once did. I learned a lot about M. Rémond last night too. He is really a wonderful man. He was in the U.S. just a couple of weeks before Germany invaded France and could have stayed in the U.S. and not had to go to war. But he knew a war was coming and that France would be defeated, but he knew he had a duty to France, so he spent 6 years at war – 2 of them as a prisoner. I've decided that he couldn't have been married 2 times before now, because from the things he said and the things Mme. Rémond said.

This morning in music history M. Handemann asked me if I were studying voice. I said, yes, and he asked me with whom am I studying. I told him and also told him that I wanted to change. He asked me if I had heard of Pierre Bernac. I said, Yes, he is one of the names that Milhaud gave Dr. Hansen and Hansen gave me. He is one of the best! I was afraid to try him at first because of the price. But M. Handemann said that Bernac is one of his best friends and is not that expensive. He's going to call him during the next two weeks and tell him about me and make an appointment for me to see him when I get back. I'm so glad.

I can't believe that I'm going to Switzerland in about an hour!

A

Magical

Christmas

Thursday, December 20, 1956

Dear Mother and Daddy,

Greetings from Switzerland! Here I am in Zurich – which I'll tell about in a minute.

I spent all yesterday afternoon after I talked with you all packing for the trip. I was so worn out and had not had any sleep in so long that I didn't think I'd make it. Finally, we were ready to go. The Rémonds were so sweet, I hated to leave them. They gave us each a box of candy, and we gave them their presents – Mme. the hose, and to the little girls we gave dolls made of soap. They were so thrilled with them. For M. Rémond we have some more razor blades, but they haven't come yet.

Thanks to M. Rémond, who carried our bags down and hailed a taxi, we got to the station in plenty of time. Mr. and Mrs. Smithers and Mr. Hochwald (the travel man who arranged our trip) met us and helped us find our little compartment and get our bags up over the seats. We left at 8:30 and sat up all night – got off the train at 7:30 this morning. It was the worst night I've ever spent, and I'll never do it again. My miserly self wouldn't let me buy a berth, but if the occasion ever arises again I'll push my miserly self aside.

By the time we arrived in Zurich we all looked like ragamuffins – tired and sleepy. We took taxis and came straight to the hotel, which is a cute quaint little place with large, roomy rooms. There are three of us in a room with three beds, two lavatories, a wardrobe, four chairs, and two tables. We ate some breakfast and came up to our rooms and went to bed. We got up at 2:00, dressed and walked to the main train station where we took a sightseeing tour of Zurich.

The tour was very good. We had a guide who spoke perfect English, French, Spanish, and of course German. There were Americans – 5 others, 1 Chinaman, 1 Indian, and two Spaniards besides us. It was a small group – perfect for a tour. We rode all over Zurich – it's so pretty, even in bad weather. We saw everything from all the modern part to the old medieval section of Zurich. We saw the oldest church in Switzerland – built by Charlemagne, visited an old museum of Chinaware in which there were a couple of those wonderful old porcelain stoves that were used to heat the houses. There was some of the most beautiful porcelain and china. I wish I could buy some to bring home and have forever. We saw the famous University of Zurich and all the different science schools. Zurich is the largest city in Switzerland, the largest industrial and educational town. The guide told us that all Zurich children must learn to swim and ice-skate. There is no juvenile delinquency in

Switzerland because (so the guide said) children are not allowed to see movies or go to dance halls until they are 18. On TV and radio they never show crimes or violence and comic strips are unknown.

After the tour, we ended at a delightful little hotel on top of high hill where we had chocolate and patisserie and we all went to the big toy store in Zurich, the most famous in Switzerland. I wanted to buy everything I saw and bring to Janet, but I didn't. I've never seen such beautiful toys. We finally left the toy store and walked home – to the hotel. We stopped on the way at a candy store and bought some of that delicious Swiss chocolate.

The river that separates the new section of town from the old one (where we are) looked so pretty at night. There is a huge tree decorated with Christmas lights on one bank of the river. Everything is decorated for Christmas. Since we're in the German section, we're naturally going to see more Christmas decor.

It seems so funny being where we can't communicate with people because they speak neither English or French. Of course many of them do.

We ate supper about eight in the hotel dining room which is just delightful. Our dinner was delicious! There are so few people here we practically had the whole place to ourselves. There was a very nice man who played the piano.

Friday, December 21, 1956

I really think Mr. Hochwald did a good job finding us a hotel.

This morning we got up early, had breakfast, and started out. Louise and Coco went to buy watches, and the rest of us went our ways. The shops here are so beautiful and things are remarkably cheap. I looked around everywhere and finally bought a gold chain to start a bracelet with. I've decided to buy a charm in every country we visit.

After spending all morning in the shops, we met at twelve-thirty to have lunch at a Guild Hall restaurant. You know the Guilds were for members of each trade – there was a carpenters guild, a shoemakers guild, etc. Many of the guild halls still stand and are now restaurants. We ate at the Zunfthaus Zimmerlenten, a beautiful old guild hall. The food was delicious! I had Geschnetzettes Kalbfleisch mit Rosti which is minced veal in a cream sauce with mushrooms with a special baked potato – not in the shell. It is a particular specialty of Zurich. I loved it. After dinner the waiter took us around to show us other banquet rooms which are 300 years old and more. It was so interesting.

After dinner we walked around the corner to the Grosmunster – the old church supposedly founded by Charlemagne, but it was locked and we couldn't get in. So we went prying around, found one of the doors; inside was a girls' choir directed by the most dynamic director I've ever seen, and they were singing my very favorite – Benjamen Britten's "Ceremony of Carols" with harp accompaniment. It was so gorgeous! I felt like I had discovered some gem or something. We stayed there until nearly four thirty listening to them. They were so, so good. But the best part was what they were singing. It's experiences like that that mean the most.

Saturday, December 22, 1956

Last night at dinner (which was not as good as the night before) we met two young men – an Australian who used to be a concert pianist, but is now an interpreter named John McCarthy, and an American who is separated from his Swiss wife and is here learning German named Chuck McDonald. They were both really nice.

This morning Louise, Coco, and I went to Lucerne – the others decided to stay in Zurich. After a little sight-seeing we ate lunch at the cutest restaurant I've ever seen. We ate a Swiss specialty – fondue – which is a cheese mix, served hot with little pieces of bread. You dip the bread in the cheese mix and eat with a fork. It's so delicious – made with white wine.

Lucerne is very small, and with the map I got at the railroad station I saw nearly all of the town. Most of the houses date from the 16th century. They are so quaint, charming – some of the houses look like little ginger-bread houses. On the old side of town there are no cars – the streets are used to walk in. All the Christmas decorations were up and looked so pretty. I visited three churches: One is a Jesuit Baroque church which took my breath away. The inside was all white and gold with crystal chandeliers. It really was marvelous. The second little church I visited was only a tiny one, but so sweet. The third one was the famous Aulis church whose two spires tower above Lucerne. Oh, I visited a fourth church – a Protestant church which was a tiny, beautiful thing – the first Protestant church I've seen in ages. I walked around prying into little narrow streets and quaint shops until about six fifteen – it was dark then, and we met at six forty to catch the train back.

Besides all the delightful buildings, I saw the old fortification walls which look like castle walls in a fairy tale. I really forgot I was in the twentieth century – and it was a wonderful feeling. I've just never enjoyed a day so much in my life.

When we got to Zurich it was snowing big huge, beautiful snowflakes. I've never seen such huge flakes before. It was the first time Louise and Coco had seen snow, and they were excited to death. We were running down the street laughing and shouting at the snow. Coco tried to catch it in her mouth. We were having such fun – everybody on the street was laughing at us and seemed to enjoy our enjoyment.

When we got back to the hotel we were covered with snow. It was nearly nine and we knew the others had started dinner so we went into the dining room to show them the snow on us. Then we rushed upstairs and changed our clothes and came back downstairs to eat.

All the tables were decorated with sprayed pine and red candles. So many people were there. John McCarthy and Chuck McDonald sat with us – they are buddies with the chef at the hotel, who is a youngish man, and they arranged for us to have a special dinner – at no extra cost. The boys also treated us to rosé wine. They really were so nice to us.

After dinner we again sang with our friend the piano player and drank red wine. The chef joined us and took us down in the little cabaret in the basement of the hotel and bought us all drinks. The strangest group of people were there – mostly young people. We decided that we were staying in a hotel on the Bourbon Street of Zurich. Late at night – rather early in the morning, all sorts of people were on the street in front of our hotel making noise and keeping sleep from coming easily. We called it a day at midnight and went to bed, after a beautiful, wonderful, exciting day that I'll never, ever forget.

December 23, 1956

Greetings from Tschiertschen! Just sneeze kind of loud and you will have pronounced it correctly. We got up this morning with much struggling to leave our soft little beds and took taxis to the train station in Zurich to catch the 8:28 train to Chur.

We were pleasantly surprised by the chef at our Zurich hotel who had come to help us off. While we were in Zurich he prepared special dinners for us, all delicious, so last night we sang "For He's a Jolly Good Fellow," gave him three cheers, and pinned a rose on his lapel. He was the sweetest thing I've ever seen. He got on the train and held our seats for us. We handed him our heavy bags through the window and he put all of them up on the racks for us. When we finally got on the train he was standing there holding our places for us. We thanked him again and again for helping us and for last night's dinner. When he left he gave us each a little present, a chocolate bar, which is really a luxury. He was so sweet and kind that we almost cried. People like him restore all faith and trust in mankind. We hated to leave Zurich and all the friends we made there.

We had a wonderful train ride through mountains and valleys covered with snow – looking just like Switzerland should look. None of us had ever seen so much snow, and the mountains are exquisite. The sun came out about 9:30 and made everything look all pink and gold, just beautiful.

The train was a little late getting to Chur, and we found out the next bus to Tschiertschen left in an hour. We were struggling with our bags when the nicest man with two precious little children came up to Eugenie and me – I suppose because we are the smallest, and said in good English that he would be glad to help us with our bags if we'd just watch his children while he carried the bags. Of course we took him up. His children were so darling and he was so nice – another example of wonderful people. The bus came and there were too many people for the places, so we had to wait for the next one. Finally at 12:45 we were on our way. We drove up a hairpin road that nearly scared us all to death. The mountains and snow and clouds were wonderful.

We all had visions of how Tschiertschen was going to look. Some people said it was lovely, some said it was awful, some had never heard of it. We drove through several tiny little villages, and each time we came to a little spot in the road we panicked for fear this was it! About 1:45 we arrived, and Tschiertschen is a little, beautiful, quaint village of about 20 precious houses, a church and two hotels, the largest of which is ours – Hotel Alpina. Tschiertschen is situated on the top of a mountain looking at the most gorgeous scene of mountains, valleys, trees, snow, clouds. The hotel is very nice and lodge-like. Our rooms are delightful – pine-paneled, lavatories in each room. Louise and I have the best room because we have a little balcony. The other people staying here are mostly older, several whole families. Everyone is either German or French, several speak English, and the woman in charge speaks English perfectly. We came in and the lunch was served immediately. It was delicious – the first chicken I've had in ages. Since we're on full pension we are just served, you don't order.

After lunch we bundled up and ran out to play in the snow. The hotel has sleds here for its clients to use, so Eugenie, Louise and I took one and climbed up a steep, steep, hill and tried to ride three on a sled. We fell off a million times and rolled in the snow, which is so deep. Once we made it all the way down the hill. It was so much fun. After our play time in the snow we came in and changed our clothes for dinner, nothing dressy, just skirts and sweaters.

After dinner, which was excellent, we came into the sort of lounge, where there are tables and chairs, a piano, a fireplace, and a Christmas tree. We all wrote letters until right now, when we're going to bed at 9:30.

I can tell this will be rest time here because there is certainly no excitement, and I'm glad, because we were so tired before we left Paris. We got no rest in Zurich, and I'm sure we won't in Austria and Germany. Everything is so beautiful and peaceful here. The scenery is so gorgeous – I just wish you could see it all. It leaves you without words because words are so little when it comes to expressing such beauty as this.

Christmas Day, 1956

I never imagined that this Christmas would be so wonderful. I've missed being at home, but everyone here is so good and kind and marvelous that it has been truly a wonderful Christmas.

I spent yesterday morning renting skis, boots, and a jacket. There is a little shop here in Tschiertschen which rents all those things. The sweet lady here at the hotel found me some ski pants that swallow me whole, but serve the purpose. My skis weren't ready until the afternoon, so yesterday morning we helped Coco and Martha get started since they already had their skis. Coco was so funny – she couldn't get up on them and we were all behind her trying to push her up. Every time she would slip, so would we, and we all ended up in a pile in the snow. It was so much fun. Then after lunch, when I got my skis, we headed for the slopes.

We had an instructor who is James Dean's double. He is the cutest thing I've ever seen. We all stood and gazed at him. He's wonderful and skiing is wonderful too, but so hard to do! We only went down tiny hills, but I took many a spill. I tried to do what the instructor said, but it's so hard! I'm glad I've tried it, though.

We skied until about 4:30 yesterday, then came in, wrote letters, and ate chocolate bars. While we were sitting in the parlor writing, our wonderful Christmas Eve began. We had been talking with a man who speaks English, who is so nice. He has his whole family here, two little boys, a little girl, and his wife, who is expecting. He told us that they were going to light a Christmas tree outside for a surprise for their children, and asked us if we wanted to go with them. Of course we did!

About 6:00 we bundled up and trudged up a little mountain in the coldest cold I've ever felt. The two little boys had flashlights to light the way. We walked about 15 minutes and finally came to a little clearing where there was a perfectly shaped Christmas tree. The wife had decorated it with red candles that afternoon. We climbed over a fence to get to the tree. There was too much wind and the candles wouldn't stay lit, so we each stood by the tree and cupped our hands around two candles. Everything was so still and quiet and beautiful. Then our friend,(I don't know his name yet) started singing "Silent Night" in German, of course. His family was singing in German and we were singing in English. It was so sweet that tears were streaming down my face. Then he read the Christmas story in German. I could understand some of it. He asked us to sing then, so we sang about five carols.

It was the most wonderful feeling in the world sharing that family's Christmas Eve. To ask us to share it with them was the nicest thing he could have done. I've never felt the Christmas Spirit – the true meaning of Christmas – quite so much. I can never say in words what I felt at that moment. The lights on the tree, the songs, the family, the unity between foreign people through a single belief, a single faith. It was truly a "mountain top" experience, to use a cliché.

We came down our little mountain to the hotel to have dinner, which was delicious, as all of them have been. I think Swiss cooking is more like our cooking than any European cuisine I've tasted so far. I love it.

After dinner we came into the parlor where everybody in the hotel was gathering. We were hoping there would be some sort of party, but we had our doubts. The man who runs the hotel came in and lit the candles on the tree. Then a woman came in and played the piano atrociously while everyone sang, all in German. We sang "Silent Night" about 10 times I think. Then a little girl played the accordion, also atrociously. While she was playing Sandy and I started talking, in French, to a very nice man sitting near us. He thought we were English because he said we were so gay, happy, and warm-hearted, and because of our accent. I guess the Southern accent is much more like the English with our broad A's and dropped R's, but the part about the gaiety was surprising, especially since our conception of English people is exactly the opposite of his idea. We talked about how wonderful it is in the mountains at Christmas and he said, "Just think – two months ago, with the wars in Hungary and Poland, we weren't even certain of having a Christmas." And suddenly I realized just how much faith and hope these Europeans have.

As the party progressed, the man who runs the hotel announced that we Americans were here and would sing for them. So we sang Christmas carols for them. We have sung so much together that now we're really good.

Everyone seemed to enjoy us so much, so we kept on singing. Occasionally we sang songs that they knew, and we had German, French, and English going at the same time. One thing led to another and we somehow wound up at the piano singing carols. Then we started on the old favorites. Louise played and we all sang, then Eugenie started playing jazz. They loved us by then.

We began talking to everyone, either in French or English, and made so many friends. First was a man from Holland who speaks beautiful English and loves Americans – a very interesting man. Then a Swiss man bought us all big chocolate bars because he liked our singing so much. He turned out to be a magician by hobby and entertained us with card tricks. Then one of the men who was sitting near us bought us all drinks. He and I became great friends. He was amazed that we were Americans because he had always thought Americans were hard, distant, and cold. He kept saying," You all are so wonderful, so warm and happy, and sing with so much heart." That was a thrill to hear. He, too, had thought we were English.

Our magician friend is the sweetest man. When he gave us the candy we sang "For He's a Jolly Good Fellow," and it thrilled him to death. He kept saying, "You're so wonderful – you have the voices of angels." We all love him. The whole evening was amazing – how in the course of about 2½ hours we made so many friends and made ourselves liked so much. I really think we've been good ambassadors for the U.S. I'm glad our group is so amiable and has so much fun. That helps to make us liked, and if I must say so, we do have a lot of talent for a group. Everyone loves our playing and singing. It was really a Christmas Eve to remember – with strange but lovable people. It's wonderful to know that people are good and kind, and basically the same.

This morning at breakfast we could tell we were a success last night because everyone came over to us and said hello, and smiled at us. I just love all these people here. After breakfast we had another ski lesson with our darling instructor. I had more trouble the first hour this morning than I did yesterday, but the second hour I did pretty well, and had so much fun.

At lunch our friend the magician was sitting all alone, so we asked him to join us. He was delighted. We found out that he is from Munich originally, lives now in Zurich, and is a teacher in a school for retarded children. He bought us wine and coffee for lunch. He speaks English awkwardly, but he goes ahead and tries, mistakes and all. He is so sweet. Once during lunch we were talking about skiing and how we all fell down all the time. He said, "It's a miracle to me. You are like six little angels who haven't yet learned to use their wings to fly." We all sort of gasped, it was so moving. We asked him to eat dinner tonight at our table, and he gladly accepted.

After lunch we all six went into the parlor, and as usual headed for the piano. We sang and cut up some. One thing led to another – it always does – and pretty soon Louise was playing, I was singing, and Martha was more or less acting a monkey. She pretended to be the person to whom my songs were directed. She had pained expressions of love, sadness, etc. She really is an actress – a comedienne. Soon we had an audience. Mr. Ackermann, the magician, and some other people from the hotel. They enjoyed us so much we were further inspired. We worked up a little pantomime – like the old time movies. Louise played the background music, Sandy was the grandmother, I was the heroine, Martha was the hero, and Coco was the villain. It was hilarious. Our little audience laughed so hard I thought they'd die. We were laughing too. Then I danced for them, then we jitterbugged and did the Charleston. This went on for almost two hours.

We were exhausted when we finally stopped. I went upstairs later to change into my ski boots and met Mr. Ackermann in the hall. He had six apples to give us. I thanked him again and again. The other girls came up and did the same. He kept saying, "It's nothing. You all are so wonderful." Yesterday and today have made me so happy that I feel like I'm going to burst.

I got rigged up to faire le ski and went out to try it again. Coco and I just weren't in the mood, so we came back, put our skis up, and went back to the slopes where the others were watching James Dean, the ski instructor, teach another class. While I was standing there this young man whom I saw the other day came skiing by. We both sort of stared at each other. In a little while he came up and started talking to me. He's very nice looking and seems to be interesting. He's Swiss, speaks German, French, and a little English. There's a dance at the hotel tomorrow night and he said he would come.

Wednesday, December 26

It was so cold yesterday afternoon that we had to come in. The temperature has been wavering between zero and five above ever since we've been here. It's always colder in the afternoons than in the mornings. We came in and sang awhile, then changed into skirts and sweaters for dinner, which was delicious. We had the most beautiful, delicious dessert – something like baked Alaska. Mr. Ackermann saw that we liked it so much, that he ordered some for us to have after church. After dinner we all went to church for the special Christmas service. Mr. Ackermann and Klaus, a boy about 17, who is so handsome and has been so good to us – especially to Louise – went with us. They helped Sandy walk down the hill, because she sprained her ankle skiing and couldn't walk very easily.

The tiny church, a Protestant one, was packed. Besides all the people who live in Tschiertschen, there were all the vacation guests. It sounded just like Broadway Methodist Church in Paducah with all the talking before the service began. Everyone had their children, and they were laughing and squealing. Finally, with church walls bulging, the service began. The altar was decorated with a huge Christmas tree, which was covered with candles that burned a hypnotizing glow. The service turned out to be Children's Hour. Little red-cheeked sweeties sang off key, another group acted a little play, an older group sang. Then the preacher, who is very young and handsome, preached. Of course I didn't understand much of it, but he read the Christmas Story, which I understood pretty well. After his sermon we sang hymns. Then the best part – a men's choir. They were all so funny looking that we could hardly keep straight faces. They couldn't get started on their song, but after about four tries they made it. They sang so loudly the roof nearly blew off. When they finished it was 9:00, and the service had started at 8:00. We couldn't stand it any longer, so we left.

When we got outside we all started laughing. Mr. Ackermann laughed so hard I thought he'd die. We nearly split our sides laughing at him laugh. He kept saying, "O God help me," and then dying with laughter. We were all so weak by the time we got up the hill, we could hardly move.

We came in the parlor and began our nightly music session. Only Klaus and Mr. Ackermann were with us, as everyone else was in bed or in the bar. We were happily playing and singing when Eugenie saw "James Dean" come in and go into the bar. We all got so excited. Finally Sandy went to see if it were really he, and it was. Finally he came out into the hall, and some of us casually sauntered out, talked to him, and asked him to come join us, which he did. We all sat around a table and stared at him. It was funny, because he can't understand our English, and we can't understand his. We had the strangest conversations, for example, he said "I like to learn foreign languages because they are such wonderful instruments for learning about people," and Martha said, "Oh, do you play an instrument?" Finally we asked Mr. Ackermann to do some card tricks – he is really good.

Our friend James Dean's name is Hans Sprecker. We all looked at him with our tongues hanging out all night – he is so darling! He works as a ski instructor and truck driver in the winter, and in the summer he works in Bern as a car mechanic and swimming instructor. If he comes to the dance tonight like he said he would, I feel sorry for him, because all six of us will be after him!

About 9:30 the lady brought in the dessert that Mr. Ackermann had ordered for us, and we all sat down and ate it, Klaus and Hans too. We got so tickled because each of us kept making little references to Hans and James Dean, which no one but us could understand. It got so funny that the men laughed too, even though they didn't understand.

After stuffing ourselves we began singing again. Klaus wanted to hear us sing our version of "Laura," which Eugenie had arranged. Then Martha wanted me to sing and Louise to play, so we went through our repertoire. More people came in and I sang practically everything I know, from the Dorothy Shay songs to "O Holy Night." They kept asking me to sing more, and you know me, I gladly obliged. Hans seemed to enjoy the Dorothy Shay songs, although I know he couldn't understand them. He bought us all beer and we sang "For He's a Jolly Good Fellow." He blushed and looked like a doll! Finally at midnight we all said goodnight and went to bed.

This morning when I got up I was so sore from all the dancing and carrying on I had done yesterday afternoon. After breakfast Coco and I decided we didn't want to ski anymore, so we took our equipment back to the little shop. Then we climbed to the top of a hill to get a good picture of the village of Tschiertschen. Everything was so beautiful this morning, the sky was turquoise blue. We walked over to watch the skiers, and I took a picture of sweet Mr. Ackermann in his ski outfit, and also of Mr. Breiner, the man who invited us to light the tree with his family on Christmas Eve. We stayed until noon, and then after lunch, which was the best we've had, I washed my hair and took a bath so I would look decent for the dance tonight. We have to leave in the morning on the 7:00 bus to Chur, where we catch the train to Innsbruck. It always happens that we have to leave at an outrageously early hour the night after a party!

December 27th

I'm sitting on the train waiting to go to Innsbruck, Austria. Louise and I are in a car with some French people and the other four are in the next car with some interesting looking men. There wasn't room for all six of us together. I don't know why Louise and I always end up together.

Last night was really something! We all dressed up and for a change looked half lady-like. Some of our friends had already left, so they never saw us as young women. Our sweet Mr. Ackermann had gone back to Zurich. We all told him goodbye, then I walked with him to the bus because I had to go to the post office and the bus stop is in front of the post office. He was so wonderful with his poor English and his contagious laugh. He hated to leave us.

After dinner we all went into the parlor and waited until time for the dance to begin. Just about the time it was to start, Mr. Stoeher, the hotel owner, said he didn't think there would be any dance because there weren't enough people. We were so disgusted, However, more people kept coming. The friend I met on the ski slopes came, Rene Buhl. He is so strange, we decided he is either half out of his mind or over-sexed! Klaus was there, and finally HE came – the adorable Hans. He was with three friends.

Some older people were there and three young Belgian boys. A French girl who was in our ski class, who looks like Gina Lollobrigida, was there with her Papa. We thought she was at least 19 and she turned out to be only 15! So – we had enough people to dance. The rug was rolled up and we put records on the phonograph. Then the fun started.

Everyone was dying to dance with Hans. He was so cute – he danced with each of us several times, but his preference was Eugenie. I danced with one of his friends a lot – he was a marvelous dancer. I asked Mr. Stoeher, the owner, to dance and he was the best of all. He asked me to dance a couple of times too. We five (Coco was in bed), Hans, Klaus, and two other boys all sat around a table drinking beer and making toasts. We all locked arms and sang, drank beer with crossed arms, and kissed each other on the cheeks. We stayed up until about 3 a.m.! Mr. Stoeher stayed up with us. We had such a good time. Hans and Eugenie were really getting along fine – all of us were green with envy. We were all quite buddy-buddy by 3 in the morning. I got to bed about 3:30, then got up at 6 because we had to catch the bus at 7!

Mr. Stoeher and Mary Ann, his sister, got up to fix our breakfast, and they also fixed us box lunches for the train, which we paid for. After breakfast we told Mary Ann goodbye, and she said she would miss us so much. It was still dark outside when we left the hotel. The moon was out, a half-moon with a ring around it. The sky was a dark, dark blue and made the snow look a luminous blue. The rays of the sun were barely evident behind the mountains – night and day at the same time. I've never seen anything so beautiful.

Mr. Stoeher carried our bags down the hill on the sled. He is so good and kind. He's big and smiles all the time, and his eyes are "the milk of human kindness." He gave us each a chocolate bar as a going away present. When we got to the bus and told him goodbye, he said that he would miss us and wanted to hear from us. We all shook hands. I was so moved, I reached up and kissed him on both cheeks. He was so pleased.

Just as we all got situated on the little bus, who should appear but Hans! He came on the bus and told us all goodbye. He's so cute, I wish we could have taken him with us! I actually cried when the bus pulled away – I love Tschiertschen so much. All the people we met were so wonderful. I'd love to go back someday, but I know it would never be the same. We ourselves created much of the feeling that was there, and I'm afraid it could never be recaptured. It's always like that. I remember trying to recapture Interlochen that summer, and how futile it was.

As the little bus went down the perilous road to Chur, stopping now and then to pick up milk cans for the farmers to take to Chur, I felt as if I were losing something. The thought of never seeing all the wonderful people again, of never seeing Tschiertschen with the beauty surrounding it, of never having another Christmas there, is just appalling. But overpowering the feeling of having lost something, of having left so much behind, is that feeling of joy, of understanding, of love, of hope, of fulfillment, that comes from such experiences.

Life, I suppose, is composed of "experiences," each one complementing the next – each building on to the foundation of a life of a being, of a purpose. I just realized this phenomenon of life after graduating from high school, knowing that things would never be the same, that friends would part, interests would vary, all would be of the past. Then after that second summer at Interlochen, I felt even more the pain of leaving friends, of never seeing them again, of never knowing what they were doing, of never having the same experience. College brought the same feelings, although not as much. And now Europe. It's almost frustrating, knowing that it will soon pass – this glorious, wonderful year, being 20, being young. Things will be so different when I come back.

When we arrived in Chur, I felt as if I had just lived a dream – as if my precious village was another Brigadoon, remote, quaint, apart from the modern, hub-bub world. Tschiertschen will always be my "Lost Horizon," my village for dreaming about, for remembering with mixed emotions, for always cherishing.

January 6, 1957

I'm on the train going home – rather to Paris now. I hate for it all to end, but I'll be glad to get back to Paris.

As the marvelous trip ends, here is my brief review of the highlights after we left Tschiertschen.

INNSBRUCK

Arriving in Innsbruck, I had to keep telling myself – you're in Austria! But then we saw cute men in Tyrolean hats and knickers, and women in peasant dress and knew we were.

A dream fulfilled: I used to dream of riding in a real horse-drawn sleigh, but I never thought I ever would – especially in Austria. When we were able to hire the driver and start our tour, we kept saying to ourselves – we're riding in a real sleigh in *Austria*! The view from the sleigh was magnificent – mountains, snow, valleys, villages, clouds. We sang songs as we rode. The driver enjoyed them so much. It's amazing how well people can make themselves understood only by smiles, nods, and gestures. We smiled at the driver and he smiled at us. When we stopped singing he turned and said "Singen" – sing – so we did – for him.

Riding up the mountain: This was an amazing adventure. We began this trek by first taking a trolley to the end of the line, from there taking a funicular up the mountain to Hungerburgen, then a cable car to Seegrube, then another cable car to the top – Halekafar. The funicular went up the mountain by rail and the cable car by cable. It was such a thrill! The view on the ride up was *so* gorgeous. We could see the two mountain ranges with Innsbruck down in between them. It was even more beautiful going down, because the sun was setting behind the mountains and there was a misty pink color hanging over everything.

Innsbruck's beautiful church. We visited St. James Cathedral – the most beautiful church I've ever seen. It has an altar of solid silver, a gorgeous pulpit of gold, ceilings paintings famous because of their beauty, and because they make the top of the church look like two domes when it is really a flat ceiling. It really is unbelievable.

MUNICH

Our arrival in Munich was notable for the very nice English speaking German boys on the train, who helped us get our bags off at the station. We've been very lucky on this whole trip finding people to carry our bags.

A museum to remember: Four of us went to the famous German Museum.

It's unique in the world, and we only had time to visit several sections. They have exhibitions of everything there from physics to agriculture. We visited first of all the room where all the old, old pianos are. There were all sorts of them – I'm dying to buy one and bring it home. The curator of that section played all of them for us and showed us the different sounds. They had all kinds – from the very first ones. We also saw the rooms where all the old musical instruments were – all kinds of all instruments. It was so amazing. I've never seen such instruments – didn't even know that some of them existed.

The Hofbrau Haus: Sandy and Martha introduced us to the famous Hofbrau Haus, where they had met some U.S. soldiers. It's the cutest place. Downstairs there are crowds of people sitting around picnic-looking tables drinking beer and listening to the Um pah, pah, band. We went upstairs, which is more "refined" than downstairs. It is a huge, huge room – decorated with Christmas trees and Christmas decorations of course. Everyone drinks beer in huge quart beer mugs – delicious beer too.

Greeting the New Year: The Hofbrau Haus looked very festive, decorated with New Year's decorations. In the huge room there were so many people, there was hardly room enough to stand. There were two smaller rooms, each with little combos and very quaint. I spent most of my time there. At New Year's beginning everyone wished everyone Happy New Year in grand style. I was very touched once, because a Hungarian refugee (she said this in German and a nice young man translated for me) came up to me and clasped my hand and said Happy New Year, blessings, etc.

HEIDELBERG

A touch of home: As the six of us were walking down the street in Heidelberg window shopping and eating, popcorn of all things (the first I've seen since I left the States), a soldier came up to us and asked us if we were from the States. We said yes, and he asked "Where?" We said "The South" and he said "Yippee! I'm from Louisiana and haven't seen a Southern girl since I left two years ago." He was so nice.

Real romantic history: Our tour of Heidelberg was very good. We had a little private bus and the first woman guide we've had, who was quite interesting. The main points of interest included the famous beer garden of the Student Prince, which isn't called that, but it is the place where Prince Charles the V used to go to drink beer when he was a student in Heidelberg, and there he fell in love with The Innkeeper's daughter. I've forgotten the author who made a story of the real love story and called it Old Heidelberg but it was from that story that Romberg got the idea for *The Student Prince*. It was so romantic seeing the house and imagining all that may have happened there.

FRANKFURT

Meeting Harvey Rappaport. Meeting Harvey was a delight. We met him at one of the places G.I.s frequent, quite near our hotel. He asked if he could buy us a Coke, so we asked him to join all of us. He was really the nicest boy I've met in long time. We all sat and talked for a while. He said he was from New Haven, Conn., was going home in a month – hated the army – as all of them did. Later, when he asked me to go with him Saturday afternoon to the snack bar at the big PX and he said he'd buy me a cheeseburger and some milk, I readily accepted!

The next day we rode in a taxi (you can tell it has become a luxury to me!) out to the PX. I had two cheeseburgers (at Harvey's insistence), French fries, chocolate sundae, and a big glass of milk – my first since I left the ship. It was so delicious.

As we walked that afternoon, and later at dinner, we discussed everything! I asked him if he were Jewish and he said yes. That led to a long discussion on religion. He told me some pretty disgusting things that have happened to him because he is Jewish. Harvey is really so nice. I'm glad I've known him.

We got up this morning at six thirty, ate breakfast, and went to the station. The train left at eight four and our long ride to Paris began, which brings me to where I started.

All of us slept most of the morning, but around noon throngs of people crowded onto the train and we had to sit up. The afternoon passed rather quickly with the aid of conversation, coffee, and songs. I love our group of six – we have so much fun together. I'm glad we'll be going to Spain between semesters and Italy at Easter together.

Later

We arrived in Paris about six twenty. Paris is so wonderful – I was so glad to get back to her! The weather is wonderful – very warm and spring like – just like last year they say. It was wonderful in January, but in February and March there was the severest cold in Europe's history!

We took a taxi home, climbed the stairs. Mme. Rémond came to the door looking very refreshed after her vacation. I would love to have hugged her, but she is so cold that way – so I just shook hands. We talked for a minute, and then came in our room. It looked so clean and neat. The bathroom too had been cleaned from top to bottom. The first thing I did was read my mountain of mail! I loved it. I had lots of Christmas cards and lots of letters. Christmas at home sounded wonderful.

Well, bye, bye vacation. It's been so wonderful. I'll never ever forget it. I love Europe and Europeans so much. It's been absolutely fabulous. Thank you for giving it to me.

Back

to

Classes

January 8, 1957

Dear Mother and Daddy,

Now my life – Monday and Tuesday and Wednesday were spent going to class, practicing, and studying. Tuesday night Jean-Louis Baut called me. I really was surprised, because before I left for Christmas vacation he called me, asked me to go out and I refused. Then he asked me to write him during vacation. I said I would – but I didn't. I really didn't care to go out with him anymore because he insisted on seeing me all the time and was so childish about it. In the first place I didn't have the time, in the second – he bored me. Well, the other day the Rémonds received a calling card from M. Baut wishing them his best wishes for the year. Mme. said that sending a card like that was so "bien-éléve." That it was almost extinct now! They were both quite impressed with Jean-Louis especially his good manners and sparkling intelligence. So of course I began feeling bad about being so mean to him. I asked Mme. what to do, and she said I should wait a while to see if he called – if he didn't I should write him a note. She said I should make it clear that I'd like to go out with him, but not more than twice a month. So I agreed. I didn't have a long wait – he called Tuesday, asked me to dinner Wednesday night and I accepted.

Tuesday night the Rémonds had guests for dinner. The man and his wife were really remarkable. He is about 50 – maybe a little over, and she is in her early 40s. He is an artist, a singer, poet, and other such little items. She is very young looking, rather slim, is the mother of 14 children and is expecting the 15th! I stared at her all night because I've never seen such a phenomenon as she! The man directs all of his children in a family choir. After dinner Louise and I played and sang, as has become our custom for all the Rémonds guests. After we performed, the man sang – not very well. The man sang some comical folksongs which don't require good singing. He did them very well and proved to be a real comic. The evening was very enjoyable.

Yesterday at Music History M. Handemann told me I could call Pierre Bernac and arrange an appointment – so I'm going to as soon as I finish this.

Last night I went out with Jean-Louis. It was the most charming date I've spent with Jean-Louis. He apparently understands that I want to see him but not very much. He was very charming and I didn't even get mad at him once. We went to a darling little Italian restaurant called The Pizza. It was decorated with beautiful paper lanterns. They played Italian music (records), the waiters were dressed in Neapolitan costumes – looked straight out of *The Gondoliers*. I had Tagliatelle Bologna – a sort of spaghetti with delicious meat sauce. For an appetizer I had snails – not at all Italian, but I love them so. For dessert I had a frozen orange piled with orange ice cream – just delicious. We finished dinner about 9:45, then ran across the Champs to the movies to see *The Solid Gold Cadillac* with Judy Holliday. The American movies all have French subtitles, so Jean-Louis could understand it too. After the movie we went into a café and had hot chocolate. The Metro had closed by the time we finished, so we came home in a taxi – really a splurge. I really enjoyed it, and so did Jean-Louis. I hope he sees how much nicer it is to see each other less and enjoy each other more than it is to see each other more and fuss all the time. I was glad to be with him again for my French's sake – he helps me so much.

I just called M. Bernac. He sounds so nice. I'm hoping to sing for him Monday afternoon. I'm so anxious to get started with him. I could just kick myself for not having done this at the first of the year – but we live and learn. I was so surprised because he spoke English to me on the telephone – perfect English. He has a very young sounding voice.

We had such an interesting conversation at dinner today. We discussed the French system of government. The Rémonds think the system is stupid as it is. No one wants Guy Mollet to stay in power after the idiotic way he handled the Suez but no one wants his job either. The Rémonds are very royalistic – they would love to have a monarch in power again – and I'm inclined to agree. The Frenchman is so independent, so individualistic, that the only way he can be led, or governed is by a strong, firm government which has not existed in France since before the Revolution. We also discussed the question of morality in France – and the question of drinking alcoholic beverages.

It is strange how people of different countries form their ideas and ideals. I always thought that the French were wrong drinking wine all the time and giving it to their children instead of milk. But I understand that it's not at all wrong – they have always had wine – it's not bad for them – it's not bad for their children. Granted they don't have as pretty teeth as American children, but they haven't been done any harm morally. All those stories about poor drunk French children who were saved by milk when Mendès-France was in power – all those stories were a farce. I like milk, but I have almost come to the point of thinking wine is preferable for meals. As far as taste goes, wine blends much better with food than milk. Drinking wine can become an art – knowing when to choose which red wine to best complement meat, and which white wine for fish or dessert or cheese.

In the Latin countries there is a difference in wine and in the alcoholic beverages – which shows the different points of view taken by Americans and

Europeans on the subject. As to other alcoholic beverages – Europeans know how to drink. They drink for the taste, for the pleasure (have I said all this before?) not for seeing how much they can hold as do many Americans. I've yet to see a "drunk" Frenchman! I remember Papa used to say that gluttony is a sin – it is just as wrong to be a glutton at eating as it is at drinking too much. I really believe that. As to morals of the French – they are no better and no worse than we. In France lovers have no inhibitions in the Metro, on the bus, in the park, on the sidewalk, but no one minds. Anglo-Saxon people condemn Latins for making love publicly, yet the Anglo-Saxon peoples do it too, behind doors, and alleys, in dark corners. In my opinion there is no difference in what is done – as to whether it is wrong or right – the only difference is the way of thinking of different peoples. The French are so grand about things especially the physical attractiveness of people. The French think nothing of saying "what a pretty bosom you have" when they pay you a compliment – many women say it. "Quelle belle poitrine" is an expression heard very often. (In fact, I've heard it from Jean-Louis, and I was concerned he would discover that I wear a padded bra when he put his arms around me!)

I can't say that I prefer the French way to ours, but one must understand the differences in order to understand the people and to appreciate their way of life. I must say the French are much more adult and realistic as a people than are Americans – except in politics!

Tonight we're going to the Sorbonne to hear M. Rémond give a lecture on Acadia, the section of Nova Scotia and Canada from where Evangeline came, and from where the Cajuns of Louisiana came. Of course Louise and I are going and so is Coco – a real Cajun. M. wanted me to sing the song Evangeline at the end of the lecture, but there is no piano in the lecture hall and it is not worth singing without accompaniment. I have to write an essay now. We don't have class this afternoon because Mme. Alvernhe is ill.

The weather has been beautiful for the past two days – but horribly cold! The wind cuts you in two. The house is freezing. M. Rémond just built me a fire in the stove in our fireplace. I have on my long underwear, socks, my wool sock house slippers, wool slacks, and two sweaters. My hands get so cold they look purple and pink spotted! But it could be worse I guess.

Friday night

This weekend, unfortunately, is not going to be really exciting like last weekend – I have not one date! It's funny – until I had several dates (with Americans – Jean-Louis doesn't count) I didn't even think about going out, but now, after having dates, I think about it too much. It's sort of like caramel pie – I can do well without it, but once I have a bite I can't stop eating it! Oh well.

Last night we went to M. Rémond's lecture on Acadia and Evangeline. It was very interesting – I was proud to be his "daughter." Coco met us there at the Sorbonne. M. Rémond was so natural he was just like he is at the dinner table with us (he talks all the time there too.) He was so nice – he paid our way on the bus. Afterwards Louise and I took Coco and M. Rémond to have coffee. He was still talking. He's so funny; he loves to be alone with Louise and me – we must make him feel younger or something. After our little coffee rendezvous we came home on the Metro. M. paid our way again – and in first class too! We really felt honored. We are getting to be such good friends now with the Rémonds – close, that is – and I'm so glad.

After lunch this afternoon Louise and I put on our slacks, loafers and socks, wool scarves, took purses and cameras and sallied forth to take pictures of la belle Paris. It was so beautiful today! It was cold but the sun was warm and there wasn't so much wind. We took some good pictures. We looked like such typical American tourists everyone looked at us and grinned, and all the boys made comments. We walked from our house down Malesherbes to the Madeleine, down Royale to the Place de la Concorde, across the Seine – taking pictures on the way. Then we decided to go pay Mike Margulies a visit. He doesn't live far from Place de la Concorde – by Metro that is. He lives in a pension – and I'm so envious of him. He has the nicest room and it's so warm! He was very surprised to see us. We had the concierge call him down, then he took us up to his room. We sat and talked, listen to his radio, ate Swiss chocolate he brought from Switzerland. We stayed about an hour then he drove us home as far as the Place de la Concorde. From there we went on the Metro and came back here about 7:00.

Paris was so beautiful today – I adored her.

Wednesday, January 9, 1957

As of yet my 1957 life in Paris has not been extremely exciting. Monday I spent in class, practicing, and washing clothes. Yesterday I spent doing the same thing. I went with Louise to The American Express to try to get the $50 for the Rémonds, but we can't get it any more. They told us when we first went in November that you can only have $50 if you're going back to the states; but we went back and were able to get it the second time. But the third time they knew us and wouldn't let us have it. It's too bad for M. Rémond's sake, but for us it's better. I have a chance to make a little more now. Speaking of money, the $100 arrived today. I did so well on my trip that I still have $145 in francs. Of course $125 of it I will pay Friday for January's rent. I also have $10 in travelers' checks from the first $400 you gave me.

Last night after dinner the Rémonds told us that now it is official and that the new baby will come in June. I thought it would come before then surely! It seems you never tell about a new baby until after a certain period has passed. They were so cute about it. I'm really afraid we won't get to see it because I think it comes around the end of June, and we will be gone then.

Oh, yesterday afternoon after class Mme. Alvernhe told us that Mme. Rémond had called to tell her that they would be away about 3 days the end of this month in order to get the children, who are at Mme.'s mother's in Bourgoyne, and bring them back to Paris. She wondered what to do about our meals. We told Mme. Alvernhe to let us do our own cooking. Louise is a good cook, and I think I can manage. Mme. Rémond had said she could leave us money to eat in a restaurant (not a very good one), so we can use that money to buy things and cook it ourselves. I hope she agrees. If she does the first thing we're going to do is have fried chicken! I can hardly wait.

Today we had music history – love that class. M. Handemann is so nice. He told me he had telephoned M. Bernac (the famous voice teacher) and he would see me in 2 weeks. I said I would like to start working soon and couldn't I possibly see him in a week. M. Handemann is going to re-telephone Bernac and see if he won't see me sooner. I'm excited about it. I talked to Johanna Hammel about it this morning. She's the graduate student from Newcomb. She came last year as a senior and decided to stay. She is studying at the Conservatoire now. She said the only voice teacher she ever heard about is Bernac – how wonderful he is, etc. I'm so thrilled about it and so angry with myself for not starting out with him – but I was trying not to be too expensive.

After class I practiced, came home and had dinner. After dinner I called David Kaufman to say Bonne Année and see how his vacation was. I said, "Well, David what do you know?" He answered, "Why don't you and Mike and Louise and I get together Sunday night?" It was such an unexpected but well-received answer. Of course I said yes. Louise was listening on the extra earphone (which all French phones have), so I had to pretend to be calling her to the phone so David could ask her. He said he and Mike had planned this last week. I take it Mike will call me soon about it. While David was talking to Louise he asked her to go to the movie this afternoon to see Mozart's *Don*

Giovanni performed by the Vienna Opera Company. I wanted to go too – so I did. I don't think David minded – I hope not. I think David likes Louise a lot. *Don Giovanni* was very, very good. It was done in German with French sub-titles. The singers were excellent. It always detracts a little though, to have someone else do the singing instead of the actual actors. The sets and costumes were scrumptious. I really did enjoy it. It was so funny – when we left David he kissed Louise on both cheeks and didn't even shake my hand! Louise was so surprised that she let out a yelp and I think poor David was embarrassed.

Thursday Morning, January 10

Guess what I did last night. I went to the movies all alone. I've been dying to see *War and Peace*, so I called Coco and Sandy. Neither of them could go. Louise had a date with Jim Long, so I decided to go alone. The theater is on the Champs and is just a couple of minutes on the Metro – which lets you off practically in the front door of the theater. There was such a large crowd there last night. The line stretched for nearly a block. But finally I got in. It was really a wonderful movie and I'm glad I went – even if I did have to go alone.

Night

We're getting ready to meet Eugenie and Sandy at the movies to see *Notre Dame de Paris*. I haven't seen a movie since I came to Paris, and then all of a sudden I am seeing three in two days! What a splurge. But I figure I should take advantage of not much homework and see some of the things I've been wanting to see.

Friday morning

Hi – Eugenie didn't come last night, but Sandy did. The movie was a big disappointment. It didn't capture the mystery and horror of the middle ages as Victor Hugo originally wrote it. I really was let down. Louise said the version with Charles Laughton was so much superior to this French version.

Monday, January 14, 1957

I've had such a big weekend – it will take me hours to tell all about it. Friday afternoon about 4:00, Hi Petter called. He and his friend had finally arrived by the hardest – they ran out of gas at Chartres, etc. Anyway, Friday night Louise and I went out with Hi and his friend Dean Lucas – a very nice young man from Ohio – a dentist now in the Army. Hi had come to get his new Simca – but it wasn't ready till Saturday. We started out Friday night in Dean's car, headed for Montmartre. We walked around up there, looked in at the art stores, etc. We drove by the Lapin Agile, but it was too early; no one was there and the entertainers weren't going to begin for about an hour. So we decided to go down to the Champs-Élysées and hunt for this little Spanish place with music, dancing, etc. that Johanna Hammel had told me about. We hunted and walked and looked for it, but couldn't find it. Finally someone told us it was closed! We were so disappointed. We then stopped in at a café and had café-au-lait and talked. Hi is really so funny and so smart. I like him so much! At about 11:30 we went back to the Lapin Agile. It's the most wonderful place – l could go every night I think. It's a little cabaret near Sacré-Cœur. It's off to itself in a sort of house-looking building, but there are only 4 rooms – the main room, the entrance hall, the coat room, and the room where they fix the drinks. The cabaret room is covered in paintings, sculpture, etc. Many of the works are original – there is a Toulouse Lautrec original among them. The reason there are so many original things is because all the artists used to be broke when they came to the Lapin Agile, and the only way they could pay their bill was by giving the owner a painting, a sculpture or something. Everyone sits around big octagonal wooden tables. The atmosphere is wonderful. Suddenly a man came in to play the piano – then another handsome man, who was just sitting at one of the tables, got up to sing. He had a beautiful voice – sang French folk and love songs. A platinum blonde and a cute old fisherman-looking man sang duets – little novelty songs and folk songs. Then everyone sang together including the clientele. It was so much fun. They sang a couple of French songs that I know. There was also a marvelous guitarist, and a cute man who told jokes. It was all so wonderful because it was sort of spontaneous. There was also a tenor in an Italian costume who had a marvelous voice. It was all very intimate. When the entertainers finished a number, the piano player would play and we would clap in a certain syncopated rhythm. Hi and Dean loved the place too. Hi speaks French pretty well, and he could understand most everything they said. The piano player had each of us give him a note. Hi gave him "mi," someone else gave him "do," another "do," another "mi" – I gave him "ti," and someone else "bb." Try that on the piano – ECCEB and Bflat. That's how he played it – he then proceeded to play a whole piece on those notes.

After all the performers had performed they asked this young man who was sitting across the room to sing. He did, and was very good. (Louise saw him Sat. night in the chorus at the Opéra-Comique.) Then someone told them that only the American women (there were two with their husbands) could sing, so they got her to sing too. She was pretty good – sang "I Love Paris" and "Summertime." She's from California. Not to be outdone – Hi raised his hand and said I could sing and Louise could play – so they took us by the hand and made us sing too. I sang "You Made Me Love You" and they loved it. They applauded till I sang again. Then I did "Hello Young Lovers" and "Getting To Know You." They really liked us. The blonde who sang (had a good voice and is very attractive) told me I had a professional poise and voice. The tenor asked me if I was singing in a nightclub in Paris. Then they gave Louise and me both a painting of the Lapin Agile. We were so thrilled. It was so much fun – the whole evening. Maybe if I keep on singing everywhere I go I'll end up with a job of some sort! We finally left the Lapin at 2:15 a.m.

Saturday morning at 11:00 we had to go to the Sorbonne and register for our exams. I have my Art History exam Tues. At first Newcomb was going to give it to us, but they persuaded the Sorbonne to give it to us. You see, you're not allowed to take Sorbonne exams unless you take the full four-course civilization course – which only Coco, Susan, and Ellie are taking because they're French majors.

Saturday Louise went out for lunch with some people from Baton Rouge who were here, so I was alone with the Rémonds. I love being alone with them – it gives us a much better chance to really talk and know each other. Madame had made me a special treat – her mayonnaise. She knew I loved it (it is the best I ever tasted!) so she fixed ham rolls filled with vegetables with mayonnaise all over it. It was the best thing we've had to eat since I've been here. We sat and talked till 2:30 after dinner! Madame has a preference for me which I didn't realize till then. Louise has said so all along, but I disagreed, but Saturday it was obvious. She said some things that really boosted my morale. They both are so good to us – even if they are sort of peculiar sometimes.

Saturday at 8:00 I had a date to double date with Johanna Hammel and her fiancé, Don Healy. Don has a friend, John Donaher, who works at SHAPE too – is engaged, but wanted to go out with them. So – we went. John is very nice, cute, and good company. He's from Pittsburgh, went to Notre Dame, was in Eddie Hannan's class. Don is from California – a big brute who is so funny. We all stayed in stitches the whole time. We went first to the section around the Bastille – which is really a rough section – especially the Communist and prostitute area – but also with some very atmospheric, odd places to eat, drink, and be merry. Everyone was hungry, so we stopped in tiny little hole in the wall and had saucisson sandwiches (sausage) and beer. Then we went to a place where there was supposed to be real Apache dancing. The first place we peered into was completely vacant. So we walked down a shiny, dark, cobblestone alley, and into another place. There weren't many people – until a tour came in. If there's something that's funny – it's to watch people being led around on a night-life tour. They filed in, were served thimble servings of champagne. With their arrival the "Apache" dancing began. It was really a farce. The ugliest men and women I've ever seen. They didn't dance – they just threw each other around. We laughed so hard – they thought they were being so sexy and they were really just comical. When the big show was over we went to Harry's New York Bar. I've always wanted to go – there's a Harry's New York Bar in just about every international city. Ernest Hemingway is always sticking a Harry's Bar in his books. It really is a nice place – the piano player plays all American bar-type music, everything is quite calm and refined. We drank German beer and sat and talked till about 12:30. The boys had to take a bus back to SHAPE at 1:00, so we called it a night at 12:30. John sent me home in cab. I offered to go on the Metro because we were so near home, but he insisted on the taxi. He took my address and phone number and said he'd call me soon – which I didn't expect him to do. I'm glad – because he'll be nice to go places with – even if he is engaged. I take it his girl is in the U.S.

Sunday morning I slept late – I intended to go to church, but didn't get up in time. Louise and I decided we would go to the Flea Market that afternoon. I thought perhaps Hi might like to join us, so I called him. He had already been last summer, but he and Dean wanted to go again. They came by for us about 2:30 – had a friend with them – Niko Something. He is a doctor about 35 years old, but looks 50. He is an Austrian by birth, an American now. His family was one of the most outstanding families in Austria when the Germans came in during the last war – thus they were among the first to be stripped of everything. I imagine the war has caused Niko to look so old. Anyhow – the Flea Market is a huge market open on Sat., Sun. and Mon. in tents. There is everything there – old costumes, paintings, and antiques. The biggest attractions are the antiques. All the dealers in Paris have a shop in town and one at the flea market. The same thing that will be for 4000f. in town will be 2000 or 3000f. at the Flea Market. It's fabulous! We spent the whole afternoon walking through all the shops. Louise bought an ancient (15th Century) cossack sword for her Daddy's collection. I of course nosed around in the jewelry, the silver, the brass, etc. They have some absolutely beautiful things at such low prices. I'm going back sometime and buy gifts for people. They have wonderful old porcelain doorknobs – everything. M. Rémond said the best time to go for buying things is on Monday because they like to sell as much as possible by then – even at no profit. He said you can get things for nothing then. I really can't explain how fascinating it is. I thought about the reaction of you, Mother, and other antique lovers. You could have a field day!

The Rémonds were out to supper, so Louise and I ate alone, then got ready for our date at 8:00 with Mike and David. They came – Mike was in his usual good, laughing mood – which is so nice to open the door to. We went to the Opéra-Comique, and saw *Madame Butterfly*. It was the very best opera I've seen in Paris. The singers were all (for a change) wonderful. The production, staging, costumes, sets, were fabulous! I was so impressed. The only time I have seen *Butterfly* was the summer the opera group at Interlochen did it. Of course this professional production was so far above Interlochen's. It encouraged me because some of the operas I've seen here have been disappointments. It was all so beautiful and fine. The music I guess is just about my favorite Puccini. I've been thinking about it all day.

After the opera we went to Pam-Pam – a place across from the Opéra where they serve American-cooked food. We went with the intentions of having a hamburger, and ended up with waffles. It was the first I've had since I left home – really tasted good. We sat and talked for about an hour. I found out more about Mike. He makes me sick he's so talented. Besides speaking so many languages, he plays, the piano, the organ, he sings, he flies a plane, etc. I'm always so jealous of people like him. He really is fascinating. We left Pam-Pam. I wanted to walk across the Seine, so we drove to Place de la Concorde and parked the car. We walked along the Seine toward my favorite bridge, Mike and I went down the steps to the walk that is right on the level with the water. We sang and even waltzed there on the smooth concrete. We walked to where we thought we could get back on the street walk, but there was an electric fence around the door. So – we walked all the way back to where we had first come down. I still hadn't walked across my bridge, so after playing on a huge statue of I've forgotten who on a horse – we walked across my bridge. The Seine was so magnificent last night. There was only a faint trace of a moon, all the lights were reflected in the water – even the little red lights of the Eiffel Tower were reflected. The wind was just being playful – the air was cold and warm at the same time. I hated to leave the scene – but we did about 2:00 a.m. We sat out front and discussed singing till 2:30. David is interested in a voice career. He says it's only the stage for him. We decided we'd get together and sing for each other soon. I've never heard him. He says he really doesn't feel ready to be heard by anyone yet, but he guesses he'll sing for me. Thus my wonderful weekend came to an end. Time flies so rapidly – I wish I could capture certain moments and hold them together forever. I wish life would slow down once in a while, but then I suppose it would be something other than life.

I practiced from 2:30 to 4:45 – I sounded better today than I have this whole year. I was so excited when I finished singing I thought I would pop. I suddenly had a mad desire for a book of folk songs by John Jacob Niles. I went immediately to the biggest music (books, sheet music, etc.) store in Paris. They didn't have anything, but said they would try to order it. I hope they can. I came home, washed a sweater (I've been washing one about every 4 days with Woolite – it really does a beautiful job), wrote this, ate supper, am here again. The Rémonds have been gone all day, but I hear them coming in now.

Louise got the news today that her mother and daddy are letting Genie, her 19 year old sister, fly over here this summer when school is out and travel with us this summer. Isn't that wonderful?

We found out the other day that we have 15 days between semesters! We finish exams the 19th of February and don't have to be back till March 6th! That means trip time. We want to go (the six of us) to Spain, Portugal, and come back by the French Riviera. How does that sound! It won't be as expensive as Christmas, because Spain is the cheapest country in Europe. We have also decided it will be cheaper to have only the rooms in the hotel not meals. Because lots of times we were only in the mood for a sandwich and we had to eat a huge meal because it was already paid for. We talked to Ellie and Susan and they got along much better eating on their own in Italy – may I go? We'll have time to see so much that I had given up hope of seeing. Then at Easter time we want to go to Italy by way of Geneva, Switzerland – which is right on the way to Italy. I want to spend the whole Easter vacation in Italy. When school is out we want to go up through Belgium to Holland, then across the top of Germany to Denmark, from there to Sweden, then Norway – sail from Norway to Scotland – Scotland to Ireland – Ireland to England – sail home from England. By the way my reservations are for the 16th of August on the Île de France.

Saturday night January 19, 1957

This morning I spent practicing. I'm becoming a real Trojan about practicing. This afternoon after lunch I went to the Comedie Française to try to get tickets for *Les Miserables* for tonight, but only very expensive tickets were left, so of course I didn't buy them. Then I went to the Louvre. I spent nearly two hours in the Italian school paintings section. Of course I didn't have time to see them all – I'm going back tomorrow afternoon to finish up. But I saw the famous da Vinci *Mona Lisa* this afternoon. She really is an interesting woman. I was surprised that the colors in the original are so somber. Mona has exquisite hands. Her smile is unusual, but I don't think it conveys any sarcasm or maliciousness at all. Rather – I found her smile one of tenderness and understanding – one of a woman who has had a rich life and experienced many things – happy and sad. Next to Mona is Titian's *Young Woman at her Toilette* – magnificent. The true color of Titian hair is wonderful – a deep auburn. I stood nearly thirty minutes admiring it. I loved all the Titian paintings I saw. Also saw other Da Vinci originals. I loved *The Virgin of the Rocks*. Also saw for the first time some Fra Angelico and Andrea Del Sarto. I've read about both of those artists, but had never seen any of their works except in black and white pictures.

When the Louvre closed at five I walked from there through the Arc du Carrousel, through the Tuileries to the Place de la Concorde, and from there home. It was so beautiful. The sun was a radiant ball of fire, sitting behind the skyline of the Left Bank. In the Tuileries the fountains were spurting water into their frozen basins – the Arc de Triomphe, the Obelisk, The Eiffel, were hazy gray shadows. The sky was still blue, streaked with pink flurries. It was so gorgeous – I only wished I had my camera.

I love to walk down Avenue Royale in front of the Madeleine on Saturday afternoons about five thirty. All the Paris elite come out – the fur-coated, perfumed, bejeweled women – the well-dressed men – diplomats and big business men – C'est formidable. By the way, "formidable" is used for everything – is translated like we say something "is really something."

Sunday morning, rather afternoon

I went to a concert this morning for the Jeuneses Musicales Françaises. It was great – I'm so glad I finally know how to make use of this organization of which I and thousands of other French students are members. This morning the orchestra played Aaron Copland's ballet suite *Rodeo*, Gershwin's Concerto in F, and Suite *Bachianas* No. 2 by Villa-Lobos. Before each piece a man came out on the stage and gave explanations of each work, something about the life of each composer. It was really interesting. The orchestra was very good – they did an excellent job of the Gershwin – the pianist was exceptionally good. It was fun to see the reaction of an all French audience (almost) to a program of all American music. The French love Gershwin, they seemed to appreciate Copland much more than Villa-Lobos. I was real nostalgic – almost to the point of being homesick – during the Copland. He knows how to express Americanism in every note of his music. The concert hall was filled – which surprised me because this was the third performance of this concert, and it was at ten in the morning.

I spent about two hours in the Louvre this afternoon; I finished seeing the Egyptian section and nearly finished the section of the 19th century French school of painting. The works in the Egyptian section are unbelievable – first because of their age and secondly because of their beauty. It's amazing to see how much of what we call "modern" is really primitive and much like Egyptian and other oriental art. The Louvre is so wonderful – the ceilings are gorgeous. The Egyptian collections are in the rooms which Charles X had fixed especially for them. In the French school of the 19th century I saw works of David, Delacroix, Ingres, Guerin, Proudhom – the originals!

We went straight from the Louvre to Salle Pleyel to the concert. We were so disappointed because Robert Casadesus was ill and couldn't play. A young woman played another Beethoven concerto. She was very good – but not Casadesus. The orchestra played the *Leonora* Overture No. 3, the Concerto and the 4th Symphony. It was a good concert, but not really exceptional.

Monday night

I am now a voice student of M. Pierre Bernac. Hallelujah!

I went to his apartment this afternoon at three thirty. He has a beautiful apartment, I had to wait a while for him to give a lesson. Then he came in and took me upstairs to his studio. He is so cute and gracious – not cute looking – attractive is the word. He is so warm and understanding. I sang several things for him. He said my singing French was terrible. I knew that. He didn't say my voice was good or bad – just that I could do a lot. He asked me what I could pay – I first said 1,000f. a lesson. He looked at me as if to say, "Who do you think you're going to take lessons from?" So I said – at the most 1500f. a lesson. Then he asked how many lessons a week – I said two. So he said – "I'll take you for three lessons a week – 3,000f. per week...at first. Then we'll make it 2 a week at 3,000f. a week." I agreed.

I didn't expect to get off so cheap – and then to have 3 lessons a week! He spoke to me in French about casual things – but about singing he spoke to me in English. I like that. He's going to Milan with my music history teacher M. Handemann this week, so I start my lessons with him next Monday. They're going to the opening of La Scala. I wish they'd take me along. Anyway, I hate myself because I haven't been taking from Bernac all this time. I'm going to really work doubly hard to make up for it.

When I came back from M. Bernac's, Madame's cousin, Marie-Lise was here to have tea. (Louise wasn't here – she had a piano lesson) I had never met this cousin before. She is about my age – a little older I guess – and so attractive. I really did like her. She's the first French girl I've found it easy to talk to. She's engaged. She's going to get some friends of her fiancé for Louise and me, and we're all going out somewhere, together. Madame looked so pretty. She had on the new black maternity suit she made. She has such a pretty face. I love her so much now.

I received a Pneumatique from Jean-Louis this afternoon asking me to come to dinner tonight and meet his little sister. He called before I came home to lunch and I was supposed to call him back but I didn't have time before I left for M. Bernac's. So I called him after Marie-Lise left. He wasn't there, his mother answered the phone. I explained to her why I hadn't called and why I couldn't come. I think she understood most of what I said. It's so hard to speak clearly on these telephones in French. She said they wanted me to come Wednesday night for dinner – I said yes. Then Jean-Louis called tonight and asked me again. Susan Shelley and his cousin Michel are also coming. I like Jean-Louis' mother so much – she probably hates me now for being so mean to him!

M. Rémond was quite amusing at the table tonight. He told a gruesome detective story, but he was funny about it. He loves to talk so much – he forgets to eat, and all his food gets cold. She interrupts his stories to tell him his food is getting cold – it makes him so angry and he gets so flustered. I love to watch him.

Wednesday, January 23, 1957

Last night we had guests for dinner. Louise and I invited Johanna Hammel, and the Rémonds invited three guests. It was so good of them to do it – they did it just for us – the dinner I mean, because we asked if we could have Johanna for dinner. They took advantage of the occasion to invite their friends to whom they owed social payments. The other guests were an elderly man and woman – I don't remember their name, but they are so nice and easy to talk with. Jacques Lauriau was the other guest. He is a friend of

M. Rémond's younger brother Claude. He's about 35, not at all attractive but very interesting.

We had our usual "guest" menu of roast beef, fried potatoes, and last night we also had Brussels sprouts. Then salad, cheese, and dessert. Mr. Rémond was sitting next to Johanna, and just about talked her ear off. I was between Mme. Gazery (I think) and M. Lauriau. For once, thank goodness, Louise and I didn't have to entertain after dinner. I think I would have screamed if someone had asked us to play and sing. We had after dinner coffee, and then everyone talked. Jacques and I talked and talked. It was the first time since before our vacation that I really felt confident with my French. He asked me to go out with him to see some of the sights of Paris when he returns from winter sports in Switzerland – which will be around the 5th of February. I said I'd love to. He's so much like Jose Ferrer was in the film about Toulouse Lautrec but he is very interesting – and I don't pass up chances to see more of Paris.

Last night Louise, Johanna, and I decided to go to Chartres this Sunday. I certainly hope the weather is good.

Pretty soon it will be money sending time again. But wait until I can write about the cost of our trip. I can go can't I? We haven't all met with Mr. Hochwald yet to get prices, etc., but we shall very soon.

Thursday, January 24 , 1957

Last night I went to Jean-Louis' for dinner. When I arrived Susan and Michel (J.L.'s cousin) were already there. Madame Baut prepared the meal for us. She is so sweet. J.L.'s little sister Florence was there in bed with a slight cold. We went in to say hello to her. I've never seen her before. She is precious – the face of an angel. She looks straight out of a Renoir painting. Before dinner we had an aperitif of that delicious port I love so much. It was so easy to speak French last night. We had a wonderful meal. First we had omelet with tomatoes and mushrooms, then sausage, ham and salad, cheese, and peach pie – rather tart. It was really delicious. We sat and talked – didn't leave the table until ten. Jean-Louis had told me that his mother said that Pierre Bernac was a homosexual. I couldn't believe it, so last night I asked her about it. She said that it was known everywhere that Bernac is homosexual and that his "friend" is Poulenc! I knew they were great friends, gave concerts together, etc. Today I asked Madame Alvernhe about it, and she said "Bien sur" he and Poulenc were homosexuals.

Back to last night. After dinner we had a drink, then got a taxi and went to Le Club Sexy – one of the most popular night clubs. It's small inside, and done all in red and black. They have the greatest jazz combo that played progressive jazz à la Brubeck and others. There is no dancing until after the show. We drank champagne. The spectacle had many attractions, the main one being Pierre Dudan – a handsome singer who writes most of his songs. He has written so many things that we sing at home even! He was really good. There was also a funny quartet, an acrobat, a mind-reader, an American with his marionettes who was wonderful. I've never seen such marvelous puppets. Then interspersed between all the above mentioned attractions were the strip-teasers. It was the second strip show I've seen in my life – you remember the first in New Orleans. And they stripped – completely! There were even men-strippers! At first I was of course shocked and embarrassed and everything else, but later it became so natural that it didn't even bother me. The women were beautiful and didn't do repulsive dances like those "things" did in New Orleans. It was enlightening to say the least! The show didn't end until three. Then we danced (on the stage) until about three-thirty. I was so tired and sleepy, I insisted on leaving. Susan and Michel wanted to stay a little longer, so J.L. and I took a taxi home. It was really a lovely evening – I enjoyed it thoroughly. Jean-Louis is really nice to me, and I'm so mean to him.

Friday, January 25

Believe it or not we went to the theater last night to see Racine's *Berenice* for 80f. which is about 25¢. We went and stood in line just before it started (faire le queue) and bought the bargain tickets – Bon Marché. They do that at practically all the theaters – put cheap tickets for good seats on sale just about an hour before performance time. Of course you're not always sure of getting a seat that way especially when the play is really popular. The play wasn't really very good, but it was interesting to see after having read it. I understood everything – I guess because being a tragedy, all the lines were spoken more slowly.

Today at noon Madame Rémond said that her cousin Marie-Lise – the one who had tea with us the other day – had called and invited me to go out with her and her fiancé and the fiancé's friend. They're going dancing tonight. I'm so tickled to be going out with them.

My feet are in such a mess! All this walking we do has really ruined them. I have huge corns on my little toes. But the worse thing is my heels. They look horrible – they're twice as big as they were. My left heel is really painful, It feels bruised. I can hardly walk in any pair of shoes. I think those "kitten" shoes helped ruin them. They were so painful to break in, but I kept plugging – determined to wear them. I don't know whether to go the doctor or not. Any suggestions?

I hate to keep asking for money, but all the shops are having their big sales now – even the big names. I'd like to look around and see what I might find. Also, I found out about a seamstress who makes beautiful suits and coats – using Dior, Balmain, etc. for patterns – and she's inexpensive. I'd love to have a coat made. I think I could get one for about $25.

Don't worry about my turning up my nose at cuisine à la Woodall. I dream about turnip greens, green onions, cornbread, country ham, corn, crowder peas, spinach, squash, green beans, riced potatoes, baked potatoes, homemade pies, and I could go on forever!

Saturday morning, January 26, 1957

Last night turned out to be below my expectations. In the first place it rained. When I got to the meeting place at the Étoile I met my date. His name is Jean-Louis something. (I can't get away from it.) He is from Algeria, has studied in Paris two years, is going to the U.S. this summer. He's ugly, short, but intelligent and rather interesting. Marie-Lise's fiancé is sort of strange – has a Jesus Christ beard – huge cow-like eyes and doesn't say much. We went to a French movie on the Champs-Élysées – *Au Traverse à Paris* – which was about the black market during the German occupation. It was a comedy, but it was so moving. I understood it very well. After the movie we went to a café for something to drink, then to this place for dancing – all on the Champs. The dancing place was real nice, sort of gaudy. The orchestra was fair. I saw thousands of cute men – and there I was with my date! He danced well enough – but!

We came home about two thirty. They wanted me to go out with them again tonight, but I couldn't bear it, so I said I already had tickets for the opera. I'm sure I'll have to go out with them next week. Oh well, I guess I just have to learn to ignore my dates and be interested only in the places and the other people. I really was a little disappointed.

That's all for now. Our exams come up the 12, 14, 15, and 19 of February – so I'm having to study more now. I'm only scared of the art history exam – it will be given by the Sorbonne, and I dread it.

P.S. Are Fords really selling as fast as *Time* magazine says they are?

Sunday, Jan 27, 1957

Yesterday afternoon I went to the concert to hear Elizabeth Swartzkopf. It was marvelous. The program was the overture to *The Marriage of Figaro*, Aria from *Cosi fan Tutti*, a new symphony by the French composer Dutilleux, five German lieder of R. Strauss, and *Le Tricorne* by De Falla. The orchestra was magnificent, especially on the Dutilleux, who was in the audience to hear the debut of his piece. But Swartzkopf was the main attraction She had so many curtain calls, finally consented to sing an encore. She's short and sort of fat, not at all pretty, but her voice is unbelievable. Her tones are the purest I've ever heard. Each note, each phrase is a masterpiece of technique and interpretation. She really held the audience spellbound. It was the best concert I've heard in Paris. I'm going to go hear her again next week when she gives a concert with only a piano for accompaniment and there is no orchestra on the program. She's going to do Shubert, Brahms, and Wolf.

As I was leaving the concert yesterday I noticed two boys as they came down the steps from the floor above me. The cutest one and I sort of hung eyes a minute, then they were in line behind me waiting to go downstairs. They looked so French – I was thinking to myself how typically French student-ish the cute one looked in his duffle coat and everything. Then I realized they were speaking American in a Virginian accent. I was so surprised, I turned around and told him (cute one) how surprised I was. He said he thought surely I was French. We began talking. He graduated from U. of Virginia, knows Hi Petter pretty well, is living over here in The Latin Quarter – will be here about two more months – then he has to go into the army. He and his friend (also from Va.) walked with me to the Metro. He took my name, address, and phone number, and said he would call me soon. He's so nice and I was walking on air all the way home.

After dinner last night Sandy and Susan and Sandy's French roommate came over. They came in our room, drank Benedictine, and talked. Sandy's roommate, Edith, is precious. She has long auburn hair and big blue eyes, speaks four languages, is studying to be an interpreter. She really is fun to be with. She was good for us because we spoke French all night. About ten p.m. we went to the Cité Universitaire to a dance at the Norwegian house. Every week a different house has a dance. It was the first time I had even seen the Cité Universitaire. It is made up of large houses for each country – U.S., Holland, Germany, Norway, Sweden, etc. It looks like a big university in the U.S.

The dance was crowded with students. The music was all American. When we first entered we were immediately whisked off to dance. My first partner was a little bitty boy who's studying to be a dentist. He was awfully nice, but a little too possessive. I excused myself and went into another room on the pretext of hunting Louise. On my way back into the first room a tall blond Frenchman asked me to dance. He could hardly believe that I was American because he said my whole aspect was completely French. Must be something to that since two people thought it in the same day! Robert Genet was the blonde's name. I spent the rest of the evening dancing with him. Since the Metro stops running at one, I told him I had to leave at twelve twenty. He said he was with some friends in his car, and would be glad to take me home. I asked if there were room for Louise too, and he said yes. About one twenty we decided to leave. His friends weren't ready, so he took Louise and me on home. He seems to be very nice – a little strange though. He's studying for foreign affairs. He took my name, address, and number, but I don't expect to hear from him.

Monday, January 28

Sunday morning we were awakened at eight by Susan's phone call telling us she couldn't go to Chartres with us. It's a good thing she called or we wouldn't have gotten up until no telling when, because the alarm clock had stopped running. We rushed like crazy to eat breakfast, dress, and get to the bus stop.

The bus had trouble after we got on – wouldn't start – so we lost about ten minutes. We finally got to Gare Montparnasse to catch the train which we thought left at nine twenty five. We arrived at nine twenty, and the train had already departed at nine fifteen. So we had to wait another hour for the next train. When we arrived in Chartres we went directly to the Cathedral from the station – it's only a few blocks away. The Cathedral is really magnificent. It dominates not only the city, but the whole countryside since Chartres is in the middle of a large plain and the Cathedral is so tall it can be seen for miles. The two towers are wonderful; one is a tower of Roman architecture and the other is Gothique. They're like two fantasies atop the Cathedral. I shan't attempt to describe the Cathedral – it's beyond words. It has to be seen to understand it.

We've been studying it in our art class, and it was so good to see things and suddenly understand what the professor was talking about. The splendor of Chartres is in the stained glass windows. They are so rich and vibrant in color – the blues are unbelievable. It's easily understood why the vitraux (stained-glass windows) of Chartres are the most famous in the world. The sculpture, too, is of course magnificent. In the crypt of the Cathedral there is a piece of sculpture from the jubé of the Cathedral that was burned in the 12th century. It is the Virgin, Joseph, and Jesus. The Virgin is leaning from her bed looking into the cradle where Jesus lies. Joseph is arranging the cover on Mary's bed. It's so marvelous, so simple and sweet. The lines are perfect. But my favorite of all the many statues is the one of Christ on the façade of the southern extreme of the transept. It's the first time I've seen any portrayal of Christ which suits exactly my conception of him.

About three there was a vesper service in the Cathedral. It was beautiful and having Chartres for a setting made it gorgeous. The organ, the boys' choir, the incense and the Cathedral itself really made one aware of God and his mysteries, of man and his potential.

Before heading back to the station, we walked around Chartres. It's a marvelous old city – many of the wooden houses from the Middle Ages are still standing. Even those that were originally around the church are still there. That's one thing that Notre Dame de Paris lacks – the old setting it was originally meant to have.

The weather was so gorgeous yesterday – the sky was the bluest I've seen since several days in Dijon. It made the old town and the Cathedral even more beautiful.

We left Chartres at six. The train was so hot and I was so tired that I slept all the way to Paris. I had not had but five and one-half hours sleep Friday night and six hours Saturday night. When we got home M. and Mme. were out. There was dinner on the table and a note telling us to heat the soup. We did and we ate. I nearly fell asleep eating. The Rémonds came in just as we finished. They had gone window shopping and then to a cabaret to see a musical variety show. That's the first time that I've known of their being out together like that since we've been here. We talked with them a while, then went to bed.

I have a lesson – my first real one with Bernac this afternoon at three thirty.

Tuesday January 29

My voice lesson with Bernac was interesting. We spent the whole lesson (a little more than thirty minutes) on exercises with vowels. I have another lesson with him tomorrow. I really do like him, his methods for breathing, etc.

After my lesson I met Louise and we had a cup of chocolate, then came home and studied. After dinner, we studied again and I was in pajamas. About nine-forty Mike Margulies called me and wanted me to go to the movies right then. I just couldn't go then for I was in pajamas and I had to write a theme for today. Then he asked me to go see *Tea and Sympathy* with Ingrid Bergman – it's the hit of the season, and I of course accepted with great pleasure. I really was thrilled because I didn't expect to get to see it for financial reasons and because tickets are hard to get. I'm sure Mike has some sort of connections because so many of his wealthy relatives live here. Anyway, the point is I'm tickled to death to be going.

About the trip to Spain. Mr. Hochwald figures it will cost around $100, because now with the fuel shortage, there are only first class trains running definitely in Spain. We probably will get a reduction because if you travel so many miles in one country you get a reduction. I'm really counting on it costing less than $100. We're getting hotels this time with only breakfast included – if we get any meal included at all. Food is so cheap in Spain. We decided we could manage much better buying our meals ourselves. We're going to try to get hotels even without breakfast. The problem is they are reluctant to accept you unless you have at least one meal there.

Wed. January 30

Last night I saw *Tea and Sympathy* – it was wonderful. Ingrid Bergman was great. She is really talented – she speaks French with only a slight, slight accent. The play is really powerful but I'm afraid it lacked something that it would have gained if it were in English. The American setting, the American situation, the American names just didn't completely adapt in French. This was especially evident in the first act. After the first act it was less noticeable. Ingrid Bergman is certainly girlish looking to be forty. After the play we went to Pam-Pam's and had a chocolate sundae – then came home. Mike and I both had classes this morning. Mike is so much fun.

Thursday, January 31, 1957

I had another voice lesson with Bernac. He really tears your voice apart, but of course that's the only way to learn. At least he does it in a nice way.

Yesterday at noon Jean-Louis called me and wanted me to go to the theater last night. Tired as I was, I accepted, since we were going to see *Amphytron 38* by Jean Girardoux with Jean Pierre Aumont in the lead, but there were no free tickets last night. Instead we went to see Shaw's *Caesar and Cleopatra*. It was excellent and beautifully translated into French. I understood more than I ever have understood before. Shaw is really a genius – sometimes very cruel with his genius. The funniest thing in the play was Caesar's favorite slave and companion Britannicus – from Britain. They had him speaking French in an English accent and it was the funniest thing I've ever heard. I'm so glad he did because without the English accent his part and purpose would have been completely lost.

After the play we walked Boulevard St. Michel to a little restaurant near the Sorbonne and Jean-Louis ate his supper. I had some ice cream and hot chocolate. Jean-Louis said that his mother said that she would be very pleased if he should marry me! I almost fainted. I told him that was so far out of the question that I didn't even want to talk about it. I really thought it was funny. After he took his good sweet time eating that meal (I was in such a hurry to leave because I was so sleepy) we took a taxi home. It was a very nice and entertaining evening. I never expected to be see my first Shavian play in French.

Our Spain trip is positive now. We changed our itinerary to make the trip less expensive and less tiring as far as trains go. The cost for trains and hotel will run about $85.00. There will be no reduction for traveling so many miles as I had thought there would be. Our meals will cost us almost nothing. Dr. Smithers said he paid 75¢ for the biggest most elaborate meal he had. He said the very highest priced meals are $1.50. We changed our itinerary also so that we could stick to the south of Spain – Andalusia – which is the really "Spanish" part of Spain. We're going from Paris to Madrid, Toledo, Granada, Málaga, Seville, Córdoba, and back to Madrid. It really sounds wonderful.

We just finished dinner. We had Louise's fruitcake for dessert. It's so funny. Louise's mother sent her a fruitcake and some date nut rolls for Christmas. She sent them in November and they came yesterday! They're just as fresh and moist as can be. The Rémonds were charmed with the cake. Then we drank liqueur and talked. We discussed religions tonight – differences in Mormons and Protestants – Catholics, etc. M. is so funny – he's really much more broad-minded than she is far as tolerance goes. He never agrees with her on big points and he gets so animated. He's usually right too – at least in my opinion. They're both so wonderful. I think not having the children here for more than a month is the best thing for them right now – really is better for us!

Friday, February 1

I had my third voice lesson today. It was a great improvement and I'm much encouraged.

This morning after class Louise and I went to Mr. Hochwald's (our travel agent) office to arrange things for this summer. He's going to draw us up a tentative itinerary, arrange things for Genie and her friend who are coming over. We wanted to go ahead and make plans because reservations are hard to get in the summer when things are so crowded.

After we left Mr. Hochwald's, we went to window-shop and headed for Dior's. It's so beautiful and exclusive. The only thing they have in the window is one pair of shoes! We were ashamed to go in looking like we did – so we didn't. We did go in some little shops near Dior's where they were having sales. We tried on some beautiful coats – on sale they were $150 and 160! We have found a place to have a coat made. We figured with material and the seamstress it would cost at the most $30. I'm dying for a straight, straight dark gray coat. They are so chic and so Parisian.

We're having the most wonderful weather now – it's almost like spring. And yesterday the Rémonds received a big supply of fuel oil – enough to last comfortably till the end of winter.

Mother, I've been thinking, since Daddy can't come over at all this summer, why don't you come anyway. You could come this summer and travel with us, but I really think you'd enjoy traveling with us Easter more than you would the summer tour. Italy is the biggest attraction of all, and we're going to have about 2 ½ weeks for Easter to go there. You could come over for a week before vacation, which starts the 12th day of April and lasts until around the 1st of May. Then you could stay in Paris at least two or three weeks more. While you were here you and Louise and I could go to the Loire Valley and visit the château country some weekend. That would be the perfect time to do that. Of course you could just come Easter and stay till I come home in August! Mr. Hochwald will arrange our trip to Italy too. He's so good about doing it and arranging things so they'll be the least expensive as possible. We always travel second class on the train and stay in middle-class hotels, but it's much more fun that way. All the girls would love to have you along I assure you. We could have so much fun. You could really learn Paris. What do you think? Spring in Paris and Italy is reported to be next to heaven, it's so divine. Come on and come, Mother.

This morning coming from the Sorbonne we rode a different bus route. I saw some marvelous sites I had not seen before. That's what's so wonderful about Paris – it's infinite. We rode by Notre Dame – which stands so proud and lies in the very heart of Paris, also by the Institute de Manse where the formidable (in the English sense of the word) Academie Française is located. Across the Seine, through the courtyard of the Louvre, I love to go there and look through the Arc du Carrousel and see in the distance – in a perfectly straight line – the Obelisk of Place de la Concorde, and the Arc de Triomphe at the end of the Champs. The Arc is magnificent. The Champs goes uphill a little so that when you look at the Arc there seems to be nothing behind it on the other side – everything seems to end there. It makes a nice stopping place. I wonder if the Arc between now an eternity looks like the Arc de Triomphe? I wonder if there is such an Arc between now and eternity?

Saturday morning

I just returned from going to market with Madame. This is the most beautiful day – so I decided since I had never been with her, I'd go today. All the marketplaces are very near here. There is a whole street with nothing but little marketplaces. They are quite modern and have just everything. Then there is a big market kind of like our marketplace where she buys the meat, vegetables. We took three big baskets to put everything in. I really enjoyed doing it. She was glad to have me along too.

This afternoon I went to Jean-Louis'. His mother and little sister were there. We stayed only a few minutes, then Jean-Louis and I went to the Bois, which is practically at his front door. The Bois de Bologne is a huge park on the western side of Paris. It was so beautiful and so warm today that I couldn't resist going. I didn't even need my coat. The park is beautiful, even in the winter. Trees, two lakes, everything. It's so vast we didn't begin to see it all. We walked around the lakes, were going to rent a rowboat, but there was such a crowd waiting for them we decided not to. We did take the little ferry across to the island in the middle of the big lake where there is a darling café – like a Swiss chalet – and we had tea there. Everybody was in the park – babies, dogs, fishermen, artists, lovers, Chinese, English, Americans – it was so warm and balmy I felt like I was in New Orleans. We were in the park from about 3:45 to 6:20. The sun began to go down and the sky was all colors. When it is pretty in Paris it surpasses everything! I'd left my big old purse at JL's while we walked so I had to go back and get it. Then he saw me home on the Metro.

For dinner tonight we had crêpes Suzette that Madame made especially for today. Today is Chandeleur Day – which has the same significance as our Groundhog Day – only Chandeleur is a Catholic holiday. Madame brought the crêpes in burning in alcohol – they looked wonderful and tasted even better. Toward the end of dinner John Donaher called me. He's the boy who works at SHAPE who is engaged. Poor thing, he's been confined to the post for 15 days now because he didn't have his pass in the PX or something. He gets his freedom Monday and we're going out Thursday night.

After dinner we rushed to the Theatre de Champs Colores to hear Victoria de los Angeles sang. We had horrible seats – the cheapest. I only saw her when she came on and off the stage. She has an exquisite voice, but didn't seem to get settled until the second half of the program. When she really sang magnificently. She's very charming and gracious.

Sunday, February 3, 1957

We did have a good dinner. I was starved to death, so as usual I ate like a horse. Monsieur was in one of his more talkative moods, so after dinner we drank coffee – the four of us – smoked English cigarettes (not me) and drank Cointreau liquor (which I love). We talked about everything. I love them so much.

I studied from about 3:30 till 5:00. Then we went to a concert to hear Philippe Entremont play Rachmaninoff's Second Concerto. Entremont is so young – my age I'd say. He plays well, but youthfully. Also on the program were Debussy's two nocturnes, *Nuages* and *Fetes*. I never tire of them. Ravel's *Valse* concluded the program. I had a hard time sitting in my seat during that "valse" – I was dying to dance.

Mother, think seriously about coming Easter – it certainly would be wonderful.

Tuesday, February 5th

The money came yesterday. $300 seems like so much, but I'm wondering if it will pay $125 for rent, about $100 for the trip to Spain (including food), and about $36 for piano rent. We haven't paid any rent yet for that piano since we've been here. It's $9 a month apiece and we've been using it four months. I think that's a ridiculous price to pay. I'm going to try to get Dr. Smithers to talk to the lady who owns the pension and see if she won't lower the price.

This is my money status: Out of the $300 I'll have $19 after I pay rent, trip (which will more than likely be a little over $100) and piano rent and voice lessons. I've still got $60 in francs which I've been saving from the last money I got. I've been saving it for clothes, but I guess I'll go on and use it if I have to.

So I'm all set I guess. I think I'm going to buy a new pair of shoes before our trip. My wedge heel shoes are just about shot, and I just don't think I'll ever be able to wear those kitten shoes again as they hurt so badly. My feet are better – I've been soaking them and creaming them all the time. If they keep improving I won't go to the doctor. But I know it was those kittens that made my heels get in such a shape.

We're still having marvelously beautiful days. I just hope it doesn't stop. And they say it's even better in April and May – marvelous – the prettiest spring anywhere – so you'll have to come, Mother.

I had another lesson with Bernac yesterday. Things are really improving, he's so good. I noticed a pamphlet on his piano yesterday written in English – about a music school for advanced Americans held each summer at Fontainebleau from July 1 to Sept. 1. All the famous French musicians and others teach there. For the pianists there are master lessons with Casadesus and Rubenstein; for theorists and composers there are lessons with Nadia Boulanger, for voice students there are master lessons with Bernac and Martinelli. It's so wonderful sounding I'd love to go, but it's out of the question of course. It's such a pity that people can't do everything they want to do, isn't it?

Last night Louise and I went to a piano recital by one of the pupils of Louise's piano teacher. The woman is well-known in Paris, played with symphonies, and is a wonderful pianist. She nearly ruined her pieces, though, by singing, rather, humming while she played in the most horrible sounding hum I've ever heard! I met Mme. Bascuret, Louise's teacher. She's in her 70's and looks in her early 50's. She's so charming, but poor thing, she's crippled so badly she can hardly get around.

John Donaher called this morning and said he was freed, so we're going out tonight – where, I don't know.

Wednesday morning

I had the best time last night! I'm so sorry John is engaged. It was just awful the way the night began. He had said he would met me at Pam-Pam's – the American restaurant. I only knew of one Pam-Pam's, so I said O.K., and didn't ask any question. After much confusion of me being at one Pam-Pam's and John being at the other, we finally connected forty-five minutes later, sat down, and had a drink and talked. He told me all about why he was "in jail" for three weeks. The army is really so ridiculous. Thank goodness I'm not a man.

We left Pam-Pam's and headed for a little place that Don Healy told John about. We had the hardest time finding it. It is very near Boulevard St. Michel, is called Cave Belie. We walked down a sneaky little alley into the place, then down and down stairs to the main room. It looks like the crypt of ancient church pillars, voûtes, etc. The atmosphere is much like The Lapin Agile. There is a guitar player, an accordionist, a folk-song singer, a comedienne, everything. Everyone sings together. I was the only American girl there and the Master of Ceremonies kept picking on me. (John doesn't speak a word of French.) He first asked me if I thought men were pigs. I said "No, not at all." He said I was wrong, then they sang a song about men and women being pigs. Later he came back and asked me to scream as loud as I could. I asked him why, and he said so we can all hear you. So I screamed my best scream and everyone laughed. Then he told me that that little scream wouldn't scare anybody. Then they sang a song about screaming. Of course I loved being the guinea pig. John seemed to get a kick out of it too. We stayed until about 12:30. John had to catch the bus back to SHAPE at 1:00, so we took a taxi to the Étoile where John left, then the taxi took me on home. I really enjoy John's company. He has so many wonderful ideas. He feels just like I do about Europe and Americans – well I guess not exactly the same way. Anyway, I wish he weren't engaged!

This morning after class Louise and I window shopped for coats on sale to get some ideas about our own. I know exactly what I want now.

At noon Jacques Lauriau called. He's the friend of the family who came to dinner not long ago, and who is so old. He asked me to go to the theater tomorrow night, so I am.

After he hung up Jean-Louis phoned – I'm going out with him tonight – probably to the theater. I don't know what I'll do next year when I can't go out every night that I want to!

Thursday morning February 7, 1957

Last night Jean-Louis and I went to the theater to see Montherlant's *Celles qu'on prend dans ses bras* "Those you take in your arms." I didn't like it at all – it's the first play I've seen in Paris that I didn't like. The theater is near Place de la Concorde, so we walked there and back. We came straight home from the Theater because I had to get to bed relatively early.

On the way home we found ourselves is the deepest conversation about love, marriage, and religion. Jean-Louis changes so when we talk seriously – he is so adult – not at all the Jean-Louis that irritates me so much sometimes. He really is so intelligent and sensitive to life – he understands things so much – he seems so wise. I feel so terrible because he loves me so much. It's almost worse to be loved too much than not to be loved at all. I hope I never forget Jean-Louis – I hope I always think of him with a tender-tender feeling – my poor little Frenchman.

Later

I had a horrible voice lesson today. My throat has not been normal these past two days and I just couldn't sing worth a fizz today. It's so discouraging.

About coming home this summer. Genie wrote Louise and said that if it were all the same to her, Genie would like to switch and come home on the boat and let Louise fly. Genie's friend would probably like to come on the boat with Genie, so I told Louise to tell Genie that I would be glad to change with Lucy and fly with Louise. We'd leave around the same date as the sailing date. What do you think? I think it would be so much fun to fly home. Louise and I are both dying to stay in New York about two days before we come home. We can stay at her friend Theresa's for no cost at all. Then I could come home on the train, plane, or you all could come to N.Y. I really think it would be better if I just came home alone, but then it's still quite a long time away. I do want to see George on my way home.

I'm sitting here waiting for Jacques to come. He's late now – I thought he'd be the extremely punctual type. I wish I knew how old he is – he practically grey-headed. People will probably think I'm his daughter!

This afternoon Madame's cousin Marie-Lise called and wanted me to go with her, her fiancé, and that ugly friend of theirs to a ball Saturday night. I said I'd love to. This ball is the biggest one in Paris – we heard about it in Dijon. It's given by the commerce school. There are 30 bands – one in each room. I'm sure it will be so horribly crowded that we can't dance, but it will be interesting to see.

Friday morning, February 8, 1957

Jacques finally came last night. We drove to the theater in his practically new car, sat in expensive seats. The play was wonderful – *Amphitryon 38* by Jean Giraudoux. Jean-Pierre Aumont was wonderful, and so handsome! The setting was beautiful. After the play we went to Pam-Pam's on the Champs-Élysées. Jacques is very good company, however he has an accent that is so difficult to understand. I noticed last night for the first time that he has a big bald spot on the back of his head! Next Friday night he's getting a friend for Louise and we're all going dancing. He's the only person I've dated who tries to go to the most expensive places – he's extremely rich. Maybe I'll make it to the Lido yet!

I'm getting ready to go to the Smithers' and get my money so I can pay my rent.

Yes, it will be warm in Spain – and we'll be in the south of Spain so we're almost assured of warm weather.

Saturday, February 9, 1957

I didn't go to the ball with the 30 bands after all. My throat isn't normal, I had studying, and it has rained all day. Somehow the idea of a large crowd of people and smoke-filled rooms didn't appeal to me at all, so when Marie-Lise called to tell me what time to meet them, I told her about my throat and that I just couldn't go. She said they had not yet bought their tickets, so it was all right. I suppose I should be ashamed to miss the biggest ball in Paris, but I'm not at all regretful. Yesterday I spent studying – except for yesterday morning when I went to the Smithers' for money and the Kodak shop to pick up my pictures.

Today after lunch Louise gave Monsieur the new Time Magazine to read an article about the "oil shortage" in the U.S. It was so funny because there was a line in the article where some man said the oil men had been S.O.B.'s to the public. Monsieur was reading, when he looked up and said "What is S.O.B.'s?" Louise couldn't think – neither could I – I kept thinking sobs, soles – then I thought – oh no – got up to see – and sure enough it was S.O.B.'s. I burst out laughing – so did Louise – then we tried to explain it to him – try to explain an expression like that to a foreigner and how difficult it is! It was really funny.

Tonight after supper we got into a long discussion on Franco-American relations, the last war, advantages of travel, etc. I'm so proud to be with the Rémonds – they are so intelligent and I learn so much from them. I wish I could have talked all night with them – we talked for about 1½ hours which hurt my study time, but was worth it. The Rémonds think that had America told Hitler in 1939 that if he touched France they would protect her, the war would have been stopped within a week. There are many Europeans who have lost faith in America and become indifferent neutralists because they have seen that America cannot be depended on – she says she'll help eventually – then makes countries wait years before she decides what to do. It's certainly a problem to ponder. I wonder if we have been too selfish with our prestige?

Monday, February 11

I had the most wonderful day yesterday! Well, not all day – yesterday morning and afternoon I studied. Then at 5:00 I had a date. Louise, Jim, John, and I had planned to go to a concert, then to the Reine Pédauque to eat a fabulous dinner. Jim ended up not being able to go, so Louise and I went with John to the concert, then John and I went to eat. The concert was excellent – Daniel Waylenberg was the soloist – they did the *Benvenuto Cellini* overture by Berlioz. The Nocturne and Scherzo from Mendelssohn's *Midsummer's Night Dream*, the Ravel Concerto for the left hand, *Rhapsody on a Theme of Paganini* by Rachmaninoff, and Stravinsky's *Firebird Suite*. After the concert John and I walked down Ave. de Kleber to the Étoile, which was illuminated – the Arc de Triomphe that is – and looked gorgeous. Then we walked down the Champs. The night was so beautiful – the moon, the stars, the light wind. We talked about such interesting things – John is so smart. We talked about war, the future, the present day political aspect – he almost made me a Democrat! We took the Metro from Franklin D. to St. Augustin, and walked from there to the Reine Pédauque. It is such a wonderful restaurant – 1550 francs for the most fabulous meal from a choice that is incredible. This is what I had: first, snails – the best I've ever eaten; then I had a dish made from lobster meat with a lobster-cream sauce that was delicious – I've never even heard of such a dish before; for the main course I had roasted chicken in a thick wine sauce with mushrooms and a tiny potato. Then came the cheese – I had camembert – the best I've tasted. For dessert I had a meringue shell filled with vanilla and praline ice cream. During the course of the dinner we were served rosé wine, red wine, white wine, champagne, an aperitif between the main course and the cheese, and coffee afterwards. When you come, Mother, we'll have to go there. I paid for my meal – that was our original agreement.

John and I talked constantly through the whole meal, which made it even nicer. I found out all about his fiancée, his family, his work, etc. I like him so much. I'm so glad we're going to keep dating. After dinner – we began at 9:15 and didn't stop until 11:30! – we walked. We walked to the Madeline, then on to the Place de la Concorde and the Seine. John had never walked down under the bridges on the level of the water, so we did that. The Seine is splendid at night with the reflections in the water from the lights of the bridges. It smelled so good with the wind blowing slightly and steadily. It was so calmly romantic and beautiful. Suddenly we realized that it was 12:45 and John had to be at the Étoile at 1:00 to catch that awful bus back to SHAPE.

We ran to the Place – no taxis. We ran up the Champs, finally got a cab, whizzed to the Étoile, John jumped out just in time to catch the bus, and the taxi took me on home. End of a perfectly wonderful evening – the very best I've had yet. John is free Friday, so he's coming in Friday morning and we're spending the day together seeing Paris – until 4:30 – when he as to go back to SHAPE.

The horrible part of last night was that Louise forgot to leave me the key after she used it, and I had to ring the bell and get M. & Mme. awake. M. came to the door with almost hate in his eyes. They make such a to-do over things like that – although this was only the 2nd time all year that it has happened. The first time Mme. forgot to leave us the key. They haven't said anything about it today, so I guess they've forgiven us.

Tuesday night, February 12, 1957

Well, I just had my first exam; we had to write a composition – either on Molière or Racine, and I chose Racine. I knew the material, etc., it was just putting it into French that was especially difficult. I did all right, but I've done better. I'm not really worried about any of my exams but art history – the only exam at the Sorbonne. It, too, will be a composition. The language again will be a problem and this time the material too. But I guess I'll pull through. We have our music history exam tomorrow morning. Susan and Eugenie are coming over tonight to study with us for it.

This afternoon I had the best voice lesson I've had yet with Bernac. It was so encouraging. I hate to tell him that I'll be gone for two weeks now!

I wore my hair in a ponytail today! The first time in my whole life! Everybody liked it, but it's still not really long enough to look good that way. I hardly know myself anymore with my long hair!

Yesterday I did nothing but go to class and study, so it doesn't take much space.

I had a letter from cousin Carole explaining all about the wedding. Sometimes I think there's something wrong with me. Everybody else at home and at school is getting married, and I'm not even interested in marriage right now! There are so many things I want to do yet before I marry. The thought of settling down, washing dishes, diapers, cleaning house, etc. seems so far off and beyond me! I'm looking forward to school so much next year – and after that – who knows?

Wednesday, February 13, 1957

Well, I had my music history exam this morning. I did all right on it, too. I just wish he had given us questions instead of a composition to write. That's the hard part, because it's in French. Susan and Eugenie came over last night, and we studied till nearly 12:00. It's been easy for me because I had a lot of it last year, and my notebooks that you sent me have just everything in them.

The morning after the exam I went to the Smithers' to practice. Somehow I always practice better on Wednesday morning than any other time.

John Donaher called me just before lunch. The poor thing – he's in the American hospital with his ulcer – they think it's ruptured. I feel so sorry for him. This means of course that we won't have our date Friday. They're going to make tests and things, so he'll probably be in for several days. I think I'm going to go see him tomorrow night during visiting hours. The funny thing is I dreamed last night that I was in the hospital and that John came to see me!

I just went out and bought some shoes. I paid almost $15.00 for them. They're plain, with a tiny heel, and they fit.

Thursday, February 14th – Happy Valentine's

No more exams until Tuesday. The exam this afternoon in Composition was sort of easy I thought. I hope I did as well as I think I did! Now I have the week-end to study.

I had forgotten that it was Valentine's today until I got a few Valentines from home. People here hardly celebrate it. Louise and I bought Mme. some carnations – a dozen – for Valentine's. She was so surprised and pleased. She thought Valentine's was only for lovers. She said no one had ever wished her happy Valentine before.

Our exam wasn't over till about 5:30. I rushed home – as fast as one can rush on a bus – and bought John a red carnation and a funny card, then ran home to eat. Madame had fixed my dinner early for me so I could get to the hospital for the visiting hours (7:00 to 9:00). I ate quickly, then caught the Metro about 7:00 – got to the hospital a little after 8:00. I love to go out there – it's so exciting with everyone going and coming. John was surprised to see me – he didn't think I would really come all the way out there. He was so cute about accepting the one little flower and the card. We talked and talked – I took my slides and my viewer and let him see them. Visiting hours are supposedly over at 9:00, but I stayed till ten, then walked about three blocks, took a taxi to the Metro, took the Metro home. I like John so much – he really appreciated my coming.

Friday morning, February 15th, 1957

I assure you, Mother, no one has any objection to your coming to Italy with us. They all said they would love to have you along.

This weekend will be a busy one with studying and social engagements. This afternoon at 5:00 I have a voice lesson, after which I'm meeting Jean-Louis for tea. At 9:30 Louise and I are going dancing with Jacques Lauriau and his cousin. Tomorrow night I'm going dancing with Marie-Lise and her friends. Sunday afternoon I'm going to the races with Jean-Louis and his family, and Sunday night I have a date with John. Really, I'm so lucky to be going out like I do and seeing things. Most of the girls in our group don't have anyone at all to date, and it really is sad.

Saturday, February 16, 1957

Last night Louise and I went out with Jacques and his cousin Pierre. Pierre is tall, bald (sort of), with a black mustache that goes clear across his face! Louise and I laughed all night at our two "handsome" men. They took us to the Club Champs-Élysées – a very elegant, expensive place for dancing. There were three orchestras which rotated – thus there was music all the time. We had a good time dancing, talking. Jacques and Pierre are really entertaining. Pierre told Louise everything about everybody. He said that he is 33, Jacques is 37, Mme. Rémond is 32, and M. is 47! I was so surprised. I never thought the Rémonds were so young. Found out also that Jacques used to date Mme.! He even thought about marrying her, but Pierre said that Mme. wanted an older man with money and a name – along came Monsieur and she married him. Pierre said he thought Madame was sorry now that she married a man so much older than she. She has practically said as much to Louise and me. After Louise told me all that, all I could think about when I looked at him was – you could be my father! Anyway – we did have a good time – it's so nice to be elegant once in a while.

Marie-Louise Bernard was just here for over an hour. We're making plans for the dance at France-Amerique which will be either the last of March or the first of April. It should be really nice.

Marie-Lise called and said she had found a date for Louise, so she's going with us tonight. That was so nice of Marie-Lise to do. She's so sweet and friendly – so much more so than Marie-Louise.

Tuesday night, February 19th

Well, I'm on the train going to Spain! So much has happened, I hope I can tell it all and tell it straight.

First of all, I got the money. Thank you. Mr. Hochwald didn't want us to pay him until we came back, so I'll use that then. Now – for my past weekend.

Saturday afternoon I spent studying for my exam. Then after supper Louise and I went to the Étoile to meet Marie-Lise and her friend. They weren't there, but Jean-Louis – the ugly Algerian I went out with before – was waiting for us. He said that Marie-Lise and Phillippe were eating in a restaurant and would be there soon. We waited for them in their car which Jean-Louis was driving. While we were waiting, Jean-Louis told us that Phillippe's sister and her fiancé were going too, but no other boys – in other words there was no one for Louise. That made us so mad, we decided we'd figure some way to get home early. Finally Marie-Lise and Phillippe and the other two came, and off we started. We drove and drove until I was sure we were out of Paris. Louise and I were still mad because they weren't even talking to us. We finally got to this neighborhood and drove and drove trying to find the place – although Louise and I still didn't know where we were going. Finally we stopped in front of an old, old house, which – as they had just told us belonged to a friend of theirs. We went in and discovered a party. The house was nice but nothing out of the ordinary. There were some boys (not so cute) and some girls – about 20 in all. We had an interesting time talking – two girls were German, two girls were English, one girl was South African (white) and a Moroccan boy. We danced and drank cheap champagne. Louise and I decided to play our sick act and go home, when four good-looking boys came in. We decided to stay. I of course noticed the best-looking one. We sort of "hung eyes" when he came in, then he sat down by me. We started talking and later danced. In the meantime, Louise was doing the same thing with one of the other boys who was attractive. Mine is named Pierre Comparet, age 23, journalist by profession, "tall, dark, and handsome" with green eyes. We were all having such a good time dancing an old French dance, laughing. Finally about 1:30 Marie-Lise and her friend decided to leave. We didn't want to go home and Pierre and Andre (his and Louise's friend) offered to take us home, so we stayed till about 2:30. Then I said I just had to leave. Andre had a car, but with Louise and the others there was no room for me. Pierre had a motor scooter – he wanted to take me home on that – so that's how I went home. All these French scooters have two seats on them because so many people have them and carry other people with them. It was really a riot trying to get on that thing in my tight skirt. Oh but it was so magnificent speeding along at 3 a.m. in the moonlight through the empty streets. We rode through Pigalle – quiet then at 3:00 a.m. I was singing and so was Pierre. It was so wonderful I thought I'd burst from happiness. We got home (Pierre lives in a hotel near our street) and stood out front and talked. Just as I got ready to go in, Louise and Andre drove up, so we stood and talked with them. Pierre asked to see me before I left for Spain, so we arranged to meet this afternoon after my voice lesson. We went in – end of a charming and fruitful night that at first had no hope.

I had intended to get up early Sunday morning, but of course I didn't get up until about 10:00, stumbled around and got dressed to go to Jean-Louis' house for lunch. I hurried to be there at noon because he had begged me to be there on time. When I got there only his mother was there cooking – all the rest of the family had gone to Mass and hadn't come back yet. It seems Jean-Louis had had a big night too, and hadn't come in until 6:00 a.m. So – I offered to help but Mme. Baut wouldn't let me, so I looked at a magazine.

M. Baut was the first one to come back. I hadn't seen him since he signed my voting papers in Dijon. He was so nice, we had a nice little chat. Soon the rest of the family – Jacques, Florence, and Jean-Louis all came back. We drank an aperitif, then sat down to a delicious meal. But better than the food was the company. I love Jean-Louis' family because they're so good to me and because they enjoy each other so much. We laughed and talked and had such a good time. I love little Florence – in the middle of the meal she turned to me and said, "Do you like to play baseball?" I told her all about when I used to play in school and she was quite impressed. We finally finished dinner and walked across the park to the race track. It was opening day and the place was packed. All the women were decked out in their mink coats – all colors – I saw my first full-length platinum mink coat. Every nationality was there too. It was such a gorgeous day – the grass was green, the horses gorgeous. Before each race we went to the ring where we looked at all the horses for the next race. M. Baut was so funny – he got so excited about betting that he would just leave the rest of us. We really had so much fun. I even won 200 francs – about 60¢! At

5:00 I had to leave to go meet John Donaher. I enjoyed being with the Bauts so much – I hope I can be with them again soon.

I left the race track and caught the Metro to Pam-Pam's on the Champs-Élysées where John Donaher was waiting for me. We walked clear to Notre Dame to see it illuminated – which took us about an hour. Notre Dame is magnificent at night. We climbed up on a wall to sit and watch the Cathedral – not that we expected it to do anything! We then walked across to the Left Bank to eat – we ate in a little self-service place for almost nothing. The food was surprisingly good, too. After dinner we walked and walked hunting for a little place where you can dance that John knew about. We hunted and hunted but never found it. By then we were both so pooped we just gave up. My feet were absolutely killing me. We ended up sitting on the steps going down to the Seine near Notre Dame and talking till nearly 12:30. I found out so much about John – we're good friends now – a perfect relationship. We had to play our old game of running to catch a taxi at the last minute. The whole day was really wonderful. (Please excuse this – but the train is really awful.)

Wednesday, February 20th

Yesterday morning was the exam at the Sorbonne. I think I did all right on it. We had an easy question for the composition – in fact – so easy that it was hard because it was so general. I finished early, turned in my paper, and went to the Smithers' to practice then home for lunch. After lunch I changed clothes, went to the American Express to buy pesatos. We got a rate of 49 to the dollar – the rate in Spain is 40 to the dollar. From the American Express I went to my voice lesson. While I was in the midst of singing, one of M. Bernac's friends came. I'm almost sure she is the same woman who accompanied Mme. Milleret on the recital she gave. Pierre Comparet was waiting for me after my lesson in front of Bernac's. He's so cute. He locked up his motor scooter, left it there, then we started walking – ended up an hour later in front of my house. We had crossed the Seine, the Champs-Élysées, everything. Pierre is really quite fascinating. About an hour after I left him in front of the house, the mailman came with a huge French bouquet of violets for me – from Pierre, wishing me Bon Vacance en Espagne. I was so excited! I've been dying for someone to buy me violets – and his way of sending them was so romantic.

Newcomb's 1956-57 JYA participants pose on the bow of the S.S. Liberté, along with program directors Dr. and Mrs. Smithers and their children plus the ship's captain and crew members.

Judy, Sandy, and Louise in front of the Sorbonne

Judy's Paris hosts,
M. et Mme. Gabriel Rémond,
dressed for a party

Judy beside the Seine, with her
favorite view of Notre Dame

Christmas in Tschiertschen

Above, the adorable village of Tschiertschen, scene of a magical Christmas
Below, first-time skiers Eugenie, Martha, and Judy, in makeshift ski clothes, with
sweet Herr Ackermann

First view of the Mediterranean, on the beach at Málaga: Martha, Eugenie, Sandy, Coco, and Louise, along with a curious Spaniard

Judy and the charming Jean-Louis Baut, ready to ride in the Deux Chevaux

Easter, 1957
in Rome

Above, Judy's mother, Alma Woodall, and Louise on the Spanish Steps

Below, Judy and Louise with American priests Keith Hosey
and John Wakeman, their special guides in Rome

Judy and Jean-Louis, in his ever-present dark glasses, taking a break at the Grand Bal at the Opéra.

Oh-so-suave Jean-Louis and his darling brother Jacques, in front of the Baut apartment in Paris

Handsome John Donaher, a very special "American in Paris," on the terrace of St. Germain

A

Spanish

Adventure

Thursday, February 21st

Dear Mother and Daddy,

After a delicious dinner last night Monsieur Rémond, bless his heart, drove us to the station. We met Sandy, Eugenie, and Martha with Mr. Hochwald, the travel agent. He always comes and helps us get on the train. (Coco comes tomorrow.) We had couchettes last night on the train – they weren't exactly comfortable, but better than nothing. We slept until about 7:00 this morning – had to get up to change trains at the Spanish border. Between our getting up and changing trains we met two Spanish boys one about 15, the other 27. The older one was typically Spanish – (we spoke French with him), talking terribly rapidly, laughing. He just sort of took us under his wing. He really is the example of the Spanish carefree living. He was on his way to Bilbao (where he lives) but decided that since we were going to Madrid, he would go too! So he did. His name is Jesus, by the way.

We sleepily got off the train at San Sebastien – rather, near there – and got on the train for Madrid. It's the cutest train – it is all in one piece – not separate cars. The cars are not completely joined – there is a little vestibule like thing in between each car. It's a first class train – really nice, with comfortable seats, big windows, waiters serving drinks, etc. We spent the whole day on the train singing, reading and talking with Jesus. He bought my lunch for me – oh – before that he bought us all breakfast, paid for our luggage, and did all the tipping for us. During lunch he told me that he adored me and he adored Eugenie. He's really a character.

All day we had the most gorgeous scenery – Spain looks just like I thought it would. The sky was blue, blue, blue – we followed the snow-capped mountains a long way – the red tiled roofed stucco houses were in every shape and form – burros pulling carts – poor people by the railroad tracks picking up coal – a young girl who looked 50 washing clothes with rocks in a wheelbarrow – tiny villages with huge churches – old Spanish estates – it was all wonderful. About 38 minutes before we arrived in Madrid, we passed the Escorial – the huge austere palace built by Philip II – the sun was shining on it making it look gold. Madrid at first sight from the train was a pool of gold and red lights as the sun slowly began to sink.

When we got into the station Stratton, Joan, and Liz were there to meet us. It was so good to see them again – and good to have someone speak Spanish for us. Sandy, Louise, and I have regular suitcases, so we went back to the hotel with Jesus in the station bus while Martha and Eugenie went with the others on the Metro. We came to our hotel, changed clothes in a hurry and went out to eat with Stratton and Joan. They took us to a place they know which has absolutely fabulous food – and it's so cheap! I had a wonderful chicken casserole, dessert, wine, and bread, for not even a dollar. I tasted some things Joan ordered, liked them so much I went back today to eat them. She first had a clam dish in a hot (with red pepper) sauce that was divine – then a pork pie (which I ate today). It was scrumptious. I had said I wasn't going to gain weight in Spain, but if I keep up this eating I certainly shall. After dinner Joan and Stratton had to go back to school (they have dorm rules), so the rest of us met Jesus – he wanted to take us all out. We first went to a place where there were Spanish dancers – but it was only after 11:00 and nothing had opened.

Explanation due: from 2:00 to 4:00 is lunch hour in Spain everything closes from 2:00 to 4:00. Then dinner is around 10:00 or 10:30 at night – everyone stays up till about 4:00 a.m. Crazy life – but maybe the best.

Jesus decided to take us to a real nightclub, so he took us to the Alcazar – only the swankiest place in Madrid. He danced with each of us, bought us drinks, etc. There was a wonderful floor show with Spanish dancers, guitarists, a quartet with the best tenor I've heard in ages. Meanwhile things were happening. A man had asked Eugenie to dance, she accepted, and boom – Jesus blew up. He pouted all during the floor show. Soon it became obvious that it was time to leave. We left and came home in a taxi – pooped. By the way, taxis are so cheap – you can go almost everywhere for about 10¢! It's incredible.

This morning we got up late, had breakfast, and set out to see Madrid. We found a policeman directing traffic who spoke French, and he showed us how to get to the tourist office. We walked there – down a lovely avenue with trees and wrought iron balconies. I really do like the Spanish architecture. At the tourist office we got tour maps of the city, took a cab, and headed for the Franciscan Church where one of Goya's frescos is. The Goya is magnificent, as is the entire church. There are six chapels each painted by famous Spanish painters – some of them Goya's contemporaries, others rather modern – about 19th century. The guide who showed us around spoke horrible French, but we managed to understand him a little. (There are some wonderful Baroque sculptures in the church.)

By the time we finished looking at the church it was time to come back to the hotel where we were to meet at 2:00. Everyone then went separate ways – Louise with Stratton to see her school, Eugenie with Jesus, Martha shopping, Sandy to bed, and I went to eat lunch. I had to go back to that restaurant where Stratton and Joan had taken us – I had to have one of those pork pies! I ate all alone and got dizzy on a bottle of wine – but it was so good. On my way to and from the restaurant I was followed by several different little men. It's so funny – men follow women all the time – whistle, make compliments, but are never obnoxious and never try to do anything out of order. I really think it's wonderful.

Oh I almost forgot. After we left the Franciscan church we started walking to take a taxi, and found ourselves in a section of Old Madrid with the narrow streets, donkeys pulling carts, flower pots in the windows. We walked into a huge market place that was absolutely fascinating. There was every kind of vegetable, meat, sausage, cheese, olives, everything. The people were wonderful, dirty, toothless, greasy-headed, but smiling and friendly. There is a much warmer attitude in general in Spain towards foreigners than there is in France. We bought some beautiful navel oranges and continued on our way.

Then we went to The Royal Palace, which is Spain's Versailles, and every bit as magnificent. No one lives there now – not since the Revolution of 36 – Franco lives in a smaller house. We were taken through with a group of Spanish speaking people, so of course we understood almost nothing, but we were lucky because one of the guards in the big banquet hall spoke a tiny bit of French, with that and what little Spanish I can understand we learned a lot. The guide was so cute, he kept waiting until the rest of the group was out of sight, then he would show us something like the real covers of the chairs which had slip covers on them. He also let us sit in the chair where Franco always sits for the banquets! The palace is really splendid – I prefer it to Versailles because it's not so overdone. Its rooms have gorgeous ceilings, the furniture is wonderful. It's impossible to describe it decently.

We left the palace and walked into the formal gardens in front of it. Two soldiers – Spanish – came up to us and started talking. Of course we couldn't understand them, but finally it dawned on us that they wanted us to take their pictures, so I stood between them and Louise took the picture. Then we started walking back toward the hotel. We stopped to take pictures of the scenery beyond the palace (it sits on a hill) and a boy on a bicycle began talking to us in English. He was German, had come to Spain to work and study. He works as a waiter. He's already studied in Paris, Stockholm, and London. He wanted us to go into the Palace courtyard and see the view from there. We had already seen it, but we went back. I'm glad we did because he told us a lot about The Civil War and showed us the bullet holes in the walls. He was really so nice. He went his way after we left the courtyard. We stopped for pastry and hot chocolate on the way. The Spanish hot chocolate is so thick you have to stir it with a spoon. The pastry is not at all like French pastry, but it's delicious.

Friday, February 22, 1957

Today we got up early, nearly missed the bus anyway to Toledo, where we spent the most delightful day! We got there around 10:30, went to the tourist office and got a map, then started out to see the city. Toledo is a magnificent city – its history dates back before 190 B.C.! The old city walls surrounding the city still stand, many were in ruins, the streets are narrow, the houses have red tiled roofs and lovely wrought iron grill work at the windows – and of course, patios. The people are picturesque too – old men and little boys drive donkeys, ride them. The donkeys are laden with baskets, pottery, etc. The whole city blends in with the surrounding landscape with the red, brown, and yellow colors.

The first place we went on our tour (a path) of the town was to the church of St. Tome where one of El Greco's most famous paintings is – *The Burial of Count Orgaz* – it is truly marvelous. We wouldn't have appreciated it fully if a Canadian couple and their guide had not come in and sat behind us. The guide explained everything fully and it was wonderful. They were following the same tour itinerary as we were, so we joined them – at their request of course! Next we went to El Greco's house – a villa thing with a beautiful patio, mosaics everywhere, tiles everywhere. Interesting furniture of his time is in the rooms. There is a fascinating kitchen with a "birthing" chair in it. Many of El Greco's paintings are in the house – one of his famous *St. Peter in Tears* is there. The guide explained things about El Greco that I never knew before. From the gardens of the house there is a beautiful view of the surrounding landscape.

From El Greco's house we went to the Synagogue del Transito – where the Jews of Toledo, before they were expelled in 1492, used to have their temple. Now there is just this one big room left, exquisitely decorated. The walls are made of a mixture of plaster and egg whites and molded into patterns of intricately woven lace. It's unbelievable. The influence and design is of course Moorish.

After the synagogue we parted ways with the Canadians, but we arranged to meet the guide at 3:30 at the cathedral so he could take us through. Then we went to another synagogue – Santa Maria La Bianca – an unusual name for a synagogue. It too is a beautiful Moorish building divided into 5 naves, with the Moorish horse shoe arches. Next we went to San Juan de los Reyes – a gorgeous Gothic church with one of the most beautiful cloisters in Gothic architecture. From there – there is another wonderful view of the valley beyond Toledo.

Our next visit was to a little old restaurant the guide had recommended where we had sausages, cheese, omelet with potatoes, beefsteak, bread, apple and wine for about 50¢! After dinner we window shopped until time to meet our guide. I saw so many things I wanted to get – Toledo is famous for jewelry, etc., but I'm so stingy I ended up not buying anything.

At 3:30 we met our guide at the cathedral – Spain's principal Gothic cathedral. Every sort of architectural influence is found in this cathedral. It is the richest cathedral I've ever seen. I can't begin to describe this magnificent masterpiece. In the museum of the cathedral are paintings by El Greco and others. I was interested in El Greco since I love his work. We saw the collection of the paintings of the apostles which I think are wonderful. Life magazine did an article about a year ago showing these paintings. It was there that I read that El Greco used lunatics from the asylum in Toledo to pose for his pictures. Our guide told us this, too. The expressions are certainly those of mentally unbalanced people, but they give a certain holiness, righteousness to the expressions of the apostles. There are three wonderful examples of El Greco's three painting periods in the museum – his Venetian period is seen in the gorgeous painting of Christ on his way to Calvary, his middle period in another *St. Peter in Tears*, his last period in which he used only blacks, browns and white in his *St. Francis of Assisi*.

In another room of the museum are all the robes worn by Cardinals and Archbishops of Toledo – splendid garments beaded with pearls, diamonds, rubies, and other precious stones. In another room are many of the treasures of the church – gold, silver, diamonds, pearls etc. One of the outstanding things in the cathedral is the transparency – a vault, cleverly pierced, which allows light to flood through, showing Christ and the Angelic Hosts flying upwards into the skies. On the opposite side the Virgin rises with her Heavenly Supporters into space, while beneath is a representation of The Last Supper.

It took us over 1½ hours to see the cathedral. When we left the guide went with us – he liked us! We went to see about our bus tickets but all were sold. Then our guide took us to the station to see about tickets on the train, which we got, thanks to him – he did all the talking for us. Then we took a taxi and the guide went too – not as a guide, as a friend, only he told us everything about the city. We drove around the road that surrounds the city (it was built just for tourists). Toledo is really magnificent from a distance. The river circles the town – on one side stands an old Moorish castle – the Alcazar rises like a ghost of war across the river. It was here the Communists attacked the little pro-Franco band of men inside the Alcazar during the Civil War. The cathedral rises up over the entire city. Beyond Toledo is the red, red earth, the green valley, the blue sky – a beautiful vista.

After our taxi ride around the city we went into a pastry shop and bought some Toledo specialties, then our guide took us into a café and bought us all a glass of wine. He begged us to stay until later to see Toledo illuminated at night, but we just couldn't. We caught the train at 7:00. I hated to leave Toledo – it's so rich, picturesque, easy-going, and beautiful. The awful old train (we rode 3rd class) took three hours to go 40 miles! We didn't get back to Madrid till nearly ten and all of us went straight to bed!

Saturday, February 23, 1957

This morning we spent from 11:00 to 2:00 in the museum of the Prado seeing wonderful masterpieces by Goya, El Greco, Rembrandt, Vander Weyden, Fra Angelico, Andrea del Sarto, Rubens, Raphael. I saw my favorite El Greco – *The Annunciation*. I didn't see all the Goya I wanted to see – so I guess I'll go back when we come back to Madrid.

After lunch Sandy, Coco, Louise, and I spent the rest of the afternoon walking around in the Flea Market of Madrid – the Rostio. There is everything in the way of antiques. Again I saw thousands of things I wanted, but bought nothing. We walked for hours looking – I want to buy a fan – saw one exactly like I want, but it was too expensive. We walked to the food market to buy some oranges. We bargained in sign language, finally bought some huge navel oranges. Then we took a cab home – and here I am. In 20 minutes we're leaving for Granada.

P.S. Spanish is the next language I'm going to study – starting next semester.

Monday, February 25

Here I am in Granada with beautiful, warm sunshine, blue sky, everything that should be in Spain. We sat up and tried to sleep all night Saturday night on the train, maybe I slept for almost three hours – it couldn't have been much more. We arrived in Granada about 9:30 in the morning, came to our hotel, freshened up, had breakfast, and started out – on foot of course – to see the city. Our hotel is nice, but right now they are making reparations and there is no hot water. Isn't that jolly. They heat it and bring it up in pots for you.

Anyway, we started out to see the city. Granada is really typically Spanish – tiny narrow streets, patios, iron balconies, donkeys, sombreros, beautiful women. We walked to the famous cathedral first. It is huge – one of the largest I've ever seen – in Spanish Renaissance style. It has a gorgeous organ – very much like the cathedral organ in Toledo. The organs in Spain have pipes that stand out horizontally instead of standing up vertically. The cathedral is really magnificent. Behind it is the Royal Chapel, built in the 15th century. There Isabella and Ferdinand are buried along with other Catholic monarchs. It has one of the most famous iron grill gates in front of the altar in all Spain. The architecture is really interesting with all the complicated voûtes and domes.

From the cathedral and the royal chapel we walked to the section where the old silk market used to be. Now there is a plaza with flower vendors, fountains, surrounded with little shops. We were trying to find a restaurant listed in our little guide book, finally asked a man directions – like everyone in Spain instead of telling us how to get there, he took us there.

A drove of men followed us to the restaurant. A word about this – men follow you every where – give you compliments – "You are very beautiful" – and that's all. If you tell them to go away they will. Well – three of the men who had followed us started talking to us in Spanish. Coco can speak it a little – I can say a few sentences and can understand some, so with that and sign language they helped us order our meal, recommended another restaurant for later on.

Finally they left us – another group of boys came in and started talking to us. They could say a few words of English. They were delighted with us – told us we all looked like Marilyn Monroe, etc. A group of about 20 boys came in, sat down in a little private sort of room that opened out of the room where we were. They must have been some sort of fraternity because they passed around a silver loving cup and drank from it, then sang songs, clapping their hands while singing. It was beautiful. One of them sang in the fashion that I adore – it's a frantic, savage sort of sound. We stayed and listened to them for about half an hour. When we got up to leave they made a toast to America and told us we were beautiful. Of course we liked that!

We left the restaurant and started for the Alhambra, which I was so excited about. On the way we came to a square – General Franco Square – filled with poor, dirty gypsies. One little boy came up and in perfect English told us how to get to the Alhambra. We walked up a little narrow, winding street until we came to the entrance of the park. The trees are tall and luscious, water runs down from little streams, birds sing everywhere. It is really a natural delight. We climbed the path and first came to the monument of Charles V. We sat on the wall and rested a little before going on. Continuing we came to the main entrance, which is in the middle of the Arab Palace, the Palace of Charles V, and the old fortress – the Alcazaba. There we parted ways, because Sandy, Coco, and I wanted to pay 20¢ and hire a guide and the others wanted to follow Louise's little book. So we hired a guide.

First, we went through the Arab Palace – the most gorgeous part of the Alhambra. It is a magnificent pink palace – a fairy tale building of lace walls constructed of plaster as only the Arabs could do it. The walls have miraculously held their colors of blue, yellow, which were delicately applied to the stalactite-like ceilings. There are rooms with vaulted ceilings inlaid with ivory and mother-of-pearl. Fountains adorn each patio – small oases in the midst of the pink desert. I could go on at length about the Alhambra – certainly would have liked being an Arab and living there!

We went through the palace of Charles V next. It was never finished, and now all that remains is a big arena/bull ring-like structure. It's interesting, but after the splendor of the Arab Palace it's anticlimactic. Next, we went to the old fortress, The Alcazar. It, too, is now in ruins, but from its gardens one has a beautiful panoramic view of Granada, the Sierra Nevada Mountains, and the Sacramonte – the hill where all the gypsies live.

Our friends from the restaurant had been following us all this time. At the fortress, we all met, and in our mixed language of Spanish, English, and signs, decided to all go together to the Generalife – the summer home of the Kings on the hill opposite the Alhambra. We started down the hill toward the Generalife – we six, our seven friends, and a group of about 12 boys who were following us. Our friends said something to them and they went away. Honestly, I've never seen such following men in my life!

We sort of paired off – I was walking with Roberto Cepeda, Louise with Carlos, Coco with Arturo, Eugenie with Julio, Martha with Alfredo, and Sandy with Pepe and somebody else who was big and fat and bothered her to death. Our friends took us through the Generalife gardens, beautiful formal gardens around the exquisite house, with luscious patios and fountains. I was so proud because I could do much better in Spanish than I thought I could. I'm so enthused – I'm going to take it next semester I think. From the Generalife, we walked down the path from the Alhambra to the road, singing songs and having a wonderful time. Then we all headed for the Sacramonte where the gypsies live and dance every night in their caves.

We stopped in a little place (a gypsy place) on the way to have something to drink. We had Spanish wine, which is delicious, but strong as blazes. Gypsies were walking up and down in the road in bright, colorful costumes – several of the children wanted us to take their pictures. They are such wild little children! And dirty – I've never seen such filth in my life! We had a good time drinking the wine, talking, and singing. All the other boys were in love with all of us by this time. We were the most beautiful girls in the world, "muy bonito," etc. After about an hour of sitting in the little wine drinking place, we went on up the mountain to the gypsy caves. All the way up they stared at us as if we were freaks – which is nothing unusual now. In the caves we had something to drink, then the gypsies started singing in the savage, frantic way that I love. Later a little gypsy boy danced for us. It was so much fun.

We stayed there about one half hour. The real dances didn't start until ten, but besides being rather expensive, we were all pooped after all night on the train, so we left. But before going home we walked through the gypsy quarter (which is unbelievably poor and dirty) to a point from where you can see Granada all lighted up. It was so beautiful – the stars were out big and bright – "the night was young and we were beautiful" they told us! We left for home soon – dragging ourselves along wearily and half dead. Finally, we got down the hill into the main street. Then the comedy of errors started. We had told the boys that we were staying at the Hotel Victoria – a nice hotel not far from our hotel. Well, they insisted on taking us to the hotel, so we told them goodnight, went in the Hotel Victoria, walked up the stairs, found a bell-boy, and made him take us out the back way. Then we skipped home. We got back to the hotel, our hotel, and there was Coco, who had gotten separated from the rest of us on her way back. She had told her friend our real hotel because she couldn't go home alone. We knew all was lost because Coco's friend would tell the others – and they thought we were going to meet them Monday at the Hotel Victoria – but we didn't worry about it.

After a wonderful night's sleep we got up Monday morning and sure enough the boys arrived at 12:00. We told them we'd meet them at 2:00 at the Hotel Victoria. They doubted us, so we vowed it. But Roberto and Carlos wouldn't leave Louise and me. Finally, we agreed to let them take us on a little tour of the city.

They took us to see one of the oldest houses in Granada, some women making lace, a beautiful courtyard, and a few other little spots. At two we went to the Hotel Victoria to meet the others for lunch. At four thirty the six of us took the bus to Cartuja – the monastery. It took only 15 minutes to go – the monastery is plain and unattractive on the outside, but the interior is beautiful! The most ornate, beautiful Spanish architecture and decoration I've seen – Spanish Baroque style. It's almost too rich and gorgeous.

We walked back to town and stopped in a darling little café and had beer and perritos calientes – Spanish for hot dogs. The boys were so cute and so nice – wanted to do anything we wanted, buy us anything we wanted to eat, etc. We decided to go to the Alhambra and see it by night – supposedly a beautiful sight. So, we climbed the hill in the pitch dark – it was so romantic with the sound of the unseen water rushing down. We went only as high as the Alhambra Palace Hotel (a plush hotel) from where there is a magnificent view of Granada. The stars were bright, the night was soft, and very Spanish-y. After star-gazing, we came back down the hill to go home.

The funniest thing happened. One of the boys, Carlos, had to go to the bathroom – we could tell by the pained expression on his face. Finally, as we passed a dark alley, he said he had a cousin who lived up that alley and he had a card he had to give him. We knew he had no cousin there. He was so funny, he ran up the street and yelled "Diego," as if he were calling to his cousin. In about five minutes he came back – a new man with a smiling face, I know exactly how he felt and how he suffered before he thought up the cousin excuse.

We walked on back to our hotel. The boys took our addresses, made us promise to write them. It was all very sweet – another sad goodbye of leaving friends – never to see them again.

In Granada, walking back from the Cartuja, we passed through the poorest living district I've ever seen. People were living in earthquake-shattered houses, pigs were roaming in the streets; skinny, mangy dogs were everywhere; dirty little children, half-naked. It was certainly eye-opening concerning Spain's prosperity.

Spaniards are so different from anyone else. They are (this is of course in the lower, average classes) much more savage and primitive. Even the children are mean to each other. It's a strange mixture of eastern and western worlds.

This morning we caught the seven-fifty-five train for Málaga. It was a bumpy, awful train, but passed beautiful scenery, mountains, valleys thick with orange trees and lemon trees laden with fruit, almond trees in bloom with the most gorgeous pink blossoms – like Japanese cherry trees. It was a beautiful ride.

We arrived in Málaga at about 11:45, came to the hotel (another plush baby, sarcasm) freshened up, and started out. We took one of the horse drawn carriages that are so plentiful here (for the tourists) and went to the Miramar Hotel, the fanciest hotel here. We were determined to have a good meal no matter what the price. I had had only one meal, if you could call it that, for three days So, we splurged. For 100p. ($2.50) we had a delicious non-olive oil meal in a swank hotel crawling with tourists – Americans, English, everything. After our meal we ran out to the Mediterranean – just a few steps from the hotel. I couldn't believe I was seeing it.

We walked along the shoreline – found a little cove where we could play in the water. Coco and Sandy waded, the rest of us just put our hands in the sea. Now I've had a foot in the Pacific and a hand in the Mediterranean. We sat in the warm sun for a while, then moved on. We walked back to the hotel, the swank one, took another horse-drawn carriage – $1.00 for an hour drive around Málaga – 3 of us in a carriage. Málaga is really pretty – ideally situated on the Mediterranean, a beautiful harbor, green, luscious trees, flowers, wonderful weather. The only thing of historical interest is the ruined Moorish fortress of the eleventh century that sits on top of a hill overlooking the city. After our ride we bought some fruit at the market, came back to the hotel. Tomorrow we catch the 8:50 train for Seville. I can hardly wait.

Wednesday, February 27, 1957

Here I am in Seville. We left Málaga at 9:00 this morning, and finally arrived at 3:00. We didn't know any hotel to go to because Mr. Hochwald hadn't heard from the hotels in Seville and Córdoba and he was supposed to wire us before we got here, but he didn't. So, we went to the Transglobe Travel office (Mr. Hochwald's firm) and found it closed till 4:00. While we were waiting all Seville passed that office, stared at us, and made comments. I suppose we did look like little lost waifs or something similar. 4:00 finally came and we went inside the office. They gave us our reservations and called a taxi to take us to our hotel – The Hotel Colon. We were so amazed to see the hotel because it really is a hotel and we have rooms with baths! We're afraid Hochwald made a mistake – we're out of our traveling element – and it's so nice. Luxury is a wonderful thing – especially when you go without it for a long time.

We came in the hotel, took baths, then dressed to go eat. We were all starving since we hadn't anything but fruit since mid-day meal at Málaga. We got all dressed up and went to what the hotel recommended as the best restaurant in town. We went in and had a beer and hors d'oeuvres, then a huge meal of tomato soup, chateaubriand steak with tomato, potatoes, and cauliflower, salad, and ice cream – all for about $2.50 – which is marvelous in comparison to prices in the States, but a little expensive for us in Spain. My stomach had shrunk so from not eating that I couldn't finish my meal. We had eaten earlier than the Spanish dinner hour, so we were the only ones in the restaurant, and being girls, all the waiters were fascinated by us. They stood around and told us we were pretty, watched us eat, laughed when we laughed, gave us every attention possible.

About 9:45 we finally left the restaurant. We had reservations at 10:30 at the El Patio – one of the two places in Seville to see real, good Flamenco dancing. We had been expecting Coco to come eat dinner with us at the restaurant at 8:00, but she never came. Louise and I walked back to the hotel to see if we could find her and get her to come to the Flamenco dances. She wasn't there, so we went to the El Patio to meet the others. There was poor Coco. She had been there since 8:30 because the hotel man had told her we went there instead of at the restaurant. The El Patio is a very atmospheric place – bull heads, shawls, etc. A wonderful little combo played for dancing. About every 20 minutes the Flamenco dancers performed. They were fabulous – best I've seen next to Jose Greco. There were about 15 of them, including a singer and a guitarist. One dancer was a boy about 16 years old who was absolutely wonderful.

The place was filled with Americans and foreigners. After we had been there a while I danced with a Spanish boy who was a fabulous dancer. Then later a little Frenchman asked me to dance. His name is Albert Garrabe, he works here in Spain for the Pepsi-Cola Company. He said he had a very difficult job convincing Spain that she should drink Pepsi-Cola instead of wine. He speaks Spanish, English, and French – but we spoke French. He really is nice. We stayed till 2:30 a.m., fascinated with the dancers – their beautiful costumes, the castanets, the hand-clapping, etc. Finally at 2:30, Coco, Louise, and I wanted to come home. Albert brought us home in his little car. He asked me if I would have lunch with him and I said yes, so at 2:15 tomorrow I'm going to meet him rather than have him call for me at the hotel. Wonder why I appeal to older men in Europe?

Thursday, February 28, 1957

Finally woke up at 11:00 this morning. We had the first decent breakfast we've had since we left Paris – in our room. (We're going all out!) Then we dressed (Louise & I) and went to the cathedral. We climbed the tower, which used to be a Moorish minaret, and had a beautiful view of Seville with the river, the bull ring, the Alcazar, and the far off mountains – perfectly beautiful.

We walked back to the hotel, down wonderful little streets, peeped into beautiful patios. Once at the hotel I started getting ready for my date at 2:15 - I got there at 2:00 - all I had to do was change shoes. Well Eugenie came in and told me that my friend had called at 15 minutes till 2:00 - of course I wasn't here. He told her just to tell me that he had been here. I realized then that he must have said deux heures *moins* quart instead of deux heures *et* quart. I was so mad at myself I didn't know what to do. I had his card, but it only had his name on it. I tried to remember the name of the hotel where he told me he was staying, but I couldn't remember. I hated for him to think that I had "stood him up." I went downstairs and had the darling boy that works at the tel. desk (he speaks English) to call about four hotels and ask if Albert were there. He wasn't.

So I went up and changed shoes again, and Martha, Eugenie, Louise, & I went to the cathedral – which is huge, the largest Gothic cathedral in the world, and the third largest cathedral in the world. The interior is quite interesting – beautiful stained glass windows – wonderful gilded wood carvings. Spanish cathedrals differ from other cathedrals in that their main altars and choirs are entirely enclosed by grill work, etc., thus breaking the fluency of the nave. The organ in this cathedral is marvelous. Everything in the way of churches is so huge in Europe, I'm afraid I'll get claustrophobia in Broadway Methodist Church! Christopher Columbus is buried in this cathedral – we paid homage to the Father of us all. We also saw the treasures of the cathedral – the beautiful robes, jewels, chalices of the church which I find beautiful, but quite un-religious, in fact almost sacrilegious.

From the cathedral we went to the Alcazar – the old Arab fortress – of which only a wall remains. Inside this wall is a magnificent palace – something like the Alhambra. We decided to visit only the gardens because we didn't want to pay to see the palace since it was supposed to be so much like the Alhambra. The gardens are gorgeous – full of beautiful plants, orange trees, cascades, pools, everything. We walked around for about half an hour or more.

We left the gardens and went outside the gate to meet Eugenie, who was playing her usual game of buying souvenirs. She was in a lovely shop where they had beautiful mantillas, matador blouses, combs, fans, jewelry, etc. Eugenie bought out the store. I almost bought a mantilla but didn't. For some reason I just can't bring myself to buy anything – but I am going to buy some gloves in Madrid. You can get kid gloves for $1.50 a pair!

After the Alcazar gardens we were quite tired, so we went back toward the hotel to get some ice cream at the restaurant where we ate last night. It really hit the spot – I was so tired and had eaten only a little bread and jelly for breakfast. We have been going on one meal a day – besides breakfast – because the cheap food is all soaked in olive oil. So we've been paying more for one good meal.

Friday, March 1, 1957

At the hotel at 7:00, I had the darling hotel boy try to call my French friend at a hotel which I thought sounded like his hotel – it wasn't. Sandy and Louise were standing there with me. The hotel boy, after calling for me, turned to me and said "Why not me?" I said, "Why not you what?"

"Go out with me tonight," he said. I laughed, and so did Sandy and Louise, because he had a wedding ring and a ring with a diamond in it on his left hand, and we all thought he was married. He kept on about my going out with him – said he would have to take me on his motor scooter. Joking – I said O.K. He said he'd see me at 10:30 at the hotel. Then I asked if he were serious – "Of course," he said. I asked him about his ring, if he wasn't married. He said no, his ring was a gift from his grandmother and "besides," he said, "one wears a wedding ring on the right hand." Which is true in Europe – just the opposite from in the States.

So – he asked me again to go out with him – and I accepted, for 10:30. All of us went out last night with friends we had met in Seville. But before our dates we went back to the Riviera restaurant to eat. I ordered less this time and thus ate more.

After dinner we went back to the hotel to meet our dates. I met mine promptly at 10:30. I boarded the motor scooter and off we went. First we went to a little café – the kind where you stand up around the counter – put one foot on the foot rail – and had coffee. Here we introduced ourselves – he is Conrado do Soto. He discovered I speak French, so since he is more comfortable in French than in English, we spoke French. I discovered that his life dream was to be a matador. He had fought in the ring – been gored and in the hospital a month with his wound – thus his parents forbade him to continue. He still dreams of it – he had his matador boots on last night. He is a perfect example of the lust for danger that seems to be typical in Spain – he is almost primitive in his savagery – also typical of Spain. We left the café, boarded the moto and headed for the Santa Cruz quarter. He left his moto near his house and proceeded to show me his neighborhood. First we went to the Plaza de Dona Elvira – a beautiful quiet little plaza with wonderful houses – bright in the light of the burning stars. There is the house where Franco's assistant spends the summer. We walked farther on – came to Conrado's street, named Death, preceded by a street named Life, and followed by a street named Glory. Conrado pushed open the door of his and other people's houses to show me the patios – exquisite, all of them. I asked him if no one ever locked his door, and he said never. Strange little quarter. We headed toward the Plaza Santa Cruz. On the way Conrado showed me the imprint on the wall near his house which a head had made. It seems that years ago a jealous lover found his fiancée with another man – killed the man, cut off his head, and hung the head on the wall. The head turned to a skull – the skull left a perfect print in the wall. Sure enough – Conrado climbed up the wall, struck a match, and there was the skull. An eerie tale. At the Plaza de Santa Cruz where the famous wrought iron 8th century cross is, Conrado picked oranges from the trees and gave me one. They are no good to eat, but they smell heavenly. We walked into the Murillo Gardens, and sat down on a bench. Not far away some little boys were playing marbles. Conrado sang Flamenco songs to me, then danced Flamenco dances for me, then showed me his matador tactics. He was fascinating to watch. We left the Santa Cruz quarter, boarded Mr. Moto, and went to the El Patio – where I had been the night before. I enjoyed seeing the dancers perform again – I was dying to try it myself. I was disappointed that Conrado was only an ordinary dancer. Guess who I saw there – the Frenchman I was to have lunch with. He obviously fibbed to me when he said he was leaving Seville that night. Suddenly he looked like a weasel to me, and I didn't even say anything to him. I must have looked pretty weasel-ish myself, because he said absolutely nothing to me either! We left the El Patio at 2:30, boarded Mr. Moto and took off for the hotel – I thought. I saw we were not going there, and I started asking – rather yelling – where are you going? No answer. So I held on and waited. He stopped in front of a market-looking district about 10 minutes later. I asked him what we were going to do there, and he said – "eat fish."

"Fish at 3:00 a.m.?" I asked. "Yes."

So, we went into another little café with a foot rail – the bill is not given to you or told to you – they write in chalk on the counter! Conrado explained that the fish market where we were was wonderful because everything was fresh – just arrived from Cadiz. He ordered the fish and some wine and of all things some radishes. I had no idea what sort of fish was coming but after a while here came a platter of little sardines – whole – eyes, mouth, everything. I had no idea how to eat them and was a little repulsed at the sight of them. Conrado dug right in – picked one up, shoved it at me, and said "Eat" – so I did. I took my cues from his, held the head in one hand, the tail in the other, and proceeded to eat the meat off the sides, leaving only the skeleton. I was amazed to find they were delicious – they had been cooked some way, were piping hot. Conrado got a big kick from watching me eat them. I could only down three. It was an unusual experience, not only because of the fish but also because of the funny people in the funny café – old men, withered, poor, singing, talking to themselves. I was the only female in the place. It was the strangest sensation to be there with a strange boy, eating strange food, seeing strange sights. I really enjoyed it. We left there, came back to the hotel. All night long Conrado had been handing me that old Spanish line of "you're beautiful, I love you, let's be married." At the hotel door he looked as if he going to cry because I was leaving. Of course I knew he has faking, but he looked mighty convincing. I don't like Spanish men – they have lines a mile long – "they love you madly." They'll never forget you, they follow you in the street, make clucking sounds at you and just about everything else. It'll be strange to come back to the U.S. and be ignored on the streets!

By the time I got to bed it was 4:00. At 9:00 I got up, we had breakfast, dressed and went to the Marie Luisa Park – the famous park of Seville. It is really gorgeous – waterfalls, flowers, a small lake, fountains, beautiful flowering trees. It was worth the walk there. We came back to the hotel at 12:30, finished our bags, called a cab, and left for the train station. At the station we met two American women traveling in Europe – one is from Nashville, Tenn., and was Kefauver's secretary. She was in Europe in '52 with the Kefauvers, she said. She had a donkey pinned on her lapel – a typical "Committee-woman" type.

While we were waiting for the train and going through the usual rigmarole about the tickets, we were entertained on the quai by a group of boys who were playing guitars, singing, and very amateurishly dancing Flamenco-style. They had come to say good-by to one of the boys in the crowd – who got on the train for Córdoba too. They were so cute waving their handkerchiefs to him as the train pulled out. We were late leaving, so we didn't get here till about 4:30 – the shortest train ride we've had yet on this trip. Once here, we hired a little man to roll our bags in a cart to the hotel because it's so near the station. We are again in a wonderful hotel – each room with a bath. I'm afraid this is going to spoil us!

Sunday, March 3, 1957

Córdoba has been the most delightful town – thanks to a boy named Ricardo Rodriguez. I'll tell you about it.

Yesterday morning Louise, Sandy, Coco, and I got up and started out to sightsee. There isn't nearly so much of historical interest here in Córdoba as there is in the other towns we've visited, but the number one to see in Córdoba is the Mezquita Cathedral – unique in the world because it was originally an Arab mosque. Charles V had a cathedral, that is the altar and choir of a cathedral constructed in the middle of the wonderful mosque. We walked down wonderful little winding streets and saw beautiful patios opening onto them. It was so typically Spanish.

We went to the Mezquita – refused to hire a guide – nothing tight about us, say? The Mezquita is a marvelous monument to Arab culture. It's a forest of columns with double arches painted alternately red and black. It's a fantastic sight to see. It's such a shame that the cathedral had to be built in the center because it spoils the perspective. If the cathedral were not there, you could see the chapel where the Koran was kept from any viewpoint, because the pillars were mathematically constructed so that from any point in the mosque one had a clear view to the Koran. There are beautiful examples of the amazing plaster work of the Arabs. We stayed there about an hour.

As we left the Mezquita we walked by the river Guadalquivir and saw the old Roman bridge. We were walking from the bridge toward the Alcazar, which was on the way to the hotel, when this tall, thin, good-looking boy passed us. I remarked to Sandy how bowlegged he was – I've never seen such bowed legs. We laughed about how he must ride bulls. Later we were perusing around the Alcazar trying to figure out how to get in, when this same bowlegged boy came up and in Spanish told us that we couldn't get in because it was under reparation. Then he proceeded to walk with us. He told us things about Córdoba, made jokes, and was so sweet. He took us down little streets that were absolutely charming – showed us some beautiful patios. He seemed to know everyone. Later he took us into a little café and bought us a glass of white wine.

He was so poor – his clothes were tattered and worn. He introduced himself as Ricardo Rodriguez, age 27. We were astounded that he was so old. He doesn't look over 24. He said he was a student. We were talking a mixture – mostly Spanish. He said he could understand a little French. I could understand him when he spoke Spanish, but I had trouble talking to him in Spanish. We left the café and he took us into a gorgeous patio with orange and lemon trees. The caretaker let us pick oranges and lemons – they were so good! The lemons were sweet – almost a tasteless sweet, and the oranges were delicious.

We walked then to the Calle de los Flores, a tiny little street where the houses are covered with vines and flowers. It's so pretty. I guess we walked for way over an hour. When we got back to our street Ricardo offered to take us to the museum that afternoon. Only Sandy wanted to go, so they made arrangements to meet after lunch. He also invited us to come with him that night and eat a typical meal which a friend of his who owned a café would prepare. We accepted, arranged to meet him at seven p.m. He was the nicest of all the Spanish men we had encountered. While we were in the café drinking white wine he made the most beautiful little speech about why he loved Córdoba and why he would always live in Córdoba – because it was simple, tranquil.

We left Ricardo at the corner of our street – he didn't want to come to the hotel – I think he was embarrassed because he is so poor and his clothes looked so shabby. We came in and ate lunch – a big meal – the first mid-day meal I've had since I left Paris. After lunch I was going to go shopping, but there were several Americans in the hotel who started talking to us – to Eugenie, Martha, and me. They were all hicks, but they were so pitiful – they hadn't seen any American girls in so long and they wanted to talk. They bought us drinks, then wanted to take Martha and Eugenie to the Mezquita since they hadn't seen it. I decided to go with them, so they took us in a taxi there.

Once there they hired a guide – which we were too cheap to do before, so I learned a lot about it on the second trip. I had to be back at the hotel at 5:15.

Later, at 7:00, we met Ricardo around the corner. Bless his heart, he had changed his clothes, put on his Sunday best. He looked so nice. His eyes just twinkled and he was so happy to be with us. He is the most sensitive boy I've met in a long, long time. We started and went to a café which a friend of Ricardo owns. We went in a little back room where there was a table, benches, and some chairs. This was where we were to eat our meal. First we drank some wine, then an old man (about 54 – probably younger than that) came in and played the guitar, which belonged to Ricardo. He was really good on the guitar – his name is Pago. Ricardo said the wife of the proprietor was going to fix the meal for us, so while they were getting things started we all went for a walk. Pago went with us and played the guitar as we walked. We walked down lovely little streets, past a Franco political party outpost, past some famous statues. The night, as all the nights were in Andalusia, was gorgeous and clear with beautiful, bright stars, and a little breeze that practically sang.

We went to another café, had more wine. Pago was still playing the guitar. Ricardo danced à la Flamenco for us, and did a few little torero tricks. Then Pago played a paso doble and Ricardo danced with each of us. He had shown favoritism for Sandy and me all along, and this kept up all evening. As we walked back to the café where we were going to eat supper he wanted Sandy and me right by him all the time. He kept saying how wonderful it was that all four of us girls and one boy and an elderly man could be such good friends, have such a fraternal feeling towards each other. He said that if we were Europeans it would be impossible because friendship between one boy and several girls, without showing favoritism or being amorous, just doesn't exist in Europe. He said he didn't want anything or anybody to displease us this night because he was like the pilot and we were his passengers. This he said all in Spanish – for me to translate! The pilot simile was a good one, because for four years he was a pilot in the army. Now he's going to aviation school for Air France. He really was so good and kind.

We went back to the café where we were going to eat our supper. Pago was still playing the guitar, poor old thing. Our meal was being prepared by the proprietor's wife and another woman. Coco was fanning the fire in the stove. The rest of us were in the little room listening to Pago and Ricardo. It was so funny because Pago couldn't understand us and we couldn't understand him. You know when people speak to you in a foreign language and don't think you understand, they are prone to shout at you. Pago would get right at our faces and shout! We'd say Si, Si – etc.

Finally our dinner was ready. We had paella – which is a typical Spanish dish of rice with tomatoes, peppers, and shrimp. It's really delicious. We also had a potato tortilla, which is an omelet filled with potatoes. It was so good. We had all sorts of wine to go with the meal. The proprietor's wife came in and we thanked her for everything. She was so pleased, even though she couldn't understand us. It's amazing what smiles and laughter can do. The proprietor came in and we sang "For He's a Jolly Good Fellow" for him. They all liked that.

Once during the meal we got so tickled I thought we all were going to pass out. Pago started it all by laughing at something. He has a contagious laugh, tears fill his eyes and he shakes all over. Of course when he started laughing so did we; then he would laugh because we were laughing. I hurt so badly after about 15 minutes of solid laughing! After dinner Pago's son, Rafael, came and joined us. I guess he was Ricardo's age. He also played the guitar. Then he and Ricardo danced à la Flamenco for us. Pago played the guitar – still. Then Ricardo and I Spanish danced together. It looks so easy, but is really quite difficult. Rafael danced with me too – we all danced paso dobles. Even the proprietor – Antonio – came in and danced with us. We really had such a wonderful time. We stayed till 1:30. Ricardo kept asking us if we were going to have good memories of Córdoba now. He was so anxious that we like everything.

Finally we started home. Louise, Coco, Sandy and I plus Pago, Rafael, and Ricardo, who wanted to take us to the Calle de las Flores, but we just couldn't do it. Poor old Pago was still playing his guitar. We got back to the hotel, and Ricardo wanted to meet Sandy and me Sunday. We thought it was best to end everything there, so we said no. I felt so mean doing it because he had been so sweet to us, but with hearts of stone we said goodnight to them, thanked them for a wonderful evening.

The next day, Sunday, Sandy and I went down for breakfast – at noon – and who should be waiting for us at the hotel door but Ricardo. We were certainly surprised. We ate breakfast, then thinking Ricardo had gone away, we started down the street to take a walk around Córdoba. At the corner waiting for us was Ricardo. Not a word was said, but he joined us. We were headed for the bull ring. Since we weren't going to see a real bull fight we at least wanted to see a bull ring – close up. Ricardo went with us. I think he must know everyone in Córdoba. When we got to the ring it was naturally locked up. We were dying to go inside, so Ricardo knocked on the door and the caretaker came. They talked, and before we knew it we were inside the bull ring – in the arena area itself! It was thrilling just to stand there and see all the horse and bull hoof prints, Ricardo pointed everything out to us – all the sections of the stadium where certain officials sit. He took us back to see where the bulls are kept before they enter the ring. We found a practice bull – you know, one of those things on wheels with real horns that the toreros practice with – and brought it into the ring. Ricardo played torero for us, then Sandy and I tried it. I took some cute pictures of our antics. It was so much fun!

We left the bull ring and started walking again. We walked through the big park, past the fancy hotel, Córdoba Palace, and ended up down by the river. Sandy and I walked down a bluff sort of thing to get to the water. There I saw sights I've never seen before. All along the river there were people – living like animals. On the road above, little goats and donkeys were driven by skinny, half-naked children, withered old men, and beaten-looking women. By the river in the side of the little hill in a tiny cave was a family of five, huddled under the straw-roof porch they had built against the cave. Donkeys stood near-by. The father was fishing in the river. The children were filthy, naked (almost), with runny noses that had dried on their faces. They all came up to us and begged. I wanted to give them everything I had. Ricardo must have known that Sandy and I were having our eyes opened because he kept looking at us as if to say you didn't know this life existed did you? I don't suppose I've ever been that close to it. Down the way was a sort of camp – people living in tiny white tents. We sat down in the grass on the bank half way between the tent camp and the cave home and talked, and watched the poorest people I've ever seen go by. The women carried things on their heads and babies in their arms. A couple of women were washing clothes on rocks in the river. You can't imagine how strange I felt sitting in the midst of all that. Oh how lucky, fortunate, and blessed we are!

We left the river and walked back to the hotel. Ricardo kept saying how sad he was that we were leaving – he had never known Americans like us. I think it was a compliment. At the hotel we said goodbye to him until 7:00, when he was coming back to go to the station with us.

In the hotel we saw Martha and her friend George, and met a couple of other Americans from Louisiana – hicks from the word go – but they had cars and they offered to take us to the station – all of us, including our bags. Of course we took them up. At 7:00 – all of us, including Ricardo, piled into three cars and headed for the station. The men were so nice; they put us and our baggage on the train, stood and waved goodbye to us until we were out of sight. Ricardo looked so pitifully sad. People are so wonderful.

On the train we sat three and three in two compartments, which we had practically to ourselves, so we slept not too badly that night. We got to Madrid at 7:00 the next morning – Monday. We went to the hotel, checked in, then went to have breakfast. We were all starving, so we went to a little place that Martha had found the first time we were in Madrid and had ham and eggs, tomato juice. Boy, was it good. Then we started our shopping. Oh – Coco, Louise, and I were going to the Escorial, but we were too tired and tired of riding on the train, so instead Eugenie, Louise, and I spent the whole morning in a record shop listening to Andalusian music. I bought the best record! I can't wait for you to hear it.

After a quick lunch, we continued our shopping. Louise and I went to the glove shop, and I bought nine pairs to bring home for the family! I'm so proud of them. They really are wonderful gloves.

Then I bought perfume – for me. I was out anyway, and perfume is even cheaper in Spain than it is in France. The stores closed at 7:30 and we did too.

The next morning after breakfast Coco, Louise, and I set out looking for botas – they are wonderful goat-skin bags used for wine. All the Spanish carry them on trips filled with wine, water, or whatever. I can't wait to carry mine to Italy. I bought three – one for me, and two for gifts. Then we went to a delicatessen and had some sandwiches made to take on the train.

The train left at 12:45, and was the roughest, bumpiest train ride I've had in a long time. We didn't change trains until 7:30 at the Spanish border, then we had compartments. I was going to buy a couchette, but I preferred the perfume, so I sat up all night. I did sleep a little. We arrived in Paris at 8:00 this morning. One of the boys we met on the train brought Louise and me home in a taxi, insisting on paying because it was a Spanish custom, and he is Spanish.

So the end of another wonderful vacation. In some ways I was disappointed in Spain, but in general she lived up to all that I expected. Her people are warm (the men too warm), generous, and incredibly easy-going. There is color, quaintness, and mystery in Spain – the Arab influence is far greater than I had expected.

Although I loved the trip, I was certainly ready to get back to Paris. When we came in we were greeted by Monsieur. Madame is at Champscenest with the children, whom Monsieur is going to get tomorrow. I wish they were staying at their grandmother's. It's been so nice here without them.

Mother, your passport surely came quickly. Yes there is a hotel just around the corner that looks very nice and is probably not expensive. The fact that you don't know any French is unimportant. I don't know much about the trip to Italy yet – I will be finding out very soon. You know of course that we don't go the most comfortable way – we never suffer, although we came close to it in Spain as far as little old uncomfortable hotels go.

About my flying home. I received a letter from Genie Slaughter's friend Lucy thanking me for switching with her. She wants to make an even exchange. I'm so excited about it. You do approve don't you? I'd love to stay in New York a couple of days with Louise's friend before coming home. I'm really excited about flying home.

Juggling
Classes
and Life

Friday, March 8, 1957

Dear Mother and Daddy,

Yesterday Madame and the children came home. The children are so healthy and much sweeter.

Yesterday afternoon we met with Madame Alvernhe at the Sorbonne to register for the new semester. We don't get our Sorbonne grades until March 15th – income tax day. I wonder why everything happens on that day? From the Sorbonne we went to Dr. Smithers' to have our composition class. Madame Alvernhe gave us our grades for that course – I'm so proud because I made the highest grade out of all of us – A plus! I was really surprised. She gave us back our exam papers – I made the highest exam grade. She also gave us back the last theme we had written – our impressions of Paris – and I had the highest grade anyone has made in that class. She told me I should frame it! I'm so proud of it.

Monday, March 11, 1957

Well, I haven't been on a lost week-end, but it's been a busy one. I'll try to resume where I left off.

Thursday night Louise and I went out with Jacques Lauriau. He told us there was another man, one of his friends, coming along with us, but he wouldn't tell us who it was. When he came to get us he was alone and we were wondering who it would be. We walked down the steps to the ground floor and Jacques stopped in front of Claude Rémond's door and made a little speech about our surprise. Just as he finished the door opened and there stood Claude, bowing to us.

We had suspected that Claude would be the one. He's quite charming and strange, not as attractive looking up close as he is from a distance. This was the first time this whole year that we had been introduced to him. We decided we would go to see *Anastasia* and then go to dinner, driving in Jacques' car.

Claude was so peculiar – he really has no manners as far as opening doors, helping with coats, etc. He walks off and leaves you much of the time. He really is peculiar. We saw *Anastasia* and I really enjoyed it. I was glad to see Ingrid Bergman after seeing her in person. After the movie we went to a beautiful restaurant on the Champs-Élysées. Claude and Jacques are really amusing together. Claude took a liking to me and I think made Jacques a little angry. On the way home Louise and I rode in the back seat, and they rode up front. I've never done that before. We never did decide if we had dates with them, which one was with whom, etc. but it was nice that way. We came home relatively early – around one a.m.

Friday morning I went to practice. That afternoon Hi Petter called me to say he had just arrived with a friend who had never seen Paris, and they wanted Louise and me to go with them. Hi had his beautiful greyhound, Cory, with him. Since they were tired of driving, and Cory hadn't been out all day, we started walking. We went to a butcher shop and bought Cory some meat. Everyone was looking at her and praising her – Hi was so proud. Earlier he had shown me a magazine about show dogs with Cory's picture in it. As we were walking we ran into the woman who publishes that magazine! She recognized Cory immediately, saying, "Mon dieu! C'est Cory!" We were very impressed. The next day we went with Hi to a huge, important international dog show, and Cory won first place among the greyhounds, making her an International Champion! It was all quite exciting.

Later I met John Donaher and we decided to go to the Château de Vincennes, at the edge of Paris. We rode one of the buses with an open-air platform, which took 45 minutes, and when we arrived the château had closed, so we just walked around and saw its handsome towers, walls and moat. Then we walked in the Bois de Vincennes, had coffee in a little café. It was so good to see John. We have such interesting conversations about so many subjects – I do enjoy being with him. We left the bois and took the Metro to go to a movie, *Written on the Wind,* a horrible movie, but it stimulated exciting conversation. After the movie John caught the bus back to SHAPE and I took a cab home.

Sunday I slept until nine, got up, bathed, dressed and met John at the Étoile at ten-thirty. We went to Notre Dame to Mass. Again it was a nice day – everyone was out sitting at the sidewalk cafés which are out again, walking their children and dogs. The other half of Paris was in Notre Dame! I've never seen such a crowded cathedral. Notre Dame is so marvelous. The organist is very exciting – the main reason for my wanting to go. I enjoyed watching the colorful service with the cardinal and choir boys, but the French are horrible in church. They talk, walk, stand on benches, push and everything else but what they should do. It isn't conducive to pious thoughts! John was so angry I thought he'd pop! After Mass, we crossed the Seine and joined the sidewalk café crowd for a cup of coffee. We then discussed religion – John explained a lot about the Catholic service to me – and the religion. Catholics are so lucky because they are so confident of their religion – all of them!

We left the café and went to the Flea Market – John had never been, and he wanted to go. I just love that place. There are so many beautiful things. Before I leave Paris I want to buy a cordial set there. They have some gorgeous ones for wonderful prices. I bought something yesterday – a little miniature in a bronze frame. It looks so much like my baby pictures and like Janet that I had to have it. It was originally 600 francs, but I bargained with the woman who owned the stall and got her down to 450 f. which is $1.30. I'm so proud of it. Mother, when you come to Paris we'll have to go there one afternoon. We stayed at the flea market until about four. We left the wrong way and ended up walking what seemed miles to my poor tired feet before we found a Metro. We took the one we finally found and came back into Paris to Salle Pleyel. We changed buses at Gare St. Lazare, where both of us beat it to the restrooms before proceeding to Salle Pleyel for the concert. Igor Markevitch is guest conducting one of the orchestras for several weeks (Orchestra Lamoureux) so we went to hear him. He's so fabulous. I've never heard that orchestra sound so wonderful.

They played a Sinfonia of Leclerc, which I don't know, and *Apres-midi d'un faune* by Debussy, Strauss' *Till Eulenspiegel* and Brahms' 1st. It was really the most exciting concert I've heard from an orchestra this year.

After the concert we went to a little Greek restaurant and stuffed ourselves until we could hardly move, with delicious, inexpensive shish-kabobs. Finally, with a struggle, we left and walked down St. Germain to a little place called Le Trou Madame. It's down in a cellar-looking place, has a fireplace, etc. It's very cute. One drinks and dances there. We had a good time, but the place is too expensive. We only had one beer apiece and the bill was more than our dinner! So never there again. We left and took a cab, played our game of taking John to the Étoile, and then me continuing home alone in the cab with my happy, contented thoughts of a wonderful weekend, of a marvelous city that shall forever be a wonderland, a fairy-tale – pure magic to me.

This morning was back to school with art history. I'm just crushed because with the new semester we have a new teacher – a woman who's mousy, dull, and never changes expression of face or voice. I loved the other teacher, M. Gaillard, so much. There were many, many new people in class today – most of them English – that is, most of the new ones were English. Lots of new American faces too. Sometimes I think I'm really doing something usual studying in Europe – then I see all these other students who are doing the same thing and doing it better and I feel about one inch high.

This afternoon after lunch I went to practice. I have another voice lesson tomorrow. After practicing I caught the bus and rode as far as Au Printemps.

Then I got off, looked in store windows as I walked the rest of the way home. Everyone was window shopping, sitting at the cafés and in the parks. I went to the little park across the street from us and sat down to watch the children play. I could hardly find a spot on any of the benches, the park was so crowded. Parks are really blessings to Parisians, who live in apartments with no sun, no grass, no trees, no flowers.

Mother, Just found out our spring vacation will be from April 12 to May 1st. You must decide if you are coming so we can make plans and reservations. Louise and I have been talking, and we want just the three of us to travel. After Spain, I think it would be so much more fun for just the three of us to go – much less to worry about. Oh, please decide soon. We could have such a good time. Also, Louise and I could leave on the night of the 11th since we don't have classes on the 12th – a Friday. Do you realize that if you got here around the 1st of April you'd be here in not more than two weeks. Please come!

I just got your letter, with the $250. Thank you. I also see that you got the letter I thought I had lost.

Mother, you must come to France. Please send me the approximate date so I can make your hotel reservations. I can meet you at the airport on any day at any time! Time is growing short, so please decide.

Wednesday, March 13, 1957

The weather we've been having is absolutely phenomenal! The sky is blue, blue, blue and the sun so bright and gorgeous. I hope it stays this way.

Yesterday morning I had my first voice lesson since before the trip to Spain. Monsieur Bernac is so kind. I had a good lesson, especially considering that it had been a long time since I had sung, really sung.

Oh – I made the highest grade in our Theater class A plus.

Yesterday morning Louise went to see Mr. Hochwald about Genie's trip, and also told him to start on our trip to Italy. We told him that you were coming and we wanted plans for three people. We said that we could use one room with two beds – double beds – or one room with three beds. Many of the hotels have such accommodations. I can't believe that in a month we'll be traveling again!

After theater class yesterday afternoon I met Jean-Louis at Sèvres-Babylone. Jean-Louis looks good. He's gained weight and it certainly becomes him. He had to go see a man about making him a neck-tie. The shop is an export-import place run by an American from Brooklyn who has been in Paris about

20 years. We talked awhile. He was still after all these years, praising Paris. He said "the only people who don't like Paris are those who don't have an eye for beauty and an ear for music." I suppose that's true, because if you have those qualities you can't help but love Paris.

After seeing about the tie we stopped at a café and drank Martinis – not the kind in America – and exchanged vacations. I think probably the most agreeable thing there is to do is to sit at a side walk café drinking, talking, and. watching people go by. We sat until time to start home so I could be here for eight o'clock dinner. Since we weren't far, we walked home. The night had become so beautiful – the moon was out, the stars were bright.

After dinner I met Pierre in front of St. Augustin at 8:45. While we were standing in front of the church trying to decide what to do, he pointed to the statue of Joan of Arc in front of St. Augustin and said that once an American came to Paris, saw the statue, and said, "Oh look, there's Ingrid Bergman!" I thought that was right cute. Finally, since I had no idea what I wanted to do, we boarded the moto and whizzed to the Bois de Bologne. There we walked along the lake, discussed the existence of God – which Pierre doubts – and other rather abstract subjects. Pierre is very sensitive to beauty, to music. We spent part of the night singing opera to each other. He has a terrible voice – most Frenchmen do, but that doesn't keep them from singing.

About eleven we left the bois and headed home, I thought. We rode down the Champs – I really felt "elegant" on the moto! Then through Place de la Concorde on down St. Germain-des-Prés. He showed me where he went to school – right across from the Church St. Germain. Then we went to a café around the corner and had a drink. There were two American girls – of the worse kind – with some Frenchmen. One girl could speak a little French, the other couldn't understand anything. The conversation was so hilarious that we were highly entertained. About 12:30 we whizzed home – à la moto. Pierre is quite charming.

This morning is a gorgeous day. I'm going for a promenade in the park this afternoon with Jean-Louis. The beau temps is really hard on the studying!

This afternoon after lunch Marie-Louise Bernard and Mademoiselle Bley and Monsieur Thomas (or something) came over to discuss our soiree plans. Mlle. Bley and M. Thomas work for the man at the American Embassy who is head of the cultural department. M. Rémond asked them to help with the soirée. They are going to contact the other groups and people who have Fullbright scholarships. The grand bal will be the 10th of May. It's going to be very elegant. We decided to have a small party consisting of our little group, some French girls, and men – American and French. The party will be the 5th of April here at the Rémonds. Mother, if you're here then it will be quite interesting for you. And guess what? Queen Elizabeth and Prince Philip will be in Paris from April 9th to the 15th or something like that. M. Rémond is in charge of receiving them. There is a reception and a church dedication. I feel sure that he will arrange it so we can go to at least one of the functions and meet the queen – or at least see her.

After our little conference I met Jean-Louis and we took the Metro to the Bois de Boulogne. It was so lovely today. It was amazing the crowd of people in the park on a week day. We hired a row boat and rowed (he did) for an hour on the lake. It was really delightful. Today Jean-Louis and I decided to tutoyer each other – that is, to use "tu" instead of "vous." That's the familiar pronoun used for intimate friends. Nowadays students tutoyer each other all the time, but Jean-Louis and I have stood by the old regime and abstained. I'm glad we did because it means so much more now.

I decided to ask him for us to begin to tutoyer, but I haven't had the nerve to do it. Finally, at the park I did find my nerve, and said, "Jean-Louis when can we start to tutoyer each other?" He said, "Why, anytime you want to – it won't bother at me at all." So I said, "O.K., let's tutoyer each other now." So – it was settled. Except for the next half-hour we obviously avoided the use of any form of "you" in our sentences so we wouldn't have to tutoyer for neither of us wanted to be the first. Finally, Jean-Louis said "tu" – we both laughed – it was like having a new toy and not knowing exactly what to do with it.

Saturday night, March 16

Well – I'm behind again – shall try to catch up. Thursday morning I spent writing a theme for class that afternoon. After class I was to meet Jean-Louis at the park at Sèvres-Babylone, but he wasn't there, so I went to the café where the girls were drinking coffee. Jean-Louis was there – we had just missed each other, he saw them and figured I would come to find them soon – he was right. Jean-Louis and I walked home from Sèvres along the Seine. I explained sororities and fraternities to Jean-Louis as best I could. They seem so ridiculous now – I'm afraid I couldn't make them sound very useful. We stopped by the bridge at Place de la Concorde to watch the fishermen fish. Miracle: I saw three men catch fish. That's the first time I've ever seen anyone catch anything from the Seine. M. Rémond never has! Wouldn't Ernest Hemingway be surprised! It was so delightful sitting there watching the fishing, watching the beautiful day end with an appropriate sunset. Sometimes I think I shall pop with emotion on seeing Paris in her splendor. We walked to the Madeleine, stopped and had a Martini (French aperitif), then walked home.

Immediately after dinner Louise and I ran to the cinema to see *Giant*. It was a glorious movie I thought.

Friday morning I practiced, talked to Dr. Smithers, and went to my voice lesson. Things are going fine.

Yesterday afternoon after lunch I took Nanou with me to buy a canvas suitcase. I decided to buy one to take to Italy. It's so much easier to handle. I'm going to take it this summer too. Nanou was so cute. She loves to go to Prisunic, a store across from St. Augustin. I bought her a little plastic change purse for 30¢ that thrilled her to death. Then we went to the park, she played in the sand, later we walked and window-shopped, ended our tour by buying some flowers for Madame. Nanou tutoyed me yesterday. When we came home she showed her mommy and daddy the change purse, then threw her arms around my neck and kissed me. Of course now I'll do anything for her.

At four yesterday afternoon we had our music history class – two hours of it. I always get embarrassed because M. Handemann so obviously prefers me to the others – and not quite just teacher-like-student preference either. After class he came up to me and told me to bring something to sing for him next time – after the others would be gone.

Before I write about today I want to get something straight. I realize fully now – in retrospect – how dangerous it was for me to go out alone like I did in Spain. I realized it the minute I got in from the date, and I vowed I would never do it again, and I won't. Somehow I forget about danger concerning people that seem nice, good. I certainly don't feel that way about everybody. I suppose I get too carried away with what goodness and trustfulness I do find in people. Anyway, I perfectly understand your wariness and uneasiness about that and I repeat – it shan't occur again.

But what hurt my feelings and rather amazed me is that you think I stay "tanked up all the time on wine and beer." I was so shocked to read that statement that I actually got sick at my stomach when I read it this morning. Perhaps you will say I stay tanked up all the time because every day, for two meals I drink wine, sometimes more than one glass a meal. Is that wrong? Thousands of Frenchmen do it every day. It's their milk. It does not make you drunk or "tanked up" unless you are a glutton about it – which I am not.

I have developed a taste for good wine, just as I have developed a taste for good beer – which happened in Germany. In general, perhaps I have a glass of beer a week. It tastes good – I drink only one glass – I do not get "tanked up."

In Europe drinking wine and beer are part of life – part of the cafés – with time out to enjoy each other's company and have a glass of wine or beer. It's like drinking Coca-Cola and lemonade at home. I repeat I have never seen a drunk European, except the bums who are often alcoholic, but they are rare. Granted, I was opposed to beer, alcoholic beverages at home. I practically never even had a drink before last year, when I did learn to like certain mixed drinks.

I think I would still be opposed to beer, liquor at home, because it's consumed with an entirely different point of view – in most cases. It's consumed for consummation's sake – to create hilarity – to make fools even more foolish. That is wrong. People must know how to be refined about drinking just like everything else. It's that way in Europe – and so am I. From now on I shall omit mentioning cafés and wine because I never want to have the hurt, sick, misunderstood feeling from a crude statement like "It seems that you stay tanked up all the time on wine and beer." I've always told you all everything – but I guess there are some things I should keep to myself alone.

End of speech. I'm going to bed now – will write about today, tomorrow. Excuse me if I've been out of line for a daughter of parents whom she dearly loves and worships, but I think I needed to defend myself.

Monday, March 18

Saturday Pierre and I had planned to ride to the sea following the Loire on his motor scooter. We were hoping for beautiful weather, but of course Saturday turned out to be the one day in the week that was chilly and grey. But, we decided to go anyway, I bundled up in slacks, sweaters, and jackets and at ten a.m. we started off. I love to ride his moto. We rode for about an hour and a half, then decided it was just too cold, and grey, and it was drizzling, to head for the sea.

We were about 30 minutes away from the little town of Chantilly, so we went there. There is a gorgeous château surrounded by beautiful moats with a gorgeous park and gardens, and elegant old stables, all in Chantilly. The château didn't open until 1:30 p.m. so we ate lunch in the meantime. Pierre was so sweet. He took me to the nicest restaurant in Chantilly – which was way too expensive. The food was delicious though. Pierre ordered us omelets – the best I've eaten – and entrecôte of beef. Then he said he wasn't hungry, so when the food came he made me eat it all. So I had a double lunch – but no complaints.

After lunch we rode to the château. The sun had begun to appear, and it made the château look like a fairy castle rising out of the water. All around the gates of the château were old women and little boys selling beautiful daffodils. As we walked across the courtyard to enter I suddenly had a mad desire to be a princess or duchess of the 18th century and ride in a carriage pulled by white horses from the stately stables.

We took a tour through the château. It's a beautiful thing, recently restored. It has the fabulous collection of miniatures painted by Jean Fouquet, the most famous 15th century miniaturist. We studied about them in our art course, and I was so glad to see them. There is also the most wonderful collection of portrait miniatures there. It really is just too charming – *ravissante* as the French would say.

After seeing the château we walked in the beautiful park. A pretty little canal runs through it, there are the first spring flowers along the banks. We came upon an old, old mill by a little stream, with a wooden wheel that was slowly turning. It was so picturesque. After about an hour of walking in the gardens and the park, we decided to leave. As we went out the royal gate Pierre bought me a bunch of jonquils from an old lady who was so cute. We boarded the moto and drove around the road that circles the château and gives a beautiful view of the entire landscape. The town of Senlis is only four miles away from Chantilly, so we decided to ride over there and visit the cathedral, which is one of the first of the Gothic cathedrals. We had studied it in art history, so of course I wanted to see it. Senlis is a calm, ancient, beautiful little town, the cathedral is certainly interesting, but not quite Gothic enough to be beautiful. The sculpture is wonderful. We left Senlis around 6:20 – headed straight for Paris, and got here around 7:15. It was such a wonderful day. All the way home we saw people riding bicycles loaded down with jonquils. I loved everybody so much. Pierre had been so nice all day, he's so cute, but I wish he'd have his hair cut. That was a stupid, selfish statement.

After lunch Sunday, Louise and I met John Donaher and John Hanna at the Étoile. John D. got John H. a date with Louise. John H. was okay but nothing special. John D. is great. We went to the Louvre for two hours, then to a concert – Igor Markevitch directing. He is here for a series of 5 concerts. I've heard the first two. The last one will be on April 7th to which we shall go, little Mother. After the concert, which was superb, we had dinner in a very cheap, but nice restaurant, and then went to the Abbaye, a little cabaret to which I've been dying to go for months. It's a tiny, tiny place with tiny tables and stools. The purpose for going there is to listen to the two guitarist singers there – one is a negro, the other a white man. They sing spirituals, French folk songs, American folk songs, and calypso songs. They really are good. The negro has the best voice and the best physique, he is very Harry Belafonte-ish – almost too at times. The place was packed to the brim with Americans, Englishmen, and Frenchmen. I had as much fun watching the people as I did listening to the singers. Guess what I had to drink – fruit juice! We stayed until midnight, then caught the Metro home. I was so glad to have gone to the Abbaye at last. Instead of applauding there you snap your fingers. It's quite "casual."

This morning I practiced from ten to twelve. One of the best practice sessions I've had. I must be in good form for M. Handemann on Wednesday.

Tuesday, March 19, 1957

Today was Monsieur and Madame's eighth wedding anniversary. They had their most intimate friends over for lunch today. Louise and I decided to give them a real nice gift, so we bought them a cake serving set – the knife and a spoon – silver plated – came to $12.00 ($6.00 apiece). They have been so wonderful to us.

Yesterday afternoon I went to the hotel around the corner to find out about your room, Mother. The name of the hotel is Le Rochambeau. I had them show me the rooms and they are really very nice. The kind I'm going to get for you is the one with a double bed and bath, but not a toilet. The toilet is just across the hall. It's over a dollar more with the toilet in the bath room, so since it's just a few steps from the door of your room I decided you'd rather save the dollar. The hotel management speaks English. The rooms are really nice. The price, not including a 10% service charge (found everywhere in France) is 1,650 francs a day – including the service charge it will be a little over $5.00 a day, which is not at all bad. That would make your bill about $35.00 for the time before we go to Italy. I hope you intend to stay at least another week after we get back from Italy. Do you? The big advantage to the hotel is that it's just 3 minutes from 3 rue de General Foy.

After seeing about the hotel I met John at the Étoile. We walked down the Champs to the American Embassy, where John wanted to have a chocolate milkshake. I hadn't had one in so long and it tasted so good. Over our milkshakes we talked about politics. John is a good friend of the Adlai Stevensons and a staunch Democrat. He knows much more (fortunately) about the Democrats than I do about the Republicans. He almost had me converted after the milkshake! Did you know that Eisenhower has not made (rather the Army has not made) one five-star general since Eisenhower came into office? I never even thought about it. John is really a good business man. His field is selling. He shall probably make a fortune if he can sell his product as effectively as he can sell the Democratic Party and the Catholic religion!

After milkshakes and politics we walked down by the Seine and watched the fishermen. I can't describe the beauty of the Seine well enough. It's just unbelievable. We walked on down by the Seine and crossed over to the Tuileries Garden, which are beautiful now with all the flowers. We sat down by one of the little pools and watched the children sailing their boats. We sat there watching and talking as the sun set. I could have sat there all night. About 7:30 we started walking again, crossed over to the Left Bank, walked down St. Germain-des-Prés till we came to the Bonne Crêpe, where we had delicious crêpes – thin, pancake-like things.

After eating we caught the Metro to the theater where *Streetcar Named Desire* (the movie) was playing. We had to stand in line about 30 minutes before we could get in, but it was worth it. That is really a classic movie. I saw the play last year in New Orleans and thought it was excellent. Tennessee Williams can really bring out the worst in people, both his characters and his audience! We didn't get out of the movie till 12:30, so John had to hurry to get his 1:00 bus. I came home in a taxi.

This morning I went to practice before my voice lesson at 11:00. It was one of the best I've had. Monsieur Bernac gave me an invitation to a concert at the American Embassy next Tuesday night given by Francis Poulenc, Monsieur Bernac, and Jean François. I'm thrilled to be going. I'm dying to see Poulenc.

This afternoon I did nothing but go to class. Madame Alvernhe gave us our grades from the Sorbonne for the art history course. The Sorbonne grades on a basis of 20. You must have 10 over 20 to pass. I had 10 over 20. I was so pleased. Newcomb will then interpret those grades according to their standards which are much more liberal than the Sorbonne. I'm not at all worried.

Tonight I'm going to bed for a change before 1:00 A.M. I have to sing for Monsieur Handemann tomorrow. I thought you might like to read the theme I wrote on my impressions of Paris, so I translated it into English.

Here it is:

> My impressions of Paris are numerous, too numerous to write all of them, but here are several impressions which I shall guard preciously for the rest of my life.

The Seine

For me the Seine is the symbol of the life of Paris. It flows through the middle of the city, seeming infinite, giving life by many ways to many people. Along the banks of the Seine the anglers stand for hours with pole in hand, waiting a gift – a tiny silver gift – from the river. At night the homeless beggars find a place to sleep under the shelter of the bridges of the Seine. The beauty of this river, in the shadow of the Eiffel Tower, which watches over the city like a great, grey phantom vigilante, gives pleasure and happiness to the millions of people who cross its bridges by bus or automobile, by bicycle, and on foot. The light of Paris, which is more luminous and delicate than the light of other cities, shrouds the Seine as if it were a holy shrine.

Place de la Concorde

At sunrise the sky is pink and grey; the street-lamps are yellow shadows in the light mist of morning. The people are grey silhouettes. The hum of life which comes with morning becomes gradually stronger, like a great Wagnerian crescendo. At sunset, the Eiffel Tower stands guard while the inhabitants of his city hurry to their apartments on the fifth floor and their flats on the ground floor.

Standing in the middle of the Place de la Concorde one sees the life of Paris: Elegance strolls along the brilliantly lighted Champs-Élysées. Poverty slinks in the dark corners; fatigue rides the buses and invades the Metro stations; Love walks languorously along the Seine. To the left is the Louvre with its incomparable treasures, the Arc du Carrousel is a shadow in the twilight. To the right is the imposing Arc de Triomphe, beyond which one sees nothing – it seems to be the end, the stopping place, the door between now and eternity. One wonders if the door between now and eternity will be more splendid than the Arc de Triomphe – perhaps Napoleon wondered the same thing when he constructed the famous arch.

The Latin Quarter

Every race, religion, political tendency is represented in this quarter. A feeling of humility and a thirst for learning dominates me when I'm in this quarter. The bearded, duffle-coated students buy the new progressive jazz records and Bartok quartets – music which is well accorded to the exciting and confusing student life.

MONTMARTRE

The two windmills which remain from the 14 original mills – the traces of a strange époque of art – Lautrec, Utrillo, Van Gogh, Gauguin, Monet . . . The atmosphere of an old world, the mystery of the little cabarets – the chords of old French songs accompanied by a guitar – the pseudo-existentialists who have just discovered Gide and Sartre and express their new discovery with their long hair, their pale faces, and their eye-makeup – the market with the sound and noise, the odor of food and of people mixed pleasantly into a rude odor.

THE CAFÉS

The cafés are the strongholds, the places of refuge. There are little cafés – the bistros where the workers drink their beer and think about Poujade. There are elegant cafés where one has the comfortable feeling of luxury that he can fall into like a feather bed. There are the average cafés where one finds the average people – where the true spirit fills the air with happiness until he thinks he shall burst! One realizes the secret of Paris: Paris is the Present – life is lived for the present – not for the past – not for the future. It's a secret which America has not yet found.

Anne Lindbergh expresses this secret of living in her book *Gift from the Sea*. She says:

"Europe has been forced into a new appreciation of the present. The good past is so far away, and the near past is so horrible, and the future is so perilous, that the present has the opportunity of expanding into a golden eternity of Here and Now. Europeans today take pleasure in the moment – even if it is only a walk in the country on Sunday, or the pleasure of sipping black coffee at a sidewalk café."

Thus – my impressions of Paris.

Saturday morning, March 23, 1957

I just can't seem to stay caught up in my journal anymore! So much has happened since Wednesday.

First of all, Mother, I'm so glad you're coming. I suppose by now you've received the information about the hotel. Now here's our itinerary for the trip:

We leave Paris on the 12th, arrive Venice on the 13th, on the 15th take the train to Florence, where we spend 5 days, then on to Rome for 5 days, including Easter Sunday, then on to Naples for 4 days, then one day in Pisa, on to Milan, arriving back in Paris on May 1st.

I think it's a perfect itinerary. Louise and I made it out and Mr. Hochwald made it just like we wanted. I'm sure going to St. Peter's Basilica on Easter Sunday will be a thrill of a life time. In Naples there is not just a lot to see except the natural beauty of the city, but it's a wonderful headquarters for day trips to Capri, Sorrento, and Pompeii. Pisa is small, and of course the leading attraction is the tower. Milan is also easy to see in a short time, and of course our main reason for going is to go to La Scala Opera. We're going to arrange to have tickets both for La Scala and St. Peter's on Easter before we leave. I get so excited about going!

About clothes: for Italy the best things will be skirts, blouses, and a few sweaters. Everyone says it is very warm in April in Italy. Suits would be fine. One nice dress will do. I'm going to travel very lightly. For Paris – bring one cocktail dress – or something cocktail-ish. Suits are in order now. You won't need a coat I don't think – if so, you can wear one of mine. You know so much about packing there's nothing I can really tell you.

About bringing me things: A new need has come up. Jean-Louis has invited me to the ball of Paris on May 8th, the ball given by the school of Political Science, where Jean-Louis' cousin goes, and his uncle is a big wig there. But you have to wear a long dress (and the men wear tails) which I don't have. I asked Jean-Louis if one to the ankles would do, and he said yes. I thought maybe you could bring the pink one for me. Of course I would rather have one made, or buy one but I'm afraid that isn't going to be possible.

Now – to get back to my life in Paris. Wednesday was the most wonderful mixed up day! Wednesday morning after music history class, I stayed at M. Handemann's and sang for him – he accompanied me. He was so enthused about my voice that he had me stay an hour and I sang practically my whole repertoire. He said he had no idea that I sang so well – that I had the type of voice he prefers and that before I go home he wants me to give a little concert at his house for some of his music friends and his wife. He asked me if I ever intended to come back to Paris. I said I wanted to, but I couldn't until after next year. He told me that whenever I came back he would do everything he could to put me in the music world's eye. He said he felt sure that after a year's more study he could even present me in the Paris Opéra!! I was so overjoyed and so thankful to hear it I was living in the clouds.

I was to meet Johanna Hammel at a café up the street after the singing session – I was so happy and thrilled that I ran all the way up the street. Everyone on the sidewalks thought I was out of my mind. Johanna was so excited to hear my news. She said that M. Handrnan was really an influential man, musically, and that I should really take advantage of his offer to help me. Johanna and I had a long talk about everything from staying on in Paris another year (she did it) to being in love, religion, life, everything. She's a wonderfully intelligent girl and I really enjoy her company. We stayed at the café until time to go home for lunch.

Wednesday night after dinner I met Pierre and we went walking by the Seine for little while. I was feeling sort of funny by then and didn't want to stay out late. We had some real interesting conversation. I found out Pierre's ambitions and hopes, and loves, etc. He's a member of the Socialist party, Guy Mollet is his boss, he intends to have Guy Mollet's job someday, he wants to own his own newspaper, he does not believe in God, he believes in a United Europe. It was really the first time we have had such serious conversations and I really enjoyed it. We walked back home through the Tuileries Garden, in front of the Louvre. It was such a gorgeous night.

Thursday morning we had class at the Sorbonne. After class, Louise, Eugenie, Susan, & I went to have coffee together. We were all talking about how sad it would be leaving Europe and how we envy the girls coming over next year.

Thursday night Jean-Louis and I went to hear the choir from Frankfurt, Germany sing a concert of four Bach cantatas at the Church St. Eustache. It was a beautiful concert. Nothing can beat a German choir for warmth and beauty. The soloists were all excellent, and quite young. After the concert I was so sleepy that I had to come right home.

Yesterday (Friday) I finally caught up on some much needed sleep. After lunch Louise and I went to look up the dressmaker, which I told you about. I was so disappointed that she couldn't sew for us. Later I took Nanou with me to pick up Isabelle from her catechism class at St. Augustin (Madame had her students and I offered to do it for her). I was so touched. When Isabelle got out of class she saw us waiting for her, and ran up to me and hugged me. She's never done that before. I was really touched by it.

At 6:30 I met John at the Étoile. We walked to the Eiffel Tower, sat by the Seine, and walked around Palais Chaillot. We were both in such a gay mood, we danced on the large square behind the Palais. I guess people thought we were nuts. Then we went to a little cheap restaurant we found and ate delicious ravioli. We sat over dinner almost two hours talking. We always have such stimulating conversations. Then we walked down the Champs, and sat in the park by the Place de La Concorde a little while, walked back up the

Champs a little, took a taxi to the Étoile, went into a café and drank coffee until his bus came, then I took a taxi home.

This afternoon at 2:30 Jacques Lauriau is coming to get Louise and me and take us to the Loire Valley in his car to see the châteaux – just the three of us. We're going to spend the night with his brother and sister-in-law who have a small château near one of the biggest ones – Blois. We'll have dinner there tonight after seeing a couple of châteaux this afternoon. Tomorrow we'll see several more, then return to his brother's for tea and dinner, and come back to Paris tomorrow night. Isn't that grand? And the weather is gorgeous!

Saturday night, March 23, 1957

Here I am in Oncques, France, a little town about 2 ½ hours from Paris. Jacques Lauriau came to pick us up at 2:30 – well he was late as usual, so he didn't get there till almost 3:00. We got in the car and started out for Château of Maintenon, to which we came about 4:15. This château belonged to Madame de Maintenon, the second wife of Louis XIV. It's a small château, very charming, furnished in wonderful taste. It is still privately owned, but in order not to pay the heavy taxes on it the owners have made it an historical monument and have opened it to the public on certain days. It has a splendid ballroom built by Louis XIV, the bedroom of Madame de Maintenon with adorable furniture – one of the most wonderful beds I've ever seen. The château faces a sort of canal at the end of which is an ancient aqueduct almost in ruins now, but it makes a very impressive decor. I would really have liked to own that château.

After the château visit we had pastry, then we climbed in the car and started off. By this time it had started to rain. We were so disgusted. We drove through Chartres. I never expected to see that cathedral again, but there it was, towering over the countryside, majestic and beautiful. From Chartres we drove on to where we are – Oncques. I was mistaken, I thought we were going to sleep at Jacques' brother's home, but we're not. We are in a darling little hotel with wonderful almost feather beds. Louise & I have a room and of course Jacques has his. When we first arrived we came up to our room and washed up, then went down stairs for dinner. We had the best dinner I've had in ages! The man who owns the place is the cook and he's so nice and such a good cook! First we had a delicious soup, then pâté, then veal with mushrooms, and potatoes that looked sort of like hush puppies, that were oh so good. Then we had lettuce salad and crème caramel, which is sort of a pudding, for dessert – all just delicious.

After dinner we went into the big room, the sort of entrance room, where there is a piano. Louise played and later I sang. The owner, the two girls who work here, and a real old woman all sat and listened and Jacques, too, of course. It had been a long time since anyone had played the piano for them and they really enjoyed it. I don't see how some people can say that the French people aren't friendly. While we were performing Jacques' brother came in with his wife and their children. They sleep here it seems instead of their home near here because it isn't heated. The home near here is their country home (they live in Paris). So we met them, talked awhile, their little girl played the piano, and we all came upstairs to go to bed. We're going to have supper at the brother's house tomorrow. It's so strange, all this. That Jacques would bring Louise and me to do all this, pay for us. He's old enough to be my father.

Monday morning, March 25, 1957

Yesterday was a wonderful day – even the weather cleared up for us. Our day started with a huge breakfast of café au lait and croissants, after which we drove to Blois and went directly to the château, which is one of the most famous châteaux of the Loire. It is very unusual. The construction lasted over several centuries, so when you enter through the courtyard, you are encircled by various architectural styles. Above the entrance is the famous statue of Louis XII on the horse that walks with both legs up on his left side. That's a stupid sounding sentence, but I hope you see what I mean. In this château Catherine de' Medici died, the Duke of Guise was murdered, and other such delightful events took place.

The construction of the château lasted over a period of centuries, therefore, there is a section built in the 12th or 13th century, one from the 14th and 15th, and the Italian influence section of the 16th century. The exterior is really impressive. The interior is rich and elegant and somewhat mysterious – especially Catherine de' Medici's little room with secret panels where this charming person hid her various poisons. The huge room reserved for the meeting of the États-Généraux (which occurred twice) is splendid – absolutely.

After Blois we drove to Chaumont. Here on top of the hill overlooking the Loire is a wonderful château, which belonged to Henry II's mistress – Diane of Poitiers. We drove along the road and looked at the château. It was dinner time then and the château was closed, so we crossed the Loire and drove to a tiny town called Ourzain to have dinner in a delightful little restaurant with wonderful food. After dinner we drove back to Chaumont to see the château.

It is very impressive with its towers, moats, and draw-bridges. It was originally a fortress. The interior is interesting, but certainly not as rich as that of Blois. As we were waiting for Jacques to buy our tickets at the entrance a bus load of American soldiers arrived. At first Louise and I decided to make them think we were French. We spoke French to each other, etc. It was so much fun to listen to the boys talk about us. They really did think we were French. After we got in the château the guides, who spoke only French, began showing all of us around. There were four American women there, one of whom seemed to know some French, but they weren't helping the soldiers at all. Finally, after hearing their pained statements like "I know this would be interesting if I could only understand," Louise and I began translating for them. They were so surprised that we were Americans! They were the nicest group of American soldiers I've met in Europe. They're stationed at Orléans and have been in France only about a week. They were from everywhere in the U.S. – were so eager to find out about France. We stayed with them and translated for them – the guide was equally pleased to have someone translate for her. After the tour we talked for a while with the soldiers, then told them goodbye and went on our way.

On the way down the hill to the car there was a field of beautiful jonquils. Of course I had to pick some. Since it was forbidden I hid them under Jacques' coat until we got in the car.

From Chaumont we headed for Jacques' brother's house. On the way we passed the châteaux of Menars and Talcy. It's so peaceful and beautiful along the Loire, no wonder all the kings and dukes wanted a château there.

As we arrived at Max Lauriau's house, he was shooting skeet with his son. They are both terrible shots! Both the daughters had girlfriends there. The youngest girl is 10, the oldest about 17. There is an older boy but he wasn't there. Madame Lauriau is so charming, has such a vivacious personality. They immediately gave us an aperitif, then Monsieur wanted us to go with him to see him feed his bees; he has about ten beehives. It was very interesting to watch. I had never been that close to a beehive before. It was getting rather chilly, so we came back to the house and soon had dinner. The house is delightful, is decorated very woodsy-ish – copper, brass, huge wooden beams. The big room, which is the living room, dining room combined has a huge fireplace and there was a wonderful open fire blazing. We warmed ourselves a little, then sat down for a dinner of cold pheasant, salad, cheeses, fruit salad and cookies, and coffee. It really tasted good. The Lauriaus were certainly gracious to have us there. Madame invited us to come back in May and let them take us on a night tour to see the châteaux illuminated. I certainly would like to take them up on it.

After dinner we drove back to Paris. The night was beautiful – stars were bright and the air was clear. It was the end of a lovely, enjoyable little weekend. The countryside (during the weekend) looked so beautiful. Spring has just begun to put on her finery. The jonquils and crocuses and other flowers that I've never seen were all in bloom. The peach and plum trees were all white and pink and beautiful. The new green was so bright and clear, the air smelled so good, the pastoral and quaint scenes were wonderfully charming. Nature certainly is wondrous.

Mother, I got your letter this morning. Of course I'll be at Orly Air Field to meet you at 12:35 p.m. on April 4th. We're going to have such a good time when you come. I can hardly wait. I wonder if you'll think I've changed much and if I look different to you. I'm afraid the color of my hair will be quite a shock!

Tuesday, March 26

First, Mother. Today at noon Monsieur Rémond offered to drive me to meet you at Orly Field. Of course I took him up on it. We'll come from Orly to the Rémonds and have lunch here – this was Madame's suggestion. I think it was so sweet of them to offer. It will work out perfectly, because after lunch, which we probably won't finish until around 2:30, I have a class from 2:30-4:30. During that time you can go to the hotel and get settled and rest. Doesn't that sound nice?

Yesterday John and I went to Parc Monceau. It's a small park, but supposedly the most elegant of Parisian parks. It's so adorably beautiful – very small, but perfectly laid-out. The flowers are all in bloom, and there are some of the most gorgeous flowering trees I've ever, ever seen. I took a few pictures of the park and of the crowds in the park.

After strolling through the park we went back up to the Étoile just in time to see and hear the ceremony for the unknown soldier, which is performed every day, but that was the first time I had ever seen it. It's quite impressive with the flowers, the flags, and the gendarme band. Then John surprised me by telling me we were going for dinner at La Reine Pédauque. I was floored! But of course I didn't object. The food was just as delicious as it was the first time I was there I can't wait for you to experience it, Mother. We ate until we could eat no more, then went for a long digestive walk along the Seine and came home.

March 27, Wednesday

All yesterday morning I practiced, had a voice lesson at 12:00. I wish I were only taking voice lessons and had all the rest of the time to practice. Yesterday afternoon we had Theater class, this morning I went to music history class, practiced and now I'm waiting for lunch.

I don't know what's wrong with me today but I'm very sad. I feel like if anyone says anything to me I shall cry. I haven't felt this way in ages.

Friday, March 29

I just finished a voice lesson. I get so excited in my voice lessons I can hardly stand it. Today we talked about Marjorie Lawrence – I'm so thrilled about the chance to study with her next year.

Yesterday was Mi-Carême (mid-way Lent), which is a celebration day in France. Since today is Isabelle's birthday the Rémonds gave her a party yesterday. Twenty-one little children came and they had such a good time. Madame rigged up costumes for all of them and they dressed up and played wedding and had all sorts of goodies to eat and drink. After class Louise and I came and joined them. Some of the parents came too, and they didn't leave until around seven-thirty. Poor Madame was exhausted. She gave Louise and me our supper then went to bed. After eating I washed all the dirty dishes. Monsieur came in and found me doing it and nearly had a fit. Then Madame came in to eat a bite of supper. She thanked me for cleaning up. Louise came in and the four of us sat down and drank coffee together in the kitchen. There is something about a kitchen that is so intimate.

We had a make-up class with Mr. Handemann yesterday. I love to go to his house – he has so many wonderful books and records. I wish I could be left alone in his library for days and explore all of his treasures.

Saturday morning, March 30, 1957

Yesterday afternoon Louise and I met Johanna Hammel and Mrs. Smithers at the Smithers' and we concertized all afternoon. Louise played, I sang, and Johanna played. Mrs. Smithers just listened. We stayed there until nearly six. It was so much fun – nothing does one's music more good than to perform for others.

After the recital Johanna took Louise and me for tea. She had invited us to her apartment for tea but we stayed so long at the Smithers' we didn't have time to go with her – so we made a date for next week.

After dinner last night I went to the Opéra-Comique by myself to see *Cavalliera Rusticana* and *Pagliacci*. The tenor in the first one ruined the whole thing – they just don't make good tenors in France! In the second one everybody was good and I really enjoyed it. Neither of them are really great as far as music is concerned but they are pleasant and can certainly be moving if done well.

This afternoon John and I took the Metro to Neuilly and then took the bus to go to Malmaison – Josephine's home which Napoleon built for her and where she lived after the divorce and where she died. It's an exquisite château with Napoleon's evidence everywhere. There are some of the most exquisite pieces of silver, gold, and porcelain I've ever seen. Napoleon's and Josephine's clothing is fascinating. It's so hard to believe that Napoleon was not much larger than I am! Josephine's bed is magnificent. Her sign, emblem, is two swans and you find them everywhere – even real ones in the little lake in the garden. It really is a beautiful country home, as it was to the Empress. I think I could have been in love with Napoleon had I lived back then.

We left Malmaison and took the bus to St. Germain-en-Laye, where Henri IV used to have a beautiful château. It has disappeared and now there is a new one – 18ᵗʰ or 19ᵗʰ century. But the big attraction is a mammoth terrace that stretches for miles from which there is a magnificent view of Paris way in the distance. It really is a fine view. The Eiffel Tower was a slight grey shadow from there. We walked along the terrace taking photos until time to catch the train for Paris, to Gare St. Lazare. We walked to La Pépinière for supper, spending more time conversing than eating. Then John walked me home and he left to catch the bus for SHAPE.

Sunday, March 31st

This has been a full day. This morning Louise and I went to Père Lachaise cemetery to visit all the famous tombs of famous people. Père Lachaise is the most beautiful cemetery. Of course all the tombs are built above the ground. The site of the cemetery is high on a hill overlooking Paris – a beautiful view from there of Note Dame, the Eiffel, the Pantheon, the Invalides. The trees are so beautiful and so are the flowers. It's not at all like being in a cemetery as far as Death goes. It seems to be a city – the inhabitants are inside their neatly constructed houses waiting to be waked up by someone. It makes Death seem so beautiful and restful – l wish I could be buried there, then I could look out over my precious Paris without end.

I really was moved seeing the graves and tombs of such men as Chopin,

Balzac, David, Géricault, Bizet, Molière, La Fontaine, Beaumarchais, Sarah Bernhardt, Oscar Wilde, Cherubini, Rossini, Delacroix, Heloïse and Abélard, General Foy, Marshal Ney, thousands of people are buried in Père Lachaise. The tombs are so interesting, and some of the epitaphs are rare. I could have spent the whole day there, but since we had to be home for lunch by one, I didn't stay of course.

We had a tasty dinner at noon, after which I ran to catch the Metro to go to the Theater National Populaire to see *Le Marriage de Figaro,* one of our theater requirements. I was late getting there, so I had to see most of the first act in the "latecomer" room where there are television sets on which the play is televised and you can watch it even though you're late. The play was delightful. The T.N.P. performs classics like *Marriage* in a renovated, rejuvenated style that is marvelous. It was so charming and delicate. It really is a masterpiece of comedy and wit.

After the play I rushed to Salle Pleyel to hear Igor Markevitch's fourth concert he's giving in Paris. Today he conducted Shubert's *Magic Symphony,* Beethoven's Fifth Piano Concerto, Satie's *Parade* and Rossini's Overture from *William Tell.* The piano concerto was fine except where the pianist played. He was horrible! I'm sure Markevitch was mortified to be on the same program with him.

When I was standing in line for my tickets to that concert, I was behind two American girls from the East, and then they sat in front of me in the concert. Listening to their conversation, looking at their dress, observing their reactions to things, I was aware of how different girls from the South are. It's rather strange to see that much difference. They seem so cold and abrupt. I think I'll discuss that point with John tomorrow.

Welcoming
Mother
(and Queen Elizabeth)
to Paris

Thursday, April 4, 1957

Dear Daddy,

Mother is almost here and I'm so excited! I just can't believe she's really coming and I don't suppose I will until I see her.

I haven't written since Sunday, and so much has happened since then.

Monday morning was that awful art history class that is so boring. Monday afternoon I had a voice lesson – which meant that all Monday morning before class, and all Monday afternoon before the lesson was spent practicing. Later I met John and we walked to the Opéra, window shopping and cutting up on the way. We saw *La Traviata* at the Opéra. It was a beautiful production as far as costumes, scenery, etc., goes, but the singing was certainly below par. It makes me so angry to think that in such a wonderful place as the Paris Opéra, the singing is usually so inferior.

After the opera, John and I decided to revisit the Abbaye. We enjoyed the performers, but not as much as the first time we were there. We left the Abbaye and walked to Les Halles, the huge street market where all the trucks from the country come in about 2:00 a.m. bringing the food that feeds all Paris. We walked there by way of the Seine – the most beautiful sight in the world at night. We got to Les Halles and walked around looking at all the vegetables, watching the trucks come in, and watching the people from the country set up their places. It was really fascinating. The meat arrived, too, all bloody and fresh. The vegetables were beautiful, huge, wonderful-looking things. John and I were the only "foreigners" there, and some of the workers made comments about lovers and how crazy we were (thinking we were lovers) every time we walked by them. We went to one of the little restaurant cafés in Les Halles – Au Chien Qui Fume, which is one of the most famous ones there. We ate the famous onion soup that is a specialty around Les Halles and drank white wine. It was certainly delicious. Then at 4:15 we called it a day, took a cab and came home. It was a wonderful evening.

Tuesday

After having slept for all of three hours I got up and did some of the work I had to do, planned a schedule for Mother and me, etc. Tuesday afternoon we had class – which I groggily attended. Tuesday night was Monsieur Bernac's concert with Monsieur Poulenc. I asked Louise, Susan, Eugenie, and Johanna to come too. The concert was at the American Embassy and was a very exclusive affair. Lots of important and intriguing people were there. Monsieur Bernac sang so well and I was so proud to be one of his pupils. Poulenc's music is so delightful. I was so happy to see him after hearing about him and hearing his music for so long. I really was thrilled to death to get to go.

Wednesday morning was Music History class and work time. Afternoon was a voice lesson. At six I met John and we had dinner before going to the Opéra to see the ballet – which was fabulous. I was so relieved because I was afraid it would turn out like the opera the other night. But it was quite good, and John and I both were really glad we went.

Today, I spent the morning getting ready to meet Mother, and helped Madame with the table. At 11:30 Monsieur drove Louise and me to Orly Field. The plane was about 10 minutes late. We got there so early, Monsieur took us upstairs to the bar and bought us an aperitif. When the plane did arrive I saw Mother get off, but I couldn't run to her because she had to come through the customs first. We were waving at each other – finally she came through the gate. We were so glad to see each other. And it was really so strange because when I saw her, all of a sudden we had never been apart. She looks so cute and good. She never changes. It's funny how you all never change for me. I wish you were here too, Daddy.

It took a rather long time to get Mother's bags, but finally we did and Monsieur Rémond loaded us in his car and drove us home. Madame had everything all ready for us. She had cooked a wonderful meal for us – unfortunately Mother wasn't very hungry. It was so delicious that I was stuffed to the gills by the time we finished.

After dinner we had coffee – then we left to carry Mother's bags to the hotel for her. Louise then went on to practice and Mother unpacked and we talked until nearly six. (She doesn't like my long hair.) Then we went to see Mrs. Smithers and leave some money to have it changed. Then we walked to Sèvres-Babylone, took the Metro to St. Michel and went to the little Greek place I know to eat shish kabobs. Then we took the Metro to Concorde and walked from there back to the hotel. We talked a few minutes, then I came home. I still can't believe she's really here. I've really got lots of plans for us while Mother's here – we're certainly going to stay busy.

Saturday night, April 6, 1957

It's so wonderful having Mother here! Wish you all could be here too.

Yesterday we had a big day. Mother slept late while I helped Madame Rémond clean the house and get ready for the party. Then at 12:30 I went by to get Mother and, according to French habits, we lingered over lunch, talking, catching up on everything. Then we headed for Notre Dame. We visited Notre Dame inside and out, and even climbed hundreds of steps up to the tower – which I have never done before – from where there is the most beautiful view of Paris. You can see everything. We also went into the room in one of the towers where the huge bell is – the bell Quasimodo rode to make it ring. It's mammoth.

From Notre Dame we went to Sainte-Chapelle. I really enjoyed re-visiting it, it's so beautiful. From Sainte-Chapelle we went to the Conciergerie, an ancient palace that served as the prison during the French Revolution. It was there that Marie Antoinette was imprisoned and tried, and from there she rode to Place de la Concorde where she was guillotined. The prison is a gruesome thing to see, but certainly interesting. All that sight-seeing took all afternoon. Then we took the bus to the Champs-Élysées, which, like all of Paris, is being decorated for Queen Elizabeth's arrival this coming Monday. By the way, Tuesday night the Queen and her company are going to make a promenade on the Seine and Monsieur Rémond has procured reserved seats for us to see her! Isn't that wonderful?

After a quick supper we hurried home to get ready for the party, which was a huge success. People started coming about nine thirty. Somehow the job fell to me to be the welcomer and the introducer but I enjoyed it thoroughly. The group consisted of the eight of us from Newcomb, Madame Smithers, Madame Alvernhe, Madame Woodall, Jean-Louis Baut and his cousins Michel and Dominique, Louise's friend Philippe and two of his friends, Robert Blake (an Englishman), Marie-Louise Bernard and five of her friends, a girl and a boy from Middlebury College, and Madame Rémond's cousin. Oh, and Sandy's friend, Michel.

It was a lovely group and we had such a good time dancing and eating the goodies. Madame Rémond had really fixed up the table nicely with Louise's help. Mother was a big hit. Madame Alvernhe just loved her. Jean-Louis was quite impressed too. When I introduced Jean-Louis and his cousins to Mother they all bowed and bent their heads down to her hand. When Jean-Louis left he kissed her hand and so did Louise's friend Philippe. I'm so glad Mother got to see our friends and see how a party with French people is. Everybody stayed until after two a.m. Finally they did leave. I walked with Mother to the hotel afterwards, then met Jean-Louis, Martha, Eugenie, and Dominique and we took a taxi to the Champs-Élysées for coffee. I came back to the hotel at three fifteen, and Mother and I went to bed – talked until nearly four.

Saturday morning we got up about eleven. I dressed and came home and washed clothes, and caught up on some of the things I'm so far behind in. At one I went to get Mother at the hotel. We took the Metro to Montmartre, where we immediately went to Place du Tertre and to Mère Catherine, a darling restaurant, where we had a divine lunch of coq au vin.

After lunch we walked around Place du Tertre – it used to be the communal center for the village of Montmartre. Then we went to Sacré-Cœur – the gorgeous white church that overlooks all of Paris. Unfortunately the weather was foggy and the view was almost imperceptible. From Sacré-Cœur we walked to the little wax museum of the history of Montmartre which I had already seen. It was still interesting the second time. We walked through Montmartre – past the two windmills that remain out of the 14 original ones.

We walked through the market place and saw all the meats and vegetables and flowers, examined the things we had never seen. Then we were in Pigalle. We walked down to the Moulin Rouge and saw it, then we went to Au Printemps so Mother could see what a French department store looks like. After more walking and window shopping, we caught the bus to the Smithers' where we met Louise and Mr. Hochwald and talked about our trip to Italy for about an hour. Then we came back – Mother to the hotel and me home to get ready to go to Maxim's.

At ten we took a taxi to Maxim's. I couldn't believe that we were there. The door man let us in, they took our coats, and ushered us to our table. Maxim's looks exactly like I thought it would – old and elegant and reminiscent of bygone days of untold wealth. The orchestra was wonderful, the people were so interesting and elegant. But the food was the best. It was absolutely delicious. We had artichokes with hollandaise sauce, turtle soup, and pigeon! I've never eaten pigeon before and it was delicious. It was cooked with tomatoes and green olives and mushrooms. It really was a supreme delight. For dessert we had lemon sherbet that was beyond a doubt the most exquisite dessert I've ever eaten. The whole dinner was marvelous and it was quite a thrill to be at Maxim's.

Sunday morning I got up and worked a little and met Mother at eleven thirty. After a nice lunch we took the Metro to the Flea Market. It was still fascinating on the third visit. Mother and I browsed and priced and fingered things all afternoon. We both hated to leave but it was sort of cold and we had tickets for the concert that began at five forty-five. The concert was the last of a series of five that Igor Markevitch has conducted here in Paris. It was certainly a triumphal finish for his stay in Paris. He is such a marvelous conductor. They did Beethoven's Ninth Symphony and it was one of the most thrilling things I've ever heard. After the concert Mother and I went to the Café de la Paix near the Opéra for some tea and pastry before the opera. Café de la Paix is one of the oldest and most elegant of Parisian cafés. At the opera we saw the *Martyre de Saint Sébastien*. It's a very interesting spectacle – music is by Debussy, there is ballet, recorded singing voices, and several recorded speaking voices. The costumes and colors were gorgeous. I've never seen anything quite like it before.

April 12, 1957

Right now I'm on the train to Italy and I can't believe it. It was such a rush to get here! I'm so far behind in this diary, I'll never get caught up.

Monday morning I took Mother to class with me at the Sorbonne. Hardly anyone was there because it was the morning the Queen arrived. I'm glad Mother did get to see it, and how class is. After class we went for a quick lunch then we walked over to the Luxembourg Gardens and Palace. Everyone was sitting in the sun trying to soak up some sunshine, all the chestnut trees are in bloom and they looked so pretty.

We left the gardens and walked back to the hotel, looking in the store windows as we went. Then we went to our respective abodes to dress for dinner. Louise and I met Mother at 7:45 at her hotel then walked to the La Reine Pédauque for dinner. In its usual style it was delicious. The wine of course is unbelievable – and it got to all three of us before we left. We were all laughing and being silly. We ate for about three hours, then walked home as fast as we could. That is really the best restaurant for the price.

Tuesday morning we saw the Queen's parade that passed right under Mother's hotel room balcony! Queen Elizabeth and Prince Philip were in an open car, with Elizabeth seated beside President René Coty, Philip seated behind with Mme. Coty. They were followed by state officials in 15 powder blue open cars, all of the same make. The Parisian women were waving handkerchiefs and calling out, "Phillippe, Phillippe, Phillippe!"

After the parade, I had a voice lesson, then I met Mother for lunch, then we walked to the American Express to see about buying Italian lira. Later I had my first voice lesson with Bernac's assistant, Madame Tilliard, who is delightful. I shall have a lesson with her once a week to work out little details about interpretation. I know I'll be able to make some really good progress with her and Bernac too when I come back from Italy.

After my second voice lesson of the day I met Mother, then we met Louise and we took the bus to the Seine. By the time we got there the crowd was already huge. Thanks to Monsieur Rémond we had wonderful places right on the banks of the river, between Place de la Concorde and the Alexander III bridge. On the Concorde bridge were French, British, and American soldiers – there for the purpose of greeting the Queen. They sang songs and led cheers. On the Alexander III bridge were all the fireworks. They were really spectacular – all colors, shapes, and sizes, including a waterfall of fireworks cascading over the entire bridge.

We had a good view of the Queen and Philip in their boat, which stopped in front of us to watch the fireworks. They are quite impressive. Elizabeth was a vision of glory. Seated alone in the glassed-in bow, on the top level, bathed in light, she was dressed in a long, white, billowing gown, a white fur around her shoulders, long white gloves, glittering jewels, and a sparkling crown. She looked like a true fairy princess.

I enjoyed the crowd's reaction to the fireworks more than the royal guests. As the fireworks exploded into various colors the crowd shouted "Un, Deux, Trois, Ooh la la!"

I wish we could have seen all of the Seine because near Notre-Dame there were little choir boys singing for the Queen. Each bridge had something of interest for the Queen and her cortège. Everybody took advantage of her coming to make it a national holiday. Everything was illuminated Tuesday night – all the monuments, which is really a beautiful sight to see. In the daytime there were the decorations everywhere – fresh flowers on the lampposts of the Champs, of the Avenue de L'Opéra, on the steps of the Madeleine. Enormous French and British flags were flying everywhere and all the fountains were turned on. It was quite an experience.

After the promenade on the Seine the three of us walked back up to the Place de la Concorde. An unbelievable crowd was there, the kind of crowd you see in movies in mob scenes. The cars were forced to stop so all the people could pass. We fought our way through toward the Madeleine. Finally the crowd dispersed enough to let us get through. We went to Queenie's and had onion soup, then came home. It was a thrilling evening. Place de la Concorde was really beautiful with all the lights and the fountains going.

Wednesday morning Mother and I ran into the Queen again! We were walking down Avenue Montaigne on the way to Dior's to see about tickets for the style show. As we were walking a crowd began to form and then the Queen passed in her Rolls Royce on the way to the Scottish Church. We had to wait while she laid the cornerstone for the Church and passed us again before the police would allow us to go across the street. Once in Dior's we were told to come back at 2:45 with our passports, then we walked up the Champs-Élysées, took the Metro to the Eiffel Tower, where we met Louise and John. We had to fight a huge crowd to get in the elevator to go up to the restaurant. The restaurant is the first stop. There's a beautiful view from there of course and we had a gorgeous day. The restaurant on that first landing was filled, so we went up to the second landing restaurant, which is not as fancy and expensive, but is just as good. We had a delicious meal and sat and talked till four. We finally left and took the Metro to the Étoile, Louise left us, and John and Mother and I headed for the Arc de Triomphe to go to the top and see the little Napoleonic museum. As we headed toward the Champs we noticed the crowd (obviously) and I asked a gendarme if the Queen was going to pass. He said she was, and that we couldn't cross the street to the Arc until she passed. So – we waited half an hour. While we were waiting the priest who holds the flag during the ceremony for the unknown soldier every night was standing by me and we started talking. He was such a cute, charming little priest. We talked all about the Queen, about Spanish, about his teaching school, we even sang songs! Finally, the Queen came by – this making the 4th time we had seen her.

That evening Monsieur and Madame dressed to go to the ball at the Louvre for the Queen. I've never seen Madame so beautiful. She really did look gorgeous. She had her hair fixed and a tiara in it. I was stunned at how beautiful she looked. Monsieur looked quite dashing in his tails. He was so proud to be going. He was so excited all week about going to the parties for the Queen. He told us every day where he was going and how favored he was to be going. I don't blame him, I would have been excited too.

After they left I got ready to meet Mother and John at the hotel (John stayed there too), and we went to have a sandwich before going to the Lido, so we finally got there at about ten forty-five. The first spectacle began at eleven – the second at one. They were both excellent – beautiful costumes, good dancing, good music, half-nude and almost nude girls but they were quite dignified in their nudity. John and I danced a little – we had champagne to drink. It was a very nice evening – I'm glad I've been to the Lido, but I don't care about going back. Almost everyone there was an American – even some of the show was announced in English. I just think there are so many more attractive "Frenchie" places to go – but as I said, I'm glad I've been.

Thursday morning I had to write a theme. Mother spent the afternoon by herself, and I met Jean-Louis at twelve-thirty to have lunch with him. I hadn't seen him for a week and wouldn't see him for three more weeks, so I felt I should do that. We ate at La Pépinière – sat and talked till 2:30. He walked me home, made me go get Louise and let him take us to class in a taxi. We got to class right on time. Jean-Louis kissed my hand goodbye, and Louise and I ran upstairs to Mr. Handemann's. After class I went by to check on Mother. She had already eaten her dinner and was planning on going to bed early.

Friday morning I went to practice, then met Mother and helped her move from the hotel to our house. After doing some packing Mother and I went for some lunch then went to Dior's where we met Louise. We went inside that divine smelling place and up the stairs to the show rooms. We had good seats. The clothes were strange and beautiful – the models were even stranger. I had to leave before it was completely over to go to my last voice lesson before we left for the trip.

An Easter Trip to Italy

April 12, 1957 (continued)

At eight we had dinner (Mother, too) at the Rémonds. It was so nice of them to ask us. At ten twenty Phillippe Moret (Louise's friend) came by and drove the three of us to the station, where we met Eugenie, Martha, Sandy and Coco and got our compartment. It had awful seats. We talked for a while, then slept – if you can call that sleeping. It was quite a tiring evening to say the least. Saturday morning we were pooped – all day long Saturday we were on the train. It wasn't too bad because the scenery was gorgeous. We went through Switzerland and finally got into Italy. The weather was beautiful. We arrived in Venice at five-thirty. Mother, Louise and I left the others and took the boat that takes you from the station to Piazza San Marco. It was a beautiful ride.

Venice is a dream city – beautiful Renaissance palaces sitting on the water – gondolas and gondoliers. We arrived at Piazza San Marco – the most wonderful piazza! The Cathedral of San Marco is beautiful – the clock with the Iron Men who strike the bell every hour is fascinating. The pigeons are almost delightful. We walked to our hotel which is just off the piazza. It's a nice little hotel. We have a room with three beds. We freshened up a little, then went to Harry's Bar – of Hemingway fame. We had a Mimosa Cocktail – champagne and orange juice. Practically everyone in Harry's was American or English. I was surprised to see Harry's so new and modern. We left Harry's and came back to the hotel for dinner. We're on half pension here which means we have breakfast and one other meal here at the hotel. Our meal was delicious. Then we all came upstairs and went to bed. It felt so good!

This morning – Palm Sunday – we had a wonderful breakfast in bed, then dressed and started out to see Venice. We crossed the Piazza San Marco which I dearly love – and went to see the Ducal Palace – which is right beside the Cathedral. It's an ancient (begun in the 11th century) palace lived in by the Dukes of Venice and her province. It is certainly beautiful. The architecture is Byzantine – which is like the Moorish architecture in Spain. Inside the courtyard you see the Renaissance façades and you know you are really in Italy. Venice, however, has more Byzantine art than Renaissance. We went all through the fabulously rich rooms of the Ducal Palace. The gold ceilings, the marble floors, the Tintoretto and Veronese paintings are marvelous. From the palace balconies there is a beautiful view of the lagoon, the Adriatic Sea and the Piazza San Marco.

After the visit to the palace we walked along the main quai and hired a gondola to take us through the little canal and the Grand Canal, past the

Rialto bridge as far as the Ca' d'Oro – a beautiful palace (when I say palace in every case but the Ducal Palace, I mean mansion). We left the gondola and started walking then. We walked back to the Rialto Bridge – an unusual bridge, because it has three walkways and in between are small buildings. There was a nice looking restaurant just below the bridge, and we decided to eat there. We had delicious food and heavenly pastry for dessert. After dinner we walked back to Piazza San Marco. The streets of Venice – rather sidewalks – are fascinating. The buildings are ancient, the canals and bridges prolific. It seems so strange to see no cars, no buses – only gondolas and other boats. Back at Piazza San Marco we visited the cathedral. The beautiful mosaics are amazing. The gold is dazzling. Under the altar is the urn containing the remains of St. Mark's body (supposedly). Over the altar is an exquisite piece of silver and gold work that is ancient. But for me the beauty of San Marco is the exterior. It's so unusual with the paintings, the mosaics, the four bronze horses, the five domes and the many statues. After visiting the church we rode the elevator to the top of the tower of the bells – the Campanile. It was built in 1152 and in 1952 it fell for no reason at all. It has been completely rebuilt now. From the top is a beautiful view of Venice and the surrounding area. The huge bells at the top of the tower are wonderful.

We came down from the tower and crossed to one side of the piazza where there are tables and chairs for coffee and. tea. We sat there for an hour and when the sun had left that side and gone to the other, we followed it and had coffee on the other side of the piazza where we sat for another hour – till five. I really enjoyed just sitting and watching all the people. The clock with the man striking the bells is so wonderful to watch. I could have sat there all day long. Venice is really a fairy land with the lagoons and gondolas. I can't imagine living here! It would be like playing I think.

Monday, April 15, 1957

Here we are in Florence – the richest city in Western civilization for art and beauty. We left Venice this morning. We checked out of the hotel at 7:30 but had to wait about 15 minutes for the boat to come. We wanted to catch the fast train to Florence, but we got to the train station just as it was pulling out.

We rallied and sat outside in the sun drinking coffee until 10:00 when the second train came. We arrived in Florence then at 2:00. The station is just a couple of blocks from our hotel, the Hotel Gioconda, small but very nice.

As soon as we were settled in the hotel we took a horse and carriage to

Piazza San Marco where we took the bus to Fiesole – a little village on one of the hills that surrounds Florence. From there is a beautiful view of Florence and there are Roman ruins of a theater, baths, a temple, and city ruins. We also saw the small cathedral and bell tower from the 11th century. The wind was blowing like 60 but we braved it and climbed up one of the highest peaks for the view which was indeed beautiful. We came down from the peak and had tea in one of the little shops. Lots of tourists were there – French, English, as well as American. After our tea we caught the bus back to San Marco, and from there we took a bus to our hotel.

After dressing for dinner we walked down the street to a wonderful restaurant recommended by Fielding called Ristorante Sabatini. We had the most delicious meal at a very reasonable price. Now we're in the hotel – freezing because there's no heat in our room. So far Italy has been sunny, but not very warm.

Tuesday, April 16, 1957

Today has been a humdinger! We started it out very luxuriously with breakfast in bed. Then at 9:00 we hit the streets to see what we could see. Louise has worked hard to make out an itinerary for us for this trip, and we followed it today. We started out by walking to the Uffizi Gallery – one of the richest art galleries in Italy. On the way we stopped in the Church of Orsanmichele (San Michele in Orso). It's a small, delicieux little church with wonderful Gothic sculpture, an exquisite inlaid marble tabernacle. On the exterior at each corner is a statue of a saint put there by one of the ancient guilds as their patron saint. For example the butchers' patron saint was Saint Peter.

We left San Michele and walked on a little farther until we came to Palazzo Vecchio. Here is the oldest plaza in Florence with the old Palazzo Vecchio, the Loggia della Signoria, and the Uffizi Gallery all right there. An equestrian statue of Cosimo de' Medici and a huge fountain of Neptune are marvelous. On the porch of the loggia are some famous original sculptures – such as Benvenuto Cellini's *Perseus*, a copy of Michelangelo's *David* is in front of the Palazzo Vecchio. To enter the Uffizi Gallery was almost impossible because there were so many people. I had the worst struggle I've ever had trying to buy our entrance tickets. Finally after pushing and being pushed, we made our way in. We spent the whole morning from 9:30 to nearly 1:00 looking at marvelous paintings of Botticelli, Rubens, Watteau, Michelangelo, Tintoretto, Andrea del Sarto, Giotto, Da Vinci, Fra Filippo Lippi, Titian, and many others. It was truly an enriching experience. I felt like I was making a new discovery every time I saw one of the marvelous masterpieces.

We left the Uffizi Gallery (which was begun by the Medici family) and went to eat lunch at a recommended restaurant, Nadina's. It was delicious, extremely inexpensive and I was absolutely stuffed. Afterwards we walked back to the Palazzo Vecchio to see it. It was once used for the City Council meetings. It is a magnificent building with gorgeous gold ceilings, wonderful paintings. My favorite part of the palazzo was the little private library of Francis I (a Medici) with all the secret doors and staircases. While we were visiting the Palazzo, Louise ran into some friends from Baton Rouge!

From the Palazzo Vecchio we walked to Ponte Vecchio – the oldest bridge in Florence. It has houses on either side of it and is so peculiar. All sorts of little silver, leather, and jewelry shops line the bridge. We looked in all the windows as we made our way toward San Miniato al Monte. We walked and walked – uphill – finally came to Piazza Michelangelo where there is a beautiful view of the city and a handsome monument to Michelangelo. We had tea in a delightful sunny café there. Then we climbed the rest of the way to San Miniato al Monte – an unusual Renaissance church with a facade and interior of inland black and white inlaid marble. It really is magnificent. The mosaic above the altar is unbelievable in its beauty. We descended from San Miniato, walked to Ponte Vecchio and walked down the other side of the street. In one of the stores I bought a grey umbrella with a silver handle that's gorgeous. After some shopping we came back to a little restaurant for dinner, which was quite good, and the bill was next to nothing.

Wednesday, April 17, 1957

Today was a whopper too! We started out a nine o'clock and went to the Cathedral Santa Maria del Fiore. The facade was completed in the 19th century. The colors are pink, white, grey, pale green. The statues are painted. too. The marble and stone are laid in geometric patterns which make strikingly unusual effects. The cathedral is absolutely huge. It's difficult to describe because it's so fantastic. However, the interior is not nearly so wonderful as the exterior. There is a beautiful dome with scenes of the Last Judgment and a very famous painting of Dante explaining his *Divine Comedy*. Right next to the cathedral is the Giotto Bell Tower – the second most famous tower in Italy. It has the same decor motifs of marble as the cathedral. It, too, is quite impressive. The most unusual thing is the series of sculptures picturing the stages of man's life and the things that influence man. In front of the cathedral is the Baptistry of

St. John, an octagonal-shaped building, again in the same marble decor. The interior of the dome is a marvelous mosaic picturing scenes from the Old and New Testaments. The three huge bronze doors of the baptistry are the most famous. They are divided in sections carved in bronze. One door tells the story of St. John the Baptist; another depicts the life of Christ; and the third, the most famous, has scenes from the Old Testament.

From there we went to the Church of San Lorenzo – a strange church because the front of it was never finished. The interior is quite beautiful however. Behind San Lorenzo is the Medici Chapel. In the crypt are buried most of the Medici family. Upstairs in a magnificent octagonal polychrome marble building are buried some of the great Medici dukes. The huge room is awesome – it's so rich and fine. In a smaller chapel are buried two of the greatest Medicis – Lorenzo and Guiliano. To commemorate their lives are two marvelous monuments sculptured by Michelangelo. Lorenzo is sculptured as the thinker with Dusk and Dawn lounging on his tomb. Guiliano is sculptured very elegantly with Day and Night on his tomb. They are really marvelous monuments.

From the Medici chapels we went to lunch, and then went to the wonderful San Marco Museum with the most precious collection of Fra Angelico paintings in the world. It really is a gem. His *Last Judgment* and *Descent from the Cross* are marvelous. In each of the little cells which belonged to the priests, Fra Angelico painted small frescoes which today are, of course, priceless.

We left the San Marco Museum and went to the Galleria Academia – a wonderful collection of Michelangelo and of 15th Century painters. The main thing in this museum is Michelangelo's *David* – a masterpiece. *David* is the most powerful man I've ever seen. He is standing – squinting waiting for just the right minute to throw the stone in the sling shot. He is the handsomest, strongest, most beautiful young man you can imagine. We also admired St. John the Baptist and the Magdalene of Fra Filippo Lippi and two Madonnas of Botticelli – with whom I have become enchanted on this trip.

We were so tired after all that museum going! We stopped in a darling place and had tea and pastry.

Thursday, April 18, 1957

This morning we didn't get started till about 10:00 when we set out to see Santa Trìnita Church. We were lured into several little shops on the way and did a little gift shopping. Santa Trìnita is a beautiful Gothic church on the inside with a Renaissance façade. The frescoes on the walls are marvelous. There is a wonderful painting by Ghirlandaio and a sculpture of two colts by Della Robbia. After seeing the church we did a little more shopping – mostly looking.

After lunch we visited the church of Santa Maria Novella – a wonderful 15th century (I think) church with frescoes and paintings. In the cloister is a chapel called the Spanish Chapel (because it was built for Eleanora of Toledo's return – she was Cosima I de' Medici's wife). This chapel is really magnificent with frescoes on the walls of allegories and church doctrines.

After the church we came back to the hotel and rested a few minutes before we caught the bus to go to Santa Croce. The Church of Santa Croce is huge and very beautiful. Besides the beautiful frescoes and paintings, there is Michelangelo's tomb representing his three talents – that of sculptor, architect, and painter. We were there just in time for 5 o'clock Mass to begin. We sat through some of it, then went back into a hallway of the church and into the Santa Croce School of Leather. It is run by the Franciscan priests, but young men and boys work there. Their work is beautiful. They make everything. The leather is some of the softest I've ever felt. We did a little shopping there too. We stayed there till nearly 6:30, then walked home – rather in the vicinity of home.

Saturday, April 20, 1957

Yesterday morning we went to the famous Pitti Palace of Florence. It's not at all attractive on the outside, but the inside is magnificent. All the rooms are gilded in gold, made of marble, etc. There is a wonderful collection of paintings – especially of Raphael and Rubens. The apartments of the royal family are of course scrumptious. The gardens are beautiful too, but they can't compare with Versailles' gardens. We spent the whole morning in the Pitti Palace. We walked from there to the Sabatini Restaurant – where we ate our first Florentine meal – and had lunch. Since we knew we would have no supper we decided to splurge for lunch. We had all sorts of hor-d'oeuvres, chicken cooked with ham and cheese, green peas (the best I've ever eaten) and dessert. We were stuffed afterwards.

After lunch we walked to the station and caught a bus in the courtyard to go to the Rifredi School of Embroidery. Mother just had to go to satisfy her curiosity about it. It took about 15 minutes to go. Once there we had no trouble finding it. We were greeted at the door by two charming ladies who run the school. They were so nice to us. They showed us tablecloth after tablecloth, but none of us liked them as well as one Mother had seen previously. After nearly an hour we left there. We came back into town and searched everywhere for my gold charm – finally found what I wanted. Then we went with Louise while she bought her father an Italian silk robe, then with Mother to buy a tablecloth.

After our shopping we had the most delicious ice cream I've tasted near the Piazza della Repubblica. Then back to the hotel to get our bags. They were ready because at noon we had to pack our things to leave so the room could be free at 3:00.

A sweet man (a porter) carried our bags from the hotel to the station. Our train was late and when it finally came there were no free seats. We had the bleak prospect of standing all the way to Rome but there were some women who were so kind. They made room for us in their compartments, even gave us their seats for a while. They were just like the Germans we met at Christmas – so kind and good. We finally got to Rome, took a taxi and by the time we got to the hotel it was 1:00 A.M. We went to bed as fast as we could.

EASTER Sunday April 21, 1957

Yesterday morning by the time we got up, ate breakfast it was after 10:00 when we got started. We started out (on foot of course) and headed for the Capitoline Hill. Our hotel is right behind the Pantheon – a mammoth building (as are all Rome's buildings so it seems) which we have only seen from the outside as of yet. We finally came to Capitoline Hill, climbed up the long flight of stairs and were in the Piazza del Campidoglio, designed by Michelangelo. Here is a beautiful view of Rome.

Walking up the stairs we passed the church Santa Maria d'Aracoeli. The Palazzo Senatorio is at the top of the piazza. It was built in the 13th century. The facade is made even more beautiful by stairs and a fountain by Michelangelo. The Capitoline tower contains the bell that has served the Italians for years and years to ring out the holidays, joyous news, sad news.

From Capitoline Hill we could see the Old Roman Forum and the Coliseum. We came down from Capitoline Hill and started trying to get down into the ruins of the old Roman Forum. As we tried to fight the terrible Roman traffic to cross the street two nice looking boys said "Prego" (the adorable word that means everything in Italian) and stopped the cars for us to cross. We said "Grazie" and went on our way.

We tried several little paths to get down the hill – finally it dawned on us that we had to walk to the paying entrance. As we walked we noticed our "Prego" friends were following us. Finally they sidled up and started talking in Italian; I told them I didn't understand. Then one of them said "Do you like Rome?" in English. I answered him and we continued talking. The other one – the tall one who Mother thinks looks like Rock Hudson – could only speak German besides Italian. Somehow though we managed to talk using French, the little Italian I know from music and the little Spanish I can use.

They came right along with us into the Roman Forum – walked over the whole thing with us, explained things – we took pictures of each other, etc. We discovered that the tall good looking one is Marcello Manca, a law student in Rome and a native of Rome. The other is in military school in Naples, but he lives in Rome too. They are so nice and polite. They were so interested in talking to Mother too. Speaking of Mother – she is really amazing. We've made her walk everywhere and she walks as much and fast as we do and doesn't get any more tired than we do.

The ruins of the Roman Forum were of course fascinating. Temples, triumphal arches, palaces, everything used to be there. To sit and look at all that and try to imagine how old it is and what all has happened in those places is really quite awesome. Julius Caesar was killed and later burned right there where we were!

We walked and walked through the ruins – our two friends going with us every step. As we walked back to our hotel we went to see the monument of King Victor Emmanuel II. It's a huge white, beautiful building with statues, sculptures, and fountains – very impressive. Italy's unknown soldier is buried there.

There are two guards who stand guard over his tomb all the time – day and night. They change every two hours. They never budge once they are on guard. We were there when they changed guards. They run – never walk – when they change guards, their hats have huge plumes in them. It really was fun to see them. I don't see how they can stand for two hours without moving!

Marcello and Vincenzio in the meantime had invited us to promenade with them that evening. It was so funny – Marcello was trying to make me understand that he wanted to go for a walk, but I couldn't understand. Finally he took my arm and demonstrated what he meant! He was so cute.

We left Marcello and Vincenzio at 1:30 and walked back to the hotel, where we were to meet a young priest who is a relative of Louise's mother's best friend. Complicated! When he arrived he was with another young priest. John Wakeman is Louise's friend's name and the other one is Keith Hosey.

They are students in the North American Catholic College. Both John and Keith were just ordained in December. They are the most wonderful two young men. John is 32, went to Rice, graduated, went to graduate school, then the army, then became a priest. Keith's life has been a little simpler. He's 25 and the most enthusiastic person – a bubbling personality. They took us all around Rome yesterday afternoon to the big five churches of Rome (not counting Vatican City's St. Peter's).

First they took us to Santa Maria Maggiore (St. Jerome is buried there). It is one of the four churches where the Pope alone says Mass. The ceiling is gilded with the first gold to come from America – the crib of Jesus is supposedly there. From there we went to Santa Croce of Jerusalem – so called because it houses a part of the Holy Cross, which was brought to Rome from Jerusalem. We saw the part of the Cross – I really believe it is authentic. There is also part of the plaque that was over Jesus' head saying "Jesus of Nazareth, King of the Jews" written by Pilate. It was quite a thrill to see that and believe that it really is a piece of the true cross.

The "next church" was the Church of St. John Lateran, but before we went there we went to the building that houses the Holy Stairs. The Holy Stairs is a staircase which was taken from the palace where Jesus was tried before Pontius Pilate. Jesus walked up these stairs on his way to stand before Pilate. During Easter Week the penitents go up these stairs on their knees. It was really a moving sight to see everyone from old women to young going up those steps on their knees.

We crossed the square and went into the church of St. John Lateran. It is the biggest church in Rome – The Cathedral of Rome. It used to be what St. Peter's is now, and the Pope used to have his apartments there. The interior of the church is beautiful with frescoes, bas reliefs and monuments. The main altar covers the wooden altar that used to be St. Peter's altar. We visited the ancient cloister of the church which was just lovely. The marble work in St. John's is really magnificent.

From St. John's we went to the Basilica of St. Clement – one of the most interesting churches of Rome. It was begun way back in the 3rd or 4th century as a house – then a church was built on top of it, then another church on top of that. The three different levels were built as Rome's levels changed. The lowest level, the house, is quite interesting. On this same level is a pagan temple of the Mithra religion. Some of their statues and bas reliefs depicting their ceremonies and rites are still there. On the second level is the ancient church of the early Christians with frescoes and one of the rarest collections of marble pillars in the world. The top level – the present Church – is of about the 12ᵗʰ or 13ᵗʰ century. It is quite beautiful with lovely frescoes, marble work.

After visiting St. Clement's, John and Keith had to hurry to be back at the College by 6:00, but they insisted on walking on to the Church of St. Peter in Chains, where Michelangelo's *Moses* is. The church is almost entirely torn apart for reparation, but one can still visit the monument with the imposing and awesome Moses. The horns of light are shining from his head – he holds the sacred tablets under his arm with a pride and a majesty that is convincing if not overpowering. His face is set in an expression that is almost stern – that shows the justice and the law that this man of God projected. The artist Michelangelo is really incredible. He is so varied in his talent. I'm so thrilled to have seen both *David* and *Moses* – his two masterpieces of sculpture.

From the Church of St. Peter in Chains we walked home via Victor Emmanuel's monument, which was beautiful in the sunset. We were so tired – we dragged ourselves to a little restaurant near our hotel and ate supper as fast as we could, because we were supposed to meet our friends Marcello and Vincenzio at 8:00 in front of the Pantheon. Mother went back to the hotel and Louise and I met them. We were 15 minutes late, but they were still waiting for us. They are so nice! We walked first to the fountain of Trevi. It was a splendid sight to see at night all lighted up – lots of people around it. Of course I immediately started humming "Three Coins In The Fountain" and I threw a coin over my shoulder into the water. It was quite romantic.

Next we walked to what is called the Spanish Steps. There is a Piazza Espagna with the church Trinità dei Monte sitting on the hill. The steps leading from the piazza to the church are the Spanish Steps. For the two weeks of Easter these steps are covered in azaleas. This year they are deep pink, light pink, and white. It was the most gorgeous sight I've ever seen. The spotlights were on the flowers and against the dark night the color of the flowers was magnificent. On the first landing of these stairs is a huge Easter egg – about 6 or 7 feet tall. We climbed to the top of the stairs, then climbed still farther to the terrace of Pincio – one of the highest points in Rome and from which you can see all of Rome. It was glorious by night. We could see St. Peter's Dome in the distance all lighted and glowing. The boys bought us ice cream sticks and we sat on a bench and ate them. Later we started the walk back – they brought us to the hotel at 11:15. They were both so nice and we enjoyed their company so much. Marcello and I had the biggest conversations which is quite a feat considering that I really don't speak Italian and he really doesn't speak English! We made a date with them for Monday afternoon at 4:00.

Monday, April 22, 1957

Yesterday morning was Easter and it certainly was an Easter to remember. At 8:30 Keith, our new priest friend, came by for us with another young priest to take us to the North American Catholic College to their Easter Mass. The North American College is on Vatican City property but is not under Vatican jurisdiction. It's a brand new (about 4 years old) school for American priests and it is just beautiful. The chapel where we went to Mass is gorgeous. The mosaic in the choir is wonderful. The whole Mass was really impressive with close to 200 young priests there in their robes – looking so proud and excited to be full-fledged priests. But the best part about this Mass was the music. The choir was the best I've heard in a long, long time. And the music! A monk had composed it, and this was the first time it has been heard. It really was so beautiful.

After Mass, John Wakeman (priest) took us around to see part of the school. He and Keith and a boy from Baton Rouge took us up on their roof and from there we saw the Pope's apartments, St. Peter's and all of Rome. At 10:30 we went down to St. Peter's, just next door, and stopped in a coffee shop. Then we went to St. Peter's. The square had already filled to the brim with people waiting to see the Pope. It was such a thrill to be there – I never dreamed I ever would be.

St. Peter's Square holds 300,000 people, and I suppose that nearly that many were there yesterday. At noon the Pope came out on the balcony of St. Peter's and was warmly welcomed by the audience. When he opened his mouth to speak I was amazed, because he has the voice of a 35 or 40 year old man – not at all like that of a man who is 81! First the Pope made a short address in Italian about the Passion week. Since I know the story I was able to follow most of it. After this little talk he made short welcoming speeches ending with the benediction in French, English, German, and Spanish. Each time he started speaking in one of these languages the people there of that tongue would cheer and wave white handkerchiefs. The Catholics would kneel on the hard concrete and cross themselves. There was a band there that played. When the Pope ended his speaking and went back inside the Church, the crowd continued clapping and cheering until finally the Pope (Papa – as the Italians say) appeared from the window of his private apartments and blessed everyone again. Then the bells of St. Peter's started ringing. The big bell is absolutely huge, and has a big booming, beautiful tone. Our priest friends had to leave us and go back to the college for their dinner, so we took leave of each other and thanked them for having shown us around.

Then Louise and Mother and I started walking toward the Spanish Steps to let Mother see the azaleas. It took a pretty long time to walk it and we were dead on our feet when we finally got in the vicinity. We found a little restaurant that had delicious food, ate, and then walked to the steps and looked at the azaleas. They are really the most gorgeous things I've ever seen. As we were walking away from the steps, who should we run into but John Wakeman with four other priests. He looked sick when he saw us because he had said that he would be busy at the college all that afternoon. He was really so embarrassed, I thought he would die on the spot. We walked on to the Fountain of Trevi. It was surrounded by tourists and visitors, but was still quite beautiful. Mother threw a coin in.

From there we came back to the hotel, changed shoes, and went to the Coliseum. It's so marvelous. It's mammoth and so impressive sitting there in the middle of Rome. It's hard to imagine the extreme horrors that took place then, the gladiators, the persecutions of the Christians. It must have really been the Colossus of the world. We left the Coliseum and walked to the Baths of Caracalla – the ruins rather. It was a much longer walk than we were expecting. When we finally got to the baths we couldn't get in because everything was locked since it was Sunday. We walked around and peeped into every peephole we could find – even walked up a hill trying to see more. Finally we gave up; by that time we were so tired we were hysterical. Louise and I got out in the middle of the street and tried to flag a taxi but all of them were full. Finally we caught a bus – the wrong one, had to get off at the next stop and take another back to the hotel. Once there we collapsed until 8:00 – then we dressed and met the other girls at 8:30 in the lobby to go out for dinner. We splurged and went to *the* restaurant of Rome – the Hosteria del Orso. It's supposed to be fabulous, and it is as far as atmosphere, music, plushiness, and service – but the food was not that extra-special. It was certainly good, but I expected it to be divine and it just wasn't. We had a grand time though eating and talking. Mother, Louise, and I left at about 11:30, but the others, having found some boys, stayed on till much later. We took a cab home and plopped into bed.

Monday morning the cute bell boy brought our breakfast in. It was real funny because all the time we were there the bell boys (who were all cute) vied to see which one would bring in our breakfast. They would come in and try to see as much as they could while they were in there. The cute one, who speaks French, even asked Louise and me to promenade with him. We told him we were busy.

We finally got up and caught the bus to go to the Appian Way. It was a national holiday and everybody and his dog was on a motor scooter going out for a picnic. We rode out to the end of the bus line and then started walking back. The Appian Way is really beautiful with ruins of tombs, arenas, etc. on either side. We passed one huge ruin where the Roman chariot races used to be. We came to the Catacombs of St. Sebastian, one of the two most famous catacombs. Unfortunately we didn't have an English-speaking guide and we missed out on a lot of interesting information. It's amazing to think the Christians actually lived down there. Signs of fish and candle holders prove their martyred existence. Over the Catacombs is a beautiful little basilica dedicated to St. Peter and St. Paul.

We left the Catacombs around 12:30 and walked a little further down the road and came to a darling outdoor restaurant called San Callisto because it's near the other famous catacombs of the same name. We had a noodle dish and some beer and continued on our way, walking around the grounds, since the other catacombs were closed. The trees there were beautiful – just like all the pictures I've seen of the Appian Way. After a while, we wanted to catch the bus to go back. We were walking in between two bus stops when one bus came along. I got out in the middle of the street and waved my arms and yelled "please stop" and the driver did and let us get on. Everybody on the bus was laughing at us.

At four o'clock Louise and I were supposed to meet Marcello and Vincenzio in front of the Pantheon. Louise's foot was hurting her so badly that she went to bed, so I went to meet them alone. I explained, in my best mixture of several languages, that she was sick and couldn't come. Vincinzio was heartbroken. He wouldn't even come along with Marcello and me. I think Marcello at first was scared at the thought of being alone with me – because Vincenzio could translate for us when we were caught in a language dead lock. Finally, however, Vincenzio left us and we caught the bus to the Coliseum. From there we took the Metro to E.O.R. – a big exposition ground which Mussolini built in hopes of having a world's fair – none of it ever came about. There is building after building there – beautiful white buildings with mosaics and sculptures – all empty. Marcello told me that they are going to be soon made into office buildings for the governmental ministries. Now the grounds are public grounds for picnicking, playing, etc. Since Monday was a holiday everyone was there – old people, young people, middle aged people, and children. We sat down in the grass amid all the Italians and watched them play and sing. Several men near us were playing accordions, one had a drum, and they were all singing. I really enjoyed being out that way with nothing but Italians. They seemed to have such a good time so simply. I enjoyed being with Marcello, who is so sweet and kind. Around six o'clock we started back – I had told him that I had to be back around 6:30 to eat dinner. He wanted to see me that night so I told him I'd see him at 9:00. He said he would come to the hotel for me because "Woman no go solo, man, yes."

For dinner we went to a little restaurant across from the hotel and had delicious food, then we came back to the hotel. Mother was sort of under the weather with the cold she has contracted and Louise had "hurt to the foot" as the French would say. I had a few minutes to rest before Marcello came.

We took the bus to the Coliseum. All the monuments are lighted at night and look absolutely beautiful with an eeriness that could only come at night. The Coliseum is magnificent by night. We walked around and also saw the Old Roman Forum – walked down toward the Baths of Caracalla too. The night was so beautiful – so was Marcello. He said the prettiest things. "I displease that you part," he told me, "I believe that I love you," he said later. About 10:30 we came home. We promised to write each other. It was the first time I ever really was honestly sad to leave anyone that I've met this year – boys I mean. I wish we could have stayed in Rome longer.

Tuesday morning we got up and went to St. Peter's. We went first to the Vatican palace and museums. We hired a guide (who wasn't the best guide I've ever had) and went through the palace. There was the biggest crowd there – pushing and shoving – which didn't make things very pleasant. The Vatican palace is beautiful, with treasures in painting, tapestries, jewels. Of course the highlight and prize is the Sistine Chapel with frescoes and ceiling by Michelangelo. It is really breathtaking – beautiful, magnificent, marvelous, and all those other adjectives that mean splendid.

It was jam-packed with tourists, which made it difficult to see everything I wanted to see and spend as much time as I would have liked to have spent. After lunch, we went to see the Church of St. Peter's. It is so huge and so mammoth that it is incredible. One of the paintings hanging on the wall, so high up it looks small, is actually the length of our living room! The dome is unique in the world it is so huge and high. The dome of the Pantheon (which I forgot to mention that we saw Monday afternoon also – that's where the Kings of Italy are buried – also Raphael, the painter) is a little larger, but St. Peter's Dome is so high up. It was designed by Michelangelo. The interior of St. Peter's is unbelievable – gold is everywhere – beautiful mosaics that look like paintings – gorgeous marble monuments. I just can't describe it really, because it's so huge and so rich and ornate it's impossible to describe. I felt extremely tiny inside it. I know that.

We left St. Peter's at 3:30 and caught the bus back to the hotel. We had to pack our things and have everything ready to leave in case someone wanted our room. Mother and I then caught the bus to the Spanish Steps. Mother had to go to the American Express. Then we did a little shopping. We were walking down the street when I heard someone call "Judy" – I turned around and there was that precious Keith, our priest friend. He was walking down the street and saw us – left his friends and ran after us. We stood and talked for a while. He said he had called us Monday to take us to the Catacombs, but the hotel told him we had gone and wouldn't be back! We were sick – because at the Catacombs we were wishing we had Keith or John to show us everything. Keith is so cute and friendly and wonderful. I'm so glad to know him and to be his friend.

At 6:15 Mother and I met Louise in front of the Spanish Steps and we went to eat dinner in a restaurant nearby called Old Vienna – with specialties of Austrian cooking, which broke the monotony of all the Italian food we've been having. We had good service and finished quickly, then caught the bus to the hotel, got our bags, took a taxi, and headed for the station. I wasn't ready to leave Rome at all. If I had heard anyone sing "Arrivederci Roma," I think I would have died.

The train to Naples was packed. Mother and I got on a first class car and paid the supplement so we could sit down. I'm glad we did because the train was an hour late. We finally got to Naples at midnight. Louise had stayed in second class and had met some French speaking Italian soldiers who are adorable and who carried our bags for us to a taxi, which brought us to our hotel – a strange little place that was locked up hard and tight. Finally the concierge (a young boy in pajamas) came and let us in. Then we found out that there were no rooms for us! We nearly died because we had had our reservations for ages! No soap. Finally a little boy who spoke no English or French came down to explain. Of course we didn't understand. Then they called another boy who speaks French. He explained that we would go across the street to a hotel owned by the same man who owns the one where we supposed to be – and spend the night there, then today (Wednesday the 24th) come back to that hotel. Of course we had no choice. The two boys carried our bags for us and we came to this hotel (I don't even know the name of it). We woke all sorts of people up to get in. A sickly, scary elevator brought us up. The boys brought our baggage in and here we are.

It's Wednesday morning now – we have no hot water. I'm sure our situation will improve however. About noon we're going back to our intended hotel.

Friday, April 26, 1957

Our stay in Naples has been thwarted by the horrible hotel we have. I told you about getting here Tuesday night and not having a room – moving to another hotel for the night. Well – Wednesday morning Marcello Sybustrini – the only person who has shown any interest in us at all – came to get us and help us get back to this damned place. When we got here they still didn't have our room. Louise and I yelled and screamed in our best French and finally they said we would have it by 3 o'clock. We left our bags there and went out to have some lunch. We tried a restaurant recommended by Fielding – which turned out to be very good. After lunch (about 3:00) we walked around to see what we could see of Naples.

The part next to the sea is right pretty with the mountains, Vesuvius, the blue water, the park with beautiful flowers. Away from the water however is not so hot. There is so much poverty and filth here. Anyway, we walked up to American Express to see about the San Carlo Opera. On the way we passed all the big ships – passenger ships. Naples is the largest Italian port for passenger ships.

After our business with the American Express we walked down the street to the most popular café in Napoli and drank tea and ate ice cream and just sat in the sun. Finally we decided to leave. We stopped in again at American Express to see about something, While we were in there, friends who graduated last year from Tulane and Newcomb came in. We talked a long time, and they gave me Lou Harris' phone number. (He's the president of Tulane's son.) I knew Lou was here, but had no idea where.

By the time we left American Express it was time to eat something. None of us were hungry and we were a little tired of Italian food, so we went to a place called The California that has nothing but American food cooked in the American way. We had hamburgers and they were delicious. I tried to call Lou during dinner, but he wasn't in.

Back to the hotel, Louise and I were supposed to go out with her friends that she met on the train. We had a knock-down-drag-out that was awful over whether or not to go. Finally they came and we went with them. Their names are Salvatori and Osvaldo. I was with Osvaldo. They took us up in a funicular to one of the high points of Naples and we could see how it looked at night – very nice with the dark water and the lights. Then we climbed up to an old castle.

Osvaldo started saying he wanted to marry me and all that (we spoke Italian & French) so we came home. Poor thing. He's in the army – lives in Rome. Salvatori told Louise that Osvaldo didn't bring any civilian clothes with him from Rome, so he went out and spent all his money buying a sweater and a pair of slacks to go out with us in. Osvaldo told me to tell my mother that he wanted to marry me – we could think about it and then he'd come to the U.S.A. to get me! Those Italians!

Yesterday morning we got up early to go on an American Express tour to Pompeii, Amalfi and Sorrento. It was really a nice tour – about 15 people were on it. We left at 9:00 and rode first past Mount Vesuvius. I was surprised to learn that it was not Mount Vesuvius that destroyed Pompeii and Herculaneum in 79 A.D., it was the twin mountain (Mount Somma) which became extinct after that eruption and 15 years later Mount Vesuvius had its first eruption. Isn't that interesting to know?

Our first stop on the tour was a cameo and coral factory. We watched the boys carving the shells to make the cameos. It was so interesting to see. It's such tedious work. They say it takes five days to make a really good cameo.

After the cameo factory, we went to Pompeii – the ancient city destroyed in 79 A.D., by lava from Mt. Somma. I was surprised that Pompeii was so large. There were 25,000 people living there when the eruption occurred. Only 2,000 were killed, and all of that 2,000 were either slaves or servants. They had stayed behind to rob and steal from the people who had fled. Their greed caused their death. Pompeii is really fascinating. The huge Roman forum is still beautiful – even in ruins. Two of the houses which were uncovered are absolute gems. The walls are covered with frescoes that are amazingly preserved. The patios, the kitchens, are all there in a petrified state. The only disappointment at Pompeii was that they wouldn't let us women see the naughty pictures in the "Forbidden" Room. Oh to be a man!

In the museum we saw some of the tools, money, pictures, jewelry, etc. that were found in the houses. The most interesting things were the body of a dog, a man, a boy, and a man's head that they found in a petrified state. To make sure they remained preserved they were put in a plastic cast. The poor little dog was forgotten when his master fled the lava, and he was found on his back with his four legs up in the air, his head twisted. The man was found lying on his stomach with his arms around his head. The boy was in a sitting position with his hands over his eyes. It really is unbelievable to think they lived in 79 A.D.

From Pompeii we took the Amalfi Drive, the most beautiful drive in Italy. The blue, blue, Tyrrhenian Sea is on one side, and the mountains on the other. All along are picturesque little fishing villages and beautiful resorts. The water is so clear you can see the bottom, even from high on the mountains. Orange and lemon groves cover the sides of the mountains which are beautifully terraced for growing the fruit trees and grapes. It really is breathtaking. At the beginning of the drive is the town of Salerno, where the Allies first landed during the last war. I've always heard about the Amalfi Drive and I'm so glad we had the opportunity to take it.

We had lunch in Amalfi in a beautiful restaurant that overlooks the sea. We had a delicious meal to the tune of a little native combo that couldn't get its harmony right to save it. A cute little boy stood on a chair and sang. He was very good – with a voice like the Flamenco singers in Spain. The only thing that ruins having musicians like that is that they come around and stand by your table until you give them money. We've never been approached by beggars and greasy men like we have in Naples. It's really pitiful.

After lunch we drove on to Sorrento, through beautiful countryside. We came to Sorrento at about 4:00 o'clock. I was disappointed in Sorrento because it was so touristy. Everywhere people were hard pursuing everybody to buy something. I hate that. It really was almost disgusting it was so touristic. After about an hour in Sorrento we drove back to Naples. We were half an hour coming back. On the way we saw old rickety carts loaded down with men, women, and children leaving the city going back to the country. They looked so primitive – so dirty. We're so very lucky.

When we got back to Naples we went to the little California restaurant and ate bacon and eggs – the first time I've had bacon since December 14th! After eating I called Lou Harris – finally talked to him. He wanted to meet me at 9:00 at the pension. We went back to that awful place in hopes of having the room they had promised us – we didn't have it. Louise and I marched into the dining room and yelled and screamed at the owner's brother – who had promised us the room. It didn't do any good – but he promised and vowed we could have the room the next day. Meanwhile we found out that you had called, Daddy, and we were all excited about that. I had to get dressed to go out with Lou, so I left Mother and Louise sitting by the telephone with that sweet Marcello, who took such good care of us. Without him we never would have talked to you. At nine I met Lou downstairs. He hardly knew me with my long hair, and I hardly knew him with his moustache! He wanted to see Mother, so we went upstairs and he talked with Mother and Louise awhile. He invited us all to dinner Saturday night. (Louise can't go – she has a date with Vincenzo from Rome.)

Lou has a little English sports car and we drove to the Naval Officer's Club in it. It was so nice – there was a good combo playing. Lou and I sat in the bar and talked and caught up on each other's activities – and on everybody at school. We stayed at the officer's club till 11:30 – then he took me to the Hotel Royal – one of the best in Naples – to hear the band and to dance a little. The music was wonderful and I really enjoyed myself. I got awfully sleepy and finally just had to go home.

Today (Friday, April 26th) we slept until about 8:30 – then Mother and I went shopping to find some shoes for me since mine are splitting, but found none that fit my feet. Later we met Louise and had lunch in a restaurant with an impossible name then Mother and I decided to go to a beauty parlor and have our hair washed – a drastic necessity. Louise went with us. After we emerged from the salon with clean hair, Louise and I walked to Vincenzio's military school to have a little rendezvous with him.

To get to the school you have to walk through a tunnel and then take an elevator to get up to the school – which is a red, old, elegant building. Two guards dressed in full garb clicked their heels and saluted us as we walked in. Inside, the cutest, tallest, handsomest boy greeted us. He had on the full dress uniform – the little sabre and the high hat. I would have loved to have seen Marcello (of Rome) in one of those uniforms! The tall cute one told Vincenzio we were there, and he came down with a friend of his – Antonio. They were dressed in their everyday uniform – khaki's, almost like the U.S. Army. We met them in the parlor, sat on a little settee and chatted awhile. The uniform really was flattering to Vincenzio. After about 15 minutes the trumpet blew telling all visitors to leave, so we did. We walked back to the popular café on the street by the bay and met Mother there. She had taken a little 45 minute walk by herself while we were at the military school. We sat at the café and ate ice cream. About 6:00 we went back to our pension with high hopes of having a decent room at last – and Hallelujah – we did. It changed our whole life. We had hot water brought up to us in pitchers, bathed a little, dressed to go to the opera.

We were in a hurry to eat before the opera, so we used that as an excuse to go back to the California and eat. We got to the San Carlo Opera House about 8:30. It's a beautiful opera house – a perfect size. It's all gold and white and plush but not at all overdone – just enough to make it elegant and beautiful. We had wonderful seats.

La Bohème was the opera – of course that was perfect, because I love it so much. I'm so glad Mother got to see it. It was the most exciting opera I've ever heard. The tenor, Franco Corelli, was wonderful. He had a beautiful voice, he was tall and big and good looking – really phenomenal. Everybody in the opera was superb, but the tenor was by far the most impressive. The staging was beautiful, the scenery too, and the orchestra was wonderful. I've never been so thrilled. The music to *La Bohème* is so heavenly anyway. I really enjoyed it. Puccini could really tear a person's heart out by the roots.

After the opera we took a taxi home and went to bed, thrilled to death with the beautiful opera – and the beds that were really beds!

Saturday, April 27, 1957

This morning we got up early so we could catch the boat to Capri. We asked the man which boat – he showed us – we got on it. It was a delightful ride. The boat is a large white one – very comfortable. When we arrived to the getting off place we remarked that it certainly didn't look like the Isle of Capri that we had seen in pictures. We asked the man if this was where we got off for Capri and he told us we weren't on the boat to Capri but to Ischia!!

We were absolutely sick. There was no way to turn back, no way to get to Capri. So we had to resign ourselves to the fact that Capri would never be realized for us. Everyone on the boat who discovered our predicament – several air force men and a couple of traveling American students who had been to Capri – told us that Ischia was much prettier and nicer than Capri because there weren't so many tourists. We were hard to convince, especially since we couldn't see the Blue Grotto, but as I say we were resigned.

We got off the boat and started walking. It really is a lovely island – the largest of the islands in the bay of Naples. It is unspoiled by tourists as yet, but someday it will be just like Capri. The vegetation is remarkable – flowers of every kind, beautiful trees, oranges and lemons, cacti, and many rocks.

The sea is of course gorgeous and the sun is wonderful. The mountains on the island are all craters. There is one volcano – last eruption is 1302. We walked till time for lunch which we had in a nice little restaurant. Pizza pie was our lunch. After lunch we hired a carriage and rode around the island from Porto d'Ischia to Casamicciola, another little village. The road follows the sea and is certainly beautiful. Large inviting-looking villas were perched on the hillsides. One could certainly live an easy, lazy, primitive life here. By the time our drive was over it was 4:20 – time to catch the boat back to Naples. Here we are on the boat. I really did enjoy the day and Ischia. I must say I never in my wildest dreams thought I'd ever be in Ischia – I never even knew there was such a place! Of course I'm still a little sick about getting on the wrong boat. But c'est la vie!

Sunday, April 28, 1957

We had a delightful voyage back from Ischia yesterday. We hurried from the boat to the place where we had bought our tickets to see where we made our mistake. Over the ticket window was a huge sign saying Capri – but on the window was a little white sign saying Ischia – which if we had seen we wouldn't have known what it was anyway. So we had nobody to blame but ourselves – except that we had asked the man for Capri and he nodded his head.

From the dock we caught the bus to Piazza Dante, went into a tiny little place to try some Neapolitan pizza, which was good but nothing like the pizza at Rizzo's in New Orleans!

After the pizza we hurried back to the hotel. We unlocked our room, opened the door and there sat two old ladies in a room with no beds! We didn't know what to think! Our mouths were hanging to the floor in surprise. We went to get the maid and she told us that they had moved us to a larger room. They had – it was really very nice – and it was the room we were originally supposed to have. Of course it was too late to enjoy the view of the sea – Mr. Hochwald had promised us a view of the sea.

Anyway – Louise dressed to go out with Vincenzio, and Mother and I got ready to go to Lou's for dinner. We were surprised when Bill Hale, from Mayfield, Kentucky, came for us in Lou's red sports car. Bill is Lou's roommate! Isn't that a co-incidence? We went to their house, which is very nice. We visited over drinks, and then had dinner, which was very good, but cold. That didn't matter, because we had a good time. After dinner we all piled into Lou's car, which is quite a feat, since it's a two-seater! We brought Mother back to the pensione, then Lou and Bill took me to the Hotel Miramar to dance. I danced with Lou, and then with Bill. It was really fun. Bill said he hadn't danced since he left the States in June! About 1:15 we left and zoomed home in the little car.

Monday, April 29, 1957

Sunday morning we got up early, packed our bags, and took a taxi to the California to have breakfast before we caught the train. We stocked up on pancakes and bacon and coffee – and it was delicious. We got to the train station, had a little man jump on the train and reserve our seats – and we were off. We discovered that the train to Pisa didn't leave until 3:30 from Rome and we arrived in Rome around 1:30. It was totally unexpected, this layover. I was really pleased to have it though. I stirred up all the Italian I could write, wrote a little speech, and called Marcello Manca on the phone. I was so proud because I could understand what he said and I could talk to him. I told him I'd be there for about an hour and he said he'd be right down. In about 20 minutes he was there. I was so glad to see him again. We took a little walk in the neighborhood of the station. Through a slight misunderstanding of languages, I discovered that Marcello is only 18!! He told me he was 21 because he was afraid I wouldn't like him if he were young. He was so cute, he kept saying "Me little," I couldn't understand why he would say he was little when he's so big and tall! Finally I caught on that he meant young and explained the difference in the words to him. As train time neared he helped us get our bags on the train. Then he stood on the platform and held my hand through the window until the train pulled away. I felt so Katharine Hepburn-ish as we waved and waved until we were out of sight. I don't suppose I'll ever see him again, and it's so sad.

At about 7:15 we arrived in Pisa. Our hotel was right across the street from the Baptistry, the Cathedral, and the Leaning Tower. Our hotel was also quite luxurious – for us. We cleaned up our dirty selves and went down to a delicious dinner, after which we promptly went to bed. I was coming down with a cold, which I still have.

Tuesday, April 30, 1957

Monday morning we got up early to see Pisa's treasures, including the Baptistry, the Cathedral, which has paintings by Andrea del Sarto, and of course, the Leaning Tower, which does look like it would topple if you touched it with a feather.

First we walked down by the Arno to see the tiny little church called Santa Maria del Spina because it once held a relic of the crown of thorns. It looks like a toy church it's so tiny. The architecture is Gothic, which even makes it more precious and fragile looking.

It was time to leave Pisa and head for Milan. Rather than fight the awful crowd we sat in first class seats and paid the supplement as far as Genoa. At Genoa we had a mad scramble to find some seats. I finally procured three in different compartments. An hour before we reached Milan I was able to move in with Mother and so was Louise. We were talking to some of the people in the compartment and found out that there are *never* any performances at La Scala on Monday – and also that there was nothing on Tuesday afternoon. Well we were so mad and so disappointed and there wasn't a thing we could do. We tried to figure out a way to stay, but we already have reservations which are paid for (for the train tonight) which we couldn't get back (our money that is). Also the Rémonds would die if we didn't come back when we said we were coming. So we had nothing to do but resign ourselves to our sad fate. I was so mad I thought I would literally pop! To think we arranged our whole trip this way just to go to La Scala – and here we are. I can't help but blame Mr. Hochwald a little for not having checked thoroughly on it.

We came to our hotel (which is no peach) and checked again on La Scala – discovered there was no hope. Then we changed clothes and went to have dinner at *the* restaurant of Milan – Giannino. It's so delightful. There's an open kitchen all glass enclosed where you can see everything they cook. It's a very elegantly modern place with delicious food. Mr. Fielding was certainly right about recommending it. After dinner we were standing outside the door waiting for a taxi and an American man from Dallas was also waiting with an Italian friend. We started talking and they brought us home in a taxi.

Wednesday morning, May 1st

Well, things always work out for the best. Yesterday, we ran into Sandy here in the hotel. She had come alone to Milan because Eugenie had gone back to Rome to be with a boy she met there, and Coco and Martha decided to stay in Naples awhile. The four of us started out walking this morning on our way to see La Scala Opera House since we couldn't hear it. I just happened to look at one of the billboards and saw that Giuseppe di Stefano was going to sing Thursday night. We talked about how wonderful it would be to hear him and lamented our sad fate of returning home without having been to La Scala. I just happened to look at the billboard next to the di Stefano one to see who was singing in *Anna Bolena* – the one playing Tuesday night that we couldn't see because we had to catch the train. I looked and I was surprised that *Anna Bolena* was being sung by Maria Callas! I couldn't believe it. I re-read the poster. It sure said Callas. I got so excited I started screaming for Mother and Louise to come look. They couldn't believe it either. All along we had been saying, "If only Callas would be at La Scala!" Well, we couldn't understand how she was there without our knowing it, but we knew we would have to stay to hear her.

The first thing to do was to try to find tickets. A sign at La Scala said it was sold out. Louise suggested going to the biggest, most exclusive hotel and trying to get tickets through them. We quickly consulted her guide book and picked the hotel nearest to where we were then – the Grand Hotel Duomo. The man who handles the tickets there was so sweet and wonderful. He wasn't even supposed to fool with us because we weren't staying at that hotel, but after our hard luck story of coming to Milan just to go to La Scala, of being promised tickets and not finding them, and of Callas' being there, of our being musicians studying in Paris, he phoned "the right man" at La Scala and got us four tickets on the first row of the top gallery – wonderful seats. He was so kind. He kept explaining that we would have to pay more there at the hotel than we would at the La Scala ticket office. We told him we understood – and when he told us he'd have the tickets for us at 4:30 we almost jumped over the counter and kissed him. We were so excited – and it all happened so by chance. What if we had chosen another hotel instead of that one!

Now that we had the tickets we had to arrange our coming back to Paris differently. First we wanted our money back on the couchettes. We went to our hotel, they sent us to the travel agent who got them for us (which was right next to the hotel where we got the opera tickets). The agent said we'd have to go to the station – so we did. There we finally got our money back for the couchettes. Then we made reservations for the train leaving Milano this morning at 10:20 and getting to Paris at 10:00 tonight. Then we had to send telegrams to the Rémonds – one to Paris and one to Champsenest – to tell them of our change of plans. I hope they received the telegrams! By that time it was 4:30, and we rushed back to the Duomo Hotel to pick up our tickets – the most precious tickets I've ever held!

Louise and I wanted to see Leonardo da Vinci's *Last Supper*, so we grabbed a bus and hurried to the Church Santa Marie dei Grazie where this masterpiece is housed. We got there just as they were closing, and we had to beg the man to let us in. He did, and we spent about three minutes in rapture looking at it. It was so badly destroyed – it was completely painted over when they discovered it, and in an effort to find it they damaged it a lot. It's been partly restored, but not completely. It really is wonderful, I just wish we had had more time to look at it.

We rushed back to the Piazza Duomo to meet Mother in front of the cathedral – the largest Gothic cathedral in Italy – and I think in the world. It's really quite a sight. It has hundreds of spires topped with the lacy work – in stone – famous in Milan. The exterior is quite impressive. The interior, too, but not in the same way. It's huge, mammoth, and massive, with a flamboyant ceiling, but hardly any decoration. Behind the main altar, in the apse, are the three largest stained-glass windows in the world. They are impressive, but not exactly beautiful.

After we visited the cathedral we went to have ice cream and coffee. Nothing tastes better when you're tired. By the time we got back to the hotel, we had about 30 minutes to get ready to go to the opera. At 8:15 we caught a taxi to La Scala. I was so excited about going. La Scala is not at all pretty on the outside, and not truly so on the interior. But that's unimportant. It was one of the most exciting musical nights I've ever spent. I discovered an opera, *Anna Bolena* of Donizetti, and I heard Callas, the most marvelous voice I've ever heard. No wonder she's so acclaimed and talked about. There are no words to describe her. She can be sweet and docile with an angelic voice, and she can be cruel, cold with a masterful superhumanly powerful voice. She's tall and slender and attractive. She of course stole the whole show, but she certainly had good cohorts. The Mezzo soprano – Giulietta Simionato – was phenomenal – so was the tenor. Had Callas not been there they would have stolen the show. Everything about it was perfect – the orchestra, the costumes, the staging, the scenery, the acting, and of course the exciting music. It was well worth the trouble we spent to hear "the terrible" Callas. It was a night I'll never forget.

This morning we got up, had breakfast, went to the station, got on the train, and here we are. This afternoon we passed through Dijon. It was quite nostalgic to see the red roof tops of little Dijon. I've decided to go back now and visit there this summer. It smelled differently now because it's spring. I suppose it was autumn that gave it the smell I thought belonged only to Dijon.

Well, our trip in Italy has been wonderful. Everything worked out for the best – even Ischia. Italy is a wonderful, fascinating, abundantly rich country that cannot be fully grasped in three weeks, but then what country can? It, like everything this year, was a lovely dream interrupted only occasionally by a slightly unpleasant incident, an unexpected disappointment, etc. I'm so lucky to be me – to be here, to have been in Italy. I'm so happy Mother got to see it too. Life is wonderful – and love and understanding makes it that way.

Preparing to Say Adieu

Tuesday, May 7, 1957

Dear Mother and Daddy,

It's been so long since I've written – not since we came back from Italy.

Right this minute Mother is in the air somewhere between Louisville and Paducah – and in several hours she'll be at home with you all. I surely was glad to have her here, and I've been so lonesome today – more than I've ever been this year.

Let me see if I can remember all we've done since last Wednesday night. Thursday I met Mother for lunch, then she did some walking in her little orbit of the Opéra, Madeleine, etc. since I had to go to classes – first to music history and then to composition. I met Mother and we went to have dinner, of all places, at the Pizza – an obviously Italian restaurant! We had wonderful pizzas – much better than those we had in Italy.

Friday morning we started out and did some shopping. First on the agenda was to buy me a pair of shoes. I was practically on the sidewalk because my two pairs of shoes both had holes in the leather – not just in the soles. Luckily we found some shoes in the first store we tried. After that we walked and looked, and bought gloves. Afterward we walked through the Tuileries (which look beautiful now), past the Arc du Carrousel and into the Louvre. I could only give Mother a running tour of the Louvre because our time was so limited, but she saw Venus de Milo, *Winged Victory*, the most famous paintings in the Italian Gallery and the 18th and 19th century French galleries. From the Louvre we went to the Café de la Paix and had tea.

At 5:15 I met Jean-Louis in front of the Opéra. It was good to see him again after nearly a month's absence. We took a walk until time for him to go to the train station – he was going to Dijon for a wedding.

Later I met Mother at the hotel. We had decided to dress up and go to the Ritz Hotel for a drink and a look at the famous Ritz. We went and were very unimpressed, so unimpressed that we didn't even stay for the drink. There's nothing very unusual about it and it was dead as a doornail. We decided then that we'd go to this little restaurant I had heard about called La Grenouille where the specialties were weird foods. I can't say about the food, but the place was certainly weird. I couldn't believe we were there when the taxi driver said "Voilà." I made the driver go with me to look for the entrance, it was so well concealed. We finally found the door and went in. It was a small narrow room with pans and stuffed animals hanging all around and it was full of people (mostly men) laughing and shouting. We were ushered deep into the room to stand and wait for a place. The men paid all sorts of attention to Mother and

259

me. They offered us seats beside them, one looked at me through field glasses, several patted Mother on her derrière as she passed by!

Finally, after causing an almost sensation we decided we had better get out of there! And we did. After a hurried walk down the side street we finally flagged a taxi. He took us to another restaurant I had heard about – this time I was sure about it – it's called Quasimodo and is on the Île St. Louis. It's a cute place decorated with scenes from Notre Dame de Paris. We had the specialties – coq au vin and frog legs, which I had never eaten before. We were the last ones to leave the restaurant, about 1:30 and took a taxi home.

Saturday morning I met Mother for breakfast before we went to Versailles. We caught the train at St. Lazare. Just as we were getting on an elderly woman came up to me and in French asked us where we were going and if this was the train to Versailles. She boarded the train when we did and sat by Mother. She turned out to be not French, but English. Her name was Miss F.A. Fash. She was an old maid, rather peculiar, but kind of cute and clever. She never left us the whole day. She toured, ate, walked, and came back to Paris with us. Poor old thing. At Versailles we went through the Palace, then ate a terrible lunch during which Miss Fash cried "Death," "Poison" at different intervals. After lunch we walked miles to see the *Le Hameau* (the Queen's Hamlet) which Marie-Antoinette had built so that she could play milkmaid and the immediate royal family could have a place to retreat. I had not seen it before, and I found it by far the most interesting part of Versailles. The gardens are beautiful, left natural. The little hamlet is adorable. There are several buildings, all thatched roofs, and there is a tiny mill, a boudoir, a dairy, a pigeon loft, a tower, and the main house – the Queen's house. The buildings surround a lake and there are weeping willows and wisteria everywhere. Even though our weather was cold and cloudy it didn't prevent the hamlet from being a real delight. I don't blame Marie-Antoinette for wanting to play there!

From the Hamlet we walked to the Petit Trianon which was unfortunately closed for reparations. Then we walked on to the carriage museum, which contains gorgeous old coaches of the royal family. There are also some sleds that are fantastique. From the museum we went inside the Grand Trianon. It's a beautiful place, but rather in need of reparation. It's more impressive on the outside I think.

We left Versailles (the park) to get the bus to the train station. Miss Fash was still with us. We arrived at Gare St. Lazare about 5:15 and Mother and I said adieu to our Miss Fash.

After dinner at La Pépinière we ran to the Metro and went to the Opéra-

Comique to see *Madame Butterfly*. This production was just as good as the one I saw earlier this year except for the soprano. She was not the same one and she was little less than awful. Albert Lance was again singing the role of Pinkerton and he is very good. The music is so beautiful that you can almost ignore a bad singer. After the opera we took the Metro and came home.

Sunday morning I slept till about 9:00, then met Mother to go to the Flea Market. Our main purpose for going was to buy the cordial set for me. We got there about 12:30 and saw that it was still there. The owner had gone to lunch, so we decided to do same. Right in the midst of the Flea Market is a little restaurant where the French people themselves go which has wonderful food at a very reasonable price. After lunch we walked around the Flea Market and bought a few little things. Finally we returned to the cordial set. After a short debate and trying to get the woman to come down more, we said we'd buy it. We had to wait while she tied it up so Mother could carry it.

By the time we got away from the Flea Market it was nearly 5:00. We came home and had tea until time to go dress to take the Rémonds and Louise to dinner. We were invited to have an aperitif first with the Rémonds, so Mother came over about 8:00 and we stayed here talking and "aperitif-ing" until 8:45. Then Monsieur got the car out and we filed in it (literally) to go to the L'Orée du Bois, the restaurant I had chosen.

It's a wonderful place. First of all it's gorgeous. It sits just at the beginning of the Bois de Bologne, it's very new, all glass enclosed, surrounded by lovely flowers, there's an orchestra – and the food is delicious. Mother and I had baby duck cooked with oranges that was "magnifique!" We all had a good time – especially the Rémonds. They love to go out and they really appreciated our doing that for them. Monsieur was in his usual high spirits and Madame was also very gay. We were the last to leave. We went to the Rémonds' to have a glass of champagne to finish the evening. Then Monsieur and I drove Mother to her hotel.

Monday morning I had to go to class, after which I met Mother and we had her last Parisian lunch at La Pépinière. After lunch we went to visit Napoleon's tomb, the only important monument Mother had not seen. Then we went to the American Express to get money business taken care of, then did a little glove shopping. We walked back toward home, stopped and had tea and pastry on the way, then to the Rémonds' to wait for Monsieur to come drive us to the Air France place where Mother would take the bus to go to Orly Field.

Monsieur came, and we drove to the air-station. After a terrible price for my beloved cordial set things were finally arranged and we accompanied Mother to the waiting room. It was 8:10 and the bus didn't leave till 8:40. Madame was expecting us back at 8:15 and Mother insisted that we go. So Mother and I bravely said good-bye to each other and I left her, looking very tiny, sitting in the waiting room.

Wednesday, May 8, 1957

Yesterday was spent writing themes, practicing, and in theater class. Last night was study time again.

This morning we had music history class, then went to the Smithers' and practiced until time to come home for lunch.

After lunch I went on to my voice lesson. Monsieur Bernac was running late, so I was about 15 minutes late starting. I had a good lesson considering that my cold has not completely left me yet. After my voice lesson I met Jean-Louis; we went to the Champs-Élysées and had tea, then returned, and here I am. Mother, you'll be happy to know that we're going to the ball – it's tomorrow night. Guess what time it starts – 11:30! And lasts until 3:30! What hours! Jean-Louis' aunt is coming by in her car to take us.

Mother, after all our money-figuring things have really been hitting my supply quickly. First that awful amount for the cordial set, then $18 for two months piano rent, and now $24 for that money on my boat ticket. That makes $77 that got away on greased wings!

The weather has been still cold, but today is cloudy and on the verge of rain and much warmer. They say this is normal for the first of May, that after the 10th it turns warm again. I wish it would hurry.

Mother, how was the trip home? It seems so strange now not to be running over to Hotel Rochambeau every day. Since you've gone home I've been thinking more and more about how nice it will be to come home again.

We're busy working on the party now – and it will take work.

Friday, May 10, 1957

Last night was the big ball – and it was really a big ball – four thousand people, about, were there. I found out that this ball – given by the École Polytechnique, is the most chic, the most beautiful ball of Paris, and I well believe it. It is very expensive – 2000 francs a ticket. Jean-Louis was lucky because Michel gave him our tickets.

Last night, I dressed, then took a taxi to Jean-Louis' house. His mother was there and so was his aunt. His aunt is just as cute as his mother. They bragged on my dress, my shoes, and my hair – which Louise fixed in a chignon and I wore a little rhinestone headband. Jean-Louis looked almost dashing in his tails. We drank fruit juice and talked until about 11:15, then his mother and his aunt drove us to the Opéra, where the ball was held.

Of course everything is so beautiful at the Opéra, it lent itself perfectly to the tuxedos, tails, and evening gowns that were filling its halls. There were tables everywhere in the corridors and in the two very large reception rooms, where the dancing was. There were three orchestras, and everyone walked from place to place, dancing to all of them. There were bars set up where you could have champagne, fruit juice, and sandwiches. All the women had on their very best of course. I saw some absolutely gorgeous gowns and some that were just hideous. We sat for a while with Michel and some of his friends, then danced, walked around, watched the people. Once, by one of the bars, I ran into of all people – Louise's Phillippe! Out of 4000 people it was certainly uncanny that I should run into him!

I'm wondering if there were any Americans or English-speaking people there because I heard not one word of English spoken the whole night, which is unusual for Paris. I really am lucky to have someone like Jean-Louis who thinks enough of me to take me to places like that. The dance wasn't supposed to be over until 3:30, but we left at 3:15 because we were both sleepy – but mostly because my feet couldn't take anymore! I really had a nice time and it was certainly a pretty thing to see – the most "elegant" thing I've been to this year.

Yesterday I received a letter from Marcello Manca from Rome. He wrote it all in English with the help of a dictionary and a grammar book, and it is the most priceless letter I've ever received in my whole life. He says such cute things as (referring to our meeting again) – "Even if it will not befall never again, I will remember you equally and you will have always sincere friend in Italy." Bless his heart.

Yesterday I also received news from Newcomb College saying they had no record or transcript of the physics I took last summer at P.J.C.! Of course I was upset. I immediately wrote to Mr. Ward and Dean Matheson about it and asked them to please send Newcomb the necessary information. I also wrote Miss Daspit, the head of the physics department at school, and told her about it. She approved the course for me, so she can help me. I wish, Mother, that you would call Dean Matheson and check to see if he has sent something. I can think of nothing worse than not getting credit for that slave labor I did.

But I think everything will work out O.K. But – do call Dean Matheson if you have time.

Yesterday morning I had a voice lesson with Madame Tilliard. She's so encouraging and so sweet. I really am glad I have lessons with her.

Well – I just came back from checking on the deal about switching reservations with Genie and Lucy and flying home. The French line says that they can switch our tickets for us – that is not the problem. But TWA airlines say that a "switch" of tickets can't be done because the tickets are strictly personal. Lucy and Genie will cancel their reservations and get the refund, but they will lose about 10%. Louise and I would make reservations on the same plane, pay for our tickets, then let Lucy and Genie give us their refund money. In the long run my plane ticket would then cost me about $40. Lucy and Genie can't get their refund money until they get to Paris – which will be June 20th. But Louise and I will have to buy our tickets before then so the French Line can have them to transfer our ticket from the boat to the plane ticket. We are going back in a week to get the final word on everything.

The whole deal is – would you pay the $40 to let me fly home, or would you rather I just come on the boat? Of course I want to fly, but it isn't absolutely necessary. About the bags and trunks – there's no way to send them on an earlier ship. I'll have to either let the French line store them, which will be expensive, or ask the Rémonds to let us keep them here. If the Rémonds keep them, the French Line will come a few days before the ship sails and pick them up. If I fly, I'll just have to let Lucy and Genie take care of sending the trunk and bags on home by express. It certainly is complicated.

About the trip this summer. I was wrong about the calculated cost for hotels and transportation being $400 – it's only $300. That's not the final word, but it won't be much more than $300.

The weather is still undecided – it's much warmer, but still cloudy and grey.

I'm going to the movies tonight with Jean-Louis to see Judy Holiday in *Full of Life*. It's supposed to be extremely funny. I hope so – I'm in the mood to laugh a lot. I'd also like to have some chocolate fudge, but I'm too fat as it is.

Sunday, May 12, 1957

Friday night I went to the movies with Jean-Louis and his mother, whom I adore. After the movie we went to a café and had some fruit juice. Madame

Baut is so cute and entertaining. She and I always take sides against Jean-Louis and have more fun arguing with him.

Saturday morning I practiced for an hour, then went to my voice lesson. It was a good one. Monsieur Bernac is so wonderful. He fussed at me for not being more daring. It was just the kind of talking-to I needed.

Saturday afternoon at five I met Jean-Louis and we went to eat ice cream. While we were there, he read me a darling story about an American girl in Paris who had a French friend – like Jean-Louis. Everything they did and said was so much like what happens to Jean-Louis and me! It was unbelievable and so charming!

Last night after supper we all sat in the dining room played "London Bridge is Falling Down" with the children. Those sessions always last rather late but they're so enjoyable. Yesterday I gave Isabelle and Nanou those two little perfume bottles – the sample ones that were given to us in that little perfume shop. They were thrilled to death and yelled to high heaven.

Monday, May 13, 1957

This morning I was so thrilled. First of all I got your letter, Mother. I'm glad to hear the flight was smooth. You poor thing with no sleep and that blessed cordial set!

After reading letters I went to practice, then to art history. I was so thrilled when the wonderful man who taught us last semester walked in. He said he would be with us for several lessons. Not one single soul left today during the lecture. If only we could have him all the time.

Just a while ago the shoes came, and I only had to pay 156 francs for them! Hallelujah – they fit perfectly. You can't imagine how wonderful they feel. Thank you so much for going to the trouble of finding them and for sending them right away. They're a Godsend.

Also had a letter from Dr. Hansen. He assured me that Marjorie Lawrence would take me next year. Also that Mr. Burnham is returning. Dr. Hansen said the opera audition rumor came in a letter to Mr. Thomas, the man who handles all the Juniors – year abroad – from none other than Mr. Handemann himself (music history teacher) who said he could present me at the Opéra in a year maybe!? Surprise, I can't wait till Wednesday morning to ask him about it.

In just a few minutes I have an hour long voice lesson with Mme. Tilliard, I'm singing well – my cold is cured at last!

Friday, May 17, 1957

First before I catch up on my activities I have some news about flying home, etc. Louise's mother checked with TWA at home and this is what they told her: We can make the exchange of the plane tickets at the loss of only about a dollar! So that makes problems vanish. Lucy's family say they will take care of all my baggage, trunk, etc., that must be shipped home to me. They are so anxious to have this boat trip they are willing to do anything, even pay any extra expense – and really it's Louise and I who are getting the best deal. That should settle all problems for me.

Now – to catch up – if I can remember.

Tuesday I had a voice lesson with Bernac – which always makes my day interesting. Then John Donaher called, making it even more interesting. He had returned from Italy with a cold. We made a date for Wednesday night. Tuesday afternoon was theater class. I dearly love Mme. Alvernhe. Her knowledge of everything has no limits. I love to listen to her. After supper Louise and I went to a concert – the Orchestra Pro Arte of Munich and Stuttgart – directed by Kurt Redel. It's a chamber orchestra, one of the most famous in the world. They played five Brandenburg Concertos (Bach of course.) It was without a doubt one of the best concerts I've been to in Paris. There wasn't a flaw – I love the Brandenburg Concertos anyway.

Wednesday morning our music history was called off and I was going to take advantage of it and sleep, but, as always, there was an interruption – the Hollins' College director called me about this blessed party tonight. So my day didn't start off as I planned it. At noon I met Jean-Louis at the Étoile and we went to have coffee to discuss the party, etc. He's so obstinate sometimes – we had a big argument and as a result I was late getting home for lunch.

Mid-afternoon I met Louise at the Smithers', and we went to an ice cream party given by Mme. Alvernhe and her daughter Claude for us Newcombites. It was very nice. They had all sorts of delicious ice cream for us and needless to say we had no trouble making it disappear. There were also fresh strawberry tarts and other such goodies. I stayed till 6:45, then left to meet John at the Étoile.

He looked so good with his Italian tan. We shared Italy all night. He called Father Keith Hosey and Keith took John under his wing, introduced him to a man from Notre Dame who took John and his friends to dinner – even offered John a job in Rome! John thought Keith was wonderful. I'm really glad they got together. John had his application to Harvard Business School with him and he wanted me to read it. We walked all the way down the Champs-

Élysées to the Tuileries Garden. There we sat by the pond and I read what he had written. He wrote an excellent application and I was very flattered that he asked me to read it. Even though his grades weren't wonderful, he still has a good chance of being accepted, and he has some very influential people on his side. I feel sure he will be accepted – he wants it so badly. We have a bet – a dinner at the Reine Pédauque: if he isn't accepted I pay, if he is he pays.

After walking by the Seine and discussing Italy till we wore it out we decided to go to Harry's Bar. We were the only ones there except the piano player, so I sang all the songs he played until finally some more people came in. We left at 11:45 and walked to my house. (Harry's is by the Opéra.) When it was time for John to get a taxi and go to the Étoile he decided he wanted me to go with him – so I did. He caught his bus at the Étoile – then the taxi brought me home.

Thursday morning we had art class and that hideous woman was there. We stuck it out though. I dread when the exam comes – which isn't far off!

After lunch yesterday I had a voice lesson – they really are frequent these days. Composition class came after the voice lesson and after class I met Jean-Louis at Sèvres-Babylone and we walked to St. Germain to have a glass of something at Deux Magots. It was so pretty at that time, about 7:00. It had been a typical day – sun, rain, sun, rain, and sun again. Jean-Louis was over being mad at me and we had a good time talking and laughing. I got home just in time for dinner at 8:00.

After dinner Louise and I rushed to Salle Pleyel to the concert celebrating the bi-centennial anniversary of Monsieur Camille Pleyel – the man who started the Pleyel pianos. The concert was given by Robert (husband), Gaby (wife), and Jean (son) Casadesus. They played a Bach concerto for three pianos (Robert and Gaby and Jean), a Mozart concerto for two pianos (Robert and Gaby), and the Saint-Saëns concerto (Jean.) It was a marvelous concert. Robert Casadesus is of course the best pianist of the family. His playing reminds me of Walter Gieseking.

This morning I went to have my hair fixed for the soirée. I had it fixed sort of like Madame Rémond had hers when the Queen was here. It's page boy – that's all I know how to describe it. It's very nice – makes me look so much older. It was so simple the way the woman fixed it – I bought some rollers and intend to fix it myself next time.

After lunch today I went with Louise to the Smithers' to practice for tonight's party. Louise and I, along with some Scottish dancers, are the entertainment.

Monday, May 20, 1957

I've had a fabulous weekend!

First about the party – it was a huge success! All the problems seem to have worked out for themselves. There were enough boys, everybody danced and had a good time. The garden was lighted and was beautifully romantic, the buffet delicious and the champagne bubbly. I see that I haven't told you anything about the house where we had the party. Louise and I went there on Tuesday to look at it, but I forgot to tell you.

Monsieur Miramon Fitz-James, one of the very richest Parisians who is also in the diplomatic service, is a member of France-Écossais, and so he offered his house to Monsieur Rémond for the soirée. His whole family lives in this huge house, and downstairs is a large ballroom where we had the party. It has four huge chandeliers, marble columns, gilded mirrors, etc. – very elegant, perfect for a party. Monsieur (he's a Count) Miramon is very charming, and he has quite a charming son who is also a Count and with whom I spent a great deal of the evening. He is not good-looking, but has a delightful personality. He speaks beautiful English – that's his major study – but we spoke French most of the time, which was flattering to me.

And then of course there was Jean-Louis, bless his heart. Claude Rémond was there, and I discovered that he is a fabulous waltzer. About 11:30 Louise and I performed. We did "People Will Say We're In Love," "They Say That Falling in Love is Wonderful," "If I Loved You," "Somebody Loves Me," and "You Made Me Love You." (Do you see hints of a central theme?) They seemed to like us very much. Then about 12:30 the Scottish dancers came. The men wore kilts and the women all wore plaid skirts. They danced several of their dances, then they taught some of the guests how to do one of the dances. My teacher was an adorable little man in a kiltie. It was so much fun! The orchestra stopped at 2:00 and most everybody went home.

Of course the Rémonds remained and so did we to see that things got picked up, etc. Claude Rémond, Jean-Michel, Jacques Miramon, and a few other people also stayed. Claude had arrived too late to hear Louise and me so we played and sang for him. Madame Rémond asked me to do a Dorothy Shay number, so I did. Finally we had one last cup of champagne, and Claude brought Louise and me home. It was a wonderful evening.

Saturday I slept late, then went "marketing" to buy food for the picnic John Donaher and I were going on that afternoon. I fixed lots of goodies and met John at 1:30. We went to the beautiful Bois de Bologne. Of course as soon as we got there the sun went in and rain clouds began filling the sky.

We really didn't think it would rain, so we made no effort to leave. Finally it started raining. Paris rain usually lasts about an hour and never is hard enough to hurt. We were under a tree, and for a while kept nice and dry. But soon the "typical" Paris rain began to lose its "typical-ness" and before we knew it, it was pouring down rain!

We ran from tree to tree trying to get shelter, but it didn't do much good. By the time we got out of the bois we were very wet. We took the Metro to the Étoile, went in a café and sat until it stopped raining. Then we took our food – which we had not yet eaten – and went down by the Seine, sat on the banks and ate it. I felt like a real hobo. By the time we finished eating and walked up the Champs, looking like tramps, it was time for John to catch the 10:00 bus to go back to SHAPE. (He had to work from 11:30 on.) So the end of a not-so-perfect-day arrived.

Sunday morning I slept late again, then dressed up and was ready at 11:00 when Jean-Louis and his brother Jacques came by for me. They had invited me to have lunch with them in a restaurant near the convent where their sister, Florence, goes to boarding school. I thought it would be just the immediate family. As usual Jean-Louis didn't tell me anything about the details.

We drove to the Bauts' apartment. There we met Michel (you remember him, Mother, J.L.'s cousin), Monsieur and Madame Baut, and Mami – the nurse, cook, governess and everything else who has lived with the Bauts since J.L. was four. We got in two cars – J.L. and I went with Michel in his little truck. We drove about 40 kilometers (20 miles) outside of Paris to this adorable little restaurant that is very rustic looking. I enjoyed the ride out so much – everything looks so beautiful

When we got to the restaurant I discovered that we were to be 13 – all the cousins, aunts and uncles. The reason for the gathering was for Florence's first communion, which was going to take place that afternoon at 4:30 at the convent. First Communions are always big affairs.

I spent one of the most pleasant afternoons I've ever spent. I was seated between Jacques and Jean-Louis and across from Michel and Jean-Louis' adorable cousin Monsieur Ougu (or something). I was teased like I've never been teased before – all the jokes were made with an American as the brunt. I really had to be on my toes to keep up with them and come back with sharp remarks.

The food was delicious. We first had a concoction of ham and paté in gelatin with truffles, and a salad of potatoes, nuts and apples. Then we had a lobster apiece – hot with lots of butter and lemon. Then we had roast beef with green beans, peas, tiny potatoes, and spinach. Then of course cheese. Then fresh strawberry tarts! We had champagne before dinner, white and red wine during dinner, coffee afterwards and then liqueur.

One of the cousins who was there is a little girl of 14 who is so pitiful. She's deformed – extremely hunch-backed – with long arms and massive hands. She's so sweet looking, so pitiful that I nearly cried when I saw her. She's an adopted child, which made her even more pitiful. Jean-Louis had told me that she is very gifted, plays the piano beautifully, and will enter the École Normale de Musique next year.

Anyway, right after the dessert, when there was an empty seat next to this poor girl, I decided to go talk to her, so I picked up my coffee cup, excused myself, and sat down by her. Everyone was watching me, but I kept calm, sat down and started talking to her about her piano, her favorite composers, her teacher, a little about what I did. She seemed to appreciate my talking to her so much. By sitting down by her, I was also seated by Monsieur Baut. Across from him were the musicians, so we talked shop a little. Finally it was time to go to the Mass, so we left the restaurant and Jacques, Jean-Louis, Monsieur Baut, and I went to the convent together. I didn't know it at the time but it seems my talking to the little girl was a very extraordinary thing to do, and they were quite impressed. M. Baut kept thanking me for having done it, and Jean-Louis said he didn't know any French girls who would have done the same. I was surprised that they were so surprised! Anyway I was moved by the whole thing.

The convent is in a little village called Verneuil. I found out today that it is one of the most chic schools in France for young girls. It's in a beautiful location, very woodsy, very calm. When we got there the little girls (about 25 of them) were all dressed in white, just like nuns. They looked quite angelic. Monsieur Baut was so proud of Florence; he pulled me over by him so I could see her better and he said, "Look how adorable my little Florence is," and she was. They repeated several vows, then entered the church, followed by the congregation.

The chapel is new and modern. The choir of little girls were singing – quite well too. The ceremony – I should say Mass – was beautiful with the girls all in white, holding tall candles, making their vows, taking communion. But it was horribly long. It lasted an hour and a half! I was worried because I had no way of getting hold of John Donaher, whom I was to meet at 6:30 at the Étoile. Mass was over at 6:00, so I immediately had to leave. I was a little angry with Jean-Louis for not having told me sooner about going to Mass, but there was nothing I could do. Michel and Jean-Louis took me back to Paris. It had taken us only 15 minutes to come from Paris, but as luck would have it there was an accident on the highway and cars were stopped for miles. We were stuck right in the middle of it all – and as a result didn't get to the Étoile until 7:30. Of course John was angry, but since I was innocent he finally forgave me.

We were going to go to the theater to see Laurence Olivier and Vivian Leigh in Shakespeare's *Titus Andronicus*, but you had to be early to stand in line to get tickets. John didn't think we had time since I was so late, so of course I just felt horrible about everything. So instead we went to the movie and saw Hitchcock's *The Wrong Man* – fairly good. Nothing to take the place of Olivier and Leigh, but we're going to try again tomorrow night.

Today was art class day. For a change the old hag was interesting. This afternoon I went to practice, then to a voice lesson with Madame Tilliard. Then I went shopping and bought a new purse, then saw about getting a bracelet for my charms. I'm having to have it made especially for me. Tonight I'm having dinner with Jean-Louis. This will be the only time he'll have the car before I leave, so we're taking advantage of it.

Wednesday, May 22, 1957

This has been some day! I didn't get to bed until 1:00 last night because John and I went to see Shaw's *Saint Joan* after not being able to get tickets to *Titus Andronicus*. At 5:00 A.M. Louise woke me up and said Madame was having the baby! I was wide awake by then. Rose Marie was filling tubs, pots, pans, everything with hot water in the bathroom. Two women, one the doctor, were here too. Of course it was a whole month in advance. Poor Madame had nothing ready. She is in the middle of re-decorating her room, so of course it was in a mess. Louise and I were excited. I was too dead though to get out of bed, and there was nothing we could do to help. Finally this morning at 8:00 Madame had a little boy – without any kind of anesthesia or anything. I heard not one sound. Louise and I had to go to class at 9:00, so we didn't get to see either of them until noon when we came back. We bought Madame some flowers and Monsieur two cigars. Madame looks wonderful – as if nothing happened. She was sitting up in bed, looking fresh as a daisy. I couldn't believe it.

The little baby is adorable. He isn't at all red – he hasn't cried out loud all day – he looks very Rémond-ish. The two girls are so excited. They run in and look at him every minute. The nun who took care of Nanou when she was born came today to stay and care for the baby. She takes her meals with us. She's so cute and clever. It really has been quite a surprising day. Tonight after supper we all drank champagne in honor of little Monsieur Rémond. I can't decide if they're happy with a boy or not. I really think they wanted another girl!

Mother, could you buy something for the baby and send it? I'm glad the baby came while we were here.

This weekend Louise and I are taking the train to Mont St.-Michel. Should be a delightful little trip.

I don't think I wrote about eating dinner with Jean-Louis and his mother Tuesday night. We ate at the apartment – a very ordinary, homey meal. Then we talked and talked. I love J.L.'s mother so much. I won't see her again unless I do as she has invited me to do and go with Jean-Louis to Vichy to see her while she is there taking treatments for her liver. You know, all French people have great trouble with their liver. I nearly cried when I told Mme. Baut good-bye, not only because it was she I am leaving, but because I'm leaving so many wonderful people and things. It's all gone by so quickly.

Madame Baut told me more about the little girl who is hunch-backed and plays the piano. Her parents are Florence's god-parents. M. Baut knew the man when they were in German prison camps together. The father of this child was a gravurist – a real artist. He adored his work, and was one of the best. While he was a prisoner he was tortured by being put into wet sand up to his neck and left for hours. If he moved he would be shot. Finally he lost the use of his hands – and now he runs a little laundry here in Paris. He found the little girl, then aged about one, in a cave where everyone else (27 people) had been killed by the bombings. He took the child, adopted her. Not only did he take her, but he took in several of his friends and their families who were left penniless and homeless, and he cared for them as if they were his – and he is of very modest means. Isn't it wonderful that people can be so good!

Friday, May 24, 1957

Here I am in Mont St.-Michel – but before I tell you about this remarkably extraordinaire place, let me catch-up on my doings.

Yesterday, Thursday, I followed my unusual routine of going to practice, then to art class, then back home. All our talk at noon was about the baby, whom they have decided to name Paul, after Monsieur's father. Madame dislikes the name, but Monsieur wants to name him that, so. Before lunch I went in to see Madame. She is doing fine – looks healthier than ever. The only thing that makes the baby look premature is that he hasn't yet opened his eyes.

Yesterday afternoon I had a voice lesson, then composition class. As soon as class was over Louise and I rushed to Theatre Sarah Bernhardt to stand in line for tickets for *Titus Andronicus*. We got there at 6:30, tickets were put on sale at 8:00. Jean-Louis brought one of his friends, who is named Jean-Robert and is the talkin'-est boy I've ever seen, and the four of us stood in line until 9:00! About 10 people from the ticket window, we were told that all the tickets were sold. Naturally we were so angry but too tired and hungry to protest much. After such a failure we had to eat, so we went first to the Bonne Crêpe to eat there. Jean-Louis and Jean-Robert refused to go in because they were too dressed up. As usual Louise and I were as un-dressed up as you could be. So we went to a self-service place and ate. We had such a good time. Jean-Louis was in rare form, and his friend was delightful. It was rather late when we finished our meal and Louise and I were both dead, so we went home. Jean-Robert left us at St.-Michel, but Jean-Louis accompanied us home. I was really disappointed in missing the play, but you can't say I didn't try my best to see it!

This morning we got up at 7:00, packed Louise's tiny bag with our pajamas, and went to the market to buy food for our trip. We figured we could save money by buying food for sandwiches and and eating just one meal a day in a restaurant on this little trip. We bought ham, sausage, bread, butter, cheese, cookies, fruit. Monsieur gave us a bottle of wine, and we put it all in my little bag. We caught the bus to the train station – took the 9:30 train to Folligny. We arrived at Folligny (which may have a population of 200) at 2:00. We waited forty minutes in a waiting room consisting of wooden benches and an old iron stove. Peasants – really peasants – sat looking at us curiosities and waiting for the train. Louise and I were so tickled at the place, at our appearance, and our sack of food. At 2:49 we took a train to Pontorson, arriving at 3:30. Then we had a wait of an hour for the bus that brought us to Mont St.-Michel. During that wait we had some of our food supply for lunch.

We were in Mont St.-Michel at 5:00. An American man – older by far than we – was on the bus. He was also waiting at Pontorson, where we heard him talking to some Americans. In order to see if he spoke French, Louise asked him a question in French about our arrival. Poor thing of course he didn't understand. Then when she repeated it in English he was so astonished I thought he would faint.

Mont St.-Michel loomed up before us, and it's quite a sight to see. A small island crowned by a huge Gothic abbey isolated in the middle of a bay of sand. The tide has not come in, so there is no water. We're hoping that in the morning it will be in. Tides are so miraculous. Why does the moon affect water like that?

The bus drove right up to the fortress (the whole island is surrounded by a wall) and we got out. The American man had gained courage, and asked us if we knew where his hotel was. Since it is the best known of all of them and since Monsieur Rémond had told us where it was, we could tell him. He's staying at La Mère Poulard, which has the most famous omelet in the world. Louise and I want to eat there tomorrow.

We started up the tiny narrow street to our hotel. Monsieur Rémond had telephoned a friend of his to make us reservations. We are staying in a darling hotel – they all are. We took the cheapest room, so we have a tiny room with a double bed – but for only 800 francs.

As soon as we got our room and put our things in it we started out walking. One can cover the entire Mont St.-Michel in no time – that is, without visiting any museums or the abbey, which we'll do tomorrow. We followed the tiny street up to the abbey, climbed up the many stairs; from the landing on the way up one can see the English Channel in the distance. It was rainy today, which gave everything a somber, mysterious, Middle Age look – all grey and dark blue, with lots of wind. Perfect atmosphere for this marvel.

Out of the walls of the fortress are growing beautiful red and yellow flowers. Some of the tiny houses have gardens on their roofs. Everything seems to have a magic spell cast on it. We ended our walk, by chance, in front of the Mère Poulard.

We were walking back toward our hotel when along came the American man from the bus. We started talking, and ended up taking a walk with him. He's from California, apparently isn't married, and is a good example of the type of American tourist so often made fun of by Europeans. But we had an enjoyable walk, saw a few things we had missed. As we started back to our hotel he asked us to have dinner with him tonight. We had to say "no" because we were obliged to have dinner at our hotel in order to have our room. He said he'd see us tomorrow in the abbey and maybe we could have lunch together. I hope he means it. We're always ready for a free meal. (Isn't that awful?)

We came back and had dinner – which consisted of one of the famous St.-Michel omelets. It was the lightest, fluffiest, most delicious omelet I've ever eaten. We came to our room and had cheese, fruit, and cookies – and here we are. I'm looking forward to a good night's sleep on clean sheets!

Saturday, May 25, 1957

This morning we got up at 8:30, dressed, and started out. We decided not to eat breakfast in our hotel because we were afraid it would be too expensive. We asked them where we could find Monsieur Rémond's friend, Monsieur Nicole. It was he who reserved our room for us at the hotel (he lives at the hotel.) He is also president of the tourist organization and the owner of the three little museums at Mont St.-Michel. We were told we could find him at the first little museum. We went in to see him and thanked him for having seen about our room, etc. He asked us if we had visited any of the places yet and we told him no, so he insisted that we visit that museum right then, as a gift from him.

The museums were very interesting, mostly because of the information given by the guides. Scenes in wax depicting scenes in Mont St.-Michel's history (turbulent enough), armor, carvings, torture instruments from the prison. The most interesting was the 13th century house of Du Guesclin, a famous chevalier. It is furnished with the original furniture – wonderful old beds and chests and copper ornaments. A darling little garden is reached from the top floor.

After our sightseeing visit we walked around the walls and took a few pictures. Then we walked down the road leading to Mont St.-Michel in order to take a good picture of the whole thing. As we walked back we saw our American man friend sitting in the Mère Poulard drinking some wine. He waved to us, so we went in and talked with him. He asked us to have a bite to eat with him, but we had already had breakfast so we had to say no thank you to the invitation because we couldn't eat a bite. He told us about a walk we had neglected to take, so we left him to follow his suggested itinerary. We told him we were planning to eat there later on and we would see him maybe then.

We walked clear around the island – rather rock. The wind was fierce and wonderful – it sounded like a typhoon might sound I suppose. The wild flowers jutting from the rocks made a wonderful sight. We climbed over the rocks, fought the wind, touched the English Channel, walked on the wet sand. The salt air smelled so good and fresh and invigorating. Just before we reached our starting point we saw some people eating their lunch in a little cove along the beach. They were taking pictures, and they asked us to come get in their pictures with them. Of course we did. They were from Normandy, and spoke with such an accent we could hardly understand them. When we told them we were Americans they couldn't believe it. They thought we were peasants from Bretagne! It was the first time we had ever been taken for peasants!

By this time we had worked up an appetite, so we went to the Mère Poulard. We had decided to splurge and have the huge 1000 franc meal with all the specialties. First I had a special sausage – delicious. After that, the world-famous La Mère Poulard omelets, which they let you watch them cook. First they beat them – eggs, yellow and white, and beat them and beat them and beat them by hand. Then they pour them in a huge skillet with a handle about three feet long. They hold it over the open fireplace and let it cook. It turns out to be the lightest, biggest, prettiest, most delicious thing you've ever eaten. Oh, before they pour the eggs in the skillet they put a huge chunk of butter in the skillet and let it melt. The omelet stood about two inches high. It was absolutely exquisite. Just as we finished our omelet, in walked our American friend. He hadn't yet eaten. We were sitting at a table for two, so he had to go sit alone. Poor thing, we were about to tell him we would eat our dessert with him, when he asked the waitress if we could move and finish our meal with him. So we did. He is so nice. He's a manager of a painting agency in Los Angeles. His name is Mr. McCauley, and he lives with his 21 year old daughter who goes to U.S.C. He seemed to enjoy talking to us so much. Meanwhile the rest of our meal came. We had filet de sole de l'Abbaye, which was the most delicious thing I've ever tasted. It made the filet of sole at La Reine Pédauque look ordinary. So you can imagine the sauce was real thick – made with butter, cream, white wine, and mushrooms. I can't describe the taste but it was heavenly. After that came the cheese, a specialty of Normandy much like Camembert, but stronger. For dessert I had raspberry ice cream – exquisite.

After eating we talked, then it was time for Mr. McCauley to catch the bus to Pontorson to go on to Paris, and for us to visit the abbey. We started to pay our bill, and Mr. McCauley took it. We protested of course, but he insisted that he pay for our lunch because he said we had been so kind to him and he had enjoyed our company so much. So what could we do? We shook hands, thanked him again for dinner, and left. He was really nice to us. Just goes to show what a little kindness can do.

Louise and I then went up to the abbey and joined the tour. You're not allowed to go in alone because it's so complicated and intricate you would surely get lost. The abbey is not by any means beautiful, but it is certainly impressive and interesting. It consists of the church, and six huge rooms which were used as reception rooms or workrooms. The style ranges from early Roman to flamboyant Gothic – cold and somewhat monotonous. But the history that those rooms have seen and helped create is remarkable and fascinating. The guide who took our group through was the cutest guide I've ever had. It took about an hour and a half to go through everything. After the visit we decided we had to have some more of the delicious Mère Poulard ice cream, so we bought some, went out on a rock facing the sea and ate it. We had seen everything we could see at Mont St.-Michel, so we decided to catch the 5:45 bus to Pontorson and spend the night there since we wanted to go to Rouen tomorrow and since there's no bus from Mont St.-Michel to Pontorson that early in the morning.

We were the only passengers on the bus to Pontorson except for a big good-natured old woman and she didn't go all the way to Pontorson. We rode all the way to the station and walked across the street to the Hotel Chatelet, which we chose because it was close to the station, and we had to get up so early.

We had no trouble getting a room. The little owner was a darling old man with a smile, a moustache, and a beret on his head. He gave us a nice room with one big bed for only 700 francs – wash basin, the essential bidet and all. We decided to walk around and see what Pontorson was like. The first place we entered was the pharmacy to buy Louise some milk of magnesia. There was only one bottle and it was so old I had to laugh. French people just never have that problem.

We walked down the main street and came to a little river surrounded by tall, green grass and wild flowers. We walked down along the banks of the river, past quaint houses and farms, cows, horses, children, beautiful little gardens. The church bells were ringing, changing tones as the wind changed. People thought we were real curiosities. We came back to the main street, took another street and passed little houses covered with morning glory vines and blooms. Down the road a man was pitching hay, and behind a garage several men were playing the game that is so popular in France – they played it all the time in Dijon. It is something like horseshoes only it isn't. Everything was so quiet and calm and at 7:00 in the evening everything is so beautiful anyway.

Sunday, May 26, 1957

Mother, do you know I completely forgot Mother's Day on May 12th – anyway Happy Mother's Day to my favorite Mama. I thought of that because today is Mother's Day in France.

This morning dawned beautifully – bright golden sunshine, brisk wind and air, birds singing. We arose at 6:00, dressed, and went down for coffee and croissants. They are so good – I do wish we had them in the U.S. We finished just in time to walk across the street, buy our tickets, and catch the train to Rouen. We had to change trains at Folligny at 7:40 and caught the train to Augustan. We arrived at 10:00 and the train to Rouen didn't leave until noon, so we decided to walk around the town.

We went down a street, looked at all the people and they looked at us. On the billboard of one of the stores were three lovely, big country girls' picture. They were wearing crowns, were stoop-shouldered – three beauty queens! How typical of the provincial areas!

We went in another bakery, bought some bread and strawberry tarts to finish our ham with at lunch today, walked farther, found a bench to sit on and ate our bakery purchases – then came back to the station and waited for the train to Rouen – which came right on schedule.

Well – now I'm on the train at Rouen waiting to start back to Paris. We got to Rouen exactly on time, checked our luggage, then set out to see as much of Rouen as we could. Right outside the train station an elderly Englishman came up and asked if he could help us. We told him we'd like to find a place to get a map of Rouen. He told us that he would walk with us to the Information Bureau, but that he was afraid it would be closed. He was so cute. He had lived in Rouen for 30 years – from 1917 till just after or before or during the last war. He walked with us to the tourist office, and sure enough it was closed. But he explained to us how to go about seeing everything. Just about that time a tour of soldiers – Americans and English from SHAPE – came along with two English girls as guides.

We decided to trail them for a while. We thanked the sweet little Englishman for his help and followed the group across the street to the tower where Joan of Arc was imprisoned for five months and questioned forty times.

The tower was part of an old château (where the English had their headquarters) all but the tower has disappeared. Poor Joan – it was so tiny. It was there that she was shown the torture implements they were going to use on her if she didn't confess that the voices she heard were the voices of the devil and not the voices of God. Inside the towers the guide spoke French to the girl who was translating for the soldiers. We played French – spoke French and listened only (at least in appearance) to the French speaking guide. That's so much fun to do and the soldiers really thought we were French. The guide (the French one) told us that today was the Festival for Joan of Arc, the only day in the year when they put flowers in the old market place around her statue and put a fire in the spot where she was burned at the stake. We were so thrilled. We had no idea whatsoever that this was Joan of Arc Day.

So we headed for the market place. All around this section are those wonderful Middle Age gingerbread looking houses that I adore. The square where Saint Joan was burned is quite impressive. In back of the station is a wonderful old house with shields bearing coats of arms of various kings (I think.) Then in the center – on a pedestal on ground level – is a beautiful statue of Joan burning at the stake. The whole side of the house and all around the statue were banked hydrangeas – blue and pink. Then on the corner of the square, in the spot where the stake stood, was a huge urn with a fire in the center. It too was encircled with flowers. The Joan of Arc celebration is always on the Sunday closest to the 30th of May because it was the 30th of May that she was burned to death. They burned her for six hours so there was not even a bone left. Then they gathered her ashes, put them in an urn and threw it in the Seine. This morning, as is the custom, a group of local girls went to the river and threw flowers from the spot where her ashes were thrown in.

We left the market place and walked down to the Seine to see the spot where her ashes were thrown. There was only an ugly statue there, very modern. So we proceeded to the cathedral. It's a huge, Gothic, flamboyant structure – not what I call beautiful, but certainly interesting. We couldn't get inside, but there were lots of people waiting at the door to go in, so we figured in about 15 minutes we could enter. Meanwhile we walked around the outside of the cathedral. Suddenly we heard a choir and an orchestra inside so we ran back around to the front. Just as we got there they opened the door and we went in. A choir was finishing rehearsing a Bach chorale, accompanied by an orchestra. We decided they were going to give a concert either this afternoon or tonight. I sat down and reserved us seats while Louise went to find out what was going on. She found out that at 5:00 three choirs (one of them a boys' choir with the orchestra) were giving a concert in honor of Joan of Arc Day. We, of course, were going to stay for it. But it was only 4:10, so we put our coats in our seats and went outside to a café, then came back inside the cathedral. The interior of the cathedral is quite wonderful: flamboyant Gothic, everything made to give the impression of great light – and it does.

At 5:00 the Archbishop, dressed in red, came in with the priests and took his velvet seat. The organist played a Fantasia of Mozart, then the choir and congregation sang a *Magnificat* by Paray. Then the choirs did a chorus from Bach's 50th Cantata. Next came the sermon. The priest who gave it was quite good – very poetic. His text was of course about Saint Joan. He spoke for a long, long time! Then the choirs and orchestra did a work by a monk, Chanoine Bourdon, called *Strophes in Honor of Saint Joan of Arc*. It was lovely – quite patriotic of course. The boys' choir and a tenor were featured in it. The last strophe was sung to the melody of the French National Anthem. It was all quite moving and stirring – especially when one loves France.

The prettiest part of the whole service was the holy sacrament. The Archbishop did the ceremony while the choirs sang *O Bone Jesu* of Palestrina (the best thing they did) and a *Tantum Ergo* by Chanoine Bourdon. Then they did a chorale from the 40th Cantata by Bach. For the postlude the organist played the Allegro from Widor's 6th Symphony. I was extremely moved by the whole service and so thankful that we were able to see it.

From the cathedral we walked down the most precious, adorable street with all those wonderful old houses and found ourselves in the middle of the oldest part of town. Rouen suffered heavily during the war, and therefore much of it is new and rebuilt. We visited another Gothic church, walked down more adorable streets – I love to do that. If you let your imagination play you can see all sorts of history passing down those streets. We visited still another Gothic church, then walked toward the station, stopped at a café for tea, then went to get on this 8:15 train for Paris.

We have truly had a wonderful weekend. We are very lucky. I can't get over our being in Rouen on the day to be there without even planning it! Rouen is one of the prettiest, quaintest towns I've visited, and I'm so glad we came. I suppose this is the last travel splurge before exams.

This trip would have cost us nothing if we hadn't had to pay for train tickets because we certainly spent nothing on food – thanks to Mr. McCauley! But it has cost over $20. But it was worth every franc!

Monday, May 27, 1957

I spent the day in the bed today. The strangest thing happened to me. I got up at 8:00 this morning feeling rather heavy and tired, but I thought it was because I had slept so well last night. I went in the bathroom, did my daily washing, and went into the kitchen to get breakfast. Louise was still in bed with severe cramps. Madame, Monsieur, Rose-Marie, and Isabelle were all eating their breakfast. I put our milk and water on the stove to heat and talked to them. They asked me about our trip and I was in the midst of telling them when I started getting dizzy. My head was swimming, my heart was pounding, I felt faint. I turned around and took hold of the door edge, but it kept getting worse. Madame said something to me, I turned to answer and my eyes were so blurred I couldn't see. I turned back around toward the stove. I got fainter and fainter. I had sense enough to say that something was wrong and no sooner than I had finished saying that, than I just crumpled to the floor. I never went completely out because I knew what was going on, but I couldn't stand up any longer – something seemed to be pushing me down. Monsieur picked me up and brought me back to bed, put some cold water on my forehead. In a minute I got O.K. I still felt weak and sickish, so they insisted I stay in bed all day. I feel much better now, but still get dizzy when I stand up, and feel drained of all energy. I don't understand what happened or why, except, as everyone has said, fatigue finally caught up with me. I suppose that's the only answer. The nun took my temperature and I had only a teeny bit, so it certainly wasn't anything serious.

Nothing like that has ever happened to me before – it sure was a funny sensation.

Tuesday, May 28, 1957

After a wonderful rest yesterday and last night I'm feeling fine again.

Today was uneventful. Voice lesson this morning – a good one, which surprised me coming after my "rest." After our lesson Louise and I went to TWA to check again on our plane tickets. Everything will work out fine – it will be a simple exchange. So don't worry about that. I'm certainly relieved.

Time is really drawing near for leaving Paris – and it's so sad. I find myself looking at things as if for the last time, seeing things I've never noticed before – tiny details that suddenly loom big and important.

Oh – for the month of June we are going to pay the Rémonds only for the room – not for the food. It was their request that we not take our meals here because of the baby. Of course we were delighted. I said the month of June – I think it will be only the last half of the month.

Wednesday, May 29, 1957

Paris is so beautiful today! This morning we had music history class. Afterwards I stayed and talked to Mr. Handemann about my musical future. He's going to call Bernac and talk about me to him. Neither of us think that my giving a recital right now, just before leaving, would do me much good. He told me to write him next year and let him know what I'm doing. He assured me that if I should come back to Paris after I finish at school he will do everything in his power to make me known. He says he knows he can arrange for me to sing for the manager of the Opéra, Georges Hirsh. He said he didn't know exactly what the chances were in the U.S. for young hopeful singers, but he said that here they are searching for good voices. That is certainly true, because there just aren't that many good ones here whereas in New York they are on every corner. And, as he reminded me, practically all the well-known singers in the U. S. got their start in Europe. I'm definitely going to inquire and investigate scholarship possibilities as soon as I get to Newcomb this fall.

After class I went to practice till lunch time. After lunch I hurried to a 2:00 voice lesson with Mme. Tilliard. She's such a darling woman. She could only take me for one-half an hour today, so I was through by 2:30. I walked leisurely home. There's such a wonderful feeling in the air these days. Everything is so pretty and I love it so.

I met John at 4:30 and we caught the Metro to Port Solferino where we took an hour and 15 minute excursion on a bateau mouche down the Seine. It was so much fun. We went past all the familiar places – up as far as Île St. Louis (where the restaurant Quasimodo is.) There was a beautiful view of Notre Dame, and I welcomed the occasion to take a few pictures. We passed the Louvre, Hotel de Ville, the Conciergerie, Place de la Concorde, – went past the Eiffel and the Palais de Chaillot – down farther than I had ever been. We turned around at the bridge where there is the original Statue of Liberty. It was from this statue that the copy was made which France sent to the U. S. and which now stands in the New York Harbor. All along the banks (which are beautiful now) were fishermen, lovers, swimmers (yes!), hobos – every kind of person. It was really picturesque. We didn't take the excursion until 6:00, so the boat wasn't crowded and of course that's the prettiest time of the day.

Right now I'm waiting till 9:30 when I'm going to meet John again. He had to go to a cocktail party, so I came back, had dinner, and now will start out again. This is the first time I've had a 'divided' date!

Tomorrow's a holiday – no classes!

Saturday, June 1, 1957

Behind again!

Wednesday night (May 29), the second half of my date with John was spent mostly around St.-Germain-des-Prés. I met him in front of Deux Magots. That's the most exciting place nowadays! Now that it's warm weather everybody is there – mostly bearded students. Lots of Americans trying to look French are there too. Everybody tries to fool everybody else. While we were there three Americans (two boys and a girl) caused quite a sensation. The two boys (one with one pierced ear) were dressed as cowboys; one played a banjo, the other a guitar, and they sang cowboy songs. The girl passed the hat to collect money from the bystanders. They were quite clever – also were brazen I think. John said they had been doing that every night in the past week.

Thursday was a holiday. Paris is extraordinaire on a holiday. About 10:30 I went to the Smithers' to practice. All the streets were quiet, hardly any cars, people were all still asleep. By the time I came home from "fairing des exercises" at 1:00 everything was buzzing in true holiday fashion. The day was a beautiful one and all the Parisians took advantage of it to promenade. Balloon and candy vendors pushed their little wagons, children played that fascinating yo-yo game. It was delightful. After lunch I went to see *Love in the Afternoon* with Audrey Hepburn and Gary Cooper. It was a charming movie. Since it takes place in Paris I loved it even more, and I got so nostalgic that I cried, even at the happy ending. The movie was over at 4:30 and I had an hour to kill before my voice lesson with Mme. Tilliard, so I walked down the Champs-Concorde-Madeleine route. I took my time and enjoyed it hungrily, nostalgically, sentimentally. The weather has been so wonderful – warm, coatless weather. It is really exquisite.

After my voice lesson I walked home leisurely. I ate dinner with Isabelle and Nanou – early, because I had to go to the Comédie-Française that night to see *La Reine Morte* for our theater course. It was a wonderful production. Afterwards – for the first time since I've been in Paris – I was followed home! The boy caught the same bus, got off when I did at St. Augustin, and followed me almost to the door, talking to me all the way. I turned and said, "Allez-vous-en" (go away!), and he finally left. When I got inside our door I realized how frightened I had been because my legs were shaking and so were my hands!

Wednesday night – June 2, 1957

Well, only one more exam to go! Yesterday (Tuesday) was study day. Rather the afternoon was – the morning was taken up in practicing and voice lessons. We studied hard all yesterday afternoon and all last night. This morning was our music history exam. It was so simple I was angry. At least it seemed simple. The subject was Berlioz – his life, works, and importance in musique. I think I wrote a good paper.

This afternoon after lunch I had a voice lesson with Madame Tilliard. Before then I worked on my suitcases and trunk. After my voice lesson I met Louise at Au Printemps and we did some shopping. We each bought a book of Paris, a cookbook, and the unique French cooking utensil for grating and straining vegetables. The book is colossal. We bought the English translation with English & American measurements. It's a huge book with everything in it – even directories for wine service, etc. It cost nearly $15.00. Certainly I'll be able to cook someday with a book like that!

After dinner tonight we played with the children some. Madame brought Paul in and of course he took everyone's attention. About 9:30 we bade everyone goodnight, and I came in and finished packing my trunk. Phillippe is coming tomorrow to transport our trunks to the Smithers'.

I got the money today – thank you very much. I thought I sent you our itinerary. I won't have the final list of hotels, etc. until June 20th at which time I shall send it to you.

The address to the hotel in Paris is: Hotel de Tours, 25 rue Jacob, Paris VIe, France. I will be there from Monday night the 17th until the 26th.

We're going to Dijon Saturday evening around 6:30. I'm looking forward to the weekend there.

Monday, June 3, 1957

Friday morning Louise, Jean-Louis, and I took the 11:40 train to Fontainebleau – the château which housed the kings of France before Versailles, notably François I. Napoleon made it his home during his reign. It is in a beautiful little town – everything has the appearance of being in miniature. When we got there the first thing we did was to hunt an inexpensive restaurant for eating lunch. We found one which had omelets and Jean-Louis treated us to wine.

After lunch we walked to the château. It's a beautiful thing with a marvelous staircase at the entrance. It was, however, not as beautiful as I had expected, perhaps I had built it up too much in my imagination. The interior is magnificent. There are some of the most beautiful ceilings and floors, made of precious woods, in the world. The François I Hall is wonderful. After the tour through the interior of the château we explored the gardens – not all of them by any means, because they are quite vast. Behind the château is the

Carp Pond (L'Etang des Carpes), a beautiful water piece with a little pavilion in the center. The pond is stocked with carp – the biggest things. When you throw bread into the pond the carp swarm by the hundreds – come to the very top of the water, and fight over the piece of bread. It's very amusing. The gardens are lovely. There are formal gardens and English gardens, beautiful flower beds, wonderful pansies.

We walked, the three of us. We usually have a good time when we're together, and Friday afternoon we were all in silly moods, and danced and sang in the gardens. Everyone thought we were crazy I'm sure. After walking until we were too tired to walk farther, we left the château and went across the street to have tea. Jean-Louis was very funny Friday. We sat for almost an hour talking and tea-drinking. Then we caught the bus to the train station and took the train back to Paris.

At the station Louise left us and went home, and Jean-Louis and I went to a little student restaurant to eat a little supper. Afterwards we went to Sarah Bernhardt Theater and stood in line for tickets for the performance that night. It was the German contribution to the international festival: the Berlin Opera-Comic Company doing *The Cunning Little Vixen*, a rather contemporary opera. I've never seen anything quite like it. The scenery and costumes were fabulous. Most of the story took place in the forest, the little fox's home, and many of the characters were animals of course, forty children played the animals. The costumes were so real you thought they really were animals. There were crickets and beetles and frogs and dragon flies, porcupines, rabbits, squirrels, everything – and of course the little fox. It really was so adorable. The music was wonderful and the singers also. The woman who played the little fox was superb. I wish Linda and Janet could have seen it.

Saturday morning Louise and I had an appointment with Madame Alvernhe at 4:30 to discuss our family problems. This is what it's all about: at first, before the baby came, the Rémonds said we could stay on until the 26th, but that they couldn't give us our meals because of the baby, etc. That suited us fine because we knew Genie and Lucy would be here, we'll be busy getting things done at the last minute, and wouldn't be here much anyway for our meals. Besides, we're going to Dijon for a weekend right after exams to stay with Jacqueline Darbois. Well, the other day Monsieur said that now that the baby had already come, etc., we could have our meals here too if we wanted, but we told him that we had already arranged not to have them here and we preferred it that way. Well, says he, that changes all. It seemed that if we didn't take our meals they didn't want us to stay here just to keep the room open because Madame wants to go to Champscenest, etc., so we either had to decide to leave the 15th, or stay and take our meals here. Well, Louise and I conferred and decided to leave the 15th because we would end up paying double for meals and we can't do that. Besides, we found a cheap hotel near St.-Germain-des-Prés where we can get a room for 325 francs a day (a piece – 750f. for the room.) We figured it up, and we live much cheaper that way than here. So Madame Alvernhe approved and today we made our reservations. We told Monsieur at noon today about our leaving and he seemed just as pleased as we were to leave. We'll pay him for half the month of June. I'm so thrilled about getting to live on the Left Bank and right at the corner of St.-Germain-des-Prés is perfect.

Saturday afternoon after lunch Louise and I met Jean-Louis at his house at about 2:30. From there we went on into the Bois de Bologne to the tennis stadium to see the finals of the French International championship. Swinn Davidson and Herbie Flam were playing. It was an exciting match. Everyone wanted Flam to win, but Davidson simply out-played him. It was the first professional tennis match I had ever seen. Before the Davidson-Flam match was the women's finals. An English woman Bloomer played the American Knodt. The English woman won. It was so hot. The sun beamed down on us and I got a little sunburned.

After the match we told Jean-Louis goodbye – he was going to Dijon that night. I left Louise and went by the Hotel Plaza Athénée, the Petters' hotel. Hi had called me Friday night and Louise forgot to tell me until Saturday at noon. I had been calling them all afternoon. I went by their hotel and left them a message, then went home. Just about the time I got home Hi called and asked me to meet them for church and lunch the next day. I was so glad to finally have contacted him.

Sunday morning I went to Plaza Athénée to meet the Petters. It was so good to see them. Mr. and Mrs. Petter both look wonderful. We left the hotel and walked to the American Cathedral, which is not far from their hotel. I'm ashamed to say it was the first time I had been. I enjoyed it so much I am going again next Sunday. It was so good to hear a sermon in English. The minister there is excellent, as are the organist and choir. I like the Episcopal church so much.

After church we walked back to the hotel. We were standing in the lobby – Mr. Petter and Hi were at the desk, when Mrs. Petter said, "Look, there's Gary Cooper." I turned, and there was Gary Cooper standing at the desk! I got so excited I thought I'd die! He crossed over in front of us and walked over to where his wife Rocky and their daughter Maria were sitting waiting for him. Needless to say I stared and gaped like an idiot. Gary Cooper is much handsomer in real life than in the movies – he looks much younger. He has such a beautiful body! His wife is very attractive and elegant, and his daughter is adorable. She's about my age I think. They left the hotel – took a taxi.

We went upstairs to the Petters' rooms to freshen up, then we met and went down to the terrace to have lunch. We had a wonderful meal, and delightful conversation. I had snails a new way: they were fixed the same way with garlic and butter, but instead of being in the shell they were on mushrooms. It was absolutely delicious. Hi had never tasted them, so he tried one of mine and joined the "I like snails" club. Then of course Mr. Petter had to try – and he liked them too.

After lunch and coffee and talk we decided to go to the top of the Eiffel Tower. Mrs. Petter particularly wanted to go. I didn't realize it, but this was her first trip to Paris. We took a taxi to the Eiffel, had to stand in line for our tickets. We went all the way to the top. I'm glad to have gone to the top of the Eiffel, but there really isn't that much difference in the top and the next to the top as far as the view is concerned.

After our ascension to the top we took a taxi. Hi had to leave to go to Tours at 5:00 and I had to meet John at 4:30, so we went in the taxi to their hotel, then the taxi took me to meet John. I hope to see the Petters again before they leave. I certainly did enjoy being with them. They're such wonderful people.

I met John in the middle of the Place de la Concorde by the Obelisk. He was there when I got there. He decided that we would go to the Folies Bergère, so we went then to get our tickets. then we went up to Montmartre. John had never been in Sacré-Cœur, so we went in the church. I noticed that in the back of the church is a copy of the statue of St. Peter that is in St. Peter's Basilica in Rome. The foot of the one in Sacré-Cœur has been worn off too. I'm surprised we didn't notice it when we were there. We left the church and walked through Montmartre, Place du Tertre, past the two windmills, down to Pigalle, where we had a little supper. Then we went to the Folies.

At intermission we left! It was awful. It had no coherence, the dancing was sloppy and the singing worse. It was so hot in the theater I was about to faint – so, I repeat, we left. The only thing that can be said about the Folies that is good, is that the costumes were beautiful. But I really don't understand how they stay in business! It was terrible showmanship. And every seat in the house was packed! I guess people just go to the Folies because it's the thing to do. Or maybe when people say, "Did you go to the Folies?" and they say, "Yes," they never bother asking, "How was it?" It was horrible, and I hope I can save my friends from being taken in the biggest tourist trap in Paris!

We left, tired, hot, and bored, and went to Place de la Concorde (by Metro) to take a cooling walk. (The weather has really been warm lately.) Just as we came out of the Metro it started raining, so we re-entered the Metro and went to a café on the Champs where we sat out the rain. We took a cab to the Étoile and John caught the 12:00 bus. I returned to my joyful little room, tired and worn out, but happy.

This afternoon Louise and I walked to St.-Germain-des-Prés to reserve our hotel room. Louise reserved a room for Genie and Lucy there too, and cancelled the reservations at Hotel Rochambeau. I'm so excited about moving over on the Left Bank. I can hardly wait. After lunch we told Monsieur about our moving, and asked him for the key to the garage so we could get our bags and our trunks and put them in our room to start gradually working on them. We're going to leave our trunks in the office at Dr. Smithers' because Newcomb rents the room for all year so we can leave them. American Express will pick them up there for the sailing date.

At 3:30 I had a voice lesson with Madame Tilliard, after which I fought the Metro crowds to Place du Chatelet to Sarah Bernhardt Theater. I bought John and me tickets for the Italian contribution to the International festival – the National Italian Lyric Opera presentation of *Lucia di Lammermoor* with Virginia Zeani and Giulietta Simionato. Zeani did the lead in Poulenc's opera that opened La Scala this year, and of course we heard Simionato at La Scala ourselves. I've always wanted to see *Lucia* and I'm so glad it's coming.

On the way home I stopped in La Pépinière and bought – a Coke! I was craving one, I was so thirsty.

Tonight is study time. Tomorrow is our first exam – theater. After the exam we have a date with Major Annan. Louise called him the other day to see when we could return his heater to him, the one he loaned us Thanksgiving. He asked us (really!) to come use the PX and then to let him to take us to dinner. Naturally we accepted!

So life in Paris is rolling furiously to an end. Oh my money status is as follows. I have $54.50 in francs, $160 in travelers' checks, $185 in money orders, counting Aunt Weda's and granddaddy's. So I have $399. I'll have to pay $75 to the Rémonds, $300 for the trip, and $32 for voice lessons. I'll have to have $407 in francs. So, figure yourself what you think I'll need. Oh – mistake – add $50 in francs since I'll have to pay for my trip to Dijon (only the train will cost me anything), my hotel bill, food, and entertainment for that last week in Paris. So, send the money you think I'll need when you want to.

Wednesday, June 5, 1957

Last night we had the best time! After our exam Louise and I went to Major Annan's hotel Littre. He was sitting there waiting for us with a grin on his face. He's so good and so dumb. He hurried us into the PX to get some of the things we needed for this summer. Then we went into his office. He gave us Scotch and waters, we sat and chatted for a long time. Finally, in his incoherent way, he told us that a woman friend of his was coming with us. He told us she was French, spoke a little English, would be 37 soon, and had studied voice at the Conservatoire. We didn't know what to expect, but when she came we were pleasantly surprised.

Her name is Colette. She's a small, cute woman with short hair, laughing eyes. We, of course, spoke French. We talked about music, about singing. She had wanted to keep on studying voice, but she had to make her living, and she couldn't do it singing. She loves life, young people, can't believe she isn't really young still. We loved her immediately. Apparently she's had a hard life, has bad health, yet she is so gay and happy.

Major Annan drove us all to a little restaurant just across the Seine on the Left Bank not too far from St.-Michel called Lucien's. It's a darling place, quite expensive, and visited only by Frenchmen, not any tourists. We had the most delicious dinner. Major Annan insisted that we have the most expensive things. First we had artichoke hearts cut like little baskets and filled with asparagus tips in vinegar. Talk about delicious! Then we had chicken cooked in wine sauce like I've never before tasted. It was garnished with curled mushrooms – a rare type of mushroom that is so rich! For dessert we had the house specialty – soufflé with an orange liqueur in it. It was the best thing I've ever, ever eaten. We had divine wine, and after dinner, delicious coffee.

Major Annan has really been good to us. He was so funny during dinner. We were talking, in French, with Colette and every once in a while she'd ask him if he understood. He'd always say "Oh sure!" and we knew good and well that he didn't understand at all! Colette is really wonderful. I wish we had met her sooner. I think she's Major Annan's mistress. She lives near his apartment. He told us they were just neighbors, but I have my doubts.

We left the restaurant and drove back to the hotel where Louise and I had left our PX purchases. On the way we passed Les Invalides. In the park there, there is a sort of carnival with all sorts of rides. Major Annan suggested

289

we stop so we did. He and Colette got in one little car and Louise and I in another – little cars on a track like they always have at carnivals. We drove and bumped into each other and laughed and shouted and had just such a good time. When we got back in the car to go on to the hotel Colette begged me to sing, so I sang all the way. Major Annan went in to get our packages, then got back in the car to bring Louise and me home. Colette and I both sang, and then Major and Louise joined in. A gay time was had by all. They walked us to our door, we thanked Major Annan for everything he has done this year for us, and they left.

Thursday, June 6, 1957

Yesterday morning after music history class I went to practice at the Smithers', then met Jean-Louis and we walked to Odeon to have lunch together. We ate at one of the little cheap student restaurants there. I love to do that. It's so interesting to watch the strange people go by. The most fun to see are the American college boys – the really young ones – trying so hard to lose their Americanisms and being so obvious about doing it.

Jean-Louis and I had a good time being with each other. I won't see him but twice more before it's goodbye forever. After lunch he came home with me, we made a date for tonight. I came in and studied until it was time to go to my voice lesson. Monsieur Bernac kept me an hour yesterday because the student after me never came. I certainly hate to stop studying with him.

At 6:30 I met John at the Étoile. John heard from the Harvard Business School and he was not accepted. Of course he's disappointed. I personally think it's a blessing in disguise, and after talking a long time about it, he decided he thinks it is too. We spent about an hour sitting in a café talking Harvard Business. Then we decided to go to the movies. John hadn't seen *Love in the Afternoon* and I loved it, so we went to see it. We got out of the movie about 11:00 and decided I should go home since I have an exam today. So, since it was a gorgeous night we walked home.

This morning we went to the Sorbonne but our art history class was cancelled – Madame le Professeur wasn't there again. After lunch Louise and I killed time until it was time to go to our composition exam. It lasted three hours – wasn't particularly hard. I think I wrote a good paper. After the exam I went to pick up my shoes. I love the little woman in the shoe repair shop, who loves to talk to us.

Friday, June 7, 1957

After dinner last night I met Jean-Louis downstairs and we went to Theatre Vieux Colombier to see *Sacres Fantomes*. It was a delightful comedy, but unfortunately I was too sleepy to see much of it. It's terrible the way I get so sleepy these days. Jean-Louis thinks I'm just bored with him, I think.

After the play I woke up a little, but not much. We stopped at La Pépinière for some fruit juice and Jean-Louis showed me the pictures taken at his birthday party. Then we dragged home.

This morning I went to practice, then came back for lunch, which Louise and I had early because we were supposed to meet Jacqueline Darbois (from Dijon) at the Marignan on the Champs-Élysées. We wrote her that we would like to come next weekend, and she wrote that she and her mother were very touched by our wanting to come and they were more than happy to have us. She said she would be passing through Paris today and would like to see us. So at 2:00 we met her. She looks the same but seems different. She's had much sorrow this winter I'm afraid. She was in love with a man here in Paris who wanted to marry her, but for some reason she just couldn't. So anyway today she said it had finished after Christmas. Poor thing she's so unhappy. She kept saying how glad she was to see us. She was extremely nervous though. I'm so glad we're going to see her. We're going next Saturday and come back to Paris on Monday night.

We came on home, and I started packing. I've packed my trunk and most of another suitcase. At 6:00 I had a voice lesson with Madame Tilliard. I've decided to keep on taking lessons until we leave, so that will mean about $15.00 more than the last figures I sent home. Mme. Tilliard keeps insisting that I must come back to France and sing.

After my voice lesson I walked home, singing all the way – I didn't realize I was singing until I noticed people staring at me. It's such fun to sing.

It was so sad packing my things today. Sad and happy too. I feel like I'm going to pop I have so much emotion stored up in me right now. I feel like the only thing that could help would be to be on a stage and dance, alone, to the "Carousel Waltz." Crazy I suppose.

Sunday, June 9, 1957

Yesterday (Saturday) I had a voice lesson with Bernac at 11:30. It was a good lesson. I sang my new Poulenc – I love it. Yesterday afternoon we stayed in and studied (for a change.) Then after dinner Louise, Rose-Marie, and I went to see *The Bad Seed*. It was a fabulously terrifying movie. What would you do if you had a child who murdered with no qualms or remorse?

This morning Louise and I went to the American Cathedral. I enjoyed the service so much. They have a wonderful choir and organist.

Today is Pentecost Sunday, so we had a very good dinner at noon. We get such a kick out of the nun who's here now. She's a different one. She's been here over a week now – she's nothing short of being dumb! She says the silliest things. We really have fun out of her.

Monday, June 10, 1957

Yesterday afternoon I met John at 3:30 at the Étoile and we went to Gare St. Lazare to take the train to Versailles. John had never been there and since last night was the spectacle of sound and light we decided to go. When we got there about 5:00, we took a tour of the Royal Apartment (the part you saw, Mother) then caught the bus to the Hameau. From there we walked up to the Grand Trianon. The garden behind the Grand Trianon is all planted with flowers now and looks beautiful.

We finished dinner just in time to go to the spectacle. It was held on the big terrace behind the château. The first part of it took place facing the grand canal – the fountain of Apollo and of Laocoön. The lighting effects were gorgeous. Over loud-speakers was given the history of the gardens, interspersed with music of the 17th and 18th centuries. The fountains rose and fell with the music, turned different colors. It was gorgeous. That part lasted about 15 minutes. Then we turned around and faced the château and the history of the château began. It was like a fairy-tale. The château was illuminated and it looked absolutely beautiful. The narrator began with the Louis XIII building, the hunting lodge that grew to be Versailles. As the history progressed the illuminations changed, the fountains were lighted. As the narrator spoke of Mme. de Maintenon, the death of Louis XV, lights inside the château, in the rooms that belonged to these illustrious people, turned on. It was really impressive. Music interspersed all the narration. There were voices of people like Louis XIV, Madame de Pompadour, Marie Antoinette, Moliere, Racine, Voltaire, Beaumarchais, Victor Hugo, Napoleon, Clemenceau. It was so exciting. I was kept busy translating for John and two American ladies near us. It was a most impressive spectacle.

It was over about 11:15. We had to run – and I mean run – all the way from the château to the train station to get the 11:40 train. I thought I would die from exhaustion. We had been on our feet almost all day and I was in high heels. We made it to the train in plenty of time, and even managed to get ourselves a seat – so we were back in Paris at 12:15.

This morning I packed some things, then went to practice. This is a holiday since yesterday was Pentecost. Paris is just like a little, small-town place on a holiday. Nobody is on the streets, no cars, nothing. Mme. Tilliard told me that during the war Paris looked like it does today – everyday. She said all the houses were shut up, no one was in the streets, only of course it was worse then.

After practicing I came home for lunch. Madame fixed one of her "summer" lunches – tomatoes, hard-boiled eggs, lettuce, cold white beans – all topped with mayonnaise – quite good. After lunch I had to go to the Smithers' and leave them the money I forgot to leave them this morning. Then I had to catch a bus to go to my voice lesson with Mme. Tilliard. I had a good lesson, then came home. Eugenie was at our house studying with Louise, so I stopped on my way home and bought three Cokes to take back for us. The man in La Pépinière who always teases me waited on me. When I told him I wanted Cokes he said "Oh – the Beaujolais Americain!" He's so cute.

June 14. 1957

Yesterday morning was one last art class. M. Gaillard was there and it was very interesting.

About 3:00 yesterday Phillippe Moret came in his little Deux Chevaux to get our trunks. It was quite a feat getting them into that little cracker box. He took us and the trunks to the Smithers'. Then poor Mr. Smithers and Phillippe carried those heavy things up all those stairs!

At 4:00 I had a voice lesson with Bernac. I asked him what he really thought of my voice. He asked in what sense and I told him in the sense of doing something with it. He said that he believes I can, that my voice has a beautiful quality, that it needs to grow a little more, that I'm very lucky to be able to study with Marjorie Lawrence, that I should wait and see how my voice develops with her before I decide to return to France or to do something else.

Sunday afternoon, June 16, 1957

Here I am in Dijon.

Saturday morning we had our art exam at 8:30 in the morning. It was on Impressionism – which we studied the least, but I think I passed it, probably by the skin of my teeth. After the exam we came home and packed our bags. Monsieur Rémond had to go to an official luncheon, so he came in and gave us each a bottle of champagne, bade us Bon Voyage, then left.

We are invited (get that) for lunch with them Tuesday so we haven't yet told them goodbye. After lunch we finished packing, then about 4:00 we left. Madame Rémond helped us take all our things downstairs. I went to the corner to hail a taxi – when the driver saw our mountain of luggage he nearly died. So we left "our house" and went to the Smithers'. Poor Dr. Smithers had to help us take everything upstairs again. By the time we got everything situated and went to pick up our shoes at the repair shop, it was time to take a cab to the Champs to meet Fabienne Darbois and her aunt at the Marignan. Fabienne has been sick and has been in Le Havre, and Jacqueline asked us to bring her from Paris with us.

We had a Coke together, then took a taxi to the station. The train left at 6:30 and it was so hot in the train I thought I'd die. Yesterday was really HOT.

Fabienne has changed so – she's almost fat now, but still sweet as pie. We had a good time talking and investigating the "treasures" in my purse.

Jacqueline was waiting for us at the station. It's so good to be back – I wish we could have lived with them all year. They're so wonderful. The children and Mami were so glad to see us and we, them. We had dinner, then went into Mami's room and watched TV and talked. Jacqueline is so wonderful. I feel so sorry for her – I wish she'd re-marry. About 11:30 we went to bed. It was raining – a perfect night for sleeping.

This morning we got up about 8:30, had breakfast, played the piano, then dressed. Jean-Louis had left me a note saying to meet him this morning at the tennis courts, so Jacqueline, on her way to the cemetery took us to the tennis courts. We met Jean-Louis, watched a match, then Jean-Louis showered and dressed and the three of us went to St. Bénigne to Mass. It's such a strange feeling to be back and to have self-assurance – to not be afraid and timid.

After Mass Jean-Louis brought us back to Jacqueline's. Everything is so pretty now here – all the leaves are thick and green and flowers are everywhere. Dijon is really pretty.

Wednesday – June 19, 1957

Back to Dijon – we were on Sunday.

After Sunday noon meal, which was delicious, Louise and I went to see Madame and Monsieur Herard. Madame wasn't there, but dear Monsieur

Herard was. He was so surprised to see us, and very happy that we came. We went into their parlor and talked.

Poor thing, he's been sick all year and he looks terrible. He said he just had too much work in his school. We had such serious, wonderful conversation. He explained the Algerian problem so clearly that I really, for the first time, understand the French point of view.

He complimented our French – said we spoke like petites Françaises. It was wonderful to be able to understand every word he said. When we were in Dijon before we missed so much of what everybody said!

We stayed at Monsieur Herard's about an hour and arranged to call the next day to see Madame. We met Jacqueline then at 4:30. She drove us to the country to visit her cousins Pierre and Claudie (married). Louise had met them before, but I never had. Their (rather Claudie's) parents have a huge country home – a little château just about 10 miles from Dijon, hidden away in a beautiful forest with flowers, birds, and beautiful views from every point. It was wonderful. Claudie is pregnant and is expecting any day now. She's so adorable. Pierre, her husband, wasn't there, but his sister and her mother were. We sat on the terrace in the wonderful sun and drank lemonades – (after a fashion – the French lemonade is not like ours) and ate brioche and talked. It was so pleasant and those people are so great. I get a thrill every time I'm engaged in conversation like that – and it's in French! That's what's so astounding and so natural.

We stayed with them until 6:30 – when Jacqueline had to be back home to see her aunt and uncle off for a voyage to Greece and Italy. Claudie invited us to dinner for Monday night so we could talk to Pierre. At first we refused because we had planned to take the 6:30 Monday evening train back to Paris, but after such charming insistence we decided to stay and go back to Paris on Tuesday morning.

After dinner at Jacqueline's, Jean-Louis came for me at 9:30. We drove around cute little Dijon, then decided to pay a visit to his friend Pierre Favreau who was busily studying for exams. He was not to be disturbed said his parents, so we crept through the courtyard and sneaked up the back stairs to his room. We renewed acquaintances, talked, laughed, and thoroughly distracted him from his work. We only stayed about 20 minutes. Then we went to Jean-Louis' house. His father and brother were there, but Madame Baut is at Vichy – for her liver. The poor French and their livers!

Jean-Louis showed me the rest of the house that I hadn't seen before. We played records, danced, ate cake and pudding, and discussed impossibilities.

It was such a beautiful night – the windows of the large dining room were opened and the scent of the roses from the garden was perfuming the house. It was so romantic. A nice ending to a beautiful friendship, a delicate, understanding love. Jean-Louis brought me home about 1:00 and we made our adieux. I won't be seeing him anymore. He said he might come to Paris today – for me to call his house and check, but I didn't. I decided things were sad enough and there's no need to prolong things. Goodbye, cher Jean-Louis.

Monday morning, just as we got up, Madame Herard called us. She wanted to take us to an exposition of Burgundian sculpture of the 14-16th centuries. Same old Madame Herard. We went to her house at 10:30 Monday morning. She hasn't changed a bit, looks fine, full of that amazing energy. We talked a while, then Monsieur Herard drove us (with Madame) to the Church Saint Philibert where the exposition was held. Saint Philibert is an ancient Roman church, which is usually closed. (We didn't see it when we were in Dijon before.) The exposition was marvelous. The masterpieces of Burgundian art were all assembled in a splendid panoply of wood and stone. So many of them were statues we had seen photos of but had never seen the real thing. Bless Madame Herard for having taken us there.

We left Madame Herard with tears in our eyes – we're so lucky, Louise and I. We have so much to be thankful for, grateful for, proud of, and humble, too.

After lunch I went to pay a visit to Madame Delmas and Lisette. I went before 2:00 so Lisette would be there. Mme. Herard had told me that Mme. Delmas and Lisette were much happier now, that Lisette has stopped making straw animals and things, and now she makes people – typical Burgundian people. Mme. Herard said they were remarkably well-done and that Lisette is doing a good business with them.

I gave them no warning that I was coming. I rang the doorbell – when Lisette answered and saw me her eyes grew wide and she said "Tiens! Quelle surprise!" Mme. Delmas was resting in the room that was mine and she jumped up. Both of them shook my hand and said such nice things. We had a lovely visit – talked long and hard. I ordered two little straw dolls from Lisette. She had sent all of her things to Clos Vougeot to an exhibit there, so she's going to make them especially for me. She was so flattered that I bought them. She's going to send them here to me in Paris. She looks so cute, she's cut her hair and she seems so happy. She's going to the Scandinavian countries this summer with three other girls in a car that one of them owns. Mme. Delmas looks good too. She has been sick this winter, but now she says she's all right. Lisette had to leave to go to work and she kissed me on both cheeks. I was quite touched. Mme. Delmas and I chatted about one-half hour more, then I left after having again been kissed on both cheeks. I was happy that I saw them again. People are so wonderful.

I met Louise at 3:00 in front of the hotel clocks. We went to buy some mustard and had it sent home. I hope you get it all right. We made one last little tour of the center of Dijon, then went home.

At 9:30 Jacqueline and Louise and I drove to Pierre and Claudie's apartment for dinner. Pierre is a doll. He looks extremely American and loves the U.S. immensely. He and Claudie are so cute together. Pierre decided we should drive to Val de Suzon for a drink, so we piled in his car and off we went. Val de Suzan is an incredible cluster of little mountains and valleys that appear out of nowhere and then disappear – about 10 miles from Dijon. In one of the green valleys is a darling club where all the Dijonites go. It reminded me of the petit hameau at Versailles with the ponds, weeping willow trees, etc., so adorable. We went in the bar and had a drink and talked. We had so much fun together. It would have been fun to have lived with them this year.

We drove back to Pierre and Claudie's. As soon as we arrived the electricity blew a fuse and we had to eat by candle light, but it was delightful. We had such lively conversation. Louise and I both did exceptionally well with our French that night. After dinner we sat in the living room and drank champagne and talked some more. About midnight we left them. I hope Pierre gets to realize his dream and come to the U.S. – he loves it so. Jacqueline confessed that if it weren't for the children, she would come to America.

Tuesday morning we had to get up at 5:30 to get the 6:30 train. Jacqueline had hot chocolate for us for breakfast. We had told the children goodbye the night before. Mami got up to tell us goodbye. It was so awful leaving her. Jacqueline took us to the station. We were all brave and restrained the tears that were filling our eyes. As the train pulled out of Dijon I felt a piece of my heart was left there. I learned and faced and loved so much at Dijon.

The train was late getting to Paris and by the time we stood in line for the taxi and finally got to the hotel it was 11:00 A.M. We moved into the little hotel – it is really little, too. But it isn't at all bad. We have a right nice room with huge windows, uncomfortable bed, and hot water. It's like one big family. There is even a little precious dog.

As soon as we installed ourselves and freshened up a little we went to the Opéra and bought tickets for the *Dialogue of The Carmelites*, Poulenc's opera. Then we went on to the Rémonds for lunch. We had an aperitif first, then

Monsieur, in typical fashion, excused himself for not lunching with us since he was going to an official dinner! So we had luncheon "with the girls." We had coffee, watched Paul take his bottle, then had to go to the Smithers' to leave money.

Poor Dr. Smithers. Someone stole his car night before last! He may never get it back! We stayed at the Smithers' until time to come to the hotel.

This morning I went to practice, croaky as a frog after a sleepless night. When I went to my lesson at 11:45 I told M. Bernac I couldn't sing. It was awful because today was my last lesson. So we sat and talked awhile. He is so sweet and kind. He was very complimentary and encouraging. When I got ready to leave he kissed me on both cheeks, and I was so moved I started crying. I couldn't stop. I cried all the way home on the bus. I hate leaving people I love.

I was so sleepy I came home and tried to sleep but didn't succeed. At 2:00 we met Dr. Smithers, Mrs. Smithers, and Sandy at the Sorbonne. Dr. Smithers took movies of us all around in the Latin Quarter. I can't wait to see them.

It's so hard to believe that I have only six more days in Paris. I can't seem to get excited about the trip this summer because first I have to get over the hump of leaving Paris. It's going to be so hard to do.

Sunday, June 22, 1957

Thursday morning Louise and I were sitting at Deux Magots having breakfast when who should appear but Jean-Louis. He had waited all day long Wednesday for me to call him and I never did. I felt sick all over when I saw him. He asked me what had happened and I told him I called him but he wasn't there, so I just thought he didn't come. I just guessed at a time to tell him I called, and it was the only time during the whole day that he left the house! Anyway I was glad to see him again.

He sat down and had breakfast with us, then we all went to a record shop and listened to some records we wanted to buy. I'm so thrilled with the ones I bought. That took us all morning. About 2:30 the three of us walked to Odeon and had lunch at the little student place. Sweet Jean-Louis paid for both of us. He has been truly wonderful to Louise and me.

Sunday, June 23, 1957

After lunch Thursday Louise left us and Jean-Louis and I walked to the

Faculty of Law where he has his classes so he could pick up something he needed. Jean-Louis made the highest grade in his class on his exam. I was so proud of him. We left the Faculty and walked down Rue Soufflot and looked in all the book and art stores. I love to do that. Then we stopped at a café and had coffee. We stayed there talking (Jean-Louis told me that I talked too much now that my French had improved so much) until it was time for me to go to meet Nancy Branick at her hotel – the Ambassador on Boulevard Haussmann. Jean-Louis accompanied me on the bus then left me at the hotel.

Nancy looked wonderful. It seemed so strange to see her after so long. Lavinia Brock is with her. Sandy met us at the hotel too and we took Nancy and Lavinia and one of their tour-friends on a little promenade. We walked to the Opéra, then took them on the Metro to Concorde, walked down by the Seine, then over to the Champs and up to a café. Then we went up to the Arc de Triomphe and went to the top, although the day was cloudy and foggy. The next thing on the agenda was a view of the little men's rooms that cleverly adorn the streets. Nancy and Lavinia had not noticed them before and they were entranced – insisted on taking pictures. I enjoyed being with them so much, but it hurt too, because they just can't appreciate Paris as it really is and it's so wonderful and unique, but unless you've been fortunate as I have and lived here, you never really understand Paris.

Monday, June 24, 1957

Thursday afternoon, after being with Nancy and Lavinia, I came back to the hotel and dressed to go to Jean-Louis' house. Louise came in and said that the hotel man had given Genie and Lucy a single room for that night with a tiny bed that they couldn't possibly sleep in. So we decided that we would sleep at Jean-Louis' house and one of them could have our bed. When I got to his apartment I asked him if we could sleep there that night and he said of course. Jean-Louis and I cooked supper at his house. I fixed scrambled eggs, ham, and we had fresh tomatoes. It was very American and it tasted so good! After dinner we listened to the radio, read poetry, danced. About midnight Louise came and the three of us went across the street to have something to drink before going to bed. It was such a pleasure to sleep in a comfortable bed after this thing we had in the little hotel!

Friday morning we took a taxi to the hotel. I had not yet seen Genie and Lucy. They both look grand. We introduced them to Jean-Louis, then the five of us went to Deux Magots to eat breakfast. After breakfast Jean-Louis left us, and we started on the hardest day I've had in ages! First we went to the French

Line to see about getting our tickets changed. Monsieur Guy Richer took care of us. I won't go into the details but the rest of the day was spent going back and forth between TWA and the French Line. Finally we got everything settled. Everything is going to work out just fine. I went to pay Mr. Hochwald for our trip. With all our sight-seeing tours, etc., it will cost us $309. That's remarkable.

At 7:00 John came to the hotel to get me. We walked along by the Seine, had coffee and talked until it was time to go to the opera. We saw *Lucia di Lammermoor* at the Theater Sarah Bernhardt done by the Italian Lyric Opera Co. whose members are from La Scala. Virginia Zeani sang Lucia and was fantastically great. I've always wanted to see the opera and they certainly made it impressive for me. After the opera John brought me home, then made a dash for the bus.

Saturday morning after my breakfast at Deux Magots, I went to the record shop and listened to a record by Patachou and one by Gilbert Bècaud and bought them both. I can't wait to hear them when I get home. Major Annan had invited all of us to come to the Hotel Littre and have lunch with him, so at 12:30 I met Louise, Genie and Lucy there. Major gets better every time I see him. He's really so nice. He treated us all to cheeseburgers and milkshakes and they were delicious. Then we all went in his office and talked. When we told him goodbye – this time for the last time – he said, "Thank you for coming into my life." I was so moved I almost cried. People are so wonderful – you can't sell them short.

At 2:00 we all went to the Smithers' to see Mr. Hochwald and get our final trip information – addresses, etc. Then at 3:00 we were back at the hotel, where Monsieur Rémond came for us in his car and took us to the Château of Vincennes. This was his way of doing something for Genie and Lucy. I had been to Vincennes once with John, but when we arrived it was closing time so we just saw the exterior. The only visit-able parts of the inside of the château are the chapel and the dungeon. It was quite interesting, but for some reason I was un-impressed.

After the visit Monsieur brought me back to the hotel because I had to meet John at 7:00. Then he took the girls to have something to drink in a café. I can see straight through Monsieur Rémond now, and though I love him in a way, he is certainly typical of an avaricious (perhaps that's a little strong) bourgeois.

At 7:00 John came over. We started out walking and ended up at a little Greek restaurant for dinner. Afterwards we walked down to see Notre Dame illuminated. I still get such a thrill to see that omnipotent building – so symbolic, so wise, so durable – made even more beautiful by the magic of lights in the night time. We walked down by the water, sat on the banks and talked and watched the tourists come by, listened to their comments, and compared them with our own impressions of Paris. When the illuminations were finished, we left, he walked me back to the hotel and John made his usual dash for the bus.

Yesterday morning about 11:00 I went to the Louvre. I had such a wonderful time. I always get more out of a museum when I go alone. I went to see the section of Le Nain, Poussin, Gelée, all of whom I studied frantically before our final exam in art history. It was such a pleasure and such a satisfaction to be able to look at a painting and think about the painter's life, his ideas, his technique and see them in his finished product. I also explored the Rubens and Van Dyke room. Rubens is marvelous, but sometimes his colors are too fleshy for me. The room where the paintings are which were done by Rubens for Marie de' Medici to depict her life is fabulous. Each painting is remarkable. Then I went down in the basement to the sculpture of the Moyen Age, Renaissance, and 17th century. I finally saw the tomb of Philippe Pot which we studied so much in Dijon. (Which reminds me Lisette Delmas sent me the dolls of straw and they are precious.) I thoroughly enjoyed my visit.

I came home from the Louvre and met John about 2:00. We took the Metro from Place de Vosges to go to the Rodin Museum. When we got there it was closed. Big squelch. So we decided to drink one of the bottles of champagne which Monsieur had given us. John and I spent 30 minutes walking around trying to find some ice to ice it down with. Finally I went in Deux Magots and asked one of the waiters if they could sell me any ice. He said I would have to talk to the boss, but he doubted if they would let me have any because they never sold, gave, or otherwise let anyone have their ice. He pointed the boss out to me and I asked him in my nicest French if I could buy some ice. He looked at me, then asked his partner what he thought, and then led me back to the counter, told a woman to fix me some ice and put it in a carton for me. While I was waiting the waiter came up and asked me if they were going to give it to me, when I said yes, he said, "Well, they just can't resist a pretty woman." They gave me the ice, and when I asked how much I owed them, they said "nothing." I told them I had my breakfast there every morning, and they were delighted. It's experiences like that that create faith in human nature.

We brought the ice to the hotel, put it and the champagne in the sink and waited for it to cool. Louise, Genie, and Lucy came back soon, so when the champagne finally was cold John opened it and we all drank it, making toasts to everything and everybody. Five people can sure finish a bottle of champagne in a hurry. We stayed here with our champagne and conversation until nearly 10:00. Then the girls went out to an expensive restaurant, and John, and I, poor that we are, went back to the Greek place. After dinner I was so sleepy that I came home, leaving John a whole hour to kill by himself before the 1:00 bus. Voilà! I'm finally caught up.

About staying in New York, I've decided I want to come home on Monday the 19th instead of Tuesday the 20th. Two days in New York will be enough. Besides I'm only going to have three weeks or a little over at home, because school starts the 15th of September. So, if you do anything about my plane reservation, make it for Monday the 19th of August.

Tuesday, June 25, 1957

It's almost over now. Paris will soon be far away from me.

Yesterday was a busy day – a leisurely busy that is so very pleasant. I spent my usual hour having breakfast at Deux Magots – watching all the people and taking in the sun, only yesterday it was the clouds I took in. After breakfast I went to the Rodin Museum to see the famous sculptor's masterpieces, which are marvelous. *Le Penseur* (*The Thinker*) and *The Kiss* and *The Gates of Hell* are really terrific. I'm so glad I finally went to see them.

I left Musée Rodin and went to the Bally store by the Madeleine to buy a pair of shoes. I tripped Saturday night going down the steps, and tore the heel (which I had just had renewed) off my high heels. I decided – rather than to pay $6 or $7 to have them repaired when it is so cheap at home – I would buy a new pair. I found a beautiful pair that actually fit – for nearly $30, so my budget took a huge cut.

At 4:00 I went to the Louvre, this time to see the Impressionists. I was so thrilled and excited to see them. I'm so glad that art has finally become an important part of my life. I wish I were filthy rich and could have bought the Cézannes, Lautrecs, and Renoirs that were auctioned last week for thousands of dollars.

I stayed in the Louvre until closing time, then caught the bus to the hotel, where I changed to meet John at the Étoile at 6:15. I was 15 minutes late because the taxi driver (I splurged) thought I had said Les Halles instead of L'Étoile!

John and I went to L' Étoile Vert to have dinner. I'm always amazed at how well one can eat there for such a low price. After dinner we caught a taxi (the driver was a charming woman) to the Opéra. Last night was the second Paris performance of Poulenc's *Dialogues des Carmelites*. It was the best opera I've ever seen or heard. The music is so beautiful and moving. I'm really proud that I am one of the first to have seen it. I can hardly wait till it's recorded. I was so surprised at the singing last night. Everyone had an excellent voice. I don't know where they've been hiding them all year! Denise Duval sang the lead, and she is marvelous. I've never been so thrilled. I feel like I'm closely associated with it after having seen and heard Poulenc, after having studied with Bernac. This has been such a marvelous musical year.

After the opera John and I took a taxi and then walked up the Champs – both of us very sentimental. We have had such a wonderful relationship – each of us has been a vital part of the Paris we both love. It wasn't sad telling John goodbye because he's going to be in London when we're there, so I'll see him then.

This morning I went to Deux Magots and had breakfast, then sat there till noon writing farewell notes to Bernac, M. Handemann, Mme. Alvernhe, and Mme. Tilliard.

A Last Tour
Before
Flying Home

Thursday, June 27, 1957

Dear Mother and Daddy,

Here I am in Brussels – but let me tell you about my last hours in Paris first.

Tuesday afternoon I was to meet Jean-Louis at 3:30, so before then I walked around in our hotel neighborhood, explored the art stores and bought a Degas print. Then I walked over to the Seine and examined the book stalls. I bought two French books – La Fontaine's *Fables* and a thing by Alexander Dumas that Jean-Louis hates. I ran into Eugenie among the book stalls – we were both lamenting our departure from Paris. I won't see her anymore till next year.

At 3:30 I met Jean-Louis at Deux Magots. We had coffee, and he told me he is coming to London to see me – Jean-Louis and John both! We walked along the Seine down to Île St.-Louis, which is so charming – you feel like you're back in the XVII Century. It was so beautiful Tuesday – we took pictures of each other, laughed, were sad a little, and loved Paris extremely. Jean-Louis has been so good to me. I miss him already. We stayed together until 1:00 when I went to the Rémonds' to have an aperitif. We had a nice conversation. They begged me to stay Wednesday until the 6:30 p.m. train so I could come to the reception they were giving in honor of Paul's birth. It was to start at 6:00, but they said I could come at 5:00 and see the buffet and have some champagne with them for a pleasant farewell. They really wanted me to stay, so I promised I would. I left the Rémonds' and at 9:00 Jean-Louis and Jacques came for me in the Deux Chevaux. They are so cute when they're together. I'm always so happy when I'm with them I'd like to be in their family I think – not as a wife – but a cousin or something. Anyway – they couldn't decide where they wanted to have dinner – so after much price examining, laughing, and general cutting-up – we went to the Pizza. We had such a good time. It's the most wonderful thing to be part of something that used to be foreign and unattainable. I wish I could bottle up all my wonderful experiences and keep them and relive them when I want.

After dinner we went to pick up Jacques' date – a cute little girl who goes to school and in her spare time works for a travel agency showing Paris to visitors. We all went to a night club called Carroll's. It is a darling place with a wonderful orchestra and excellent entertainment. The star was a cute girl singer who was really great. We had champagne, danced – and stayed until 3:30. I got home about 4:00 a.m. and plunked into bed.

Yesterday morning – Wednesday – I woke at 8:00 when Louise did and since I couldn't go back to sleep – I got up. I packed my bags – went to the Smithers' and fixed my bags there and my trunk. Louise came to the Smithers' while I was there, and we returned to the hotel together. Phillippe Moret came to take Louise to lunch, so I told him goodbye. Louise didn't want to stay for the reception, so they were going to take the 2:00 train. So – I left the hotel about 1:00 and went to Jean-Louis' with all my bags, and had lunch with him and Jacques at the apartment. We went to a nearby delicatessen and bought everything already cooked and had it brought to the apartment. We had such fun together. Jacques said he wants me to marry Jean-Louis so he can come to the U. S. and visit us. I told him that if I married Jean-Louis we'd live in France – but Jacques said he wouldn't permit that. He was very funny talking about it.

We stayed at the apartment until about 3:30. Then Jean-Louis drove Jacques to Concorde and took me on to the French Line where I had to get some more stickers for our bags. Then he drove me to the Smithers' so I could put the stickers on the bags – then he drove me to France-Amerique to the Rémonds' reception. I was the only one there at that early hour, but it was perfect that way. They were so glad I stayed. We drank champagne together. They told me how they enjoyed me and how I had become a member of their family. Maybe the champagne and sentimentality mixed did it – but I was very touched. Madame looked pretty – she had on a new dress she made – of shantung – yellow print like that yellow taffeta of mine. The buffet was beautiful – I've never seen such darling sandwiches. They really did themselves proud. Nanou and Isabelle were there, both were dressed up and looked very cute. I took pictures of them all. I only stayed about 40 minutes because I had to catch the train. When I left they both kissed me. They've been so good to me. They said that if I come back to Paris they are at my disposal for any help I might need, etc.

Jean-Louis picked me up at 5:40 – we picked Jacques up at 5:45 and we sped to the Gare du Nord. They helped me get all my things on the train – then we stood on the quai and talked. About five minutes before train time we discovered that my things were on the wrong train, so we ran like crazy to change them – then got back on the quai to say goodbye. I was so touched when Jacques kissed me on both cheeks. I was so sad, I couldn't hold back the tears – I was standing by the window and Jacques and Jean-Louis disappeared. Sacré-Cœur was visible high on Montmartre and Paris quickly slipped away from me. I love her so much. I thought about how lucky I am to have known her. Even if I never see her again – how wonderful it is to have her in my heart and mind and thoughts.

In four hours I was in Brussels. It was a beautiful trip – the countryside looked gorgeous in the sunset. It was 10:30 when we arrived. I was in a compartment with a young Belgian priest who was coming from two years in Italy – in Rome. His brothers met him at the station and they all helped me carry my things and find a taxi.

When I arrived at the hotel Lucy, Genie, and Louise were all in tears, yelling and screaming at me. Louise had given me a plastic sack to take up in our hotel room in Paris as she was going out with Phillippe. She told me to put it in a brown paper sack on the bed. I had to leave in such a rush that I didn't put it in the sack, but by the sack on the bed. When Louise returned to get the sack (the brown one), she didn't look to see if the plastic sack were in it – she just took it for granted it was since it wasn't on the bed. This plastic sack contained most of our train tickets, hotel reservations, Genie's boat ticket, etc. When she arrived in Brussels without it they all panicked and had hysterics and of course it was all my fault. I immediately called the hotel in Paris. It seems the man who cleans up had come in to clean the room and had thrown the sack and the things in the trash can. I made him go look and he found everything still in the trash can. So I told him to make a bundle and I would send a friend to get it immediately. I called Jean-Louis and asked him to go to the hotel, get the things and send them to us here. Bless his heart. Well of course I was worried and was relieved the things were found. I admit it was wrong of me not to put them in the brown sack, but how could I know someone would come throw them away? The phone calls cost me nearly $10.00, but Louise and Genie and Lucy wouldn't help pay for them a bit because they said it was all my fault that it happened! They were all mad at me and Louise threw a fit like the Italian one. She accused me of trying to get the best of people, of trying to outdo everyone. She admitted to being jealous of me but she said she's jealous because I brag all the time. She says I deliberately do mean things and that I don't want her to have friends. I don't believe any of it is so. Is it? I feel sorry for Louise. Last night had there been any way, I would have returned to Paris, gotten my money back from Mr. Hochwald, and traveled by myself this summer. I don't know if I can stand it or not. I never knew people could be so jealous and conniving and selfish until this year.

This morning I slept all morning because for two nights I had nil sleep. I had breakfast in bed. Now that we're in the Benelux countries breakfasts consist of rolls, butter, jam, ham, cheese, egg, and coffee! It was delicious. I washed my hair then met the girls at La Grande Place. I'm sleepy – I'll finish tomorrow morning – La Grande Place is Brussels' oldest square. The town hall, the old guild halls, etc. are situated there. All the buildings are trimmed in gold – very impressive. We had lunch in a little restaurant for a little price. Then we walked past the huge Gothic church, up to the park of the royal palace. In the park at 3:00 was a band concert, so we decided to attend. It was very good. More than the music, I enjoyed watching the people – we humans are always so amusing at band concerts. After the concert we walked to the Royal Palace. We started to enter the gate of the palace when one of the guards stopped us and told us we couldn't go in. We were so surprised – after all we always visited the royal palaces. Then it dawned on us that Belgium's King Leopold lives in his palace! We felt so stupid. We started laughing and the guards, who knew that the light had just dawned on us, were all laughing too. So – we went from the royal palace to a museum nearby – but it was getting ready to close – so we left. From there we walked to the awful little statue for which Brussels is famous – of the little boy going to the bathroom and from there back to the hotel. We stopped on the way in a café and tried some Trappist beer that Fielding recommended. I liked it. By the time we got to the hotel it was 8:15. I undressed, wrote letters and went to bed early – about 10:30.

This is awful to say, but I'm not much interested in Brussels. Maybe because my heart is in Paris still. Tomorrow we're going to Bruges and the next day to Ghent I think I'll like them better. I'll be glad to get to Holland.

Do you realize that in exactly seven days (this is Friday, June 28th) I'll be 21 years old!!!

Mother – I don't know why I never mentioned about the baby things coming. They did and they were precious. Madame was so thrilled with them. She said they didn't have things like that in France – plastic-lined pants, etc. She will probably write you a note or something thanking you for them.

Sunday, June 30, 1957

The weather has been so hot – not really hot by summer-in-Paducah standards – but hot in comparison with what I've been used to for the past nine months. It certainly makes it hard on the sightseeing.

Friday we did absolutely nothing but catch up on letter writing, wash clothes, and walk around the city a little. We had a whopping dinner at noon at a little restaurant that specializes in Viennese and Jewish food – for only a dollar. That's all that Friday holds as being memorable.

Yesterday we got up at 7:00, had breakfast, and took the 8:47 train to Bruges, about an hour's ride. Bruges is delightful – a medieval city à la Flammand that has scarcely changed. None of the buildings were later than 16th century. From the station we took a bus into the heart of the town – the market square. Market day was on in full swing. We stood watching – very amused – a man selling quilts. It's much better than a circus. We walked around the square investigating all the wonderful buildings – mixtures of Gothic style and Flemish characteristics. Then we walked to another little square called the Burg. Here is the town hall and other municipal buildings. Just as we arrived a wedding was coming out of the town hall, so we of course joined the crowd and watched the procession come out. European weddings are so different from ours. In the case yesterday the bride and groom didn't even leave the church together. The groom is always so neglected.

After the wedding processed we went inside the town hall and up to see the Gothic chapel that is perfectly beautiful. I could see knights and ladies standing in that room by the huge open fireplace – maybe with a roast pig with an apple in his mouth being turned on the fire.

We left the town hall and walked down a little street that took us to one of the canals that runs through Bruges. We decided to take a ride in one of the motor boats along the canals and see Bruges that way. It was a delightful excursion. Bruges is really adorable. There were so many beautiful little scenes along the way.

After our excursion we walked to the cathedral. We got inside and discovered we had come upon another wedding – so we watched it too. Then we had ham and cheese sandwiches for lunch in one of the cafés.

After lunch we took the train to Ghent, about one-half hour from Bruges. It's the same sort of medieval wonder that Bruges is, only larger. We took a trolley to the center of town and walked to the Cathedral St. Bavon where one of the art treasures of the world is: an altar piece of 20 hitched panels done in oil representing the adoration of the lamb by Van Eyck. It is really marvelous. It has had a stormy history – Hitler had it stolen and it was later found in a salt mine. It is really wonderful. There is also a Rubens in the cathedral that is splendid.

From the cathedral we walked down through the center of Ghent. Wonderful buildings crowd against each other in a colorful array of the Middle Ages. You think you've stepped back hundreds of years into history. Not far from here is the Château of the Counts, a wonderful, massive château-fort completely surrounded by water. It was the center of Flemish history ages ago. From the château we then headed back toward the town center.

We came upon a market that had the best looking fruit I've ever seen. Nearby was a little shack fixed up on the inside like a little bar – so we went in and had a Coke. We were all about to drop from thirst. We've been thirsty ever since we got to Belgium and we've been guzzling water like ducks. Everyone is astounded that we drink the natural water because they claim it has too much limestone for drinking. All the natives drink that tortuous mineral water.

After our Coke we took the next train back to Brussels and got back about 6:00 – tired, hot, and thirsty. I had bought a little jar of peanut butter in Ghent – the first I've seen in ages and I just couldn't resist it – so I went with Lucy and Genie to buy their chocolate bars and I bought some cookies to spread my peanut butter on.

It's 11:00 (nearly) this morning and I'm not yet out of bed. We're going museum seeing today. I'll be glad when tomorrow comes and we go to Amsterdam.

All the tickets came yesterday – that precious Jean-Louis. So everyone is happy I suppose.

Well, it's Sunday afternoon now and we're tired and burning up. I never dreamed I'd be so warm this summer. I can only wear one thing during this heat because all my other clothes have three-quarter length sleeves, etc. I made myself a skirt in Paris by cutting off the top of that blue Lanz cotton dress. It was too short-waisted and is much more serviceable as a skirt. That has been my uniform.

This afternoon we walked to the Beaux-Arts, a marvelous museum with paintings by the Dutch masters as well as Spanish, Italian, & French. We spent two hours there, then walked back via La Grande Place so we could look at the menu (rather the prices) of the most famous restaurant in Europe (so says Fielding): L'Épaule de Mouton. It's very expensive, but we made reservations for tonight. The à la carte menu starts at almost $2.00, so I'll have to take whatever that is. I've set myself a limit and after having to pay that phone bill, I can't afford to cash more money just to eat on.

We continued back to the hotel. It's so hot it's terrible. I had forgotten what hot weather was. Anyway we are back in the hotel trying to keep cool, and waiting for dinner time.

It's Sunday night – and we're so hot we're going to sleep in our underwear. I just don't think I can take a whole summer of traveling in heat like this!

We went to L'Épaule de Mouton tonight and it was worth the dollar I had to borrow in order to get out! It's such a famous restaurant – there are all sorts of pictures of movie stars and diplomats having their dinner there. We were disappointed though, because during the whole time we were there we were the only customers. The staff of four waited solely on us. Of course we had to plan carefully in order not to break our banks. We went through the usual trading, dividing, etc. Lucy and I split a dozen snails; Genie had a dozen all alone and nearly choked trying to get them all down. They were delicious escargots – and so big! Next Lucy and I split an order of sole Herald Tribune, which was sole in a cream-wine sauce with lobster meat, mushrooms, and truffles. On the side were some creamed potatoes put in the oven and baked. It was so delicious and so filling, I thought I'd never get through it all. Louise and Genie split the same thing. Next we had dessert. Louise and Genie ordered one order of Crêpes Mikado, which are crêpes filled with a creamy melted chocolate sauce, and Lucy and I ordered one order of crêpes clairettes – crêpes flamed in three kinds of liquor, an orange liquor predominating, with shredded candied orange peel on top. Then of course we split each order four ways and each had some of each. It was absolutely the most divine dessert I've ever eaten. The crêpes were so heavenly that we were oohing and aahing with each bite. Of course we were too stingy to order wine, so we drank water like fish. We had a pitcher of water filled four times! I think they were expecting us to swim out. When we left, with the contented smiles of those who have been well replenished, we told the boss, the waiter, the waitresses how much we enjoyed it. They smiled and bowed and helped us. All in all my dinner was $5.00 + 2 cents and it was certainly worth it.

We walked out of the restaurant and into Le Grande Place. It's illuminated tonight and looks like something from a fairy tale. The sky was a deep, velvety blue; as Genie said, it looked like pictures of Christmas night, when all is bright. It really was a beautiful sight. Everyone was sitting around in the cafés, talking and drinking and enjoying the end of their Sunday holiday for all it is worth.

Monday, July 1, 1957

Greetings from Amsterdam!

We arrived this afternoon about 4:00. It took 3 hours from Brussels. The train ride was nice – we saw beautiful Dutch countryside and lots and lots of real windmills.

I like Amsterdam – especially the people. They are so friendly and so anxious to be helpful. And quite good looking. When we arrived we came straight to our hotel – a small, very clean, very comfortable hotel. We're on the troisième étage – which means three tortuous escaliers to climb – and we had to carry our own luggage!

After getting our things settled the hotel woman gave us a map of the city and we struck out. We were amazed at the numerous cyclists on the streets. Everybody rides bicycles. We walked down through the center of town, across canals, past wonderful old buildings, and at 6:00 we came to one of the boat docks where one can take a one-hour tour of the canals and the harbor. We scurried on the boat that was just leaving. The guide was a girl, very attractive, of about 23 or 24. She seemed to like us and after the tour we talked – mostly about Paris, because she had spent several months studying there too. She said she knew we must be students because we looked intellectual. She gave us some names of student restaurants here for us to try.

The boat tour was wonderful. The canal system is so interesting. I was amazed to learn that they change the water in the canals every Thursday! The houses in Amsterdam are fascinating. I enjoyed the ride through the harbor best. Just beyond the harbor lie the North Sea on one side and the Zuider Zee on the other. Ships from all over the world dock there. It was fascinating.

After the boat trip we walked to the restaurant, Porte van Cleve, for a steak. Their steaks are famous and they begin at low prices. We had a wonderful meal of steak, potatoes, and spinach for less than $1.25.

Tuesday, July 2, 1957

This morning we went downstairs to a scrumptious breakfast of ham, cheese, white light bread, toast, raisin bread, pain d'épices, butter, jam, and coffee. It was really tasty. By the time we got away it was after 10:00 a.m. We went straight to the Municipal Theater to buy tickets to two performances this weekend of the Holland Festival. (During the months of June and July Holland has a huge festival and every night in the major cities there are operas, ballets and theater with guest artists.) We bought tickets for the Netherlands Ballet Co. and also for Stravinsky's *The Rake's Progress*. I've been dying to see this opera – it's rarely done.

After buying our tickets we took the trolley to the tourist-travel bureau that made our reservation here through Mr. Hochwald. We investigated their tours and decided to take one tomorrow to Aalsmeer (the flower market of the world), the Hague, Delft, and Leyden. We had planned to go there anyway and this tour is inexpensive and we'll get to see more of the countryside. We signed up, then went to the train station and found out schedules and prices. We plan to go to Spakenburg, Alkmaar (the cheese market), Marken and Volendam, and Utrecht as well.

Since we had filled all our days up with touring, we decided that we'd better see the parts of Amsterdam today. First we thought we'd like to go to a diamond cuttery. We happened to be standing right in front of the Victoria Hotel (a very expensive one) and decided to go in and ask for information. The man behind the reception desk was so cute. He said that since I had asked him so nicely he'd have to give me a card, so he wrote his name on a card which permitted us to go in one of the diamond factories and watch them cut diamonds.

We took the trolley to the factory but they were closed for lunch until 1:00, so we whiled away 30 minutes in the street market. The fruits and vegetables were superb. I love markets. The best thing about this one was the flowers. Roses, daisies, sweet peas, lilies, iris, marigolds – everything in every color. I had never seen some of the varieties.

At 1:00 we went back to the diamond cuttery and they ushered us in. A girl took us around and showed us the way it was done. It takes so long to cut them! As we left they told us about the International Diamond Exposition just a few blocks away, so we decided to go. Almost every country has an exhibition, and I've never seen such jewels. The Hope Diamond is there too. Remember when we saw it in New York?

We spent about 45 minutes in the diamond show, then walked to the National Museum. Here we spent an hour swimming in Rembrandt and other Dutch masters. The biggest treat, however, was the little room with one Murillo, one Velasquez, one Goya, and one El Greco. (I suppose that's heresy in Holland!) We had thought there was some Van Gogh in that museum, but we discovered it was all in the Municipal Museum, which wasn't far, so we walked there.

I spent the most wonderful museum-time I've ever had. They have a fabulous Van Gogh collection – six big rooms. Some of the paintings I had seen in New Orleans when the collection came there. I have just finished reading *Lust for Life* and so the paintings meant even more to me. I couldn't resist buying a print of the *Tree in Blossom – Souvenir de Mauve*. I almost bought it in Paris but it was too expensive. It was several dollars cheaper here, so I bought it and had it mailed home. I just love it.

We stayed in the museum until closing time, then came back to the hotel, exhausted. We have been on our feet all day long!

Lucy, Genie, and I went out to eat tonight at one of the little restaurants recommended to us by the guide on the boat tour yesterday. Louise is on her starvation diet, so she didn't go. We thought we'd never find the place! After much misdirection, we finally found the restaurant tucked down in a basement sort of thing. The owners of the restaurant were so surprised to see us. I wouldn't doubt but that we were among the very first American girls to go there. No one but students work there and mostly students eat there. It's a cute place, very clean and the food is delicious. There is no menu – only one dish. We had steak, fried potatoes and apple sauce – enough for two men – for about 60 cents! The owner explained in his halting, adorable English how the place works. He kept saying "You come back every night?" We told him we couldn't come back every night, but that we promised to return.

When we left the restaurant we discovered we were only a five minutes' walk from our hotel. We had walked in a circle trying to find it!

Wednesday night – July 3, 1957

You are about to receive the last letter I shall write in my 20th year. I don't know why, but becoming 21 tomorrow is so momentous. It closes a door and yet it opens one too. I can truly say this 20th year of my life has been so full and so rich that I hate to leave it. It's like leaving a good friend and knowing you'll never see him again.

Today was a full day. After breakfast we caught the trolley to the travel office where we joined the people who were going to take the tour with us and we all boarded the bus. Our first stop was Aalsmeer, the flower market. I've never seen so many flowers! Thousands and thousands, all lying in huge bunches on tables ready to be auctioned, then shipped to all parts of the world. Carnations, roses, lilies, orchids, daisies, sweet peas of every color and form – many varieties I've never seen. I could have stayed there forever. I always feel so frustrated when I'm with so many flowers because I want them all – I want to hold them all, smell them all – and it's so impossible. We went in the auction room and watched them auction the flowers. That was very interesting.

We left Aalsmeer and continued on our way through the lovely Dutch countryside. Windmills were everywhere. At about 11:30 we stopped in a little fishing village for coffee. Three beautiful windmills were nearby, so we had beautiful picture opportunities.

After coffee we drove through Leiden, famous for the oldest university in Holland. We arrived in Delft for lunch. Just as we arrived, a storm broke and it poured down rain during the whole time we were eating, but when we finished our lunch, the rain stopped, the sun re-appeared – uncanny.

From Delft (where we loaded up on the best Dutch cookies!) we continued on to the Hague. We drove through the city looking at the government buildings, the old city walls, etc., then went to the Peace Palace. We left the bus and took a tour of the palace. It is really very beautiful. Next we drove along the beach of Schweningen, the most popular of all Dutch beaches. On the way we passed a village where the women were dressed in their old habits and were sitting in the fields mending the fishing nets. The beach was attractive, but just like all other beaches.

Madurodam was the next stop. This is a miniature city – everything is to the scale of 25% of its actual size. There is an airport, a train station, a miniature Peace Palace, department stores, churches, schools, lakes, cattle, people on benches – everything. It really is adorable. I kept thinking of Disneyland.

From Madurodam we came back to Amsterdam, arriving about 6:30, then we hurried home, washed up, changed clothes, and went to the Netherlands Ballet. It was excellent, all modern – even the version of Mozart's 29th Symphony. Also they did *The Hat* with music by Shostakovich and *The Firebird*. I really enjoyed it.

Friday, July 5, 1957

I've been 21 all of two days now, but I don't feel a bit different!

I spent the quietest, calmest birthday I've ever had. Yesterday morning Louise went to the American Express to get them to recommend a dentist to have a tooth filled. By the afternoon she went to bed with her toothache and Genie, Lucy, and I went to the antique district to browse. The antique shops are marvelous. After antiquing and not buying anything we decided to go to the pastry shop that we had been noticing and to try some of their wares, which included some of the best looking ice cream I've ever seen. Our exploit turned out to be very rewarding. It was the most delicious ice cream – orange and vanilla – that I've ever eaten. After our pastry visit we parted ways.

I walked slowly all the way back to the hotel, looking in windows, watching people, and generally enjoying being alone. I thought about being 21 – about my birthday, and how funny it is that you are always giving me things for having come into the world, when it is I who should be giving to you for having brought me here, for having given me so much. Sometimes it frightens me that I am so fortunate. Yesterday I was extremely "homesick." I've been quite ready to come home ever since I left Paris, but yesterday I was worse. I'm so glad your letter came yesterday. It helped cheer me up.

We all dressed up and went to a Bali restaurant for dinner to sample one of the Javanese feasts that Fielding raves about. It was certainly unique. The waiters are "genuine" Javanese. They wear colorful kerchiefs on their heads and white suits. We ordered the traditional rice table – which came to Holland by way of the Dutch East Indies. The waiters brought three little tables alongside of our table. The little tables were loaded with dishes. Into our soup bowls they put rice, then began serving us a spoonful of every dish on our rice. We all sat, dumbfounded with our mouths drooping at the sight of so much food. Each morsel was different, exotic, and bewildering. It took ages to eat it. I tried everything, liked most of it, and was thrilled to have had the experience.

The hotel woman had put our bottle of champagne in the ice box for us while we were at dinner, so we got it and brought it up to the room. Louise opened it and the cork shot to the ceiling and we had a well-soused floor. We decided to go downstairs and invite the woman and her husband (the hotel owners) to join us in drinking our champagne. They were real flattered. The man, a Dutch Ezio Pinza, said he never touched alcohol, but that this was a special occasion, so he would. We had a nice, friendly time. "Ezio Pinza" also sings – in the winter he sings in the operas here in Amsterdam. They are both very nice and so kind – and young too. Finally we called it a night and went to bed. So I spent a unique birthday. I'll probably never have a similar one.

Today we went to Alkmaar, the cheese market, which is only on Fridays. Today was the very first running of "The Cheese Express," a special train for Alkmaar. On the train we kept noticing a funny blond-haired man who kept walking up and down in the different cars and stared at us all the time. Finally he came up to us and asked if we were English. When we said no, that we were Americans he explained (in English of course) that he was the reporter from the local Alkmaar paper and since this was the first day for the "Cheese Express" they wanted a story. Then he asked if he could take our pictures with the girl, dressed in her costume, who passed around samples of cheese. Of course we said yes. His photographer took several pictures, then one reporter asked all about us and our impressions of Holland. He said he would send us the newspaper with our pictures, and if possible, the actual photo. So we were quite thrilled and flattered.

When we arrived in Alkmaar about 45 minutes later, we followed the crowd – and I do mean crowd – to the market place. What we saw on the way was quite delightful. The open air market is in the middle of the town square. There were so many people that we couldn't see anything. Then we spotted our photographer friend; he came over to us and we told him we couldn't see a thing. He said "Come with me," so we followed him. He pulled us through the crowd, talked to a policeman, and before we knew it, we were past the crowd, right in the middle of the square walking around as if we owned the place. Policemen would stop us, but our friend would say something to them and they'd let us pass. Friend Photographer explained everything to us. The cheese is all in big balls, like huge grapefruits, and it's rolled into the center on carts. The men who take care of it (called porters) wear white suits and straw hats – either yellow, green, or blue. The color of their hats distinguishes the companies for which they work. The buyers of the cheese taste it, feel it, then it is weighed. It is all quite exciting. Our friend used my camera and took our pictures with two porters, each of us holding a huge cheese ball. Friend took us into the room where visitors could pay 7 cents and taste the cheese. (The girls serving it were all in their native costumes.) The cheese was delicious. Our friend had to go to work, so we shook hands, thanked him for everything and left the market. We headed for the train station, stopping on the way to buy a milkshake. Everybody here drinks milk – it's amazing to see that again. The children all look so healthy and pretty. I really believe in the power of milk – especially for children.

At 12:45 we took the train to the little town of Hoorn and from there we were to take the bus to Vollendam and Markam. When we arrived in Hoorn we found out that the bus didn't go to Vollendam for an hour and a half, so we started out to see Hoorn. It's a delightful little town, completely untouched by tourists. No one spoke English. We decided to eat a little lunch, finally found a little lunch room with the cutest old man who got out a tiny English-Dutch dictionary to see what we wanted to eat. We ordered ham sandwiches and chocolate milk. He was so cute. Knowing we were Americans he thought we would like "rock and roll" music, so he switched the radio from "The Carousel Waltz" to some hideous thing. We all protested and he very gladly changed it back to the soothing music of *Carousel*. He gave us a little card for a souvenir and we discovered that this is Hoorn's 600th anniversary. That's why the town was all decorated with colored lights and flags and flowers. We stayed at the lunch room a long time after we had finished our sandwiches simply because of the cute old man. When we finally did leave we waved goodbye to him – he grinned and said "Bye-bye."

We waited for the bus in the park by the train station and sat in the grass under a tree until the bus came. It was one of those "local" buses that is very similar to a horse as far as riding it is concerned! But it was pleasant because the countryside is so delightful. We passed fields and fields of flowers all colors – a beautiful panorama. We had to change buses once in Edam (where the cheese comes from) before we came to Vollendam.

Vollendam is a fishing village on the Zuider Zee where the people still dress in the traditional costumes. Unfortunately it has been horribly tourist-ified and is almost disgusting.

We soon took a boat from Vollendam and crossed to the island of Markam, another fishing village where they still dress as their ancestors did. Tourists have not yet spoiled this delightful place. All the women wear the starched lace big hats and pigtails. They are very old looking, even the young ones. The men wear baggy pants, and smoke long pipes. They all – men, women, and children – wear wooden shoes. I don't see how they do it. Some of the children were adorable. One friendly little blond girl ran up to me and grabbed my arm and said "What is the name of you?" I told her "Judy" and she and her friend repeated it over and over, then laughed at the sound of it. We walked all over the island and saw the first "Dutch doors" we had seen. It was all quite enchanting.

Sunday, July 7, 1957

It's so hot – even in Germany! We arrived in Bremen this afternoon with no relief whatsoever from the heat.

Last night we went to Poort Van Cleve for supper. We really bit off more than we could chew. First we ordered a fried cheese curd, which was one of the best concoctions I've ever tasted. Then we ordered pea soup. When the waiter brought it we nearly died – it was in bowls that held a quart of soup! We struggled for 45 minutes trying to eat it all. It really was divine, but too much! We just couldn't finish it.

We had to hurry to catch the trolley to get to the opera. We just made it. Our seats were good – in the rafters, but we could see perfectly. But it was just unbearably hot. The opera – Stravinsky's *The Rake's Progress* – was superb.

I love the music, the production was excellent and so were the singers. It was certainly worth the painful heat.

After the opera it was pouring down rain. We had planned our funds to the penny to last us through taxi fare for the train today, but we had to get home from the opera and the only way was by taxi. So we ran across the street to the American hotel and Genie changed a dollar bill – so we took a taxi back to our hotel.

This morning we took the 8:00 train for Bremen. We had a hard time with the conductor over our seat reservations because he insisted that today was the 6th of July, not the 7th. When he finally realized his mistake he got so embarrassed. Once the train got started he kept coming in our compartment talking to us and making sure we were comfortable.

We arrived in Bremen about 1:30, so hot and dirty we came straight to the hotel and spent the rest of the afternoon washing and trying to get clean. At 6:00 we were so starved since we hadn't had anything since breakfast, so we dressed and went out to find a restaurant. We went to the main square and found a wonderful restaurant with low, low prices. We feasted on weiner schnitzel. I do love it. After dinner we walked home, stopping and looking in all the store windows. Bremen is a small town – a mixture of old and the new, thanks to the war. We haven't seen much of it yet, but starting tomorrow we shall.

Tuesday, July 9, 1957

Did you know that this is the hottest summer Germany has had in 52 years! It has rained a little today, however, and the heat has disappeared – thank goodness.

Yesterday was a very pleasant day. We walked over to the tourist office for a map and some information on the city. I was surprised to find that Bremen is the second largest port in Germany. We started out walking to see what we could see. The most beautiful part of the town is the market square, where a market is still held every day. Here is the old town hall, the 13th century cathedral, an old Guild Hall. The buildings are beautiful. Also on the square are the remains of what must have been a beautiful building destroyed during the war. We decided to try some of the delicious pastry in one of the nearby shops, so we bought some apple strudel, some butterkuchen, and some raisin bread. Then we went to a rathskeller and drank coffee and ate our pastry.

After our "lunch" we discovered the most delightful street – only for walking. All the buildings and houses are just as they were in the Middle Ages, in design at least, for some were destroyed and had to be rebuilt. Many of the merchants' homes used to be along this street. One home is still just as it was and is now a museum. It is furnished with things from many old guild halls and homes. The furnishings are beautiful – everything is late Gothic, Renaissance and early Baroque.

After visiting this museum we decided to take a boat tour of the harbor. We walked to the landing, boarded the boat, and off we went. We were the only Americans on the ship – everyone looked at us, smiled, and probably thought we were English.

The boat tour lasted about one-half hour. I understand now why so many things were destroyed in Bremen, it being such an important port. There was a girl on board who snapped everybody's picture and when the tour was over the pictures were put up on a board for sale. Of course nearly everyone bought their own picture, including us.

After the tour we went to the official town Rathskeller for dinner. It's the oldest of its kind in Germany. There are huge wine barrels, as high as the ceiling, all over the place. It's really adorable – not the appropriate word, because it's too large to be adorable. The food is delicious there. There are so many restaurants in this town – and you can feast so cheaply. Last night I had paprika-schnitzel with potatoes and salad, huge helpings of everything, for about $1.50 – and that is one of the more expensive places to eat. I really do like German cooking.

We're going to Hamburg tomorrow and Lübeck Thursday. Friday we'll spend from 8:00 a.m. to 7:00 p.m. on the train going to Copenhagen. I didn't realize it would take that long!

Every night I think about coming home. I can hardly wait – only about 40 more days now. Isn't that awful? Here I am on this wonderful trip and all I can think of is coming home.

Friday, July 12, 1957

I'm on the train to Copenhagen. I have so much to tell I'll never get it all down on paper. The last time I wrote was Tuesday. That night Louise and I were in our pajamas in bed reading. We had decided not to eat supper. Lucy and Genie came in – they had eaten at the hotel and had had sauerbraten! Louise and I immediately jumped up and dressed and ran downstairs to eat sauerbraten. We had hunted for it everywhere when we were in Germany and had never found it. It was divine. I think the hotel people were real pleased that we finally ate a meal in the hotel.

Wednesday morning we caught the train to Hamburg. We got a map, started out and hunted for antique shops and I think we found every antique shop in Hamburg. We found a little restaurant for lunch. Just as we were finishing lunch a dark-skinned young man who had been sitting at the bar came up to us and in perfect English starting talking to us.

He is an East African from Kenya. He has been in Hamburg only 4 months – he's in business there. He was very anxious for us to see Hamburg, and suggested all kinds of places for us to go. We told him we'd like to go to the city beer-hall so Genie and Lucy could see what they're like. After much talking he said that he could meet us at 7:00 and take us there himself. We agreed, but first we had to find out if there was a late train back to Bremen. So he took us a few steps down the street to his office and had his secretary call the train station. There was a train at 11:50. So we arranged to meet our friend – his name is Paul Gajjar – at the train station at 7:00 and we left. We walked down to see the beautiful city hall, then decided to take a ferry tour that took us past the beautiful homes of Hamburg, embassies and mansions.

After the tour we decided to go to the zoo, one of the largest in Europe. It really was fun since the girls had never been to a really big zoo before. (I've never seen anything to compare with the St. Louis Zoo.) We stayed until it was time to meet our East-African friend at 7:00. We were a little late, and when we got there we found him with two friends – one a young German and the other a 35 year old, grey-haired Pakistani! They both spoke English of course. They said we would go first with Paul to a business engagement for 10 minutes, then on to the Beer Hall. We piled in the young German's car – his name is Wolfgang Meyer – and off we went. Soon we stopped in front of a house, Paul got out, entered, and soon returned with a German man of about 50 who wore a hearing aid! We really made a crew!

Then we split up and went four and four in the young German's car and the old German's car. We went to Paul's apartment. They said we must have some dinner first, so the Pakistani prepared us some Pakistani food. We had such a good time. They were all so nice and interesting. All of them are in the export-import business. It was such a strange group, but so much fun. (I repeat.)

After we had eaten we all washed our own plates, then piled in the little cars and went to the Zillerhal, the Beer Hall. It is just like the ones I went to in Munich and Frankfurt: in the Bavarian style with a band in Tyrolean costumes and huge beer steins. They are the most fun places I've ever been to. Everybody sings, dances, and generally enjoys himself. We danced, made toasts, climbed on the tables and sang (like everybody else). I danced with several people I didn't know (it's perfectly in order to dance with strangers there). It really wasn't dancing, it was jogging along – more fun. We were so unhappy when the hour to leave came.

Our four assorted friends didn't want us to leave, but finally we persuaded the old man to drive us to the station. He was such a cute old man, he'd laugh and get so red in the face and then laugh some more. Unfortunately we hit every red light on the way to the station. We arrived just at the hour the train was to leave, so we jumped out of the car, ran to catch the train – and just missed it. We were so upset, but the interpreter came up to us and told us there would be another one in 10 minutes.

By that time our four friends had arrived and were begging us to let them drive us back to Bremen. But we insisted on taking the train, so as it pulled out we were thanking them for the wonderful evening and saying goodbye. I was so sleepy I slept all the way on the train from Hamburg to Bremen. When we got off the train at Bremen there stood the East African, the young German, and the Pakistani. I thought I was having a nightmare. They had driven all the way from Hamburg to Bremen to take us to coffee. In little Bremen everything is closed at 1:00 a.m. and the only place where we could drink coffee was at the Excelsior, so we went there.

We climbed two flights of stairs and found ourselves in a night-club. A girl was singing and doing a semi-stripper's dance. It was so funny to see Lucy's reaction – I'm sure she's never been in place like that before. It was funny, too, to go there for a cup of coffee. We drank our coffee, watched the floor-show and left about 3:00.

They begged us to come to Hamburg the next day, but of course we couldn't. The young German, Wolfgang, was the nicest of them all. He had taken a fancy to Louise, and asked her if he could come back alone in his car and take us all to Hamburg and the near-by places. She accepted on the condition that he come back alone. Thursday at noon he appeared – alone. He wanted to take us up to Bremerhaven, the large port, and then on up to the tip of Germany to the North Sea. Off we went.

It was wonderful to see the countryside – it's very flat in that region with beautiful farmland. It was such a beautiful day, and we really enjoyed riding in a car. We came to Bremerhaven about 1:30. It's a big port and a U.S. army base. We drove down to the harbor, watched them load ships, then went to a restaurant there on the harbor that looks out over the water. We had a wonderful meal, then headed for the tip of Germany – Cuxhaven – on the North Sea.

As we left the harbor we saw a huge ship loaded with American soldiers on their way home. We waved and yelled Bon Voyage to them. It was such a thrill seeing them. I've never seen a whole shipload of soldiers before. It made me proud to see them – and I felt love and pity and companionship for them all.

We drove on to Cuxhaven and it's really beautiful up through there. We went through lots of cute little villages. At Cuxhaven we went to the beach. It's strange because when there's no tide the water is so shallow that you can walk out for miles. There is even a horse and buggy that goes out to an island near-by!

I wished we had time to stay and sun, but it was late in the afternoon and rather cool. We left the beach and Wolfgang drove us on to a harbor where the Elbe River runs into the North Sea. A steamer was coming in on its way to Hamburg – an impressive sight. It was about 7:00, so we started back to Bremen and arrived around 9:00. It was such a wonderful day and wonderful of Wolfgang to do it. He is really remarkable. He's only 25 – his father was killed in the war, and he remembers so much of that horrible thing. He speaks English and Spanish and some French, he loves America and Americans. It always amazes me to see people like him.

This morning we caught the train for Copenhagen. I've been having the best time talking to 18 French boys who are on their way to Oslo. At present the train is on a ferry boat in Denmark. I've never seen a train on a ferry boat – amazing how it works!

Oh – something I saw yesterday for the first time: a chimney sweep – he was all dirty, had his little sticks with the broom-like thing on the end, wore a top hat, and was riding a bicycle. So adorable but a little pathetic.

We're in our hotel now in Copenhagen – it is delightful. The most adorable fat man who speaks just enough English to get by on seems to be the owner-manager. He was so thrilled because he had mail to give us. We are on half pension here in Copenhagen. The man was so anxious for us to eat immediately. We followed him into the restaurant, and the most wonderful fat woman greeted us with a smile and her best "Welcome to Denmark." She was so sweet. They apparently had dinner waiting for us. We walked to the dining room, where there were four men and women who all gave us a hearty "Good Evening." To top it all off, the big jovial woman brought in fresh strawberries for dessert. We were so excited we nearly died. They all got a huge kick out of our strawberry enthusiasm.

Saturday, July 13, 1957

This has been such a wonderful day!

We started off with a delicious breakfast of sausage (cold), cheese, three kinds of bread, butter, jelly, Danish pastry, and coffee – it really was delicious. Then we walked down to the big square and took the Bennett Tour Bus. We have three tours here in Copenhagen already paid for. I feel like I'm getting it for free! This morning was a two-hour tour of the city and the harbor, which was excellent. We saw the famous fountains, churches, palaces, the fish market, the meat market, the Royal Palace, and of course the Little Mermaid in the little harbor, of Hans Christian Andersen fame. She really is pretty. The tour gave us a wonderful overall view of the city.

I really like Copenhagen. The happiness and good-nature of the people seems to permeate the entire city. There is a feeling of mirth that grabs you.

After our tour we went to change train reservations (the agency made a mistake and reserved us 1st class seats and we have 2nd class tickets), then went to the American Express to change money. We were hungry and decided to go to the famous zoo (again) and eat in one of the many restaurants there. We had Danish open-faced sandwiches. I had a ham and scrambled egg sandwich. The eggs were cold and looked like custard. It really was delicious. We also tried some delicious Danish beer, but it's too expensive to try again!

After our zoo visit we took the bus back to the hotel and rested a little. After dinner we went to the Charlottesborg Opera, staged in the courtyard of Charlottesborg Palace. They did Pergolesi's *Il Maestro di Musica* and a ballet to Vivaldi's *The Four Seasons*. The ushers, men and women, were all dressed in 17th century costumes, as was the orchestra and the conductor. The Pergolesi was delightful and the singers were marvelous – one of the best sopranos I've ever heard. A treat indeed. The ballet was unfortunately not in the same class with the opera. The music was good, but the dancing was horrible. The delightful thing about it all was its trueness to the 17th century and being out-of-doors was so pleasant.

Monday night, July 15, 1957

I don't see how people can stand touring Europe on a bus. Our tours have been wonderful, but the bus is so tiring and dull. Trains are more fun!

Yesterday at 10:00 a.m. we boarded a bus with about 25 other Americans for the Castle tour of North Sealand.

North Sealand is the island where Copenhagen is in Denmark, and this island, like most of Denmark is chock full of castles. First we drove past the Sorgenfri Palace, where Prince Knud, the King's brother resides. The most wonderful thing about Danish palaces and castles are the grounds and gardens. Next we passed an open air museum of a Danish farm, with the buildings and barns just as the old Danish farms used to be. We drove through beautiful countryside, past cool lakes and green forests and came to Frederiksborg Castle, now the National Museum. It is a beautiful, really magnificent Renaissance castle with the wedding cake towers typical of Denmark. The castle is made of brick, a change from the German and French castles. It really is an exciting castle – the interior is very interesting. The furnishings are beautiful with china and porcelains and crystal collections that are gorgeous and tapestry, leather, and wood-work that is exquisite.

On the way out of the castle gate a little 12 year old Dane asked Louise and me for our autographs and gave us his in return. I'm going to send him a post card soon.

After visiting Frederiksborg Castle we continued on our tour. We drove past the summer residence of the King of Denmark, overlooking the beautiful lakes. Our next stop was Hellebaek on the Baltic, where we had lunch at a wonderful hotel overlooking the sea, across which we could see the coast of Sweden.

After lunch we drove on to Kronborg Castle, the setting for Shakespeare's *Hamlet*. It's exciting to see and associate with Hamlet, but the poor old edifice has lost much of its beauty. It still gives a good idea of the Nordic style of architecture – the dark, somber, coldness of the interior.

We came back to the hotel and rested a little before dinner, then afterward we walked to Tivoli Gardens, which is just about 10 minutes from here. Tivoli certainly has a right to be famous. For an amusement park it is terribly refined and is in such good taste. Beautiful flowers are everywhere. Lighted fountains play and all the restaurants and beer gardens are aglow with hundreds of multi-colored lights. There are all sorts of amusements – games, rides, foods, etc. A beautiful lake lighted with Chinese lanterns, a lighted pagoda, and many pavilions add to the romantic loveliness. Free concerts are given by the Symphony orchestra in the huge, modern, beautiful concert hall; lighter music is played in one of the pavilions. The place was jammed packed last night, but it was really fun.

This morning we boarded a bus for the tour of South Sealand. We drove on along the Baltic coast and onto the peninsula where we stopped at Vallo Castle, once a manor but now a residence for unmarried ladies of noble birth. Later we came to a beautiful little farm that we visited. It, like all the farms we've seen, was spotless – even the pigs were clean! We learned all about the Danish farmers' problems and the crops. This farmer was experimenting with some crops and he had a little field of corn, the first I've seen in all Europe. I just can't stress enough the utter cleanliness of the farm. The flower garden of this farm is unbelievable. Such beautiful flowers so artistically planted I've never seen. That's what I love about this country – flowers everywhere plus spotless cleanliness and neatness.

From the farm we continued on through beautiful fields of rye, sugar beets, clover, and beans to the chalk and limestone cliffs of Steons and the Hojrup Church which was built so close to the edge of the cliffs that the altar and the chancel have fallen down into the sea.

I've really learned a lot about Denmark. It is certainly the most advanced country as far as social welfare is concerned. No one lacks anything. There is a marvelous old age pension system, housing projects and schools. It sounds almost perfect.

Wednesday morning- July 17, 1957

We were supposed to leave on the early morning train for Stockholm, but there were no vacant seats, so the travel bureau made us reservations for the 11:30 a.m. train – which won't put us in Stockholm until 10:00 tonight. I dread spending another full day on the train.

Yesterday afternoon after lunch Louise and I went to wallow in the lap of luxury and indulge in a Danish bath. Neither of us had any idea of what it would be like. As soon as we arrived we bought a ticket for a super bath with massage and sleeping room. We went upstairs to the women's part and were met by a woman in a white uniform who ushered us into a little booth with two beds in it. There we disrobed and put on a huge terry robe and wooden slippers. Shower caps were put on our heads. We were immediately taken to a door, relieved of robes, and pushed stark-naked into a room so hot with steam that it was unbearable. Sitting on one of the benches, as naked as we were, sat an elderly fat woman from California who talked to us the whole time we were in there. We were supposed to stay in there about 35 to 45 minutes, but after about 20 minutes we couldn't take it any longer. I was one big puddle and we were gasping for air like birds do in hot weather. So we went into another steam room, one less hot than the first one. Here we sat in burning steam for a long time, again chatting with the woman from California and a Danish woman who has come once a week for ten years! Finally one of the women in white came to get us. It was time for the massage – this was what I was waiting for. They put us each on a table and started to work. I was covered in oil and then rubbed in every spot on my body where there is flesh. It was divine! Except I discovered that I'm extremely ticklish and between my laughing and Louise's laughing we had the whole place in stitches. Of course we were the only young people there – probably the first to come. All the old flabby ladies looked at us as if we were crazy. Anyhow, after about 30 minutes of wonderful massage, we were scrubbed head to toe with lathered straw and hot water. Then we were put in a hot shower with water also coming up from the floor, then the hot water changed to cold after a few minutes. Then we had to step into a pool of cold water and swing through it, hanging onto a rope like a monkey! Then we were dried, taken to our sleeping room, wrapped up in sheets and blankets and left alone. We slept for about an hour. It was quite an experience – and it didn't cost quite $2.50.

After the Danish bath I went to buy a charm, then came back and washed my hair. Louise had hers all cut off and it looks real cute.

Friday – July 19, 1957

Wednesday I spent on the train coming to Stockholm. It was a delightful train ride thanks to the clean train for a change. We didn't arrive until after 10:00 p.m. It's so amazing – at 10:00 p.m. the sky is still light – and the sun comes up about 3:00 a.m.! Our hotel is just across from the station, so we struggled over with our bags.

Thursday (yesterday) morning we headed for the tourist center in the main park of the center of town. The people in the tourist center are so gracious. We got all sorts of information and arranged to take part in the "Sweden at Home" program, i.e., we would go to someone's house for tea, or dinner, or something.

After our information session we decided to go to the famous Saltsjöbaden beach and had the most enjoyable little jaunt to the beach – 30 minutes away. The countryside we passed on the train was beautiful. We came to the beach and warily made our way to the beach house. I say "warily" because at Saltsjöbaden the beach is divided into 2 sections – one for men and one for women (what else?) and in these sections one goes à la nude. We were panicked that any minute we'd step into the wrong section.

We finally found the entrance, paid our fee, and I rented (for a dime) one of those gorgeous old wool suits that does so much for my poor little neglected chest. In between the two nudist sections of the beach is a part where one wears a suit and this part is mixed. Naturally that is where we intended to install ourselves. But first we had to go into the bath house and change. The minute we stepped through the door we were hit in the face by nude women – all old and flabby. Nothing could have been more repulsive. We dressed as hurriedly as possible with as much modesty as was permitted, and quickly headed for the "mixed" section.

Here old and young were sporting bikinis – men and women too. Little children took full advantage of the wonderful sun in the raw. At first I felt as crimson as my bathing suit but after a while it seemed quite natural and I didn't even care if my flatchestedness was so obvious. The sun was divine and was cooled by a balmy breeze, which felt so good.

We left the beach and took the 5:00 train back to Stockholm. It was so pretty when we came back. The city is built on several islands, and the water reflecting the beginning of sunset was so beautiful. The colors aren't warm here – they're cool and pastel and silvery – quite romantic.

This morning we had to be at the tourist office to pick up our invitation for tonight, which was for tea at 7:30 p.m. with a Miss Karin Pehrson. We walked around window shopping until noon, when we took a tour of the city on a street car. It was a good tour, but the guide was bad, the weather was worse, and I just couldn't keep my mind on what the guide said. I did learn that Sweden has a fabulous socialized medicine organization. There is a hospital here with 1600 beds, just as many employees, and the corridors are so long that the nurses have to ride special kinds of bikes to go to and fro.

After lunch the other girls decided to go perfume shopping and I had to go to the beauty parlor to have my hair colored. I tried two recommended salons but they were full. So I went to the Grand Hotel and tried there. They weren't going to take me, but a wonderful woman from South Carolina with whom I had been talking insisted that I take her appointment which was right then. Naturally I refused, but she was so insistent – practically pushed me in the chair – so I accepted it. After she left I was treated like dirt – absolutely ignored – and stayed there from 3:30 till nearly 7:00! I was so angry. I got back to the hotel, raving and ranting the way I can when I get so frustrated, just in time to change and go have tea. It took us ages to get there – it was in a suburb of Stockholm way out of the city. Miss Karin Pehrson lives in an apartment with her sister and she turned out to be delightful. She's smaller than I, blond, blue-eyed, very cute, 28 years old. She works as a secretary. The apartment is small, neat, and spotless.

She speaks English, but not well, and it was a strain on everybody, but so well worth it. She was so sweet it nearly made me cry. She served us coffee and cookies and then brought out strawberry cake she had made for us. We discussed everything and she said such cute things. We really had a good time. This program of hospitality is wonderful. Talking to her made up for my anger at the beauty salon and she made everything right again. She made us all feel so humble in our good fortune. She looked upon us as goddesses or something having our opportunities for travel. We sometimes forget how fortunate we are and when we remember it's quite overwhelming. When it was time to leave she walked with us to the train station. She waved goodbye to us. It was so sad. People are so good. More and more my faith in man is strengthened. The good always overshadows the bad, and God becomes so evident in man. That godliness of man is what I believe in – it seems to me it's what we must believe in, in order to live in the world.

Sunday, July 21, 1957

Pretty soon we'll board the train for an all-night ride to Oslo, and I dread it. I haven't had to suffer one of these rides since our first night on the way to Italy.

Yesterday was a terrible day. We went out to Skansen – the huge outdoor museum with whole ancient farms from all parts of Sweden, including Lapland. The park is beautiful, and it could have been most enjoyable, but it was raining when we got there, and we just couldn't seem to muster up much enthusiasm paddling around in the old rain. We did see rather much of it before we gave up and came back to the hotel. It rained steadily until about 5:30 so we stayed in our rooms. Louise and I drank coffee and talked – we're both so excited about coming home.

When the sun appeared we went to a little restaurant nearby and had our dinner. The food was good and cheap. Then we walked down the big, busy, main street to go to the movies. I hadn't seen one in so long and we were all kind of excited about going. We saw Audrey Hepburn and Fred Astaire in *Funny Face*. I loved it – not because it is just a good musical, but because it takes place in Paris and the photography is marvelous. I was teary-eyed the whole way through and terribly sentimental. It really is a beautiful movie.

This morning we took the 40 minute boat ride to Drottningholm Palace, the summer home of the royal family. It's beautifully located on the lake with green, cool woods, pretty formal garden, etc., but the interior is terrible. All junky Italian over-done Rococo. We took the 3:00 boat back to Stockholm. It's a beautiful day, and Stockholm looks wonderful in the sunshine. Stockholm is called "The Venice of the North" and today I could see from where the name came.

I don't know how I'll live until plane time August 16th! I'm so anxious to come home I can't think of anything else!

Tuesday, July 23, 1957

Here we are in Oslo, Norway. Imagine – I'm in Norway! We arrived at the un-godly hour of 8:00 a.m. after having spent the night on the train. We were quite fortunate because the train wasn't crowded and we each were able to stretch out on a whole seat and sleep. But that sort of sleep is never very restful and we were very tired when we finally got to the hotel, only to be told that we couldn't get into our rooms until about 1:00 p.m.

We came on upstairs to the restaurant where a scrumptious smorgasbord breakfast was waiting. There are cereals, prunes, sausage, ham, fish, salads, all sorts of breads, cheese, and cookies every morning and also soft-boiled eggs. It's incredible, and saves us money since after such a huge breakfast we can't possibly eat any lunch! Anyway, after we had breakfast we went into the lounge and slept in chairs and on the sofas, read about the city, and generally killed time until finally, around 12:30, we were able to get in our rooms. Then we had a washing session – we all took baths, washed clothes. By the time we had house cleaned it was 3:30. We dressed and went window shopping and looked at the famous Norwegian enamel jewelry until about 5:30, when we gave in to the call of our stomachs and went for dinner. We dined in a precious restaurant called Blom – it's a sort of artist's hangout, or rather it was until Uncle Fielding got hold of it. The food was delicious. I had the first steak worth shouting over that I've had in a long time.

After dinner we caught the trolley to Frogner Park, where *Peer Gynt* is being given in the summer theater. We went because we read they were doing Ibsen's *Peer* with Grieg's music. Much to our dismay there was no music at all and of course the play was in Norwegian so we understood nil! It would have been very good if only it had been in an understandable tongue! We stuck it out almost to the end, but it was hot and the benches were very hard, and finally the can't-take-it-any-longer point arrived and we left. I was so disappointed because I wanted to hear the *Peer Gynt Suite*.

This morning after a whopping breakfast we went to Bennett's travel bureau and bought tickets for the grand tour of Oslo which started at 10:30 and wasn't over until 6:00. By bus we first went to see the ski jump at Holmenhollen. I don't see how skiers ever have enough nerve to slide down one of those things! We took an elevator to the top of the jump from where there is a beautiful view of the city and the surrounding fjord. It must be a glorious sight in the winter.

From the ski jump we drove out to Frogner Park to see the sculpture of Norway's celebrated 20th century sculptor, Vigeland. He has placed 30 years' worth of work in this park. His things are quite controversial; some think they're atrocious and others consider them masterpieces. I was just quite taken by most of the things. I say "things" – they're all statues depicting the many facets of life, the cycles man follows. I really liked most of what I saw.

After our Vigeland review we drove to the peninsula where most of Oslo's museums are located. First we were to have lunch in the restaurant of the out-door museum. Lunch wasn't included in the tour price, so we didn't indulge. We sat under some of the beautiful pictures instead while the others ate. After lunch we visited the 13th century Stave Church used by the Vikings in the North of Norway, and one of the old houses. This was very interesting.

In the meantime I became acquainted with the two French families on our tour. One of the families – a girl, Annie, about 18 and her parents – lived only a couple of blocks from the Rémonds. They were so nice. We became very friendly by the end of the tour and Annie gave me her address and phone number for when I return to Paris, and I gave her mine. They have been to the U.S. before and plan to return not too far in the future.

The museum with the Viking ships was wonderful. The two ships (and the remains of a third) are beautiful, and quite awesome in their antiquity. Besides the ships there are beautifully carved chariots and sleds found in the Viking burial mounds.

From here we went to the museum of the famous Kon-Tiki raft that made the 101 day voyage in 1947 from Peru to Polynesia by drifting with the ocean current. I've heard and read about this raft and was quite thrilled to see it. It's so adventurous looking and so amazing. Thor Heyerdahl made it all himself: it's all tied together – there is not one nail, tack, etc., in the whole thing. I really think it's lovely. There were four fake sharks lying on the deck which I thought overdid the effect, but the guide explained they were there for a purpose. It seems the crew of six took to catching sharks by the tail, pulling them on deck and killing them in order to get rid of a few of the sharks that surrounded them constantly and to provide shark food for the new batches of sharks that would arrive!

Next we went to see the first polar ship, used in 1893 by Amundsen and the first men to reach the North and South Poles. The boat is extremely interesting – contains souvenirs from these men's expeditions to the poles.

After this we took a boat and started the two hour boat trip through the fjords of Oslo. It's lovely country – the lake (the fjord rather), the pines. We passed Sonja Henie's mansion. I must say the Oslo fjord is not spectacular. The real fjord country is around Bergen. While we were in the middle of our boat tour a terrible storm came up and it rained like I've not seen since I left New Orleans – lightning and thunder, too.

It got so bad you couldn't see out the windows. Since we couldn't see a thing we all sang. It was quite fun. An American boy and I sort of led the singing. It took everybody's mind off the rather scary weather. Finally it slacked off enough for us to go back to the boat dock. We had to walk in the rain from the dock about three long blocks to the restaurant we had chosen for tonight.

Wednesday, July 24, 1957

Our stay in Oslo is almost over. I really like Oslo – the climate is nice in spite of the rain – the scenery is gorgeous. But I'm glad to be moving on to Bergen.

Today we visited the Oslo City Hall, a magnificent building which was inaugurated in 1950, which is quite modern. The interior is beautiful with mosaics and murals à la the United Nations Building. After a little shopping – rather looking – we went to the Oslo Cathedral, a Protestant church, almost the oldest in Oslo. (Norway is Lutheran Evangelical.) The cathedral is a very nice mixture of old and new, due to restorations made about 10 years ago. The organ of the cathedral is huge – it goes through five stories and has 6000 pipes and 101 registers! The organist was practicing while we were visiting the church and it was a thrill to hear.

From the church we walked to the Ackhus Castle, which stands on a hill overlooking the harbor. It's a medieval castle that is nice to see on the outside, but the interior is not very interesting. Louise and I went post-card buying, and I also bought some more pocket-books to read on the train, among them Anne Morrow Lindbergh's *Gift From The Sea* which I have already started and I think it's so beautiful.

We came back to the hotel about 4:30, made reservations for dinner tonight at LaBelle Sole – *the* restaurant in Oslo. At 6:30 we took a taxi (splurge) to the restaurant. The handsomest head waiter showed us to our table and we began our feast. It was really divine. It's a shame food is so important and fattening and expensive at the same time! We lived our evening to the hilt and even took a taxi back to the hotel.

Now I've packed, and here I am. Our train leaves at 10:00 in the morning and we'll be on it all day. The scenery is reputed to be magnificent, so I don't mind.

Friday, July 26, 1957

Bergen is the most delightful place! We arrived here last night around 9:00 after having spent the most luxurious train ride ever! Unbeknown to us, we had 1st class seats already paid for and the car was like American trains! To make it perfect, the scenery from Oslo to Bergen is magnificent. The entire line runs through the mountains. We passed rushing waterfalls, grazing mountain goats, great patches of snow and ice. Toward late afternoon all the mountains were snow-capped. Tiny villages dotted our way and at the stations we saw hikers with their walking sticks and knap-sacks on their backs. The lakes were an emerald green and sometimes bright blue. The larkspur, the daisies, yellow wild flowers brightened the deep, rich green of the tall grass and evergreen trees. It was really breath-taking. At one station a girl got on the train carrying a reindeer skin – antlers and all! Unfortunately it's the closest I've come to an un-captured (meaning zoo-kept) reindeer.

Bergen's location is perfect. It's shaped like a horseshoe surrounded by tall mountains except for the opening to the sea that is the harbor. The clouds hang so low around the mountains that the tops of them are sometimes quite invisible.

This morning we went first to the fish market, located on the harbor. Thousands of fresh fish lie waiting the customers. The market was packed and very exciting. From the market we took a walk through the old section of Bergen, which is filled with delightfully gay wooden medieval houses – quite picturesque. We got our tickets for a tour tomorrow of the fjords, then had lunch near a beautiful park where a little band was giving a concert of Rodgers & Hammerstein.

Well, I'm thoroughly disgusted! We had planned a delightful evening of a lovely dinner way on top of one of the mountains of Bergen. We took the funicular to the tip top where I was enraptured by one of the most beautiful sights I've seen. The town of Bergen looked like a toy town – so far from it we were. We could see past the mountains to the sea and over mountains where nestled scattered villages. The sun, which has been teasing today, decided to come out, and the reflection of the sun on the water, plus the position of the sun created a celestial effect that was stunning.

After gazing at the beautiful glories of nature we entered the restaurant and prepared ourselves for what we expected to be a delicious meal. We started out with delicious tomato soup and waited eagerly for our succulent white grouse with vegetables. It came and was so horrible I just couldn't eat it. I won't go into details, but it was vraiment insupportable. So we stalked out and home again by way of the funicular – very angry at the restaurant.

Saturday, July 27, 1957

Today we took a whole-day trip to see the countryside around the fjord of Hardanger. We were on regular rural buses for most of the time. We stopped for lunch at a tiny village but we had confiscated enough meat and bread from breakfast and had bought fruit for lunch. It was lots of fun and broke the monotony of riding and was of course economical. The whole day was spent amid gorgeous scenery – mountains (snow-capped and green), fjords, lakes, fabulous waterfalls, quaint cabins, hardy Norwegians all wearing their beautiful sweaters. The green of the valleys is so deep and rich and pure that it's unbelievable. It was worth the 9 hours of riding.

Sunday, July 28, 1957

Well in an hour I'll be on the boat to Scotland. I can hardly wait.

This morning after breakfast we caught the bus to go to Trollhaugen – Grieg's home. The rural bus doesn't go directly there, so we had a fast 15-minute walk from the bus stop to Trollhaugen, which is in the village Hop. Trollhaugen means Troll's House.

It is situated on the most beautiful site, high on a hill overlooking the lakes, islands, mountains and Bergen. The grounds of the place are beautiful. The house is white frame, in the quaint Norwegian style, and is trimmed in green. The interior is pine paneled with beautifully hand carved furniture. There are photographs, clothing, souvenirs of Grieg and his wife, his friend Ibsen, manuscripts, gifts. It's very exciting. His and Nina's grave is beautiful. They were both cremated and the urns that contain their ashes were put in the side of the cliff overlooking the sea. The epitaph is a single:

EDUARD

NINA

GRIEG

It is very impressive. On one side of the house, down by the water is Grieg's studio, where he composed – one room with a piano, couch, books, stove. It's rewarding to know that, in spite of his illness, Grieg lived a very happy life. He enjoyed his success, and was materially comfortable. It's certainly an insight into his music to see where he lived and worked.

Sunday night – July 28, 1957

Well – it seems like old times. I'm on the ship headed for England – the S.S. Leda. It's a rather large ship, very comfortable and new. We sailed at 4:00 this afternoon, watching Bergen fade into the distance. It was cold and windy and the smell of the sea was delicious. We read for a while on deck, then had a tasty supper. We are in a large room for eight. It's certainly more comfortable than our quarters on the Liberté! Next letter will be from Scotland and in three weeks from tomorrow night I shall be home! Can't wait!

Monday, July 29, 1957

I'm in Scotland and it's so exciting! I was more thrilled on seeing Edinburgh than I have been all summer.

We landed this morning in Newcastle; by the time we went through customs it was noon and we took the 12:40 train into Newcastle proper. There we had an hour and a half wait for the train to Edinburgh. While we were waiting I headed to the post office and I asked a man who was passing by where it was. It was strange that I no longer needed to say, "Do you speak English" or "Parlez-vous Français!"

He was a lovely man who walked me to the post office a block away. He thought I was Scottish by my accent – he said. He was surprised that I was American, pleased that I was Kentuckian. He told me that Americans were not called 'foreigners' by Englishmen – only Europeans are called that. I thought that quite interesting.

We left England and arrived in Scotland at 6:15. The train ride was along the coast and was delightful. The countryside was the prettiest yet. We took a taxi from the station and came to our hotel – a very nice one, as they all have been this summer. We went to dinner in the small inexpensive dining room at a hotel across the street, then we decided to take a walk along Prince's Street, the main thoroughfare. Edinburgh looked beautiful – the sun was just going down and the red and gold light was filling the sky in true splendor, casting shadows of pink and gold on the old castle high on a bluff overlooking all Edinburgh, where Edinburgh Castle stands at the top of everything.

Here is a rough picture of how things are: The famous mile from Holyrood to Edinburgh Castle is on a hill, and one can see it from Prince's Street. The park is gorgeous with beautiful flowers and trees and grass. The monument to Sir Walter Scott is about in the middle of it all. The towers and steeples and old grey stone in the setting sun made a beautiful and impressive sight. Naturally, I didn't have my camera at such an exquisite moment.

We walked for a long time looking in shop windows but the most fun was listening to the Scottish people talk. They roll their R's and sound so cute. They are ruddyskinned, mostly fair, and seem to be always smiling. There was a feeling in the air that was almost exhilaration.

Tuesday, July 30, 1957

This morning we went to the American Express to cash money and to sign up for a tour of the city. Then we went to do a little shopping. With all the lovely plaid tartan shops everywhere we had to go in them. We visited several shops just to look at plaids and find out their names and quickly passed the morning that way. After lunch we went to join the American Express tour – which took us past the houses of Sir Walter Scott, Dr. Alexander Graham Bell, Robert Louis Stevenson, the real Dr. Jekyll (?) and Mr. Hyde, Sir Johnston Youngs (inventor of chloroform) and John Knox. We went to the famous Holyrood Castle, where the royal family lives ten days out of every year and where Mary Stuart, Queen of Scotland, spent so many of her tear-stained years.

We went through the castle, which is not at all beautiful physically, but the history that haunts its walls give it an indescribable beauty. English history is so exciting. From the castle we went to St. Giles Cathedral, the home of the Presbyterian church. The structure itself dates from 11th century. Inside this church is the Thistle Chapel, a beautiful Gothic chapel, all done in wood with the sweetest little angels everywhere. One adorable one is playing the bagpipes. The Order of the Thistle is the highest order in Scotland and those who hold the order are made knights. Once a year the Queen holds a service in this chapel and knights the new Knights of the Thistle.

From here we went to Edinburgh Castle and rode along the famous mile to get there. The "Mile" is wonderfully preserved and creates a delightful ancient atmosphere. Edinburgh Castle contains the crown jewels of Scotland – really beautiful, and the only original complete regalia in Europe. Also here is the room, a tiny one, where Mary Stuart gave birth to James VI of Scotland and James I of England. We climbed to the highest point of the castle and had a beautiful view of the city. Edinburgh calls for lots of time to see it.

I nearly forgot to tell the most exciting part of the day. This morning as we were walking to the American Express, we heard the sound of bagpipes coming from the distance, so we started toward the sound. Coming round the corner was a band of pipes – all dressed in kilts and the full regalia – and playing real bagpipes! Behind them were soldiers in plaid breeches and hats. We ran along beside them taking pictures and being charmed by their presence. I think we were the only ones on the whole street thus taken by the splendid sight – and a bonny sight it was!

As we were winding our way back from American Express we happened to look down into the amphitheater of the park, and there were girls dressed in kilts, doing Scottish dances. We watched them for a long time – it looks like such fun!

Thursday, August 1, 1957

My thoughts have been at home today celebrating your birthday, Mother. The pleasant thought is that I will be at home when the next birthday in our family comes around!

Yesterday afternoon we left Edinburgh and went to Aberdeen. We got there late in the afternoon and by the time we got settled in the hotel it was about 7:00. We decided to call it a day and get up early this morning to see some of Aberdeen, so we did. The people in Aberdeen are so cute. The station master called me "lass" and said he'd help us in a "wee minute." Most of them sound just like Robert Burns' poetry when they talk!

This morning we took the double decker bus out to old Aberdeen to see St. Machar's Cathedral, a 14th century church that has been Catholic, Episcopalian, and Presbyterian. It's a lovely old thing with a heralded ceiling that is wonderful. The best part about going out there was seeing "Old Aberdeen" with its narrow cobble stone streets, the typical English houses with walls around them and the sea in the distance.

On our way back to the main part of town we saw the ancient King's College, a beautiful place, and the Marischal College, an imposing white granite structure with Gothic decorations. We visited the old market square surrounded by the municipal buildings with their turrets and towers. Public executions took place in this square as late as 1857!

We stopped in for lunch in one of the "peoples" restaurant and tried roast beef and Yorkshire pudding. I was expecting Yorkshire pudding to be something to shout about, but it turned out to be a scrawny little thing of potato and bread made into a pudding. I'm convinced we didn't have the real thing.

Our train left Aberdeen at 3:30 and brought us to Glasgow at 7:10. We have a nice hotel, very reminiscent of the one in Amsterdam. We had a bowl of delicious soup for supper, then came upstairs and took baths, washed clothes, etc. We found out today that in the British Isles baths are free! Here we've been sneaking around getting our baths free – and they are free all the time! Makes me feel better to know I haven't really cheated.

Friday, August 2, 1957

Today we took a bus tour of the Trossachs country of Rob Roy fame and of Five Lochs (Scottish for lakes), among which is the largest of Scotland's lochs – Loch Lomond. We left the city at 11:30 and didn't return until about 7:00. It was a wonderful tour.

The Scottish countryside has everything. We drove through forests, hills, even mountains and the lochs. I finally saw the famous heather growing on the hillsides, a beautiful sight indeed. We passed many gorgeous old manor houses settled back amid trees and lovely gardens. The cottages along the wayside looked so quaint. Sheep like I've never seen before were grazing in the fields. We stopped in a little village called Callandar for lunch and we made another stop at the beginning of Loch Lomond for tea. The day was beautiful and not too hot, so everything worked out beautifully.

When we got back we decided to go to the neighborhood theater and see *Kismet*. I thought it was quite good but not so the others.

Of what I saw of Glasgow this morning it is atrociously ugly. I remembered that we decided to come here only because of the nearby lochs and lovely countryside. Luckily our hotel is in the only beautiful section of Glasgow. It's on a private drive where only homes are and the drive is just above the Botanical Gardens – so from our window Glasgow looks lovely. Tomorrow night we sail to Ireland and we have to sit up all night. UGH! and double UGH!

Sunday, August 4, 1957

The top-'o-the evenin' to ye from Ireland!

Yesterday morning was leisurely – breakfasting, and packing our things – then we set out for a seafood restaurant called Rogano's. This wonderful establishment is not only modern and very attractive, but the cuisine is yummy. At last I was able to have broiled lobster and it was divine.

After lunch we tried to get a tour of the city, but all the buses were filled. We were disappointed. Because it was Saturday afternoon and all the antique shops were closed, we decided to go to a movie, *Teahouse of the August Moon* – I saw the play in New Orleans, but that didn't keep me from enjoying the movie. It's a really wonderful story with such a beautiful lesson to teach – if one is willing to learn it, that is.

After the movie everyone had a headache. We went back to the hotel and had some tea. Then it was time to take a taxi to the boat for Belfast. We arrived none too soon because we were too late to book berths on 2nd class. We didn't know you could book them at the last minute. The second class quarters were just awful. There were only benches, and the crowd was a motley crew. It was hot and dirty and really unbearable, so we got off, bought 1st class tickets by paying a supplement, and re-boarded the ship. All the 1st class berths were taken too, and we had to fight, nearly, to get chairs to sit in. We ended up spending an absolutely sleepless night stretched out on chairs. I think I did sleep from 3:00 a.m. till nearly 5:00 a.m. Then we ate breakfast, and at 6:30 a.m. we docked in Belfast.

Monday, August 5, 1957

Needless to say we all felt pretty awful when we arrived in Belfast – tired and dirty and everything else that goes with sitting up all night. We got to the hotel and naturally our rooms weren't ready, so we slept a while in the lounge. Finally when we could have our rooms, I took a bath, tried to sleep but couldn't. We decided to go to church at the Presbyterian church near the hotel which is dedicated to the seamen.

After church we came back to the hotel for lunch, then went to the bus station and took a tour bus to see the countryside, particularly the Glens of Antrim. Unfortunately, the day was hazy and cloudy and we couldn't profit from all the beautiful views that surrounded us. However, just as we arrived at the most famous glen, the sun came out and was beautiful. Now I never knew just what a glen was, but after yesterday I suppose I could say a glen is a deep narrow valley through which runs clear water, waterfalls, and which is thickly wooded and is full of real, genuine, Irish shamrocks. We walked through the Glen – 1½ miles – along narrow paths and wooden foot bridges. It really was a gorgeous place. The shamrocks grow all sizes. They are beautiful, but sometimes it's hard to tell the difference between shamrocks and clovers. The Glen is just the sort of thing one expects to find in Ireland – I could stretch my imagination and see the Leprechauns sitting under the trees in the shamrock patches. After the 1½ mile walk we took afternoon tea at the café at the end of the Glen. Afternoon tea is equal to a meal, really.

Then we continued along the coast of Northern Ireland. The countryside really is beautiful. I've described countryside so much lately that I'm stale at it now so I won't go into details. I do expect to be more impressed with the surrounding parts of Dublin.

When we got off the bus near our hotel we saw Salvation Army bands, soap-box preachers, and other variations of revival groups on almost every corner. Such singing and shouting you've never heard! I felt like I was in *Guys in Dolls*.

Wednesday, August 7, 1957

I've had the most marvelous time in Dublin – but before I tell about it I must catch up.

Monday, the 5th, we spent the morning doing our little travel chores and after lunch at the hotel we took a taxi to the station to go to Dublin. We had to play the un-amusing game of dashing with bags in hand and competing with hundreds of others to find a seat. That "game" always brings out the "Yahoo" in men – almost as badly as the "Yahoo" Swift saw.

But the trip to Dublin was quite pleasant. The Irish countryside works as a balm for creating peacefulness in the midst of a great rush.

When we arrived in Dublin we were dismayed to find that no taxi would take us to our hotel because of a union feud. It seems there is one taxi company, owned by a Belfast man, which all Dubliners, being true Southern Irish, despise. The Cumberland Hotel (ours) gives its trade to the Belfast company and the only way the Dubliners can fight back is by refusing to carry people to the hotel. Finally there appeared a man who said that since the union had not officially banned our hotel, he would take us. It really was kind of him, because he could have had some trouble, I suppose, from his union.

We finally arrived at the Cumberland Hotel. We were a little disappointed in the dirty mess of Dublin's streets – we had hoped for a clean, beautiful city. Of course our abode was not in the best section!

Genie, Lucy, and I were a little hungry, so we decided to hunt for a place where we could get a sandwich. We found the largest street – O'Connell – and proceeded to look for a place recommended by Fielding. Luckily for us, we were tired and came to a large café/snack place, and went in. We couldn't find places at first, but finally got settled and ordered. About four tables down from us sat three young men who watched us intently and smiled. I couldn't be sure of this fact, however, because I didn't have my glasses on and neither did Lucy or Genie. I sort of forgot about these three, although I was conscious of being stared at the whole time.

Finally I overheard a waitress talking to our waitress about us. Then our waitress came over and said that the three "young gents that're askin' about youse." I asked what they wanted to know, and she said they were very anxious to meet us and would like to take us to a dance that night. Of course we said no, we were afraid not. But the waitress returned, after having conferred with the waitress who was serving the three boys, and said, "If you'll just smile a little, they'll come over to meet cha I'm sure."

We laughed – it seemed so strange to be "solicited" by waitresses! I asked if this was the usual thing, and she said, "Oh no! This don't never happen! But them boys is the loveliest of boys. We wouldn't recommend them if they wasn't, 'cause we don't like men much. But if ye'll meet 'em you'll thank us for a good time!"

We couldn't help but laugh. By this time the "three young gents" were all turned around looking at us. They seemed so nice and not at all bad looking. But being the "reserved" young maidens we are, we cast not a glance in their direction. Finally the "middle-girl" waitress returned and told us the boys would see us at the door as we went out. I think the waitresses were more keen on our meeting them than anyone!

Well, the time came to leave and we got up as inconspicuously as possible, walked out without a turn 'o the head or a flick o' the lash.' But once on the street we knew they were behind us. We came to the curb and as fate would have it, we had to wait for a red light which gave the boys their golden opportunity and they took it.

They stepped up, introduced themselves and asked us if we wouldn't like to go out. They were so unabashed and cute that we burst out laughing and so did they. We thanked them for their invitation, but told them we were very tired. They said they understood perfectly and wouldn't persist, but could they walk us to our hotel? We said yes and they joined us.

They were so nice. They confessed that that was the first time they had ever done anything like that! They were so interested in our seeing Dublin and having a good time, and were so upset that we weren't staying longer. By the time we reached the hotel we were great friends. They all are of the so-called working class, and while they are very young, they've been making their own living for a long time. Their names are Liam Quinlan, and John and Roger Higgins. They are all blonds with blue eyes. Liam is the best looking, with the most personality. Roger is so timid he chokes on his words. By the time we got to the hotel, Liam had decided that he could get a car for the next day and they could take us sightseeing in Dublin if we would be willing. We told him we'd be willing and we were. He said he'd call us at 8:30 the next morning and tell us if he had the car. We bid them good-night and went into bed after telling Louise about our new-found friends and plans.

Next morning at 8:30 Liam called and said he had the car and they would be at the hotel in about 35 minutes. They were 45 minutes late and we had almost given them up. It seems they had trouble getting the car at the last minute. They were so cute – you should hear them talk! They have the most lilting accent, even if they do use terrible grammar occasionally! So we started out.

First they presented us with a sack full of plums in case we were hungry. They wanted to take us wherever we wanted to go, so we told them the places we wanted to see. We were squeezed in the little car like sardines, but it didn't matter. First they took us to see Trinity College. The cutest little guide took us around. He wouldn't have anything to do with those Yank tourists, but when he found out we were "Yanks" he was quite pleased. He really was a gem.

It was very interesting to see the college, especially the famous library with some of the most ancient books in existence. From Trinity College where the statues of Goldsmith, Moore, and Burke bid you adieu, we went to St. Stephen's Green, Dublin Castle with the Royal Chapel, the State Apartments, the Four Courts, the old Abbey Theatre, Guinness Brewery – which we couldn't go in because Liam works there and he was supposed to be sick that day!

We rode down O'Connell Street and out to one of the world's largest enclosed parks where we saw herds of beautiful deer. I don't remember the order in which we saw these things or terribly much about them because I was too engrossed in talking with these three wonderful, good, happy, young men.

After our touring they insisted on taking us to lunch. When I say "insist," I mean it forcefully, because we protested with all our might, to no avail.

We went to a restaurant far too expensive for their means, but they chose it, so what could we do. We had to split up for eating – Genie, John and Roger and I were at one table and Louise, Lucy, and Liam at the other. During lunch we learned their ages: Liam and John are 23, and Roger is 21. Roger lost some of his timidity at lunch. We also learned that they are avid athletes in their spare time, and all belong to a total abstinence club, and none of them smoke. They were horrified when we spoke of dieting, and stupefied when they saw where all we have traveled this year. By the end of lunch we all felt as if we had known each other forever.

After lunch we had some shopping to do. The other three wanted to look for material, and I had my usual doll and charm to shop for. The boys decided to go with me since my shopping seemed the simplest, so we took the other three to one of the shops they wanted to inspect, and arranged to meet them in two hours. Then we went doll hunting. They were amazed that anyone could be so particular as I was about buying a simple thing like a doll! We had so much fun together.

Finally John decided to take the car and go park it by Stephen's Green and wait for us, because we were too close for comfort to the place where he worked – they were all "sick" that day. So we started charm hunting. I decided to buy a little harp – the Irish coat of arms which also appears on the money. We tried several stores before we found what I wanted. When I decided to buy the one, Liam thrust his money into the man's hand before I could bat an eyelash. I tried to make the man accept my money and give Liam's back, but of course he wouldn't. Liam insisted that he wanted me to take it as a gift from him, so I would remember him. It was so sweet – I nearly cried. Thank goodness I chose an inexpensive one! I forgot to say that during lunch John was showing me his athletic badge and explaining it to me. The inscription is written in Irish and he taught me how to say it. Then he insisted that I take it to remember him by. What could I do but accept it!

After the charm and doll were procured we went to some antique shops, but I found nothing, so we considered my shopping done. We walked to Stephen's Green and met John, then drove out to where the famous Dublin Horse Show is but unfortunately all places were sold way in advance. The three Irish wonders are sympathizers of the IRA, and they explained or rather tried to explain some of the workings of this organizations – the raids in

Northern Ireland and the imprisonments. It's quite exciting but at the same time rather appalling.

They are also fans of Al Jolson, so we sang all the songs he sang and a few others to boot. Then we parked the car in front of the place where we were to meet the girls, and waited. During the time we talked about the kind of people you meet, the type of boy I wanted to marry, the girls they wanted to marry, friendships, etc.

Then Liam paid us the most beautiful compliment. He said, "You're really amazing girls." "Why?" I asked.

"Well, you've traveled all over, the world and you're so natural and you don't brag or anything." Suddenly I felt so humble and grateful. I wanted to give him the same opportunity to make them know what they and many like them mean to us. I think they felt what I wanted to say even though the words I uttered were quite inadequate.

Soon the girls came back, and we squeezed up in the car again. They decided to drive us outside Dublin to a little seaside resort town called Bray. It took about an hour to get there. We sang and laughed on the way and they pointed out interesting sights. When we arrived in Bray they decided we were starving, which we weren't at all. They took us into a little hotel and when we ordered afternoon tea they nearly died!

"Ye'll starve yerselves!" they cried, but they ordered the same. We sat for ages. We had scones for the first time, which are sort of like our biscuits. We talked and joked for a long time. Liam is really precious. There was a piano at one end of the room, and since not many people were there Liam asked if we couldn't play and sing. The waitresses said "of course" so we all moved down to that end and gathered around the piano. Louise played and we all sang, then they made me sing alone. Soon the other customers were listening and all the waitresses had come to hear. We sang like that for way over an hour. It was such fun to hear the boys in their Irish tenor voices singing with all their hearts. We finally ended our "Sing Song" as they called it with "God Bless America" and the Irish National Anthem which they sang in Irish. When we left the café, everyone bade us a warm good-bye.

Outside the weather was beautiful. It had been cloudy most of the day, but then, about 9:00 p.m., the sky turned all pink. We were still in high spirits from singing – it's such a healthy pastime – so we decided to rent a rowboat and go out on the water. This was quite funny. The poor boys were rowing against the tide and singing all at once. They were so breathless when we finally came ashore but that didn't prevent them from showing us their athletic prowess and they leaped over fences, ran races and even had a somersault race for our benefit.

We, in return, Spanish-danced for them (in our inimitable fashion). We held carnations between our teeth which they had picked for us. They were so amused with our talents! It was after ten when we got back in the car to come back to Dublin. Liam decided it was better if I sat in the front seat with the three boys – it really did give more room since the front seat is bigger than the back one. His next decision was that his friend would probably let him keep the car until this morning so he could drive us to the boat. So we drove by the friend's house and the friend said "yes."

Then we went back into Dublin to O'Connell Street to the café where we met. They wanted the waitresses to see us three together but they weren't there, so we didn't stay. We went back outside and had a street photographer take our picture all together. The boys are going to send them to us. Then they brought us home. We thanked them the best we could with words and bid them good-night! It was a wonderful day, full of happiness and contentment at having made such wonderful friends. I'll always have a soft spot in my heart for Dublin because of Liam, John, and Roger.

This morning we awoke very early, had breakfast, carried our bags downstairs and waited for the boys. They came only a little late and we loaded the car with our bags and ourselves and left for Dun Laoghaire. We had almost no time to talk with the boys because we had to line up immediately to get on the boat. There was no way to tell them how much we liked them and appreciated them – we did our best, but words are so puny sometimes. We told them good-bye and boarded the ship. People are grand.

The little man who took tickets talked with me and when Irish jigs were played on the record-player over the loud-speaker he took my arm and danced with me. Suddenly I was filled with panic. I'm on my way to the end of this year, the very end. I can't believe it. It's been so wonderful – I well up with emotion when I think of it. I want to keep it to myself and share it with the world and cry and laugh and be 15 feet tall and feel an inch high in worthiness. It's almost too big for me. Sometimes I think I'll pop with gratitude.

Friday, August 16, 1957

My poor diary has really suffered these past nine days! But life in London has been so busy and complicated – I haven't had a minute to write. I'm not even going to try to remember things in the order they happened.

We arrived on the night of the 7th and who should be standing at the door of the hotel – quite accidentally – but Jean-Louis. You see, I had written him telling him not to come and I gave as an excuse that I was so anxious to get home I was skipping London (because I knew John was coming).

Then in Dublin I received such a pathetic letter from J.L. begging me to come and saying he would be in London and at our hotel whether I came or not, so I of course wrote him saying plans had been changed and I would be here. So we saw each other the 7th, the 8th and the 9th. Then life became really complicated!

John had no idea that Jean-Louis was here while J.L. knew about John. So naturally when I told John about the situation he wasn't too happy, but I'd rather skip the details which caused many hurt feelings, tears and very sleepless nights for a while. Eventually things worked out and everyone was happy. Although I must admit it's high time I quit trying to please everybody at the same time and thereby causing un-paralleled confusion!

London – in spite of the worst weather conditions – is enchanting, largely and especially because of the people. The English English is a lovely sound. My favorite sight is the typical Englishman looking drably dapper in his black suit, black derby, carrying his black umbrella (at all times a necessary accessory) and his dark brown menacing briefcase. And his counterpart the English woman – stunningly attractive in her well-tailored outfit. I have seen some of the most beautiful women in England! Then of course the Cockneys are a delight to hear – jolly well hard to understand at first as they spit out a strange language without any "aitches." The people are extremely friendly and so very eager to help.

The first few days, every time I took out my map to find directions there was immediately an elegant Englishman by my side saying, "May I help you, Madame?" or "Where would you like to go, my dear?" The expression "my dear" seemed awfully intimate at first, but I soon learned it means more "my child" than "ma chère."

And speaking of elegance – the English certainly possess that quality. There is elegance in the way they drink the inevitable cup of tea, the way they read their paper, the way they spill out the well-known understatement, the way they queue for a bus, the way they carry themselves, the "cheerio" they give their friends on parting.

I became acquainted with the all means of transportation. Thanks to John and Jean-Louis, I met the taxi, a roomy vehicle with enough space to dance in – and no exaggeration. They too are elegant and recall days long past. The buses are the famed two-story ones, and of course I preferred riding on the second story. It's like being atop an elephant (I imagine) and they are quite capable of undulating as much as an elephant might. It's really delightful riding so high up and seeing everything and you feel a kinship to everybody else who is isolated (as it were) with you on top of the world of motor vehicles. The subway – or "Tube" as it is called – is a wonderful system. It's a little more difficult to catch on to than the Metro of Paris, but once learned it is to be appreciated.

English food is very simple, but very good. Roast beef with Yorkshire pudding and roast potatoes and cabbage is the old mainstay as far as dishes are concerned. Owing to the fact that I was so busy doing everything else, going back and forth between being with John and being with Jean-Louis, eating was quite an incidental factor. Jean-Louis and I splurged one night and went to a very nice restaurant – very elegant and comfortable and had delicious seafood. And one night John and I indulged in delicious steaks.

There is so much to be seen in England – one must stay here a really long time to get beyond the surface. In London itself there are of course all the famous and historical places: Buckingham Palace, Whitehall, Westminster Abbey, Parliament and Big Ben, the Tower Bridge, the Tower of London, St. Paul's Cathedral, Trafalgar Square, Piccadilly, the Mall, and the museums. Most of my sight-seeing was done with John – things just worked out that way.

We saw Buckingham Palace by day and by night – it's lovely at both times of day with the bright red flowers in front and the adorable guards in their high bear-hats and bright red coats that match the flowers. Whitehall is loveliest at night when it's illuminated. The guards are there always – two in front astride great black horses. The Changing of the Guards at Whitehall is very colorful, although difficult to see because of hundreds of wide-eyed, elbowing tourists – who seem to lose all manners at such occasions. Westminster Abbey is magnificent and to imagine the coronation taking place there was quite exciting. The Henry VII Chapel is a gem, and seeing the tombs of Mary Stuart and Elizabeth I was strangely thrilling. Of course the Poet's Corner was infinitely fascinating. The Abbey as an architectural piece of art is certainly worthy of its fame and praise. One could spend hours there. It must be a thrill of a lifetime to witness a coronation there. (Understatement)

The Houses of Parliament with Big Ben at one end are a spectacle – a beautiful one. The Thames of course runs right alongside them, and at 9:00 in the evening with the sun setting (which it managed to do several evenings although it never seemed to have risen) behind the Parliament, there is one of the most stunning sights in Europe.

The Tower Bridge and the Tower of London make beautiful silhouettes against the sky. They are the most reminiscent of the Middle Ages and Elizabethan times. The day John and I went to the Tower there were mobs of people there. A Beefeater guide in his "Yeoman of the Guard" uniform took us around. Besides the Beefeaters, there were guards in the high bear-hats. It was all quite colorful.

St. Paul's Cathedral, Christopher Wren's claim to fame, was a big disappointment because it was a miniature St. Peter's, a reminder of St. Sulpice and the Pantheon all in one. St. Paul's is situated in the midst of devastation from the bombing in the last war.

Trafalgar Square, with Nelson high on a column overlooking London while four regal lions roar at the foot of his pedestal, is always crowded with people and pigeons. It's nice at night when the fountains play to the illuminations. Piccadilly Circus is exciting all the time. It is called the Times Square of London, and so it is. Flower women are everywhere trying to sell their little nosegays. The bright neon advertisements flash on and off and are really quite clever. It is always crowded and seems much like the midway of a carnival and is as much fun!

One of the most wonderful things in London is the famous Wallace Collection, one of the richest private collections in the world of priceless paintings, chinaware, furniture, arms and armory. The painters include Rembrandt, Rubens, Fragonard, Watteau, Boucher, Murillo, Frans Hals and the English – Turner, Gainsborough and Reynolds. I couldn't resist buying two Reynolds prints – *Miss Bowles* and *The Strawberry Girl*. There are also a couple of Velasquez works there. It was a marvelous experience to see it all. It would take a day to see it all and be completely satisfied.

On Tuesday, Jean-Louis and I went on a tour to Oxford, Warwick Castle, and Stratford-upon-Avon. Unfortunately, the weather was rotten, but we still enjoyed the tour. It was interesting to see Oxford. We visited only Queen's College, and learned about the tutorial systems. The town of Oxford is very old and full of wonderful Elizabethan homes, old churches. I enjoyed the visit to Warwick most of all. The Castle is still in perfect condition. There is a collection of Van Dyke, Holstein, and Rubens there that was worth the trip to see. I was greatly disappointed in Stratford-upon-Avon simply because the tourists were so thick you could see nothing but them! Shakespeare's birthplace was crowded, too, but I enjoyed seeing how he might have lived.

Anne Hathaway's cottage was adorable, but also overrun with tourists. Jean-Louis made clever jokes about "the God Shakespeare." He said he must initiate a similar idea of deity and create pilgrimages for Molière, Racine, Corneille, and the many other great French writers.

Everyone on the tour believed I was French because they heard me talking with Jean-Louis. There was a Brazilian family on the bus with whom I became friends. When they found out I was American they couldn't believe it. I was flattered – especially considering the Americans who were with us on the tour. One was a man who had the audacity to ask a tall white man from South Africa what he "talked" in his country! When he asked that I nearly died from embarrassment. One little English lady couldn't believe that I don't have any French ancestors. I had a good time talking to everyone. Jean-Louis was thoroughly disgusted with our lunch companions – two American girls and two women who could only talk of how much they had purchased in every country. It certainly was disgusting.

Jean-Louis and I had sad farewells. It was really hard to leave such a wonderful, loving, generous friend, but my excitement at going home made it less sad.

On Thursday John and I (and Louise, Lucy, and Genie), took a tour to Canterbury – the oldest Cathedral in England and the scene of Thomas Becket's murder.

I then had time to burn, so we went to the movies and saw *The Prince and the Showgirl*. It was delightful and very appropriate with its London setting. Then John and I had our emotional goodbyes. We loved each other, but goodbye in London wasn't as sad as it was in Paris.

At 8:00 we went to the air terminal and caught the bus to the airport. Our flight was delightful. We left London at 10:00 p.m. on a TWA Jetstream flight non-stop to New York. It was smooth as silk and quite enjoyable. I was sort of numb with excitement but it was a nice feeling to be going home. At 8:00 a.m. the 17th, we landed at Idlewild in New York. After the lengthy customs routine I met Bill Mount who, bless his heart, had been there since about 7:00. (Plane was an hour late.) Bill took Louise and me to Teresa Lurry's apartment. Teresa was so good to us. I cleaned up a bit, changed clothes and met Bill about noon. We drove around New York and through Central Park.

Around 6:30 we went back to Teresa's and had drinks with Teresa and Louise. I changed clothes again and Bill and I went to the wonderful German restaurant Luchow's. The food was divine – sauerbraten and all. After dinner we went to see *The Most Happy Fella*. We had wonderful seats. Robert Weede was terrific. It is one of the best musicals I've ever seen. After the show we walked through Times Square – one certainly sees a jumble of people there! Then Bill and I decided to drive across the East River and look at New York – it's strange how lights at night can be so beautiful.

Sunday was spent walking, driving, talking. We window shopped on Fifth Avenue, ate in an automat, and rode the subway. We came in early and found Louise and Freddie listening to the hi-fi set in the studio parlor. We came in early because Bill had to go back to East Orange.

Next morning Bill and I met at the air terminal around 10:30 and took the bus out to La Guardia. At 11:00 something we took the plane headed for Nashville. We got as far as Washington D.C. when the plane had engine trouble and we were grounded. So I missed the proper connections from Nashville to Paducah. I called home to relate this cheery news and my sweet Daddy decided to charter a plane from Paducah and fly to Nashville to pick me up.

Bill and I arrived in Nashville about 5:30. Daddy was waiting for me. I was so excited to see him. A year is a long time. Bill and I bade a hasty farewell and Daddy and I boarded the little plane with the pilot. Then the fun started. The pilot insisted that I fly the plane home. Not having ever flown a plane, I was slightly panicked, but with the pilot telling me all the moves to make, I did beautifully – even landed the plane myself!

Mother and Janet and Linda and Tippy were all at the airport waiting for me. Needless to say there was a joyous reunion. We drove home for supper and Mother had everything I love – green onions, turnip greens, country ham. After supper all the relatives (27 in all) came over to celebrate Daddy's birthday, and to say hello to me. We served ice cream and cake and talked, talked, talked.

And so ended the most wonderful year of my life, which I can't adequately describe to those who question me about it. But I shall remember, every moment of it and it will enrich my life forever.

How lucky and fortunate can one be?

Judy

The End

About the Author

Judith Woodall Hauman Dye is a Phi Beta Kappa graduate of Newcomb College of Tulane University. Following her studies at Newcomb, she received a Woodrow Wilson Fellowship for graduate study, and earned her Master of Music Degree from the University of Michigan.

During her singing career, she won the Detroit Grand Opera Scholarship Award, was a finalist in the regional Metropolitan Opera auditions, and a runner up in the WGN Chicago radio opera auditions.

She performed roles in opera and musical theater, has appeared as soloist with symphony orchestras and in concerts and recitals throughout much of the U.S., including venues in New York City, and at the Kennedy Center and the National Gallery of Art in Washington, D.C. She appeared as guest artist on the Carras Cruise Line, and she has been seen and heard on both public television and radio. In addition, she served on the faculty of the University of Toledo.

Judy was a recipient of the Outstanding Women of Toledo Award, and of the Community Achievement as an Artist Award given by the Toledo Arts Commission. She also served as a volunteer art and music docent at the Toledo Museum of Art.

The mother of two daughters, Constance Hauman of New York City, a singer and composer, and Carrie Hauman of Los Angeles, an artist and writer, Judy currently lives in Toledo, Ohio with her husband, Nicholas Dye.